1985

Eagle Defiant

Eagle Defiant
United States Foreign Policy in the 1980s

Edited by

Kenneth A. Oye
Princeton University

Robert J. Lieber
Georgetown University

Donald Rothchild
University of California, Davis

Little, Brown and Company
Boston   Toronto

Library of Congress Cataloging in Publication Data
Main entry under title:

Eagle defiant.

Includes index.
1. United States--Foreign relations--1981-   --Ad-
dresses, essays, lectures. I. Oye, Kenneth A.,
1949-   . II. Rothchild, Donald S. III. Lieber,
Robert J., 1941-
E876.E23 1983   327.73   83-718
ISBN 0-316-67731-0 (Pbk.)
ISBN 0-316-67732-9

Copyright © 1983 by Kenneth A. Oye,
Robert J. Lieber, Donald Rothchild

Library of Congress Catalog Card No. 83–718

ISBN 0-316-67731-0 {PBK.}

ISBN 0-316-67732-9

9 8 7 6 5 4 3 2 1

MV

Published simultaneously in Canada
by Little, Brown & Company (Canada) Limited
Printed in the United States of America

Acknowledgments

Definition, page v, of *defy* from *The Random House Dictionary of the English Language.* Copyright © 1981 by Random House, Inc. Reprinted by permission of the publisher.

Table 2-1, page 36, from National Opinion Research Center, University of Chicago, General Social Surveys. Reprinted by permission.

Table 2-2, pages 50–51, from Lloyd Free and William Watts, "Internationalism Comes of Age...Again," *Public Opinion*, Vol. 3 (April/May 1980). Reprinted by permission of American Enterprise Institute for Public Policy Research.

Table 2-3, page 60, from *Los Angeles Times/Cable News Network* poll conducted March 14–18, 1982. Reprinted by permission.

Excerpt, page 119, from Leonard Silk, "Looking for a Way to Subdue Currency and Interest Discord," *The New York Times* 5 June 1982. © 1982 by The New York Times Company. Reprinted by permission.

Excerpt, page 123, from Robert Dole, "Reciprocity in Trade," *The New York Times*, 22 January 1982. © 1982 by The New York Times Company. Reprinted by permission.

Excerpt, page 223, from George F. Kennan, "A Risky U.S. Equation," *The New York Times*, 18 February 1981. © 1981 by The New York Times Company. Reprinted by permission.

Preface

de·fy *v.* **1:** to challenge the power of; resist boldly or openly **2:** to offer effective resistance to **3:** to challenge (one) to do something deemed impossible.

The editors and contributors to *Eagle Defiant* are as concerned with surveying the domain of choice open to *any* administration as with evaluating the specific choices of the Reagan administration. While drawing attention to tactical and stylistic deficiencies of Reagan administration foreign policy, we seek to place the policies of the administration into structural and historical perspective.

The policies of the Nixon, Ford, and Carter administrations and the initial policies of the Reagan administration define two sharply divergent responses to fundamental changes in the international environment. The administrations of the 1970s adapted to the secular decline of American economic and military power and to increasing international economic interdependence. Their rhetoric was attuned to the politics of "limits" and "complexity." Their security policies of retrenchment and their international economic policies of multilateral management were part of an implicit over-arching strategy of adjustment to what they saw as the end of the post World War II era of American preeminence.

The Reagan administration sought to defy constraints that earlier administrations had accepted. The initial foreign defense policies of the Reagan administration constituted an indictment of both the need to adjust and the methods of adjustment. First, to restore the United States to a position of primacy in international relations, the administration offered what it saw as interlocking programs of military and economic renewal. The "supply-side," domestic economic program promised noninflationary growth, and the defense program redirected a larger share of American resources into military expenditures. Second, the administration retreated from the managerial international economic approach of the 1970s and sought to reconstruct American foreign economic policy around laissez-faire principles. Finally, in international security affairs, the administration reversed the 1970s policy of retrenchment by mounting an offensive against revolutionary change in the Third World and by heightening political, economic, and military pressure on the Soviet Union. The initial Reagan administration approach to international affairs assumed the possibility of returning to a position of preeminence and the desirability of returning to the policies of an era of preeminence.

The editors of this volume asked each contributor to regard this foreign policy experiment as a source of information concerning the nature of the constraints and tradeoffs that are likely to shape the agendas and responses of administrations through the 1980s. The policy reversals, failures, and successes of the first two years of the Reagan administration may contribute, albeit inadvertently, to a redefinition of the possible and the desirable for the balance of the decade.

Eagle Defiant is designed to provide a comprehensive assessment of these wider implications of the Reagan administration foreign policy. Part One, "An Overview," places the foreign policy of the Reagan administration in an international and a domestic context. The two keynote chapters lay out major themes of policy and describe major constraints and tradeoffs limiting implementation of policy. Subsequent chapters of the book juxtapose foreign policy with the often inconsistent requirements of crosscutting functional and regional concerns. Part Two, "Functional Problems," examines policies on defense, international economics, and energy. Part Three, "Regional Problems," examines policies toward the Soviet Union and Eastern Europe, China, Western Europe, Latin America, Africa, and the Middle East.

The writing of this volume has been a collaborative effort from the beginning. Each regional and functional specialist proceeded with sensitivity to contradictory and correlative interests across a broad spectrum of issues. Preliminary drafts of chapters were presented and discussed at a meeting of contributors at the Carnegie Endowment for International Peace in July of 1982. Chapters were subsequently revised to incorporate themes that evolved from these discussions and to treat developments that occurred in the second half of 1982. We aimed for a publication date late enough to acquire a firm sense of the fundamental strategies and rationales underpinning Reagan administration foreign policy, and early enough to contribute to the ongoing debate over the appropriateness of these policies.

We acknowledge with gratitude the hospitality of Thomas Hughes and the Carnegie Endowment for International Peace and the able comments and criticisms of our discussants, Thomas Hughes, Lawrence Caldwell, and Lawrence Krause. The editors and contributors assume sole responsibility for the views expressed in this book.

Kenneth A. Oye *Princeton, New Jersey*
Robert J. Lieber *Washington, D.C.*
Donald Rothchild *Davis, California*
January 1983

Contents

Part I: Overview

Part II: Functional Problems

Part III: Regional Problems

I

Overview

1

International Systems Structure and American Foreign Policy

Kenneth A. Oye

I: Introduction

Contrary to conventional wisdom, Reagan administration foreign policy differs in many crucial respects from the foreign policies of the administrations of the 1970s. Through rhetoric and action, the Nixon, Ford, and Carter administrations struggled to adjust to emerging limits of American economic and military power. The Reagan administration approach to foreign affairs is predicated on the assumption that the United States can reassert American influence while reversing secular tendencies towards the international diffusion of power.

Richard Nixon and Henry Kissinger spoke pessimistically of the inevitable "end of the postwar world." They formulated a narrowly realpolitik foreign policy to control America's descent into an uncertain future. Jimmy Carter spoke with mild optimism of a "new world" where "we can no longer expect that the other 150 nations will follow the dictates of the powerful," and added a soupçon of idealpolitik to increase the palatability of a fundamentally realpolitik foreign policy. Although every new administration seeks to distinguish its foreign policy from that of

Kenneth A. Oye is an assistant professor of politics at Princeton University and an editor of World Politics. *He coedited* Eagle Entangled *and is currently completing a book on international political economy during the inter-war period.*

The author acknowledges with gratitude the cooperation of officials in the Executive Office of the President and the Departments of State, Treasury, and Defense who kindly granted interviews on a background basis; and the co-editors and contributors, colleagues at Princeton University and the Brookings Institution, and Thomas Hughes and I. M. Destler of the Carnegie Endowment for International Peace for their comments and advice on early drafts of this essay.

predecessors, rhetorical and substantive differences should not be permitted to obscure the fundamental continuity of American policy during the 1970s. In security affairs, these administrations narrowed the definition of American interests and commitments in peripheral regions, shifted a greater share of the burdens of containment to China and Europe, and acted on limited areas of mutual interest with the Soviet Union, particularly through strategic arms control negotiations. In international economic affairs, these administrations gradually increased the scope of multilateral political management to address problems that arose as a consequence of increasing economic interdependence and decreasing American power. Their rhetoric was attuned to the politics of limits, and their actions were rooted in a strategy of adjustment.

By 1980, the strategy of adjustment had proved frustrating and alarming to a nation with expectations conditioned by a quarter century of American preeminence in international relations.* Mass concern was mirrored in the statements of one of the architects of adjustment. Ten years after developing policies suited to the "end of the postwar world," Henry Kissinger spoke of a "world out of control, with our relative military power declining, with our economic lifeline increasingly vulnerable to blackmail, with hostile radical forces growing in every continent, and with the number of countries willing to stake their futures on our friendship declining." [1] The Reagan administration shared this image of a weakening America in a fundamentally hostile world.

In April of 1981, then Secretary of State Alexander Haig pointed to "fundamental movements" of international politics.

> Disruption from abroad threatens a more vulnerable West, as we draw energy and raw materials from regions in which the throes of rapid change and conflict prevail. Soviet military power grows relentlessly as Moscow shows an increasing willingness to use it both directly and by proxy and obstructs the achievement of a more just international order. We must understand that these conditions are interrelated; they play upon each other; and the danger is therefore all the greater. If present trends are not arrested, the convergence of rising international disorder, greater Western vulnerability, and growing Soviet military power will undo the international codes of conduct that foster the resolution of disputes between nations.[2]

The Reagan administration's response to what it saw as a catastrophic erosion of American military and economic strength rested on the premise that the causes of the problem could be found not in long-term cycles of hegemonic decline but in the programs of previous administrations. Insuf-

---

* William Schneider examines public reaction to the strategy of adjustment in Chapter 2, "Conservatism, Not Interventionism: Trends in Foreign Policy Opinion 1974-1982."

ficient military spending and mistaken economic ideology were the primary causes of the recession of American power. The administration's two core programs — accelerated defense spending and Reaganomics — would restore American military strength and inflation-free economic growth. Over the long term, these programs would reverse tendencies toward international power diffusion and thereby obviate the need for adjustment and retrenchment.

Indeed, the Reagan administration saw the 1970s strategy of adjustment to declining American power as contributing directly to the deterioration of the United States' international position. Each element of the 1970s security strategy was to be reversed. The very concept of peripheral regions and interests was rejected. The Reagan administration believed that the reassertion of American power to stop Third World revolutions was central to deterring adversaries and restoring the confidence of friends. While not objecting to a policy of shifting some of the burdens of containment to China and Europe, the administration believed that the United States had gone too far in bending American policy to fit the preferences of its allies. Initial policy on China and Europe sought to reconstruct these strategic relationships around the Reagan administration's conception of strategic interests.* Finally, the administration rejected the 1970s conception of Soviet-American mutual interest. At a minimum, a more assertive United States, bargaining from a position of military strength, would wrest additional concessions from the Soviet Union in areas such as strategic arms control. At a maximum, American political, economic, and military pressure would be sufficient to force the Soviets to choose between external retrenchment and internal collapse.†

The initial administration strategy for international economic affairs relied, both conceptually and practically, on domestic Reaganomics. The policies of the 1970s — increasing multilateral political management of the international economy and increasing United States government involvement in international economic affairs — were seen as having deleterious effects on the ability of private firms to respond to market incentives in an economically efficient manner. The administration's central objective was to increase the freedom of action of private firms in private markets by using United States leverage to prune away international and foreign

---

* The disjunction between American and allied strategy compelled adjustments in administration policy towards Western Europe. Miles Kahler examines the evolving Atlantic relationship in Chapter 9, "The United States and Western Europe: The Diplomatic Consequences of Mr. Reagan." The administration's initial stand on the Taiwan question strained relations with China. Banning Garrett analyzes the slow ascendance of realpolitik in Chapter 8, "China Policy and the Constraints of Triangular Logic."

† Alexander Dallin and Gail Lapidus assess the feasibility and desirability of this approach in Chapter 7, "Reagan and the Russians: United States Policy Towards the Soviet Union and Eastern Europe."

restraints and by reducing the role of the United States government in international economic affairs. This strategy was predicated on the assumption that domestic Reaganomics would succeed in boosting American productivity and in stimulating noninflationary growth. Greater American competitiveness would negate the need for governmental defense of American commercial interests, and noninflationary growth would eliminate many of the international financial and monetary problems that seemed to require multilateral management during the stagflationary 1970s. The administration's laissez-faire strategy departed sharply from the managerial policies of the Nixon, Ford, and Carter administrations.

Behind every colorful debate over the feasibility and desirability of contemporary American foreign policy sits a corresponding dry academic discussion of the causes and consequences of changes in international systems structure. The success or failure of the Reagan administration's foreign policy experiment, and even the extent to which the administration will persist with the initial defense and economic programs and the security and economic strategies, hinges on the answers to two key questions.

First, what are the causes of the erosion of American economic and military power? The Reagan administration assumes that the choices of previous administrations account for the recession of American power, and that therefore the administration's military and domestic economic programs can restore the United States to a position of preeminence in international relations. Scholarly theories of hegemonic decline provide a historical and theoretical framework for explaining tendencies toward the international diffusion of power and for evaluating the Reagan programs. Section II of this essay examines the causes of American decline and assesses the likely effects of the Reagan administration's defense and economic programs on the international distribution of power.

Second, what are the consequences of the international diffusion of power? The Reagan administration believes that American decline is potentially catastrophic, and this view lends an understandable urgency to their military and economic programs and colors their core international security and economic strategies. An often neglected second aspect of international systems structure — the configuration of international interests — provides a key to assessing the consequences of power diffusion and to evaluating the Reagan administration's security and economic strategies. Where American interests conflict with those of other states, declining American power will have adverse effects on the United States. The Reagan administration's foreign policy is, of course, sensitive to this possibility. Where American interests partially complement those of other states, receding American power will give rise to tricky dilemmas of collective action. The mere existence of a mutual interest does not guarantee the realization of a common goal. Policies attuned to the multilateral pursuit of mutual interests offer hope of blunting the effects of changes in the international distribution of power. Reagan administration policies toward the nations of Western Europe and on international economic matters are, I argue, insufficiently sensitive to this concern. Finally, the configuration of international interests is not static. American policy can have profound effects on how other nations define their interests. Reagan administration policies toward the Soviet Union and particularly toward revolutionary nationalist states in the Third World heighten, and even create, conflict and often operate to the detriment of the United States. Section III of this essay examines the configuration of international interests exposed by the recession of American power and evaluates the Reagan administration's core security and international economic strategies in light of the structure of interests.

II: Hegemonic Decline and Strategies of Restoration

In the thirty-five years since the end of the Second World War, American military and economic preeminence has clearly faded. Western Europe, Japan, and the upper tier of the developing world grew more rapidly than the United States, and American comparative weight in the international economic system declined. The Soviet Union's military capabilities grew more rapidly than American military capabilities, and the United States' comparative weight in the international security system declined. The erosion of American hegemony reflects the dispersion of power as other nations' capabilities have increased relative to those of the United States. Power, defined in terms of ability to influence or control events, cannot be directly measured. Imperfect surrogates can provide a crude sense of the changing American position in the international system. Before turning to the problem of explaining power redistribution, it is useful to assess the magnitude and timing of shifts.

Gross Domestic Product provides a basic measure of the resources a nation can choose to apply to military programs, consumption, and capital investment. Table 1-1 on the next page presents estimates of percentage shares of gross world product for 1950, 1960, 1970, and 1980. Discrepancies between the two overlapping series reflect the intrinsic imprecision of the exercise, and give warning of the many opportunities for chicanery in comparing disparate national incomes. Nevertheless, the trends are clear. The American share of world product declined sharply during the 1950s, and more slowly during the 1960s and 1970s. How do the shares of the two competing security blocs compare? The product of the Western advanced industrial states dwarfs that of the Soviet bloc, and the ratio of Western to Eastern production has remained fairly constant over thirty years. The declining weight of the United States in inter-

TABLE 1-1. Shares of Gross World Product (Percentages)

	Council on International Economic Policy Series			Central Intelligence Agency Series		
	1950	1960	1970	1960	1970	1980
Developed Countries	67.4%	65.2	64.5	66.5	65.7	62.7
United States	39.3	33.9	30.2	25.9	23.0	21.5
European Community	16.1	17.5	18.4	26.0	24.7	22.5
Japan	1.5	2.9	6.2	4.5	7.7	9.0
Other	10.5	10.9	9.7	10.1	10.3	9.7
Less Developed Countries	9.1	9.5	10.0	11.1	12.3	14.8
Communist Countries	23.5	25.3	25.5	22.4	22.0	22.0
Soviet Union	13.5	15.5	16.5	12.5	12.4	11.4
China	4.0	4.5	4.0	3.1	3.4	4.5
Other	6.0	5.3	5.0	6.8	6.2	6.1
Gross World Product in Trillions of 1980 Dollars	$2.4	3.9	6.3	5.0	8.4	12.2

SOURCES: U.S. Council on International Economic Policy, *The United States in the Changing World Economy* (Washington: GPO, 1971) Volume II, Chart 1. U.S. Central Intelligence Agency, National Foreign Assessment Center, *Handbook of Economic Statistics 1981* (Washington: GPO, 1981), percentages calculated from Table 9. Gross World Product for C.I.E.P. Series derived by dividing U.S. GNP in 1980 dollars (*Economic Report of the President 1982*, Tables B-1 and B-3) by the C.I.E.P. estimate of the U.S. share of Gross World Product. European Community adjusted to include the United Kingdom for all years in both series. Some of the major disparities between the C.I.E.P. and C.I.A. figures for the overlapping years of 1960 and 1970 appear to rest on the following factors: (1) European Community and Japan — Exchange rates used to value national product in dollars; (2) Less Developed Countries and China — Quantity and value of subsistence sector plus exchange rates; and (3) Communist Countries — Quantity and value of production in command economy plus exchange rates.

national economic affairs is revealed clearly by comparing the American share with those of Japan, the European Community, and the developing countries. It is important to keep in mind both trends and final position. Even after decades of relatively rapid growth, the nations of the Third World account for less than 15 percent of world product, while the developed Western nations account for over 60 percent of world product.

Military spending and personnel provide a crude measure of military capabilities. Barry Posen and Stephen Van Evera provide an extended assessment of the *adequacy* of American and allied military forces for varied contingencies in Chapter 3, "Defense Policy: Departure from Containment." As they note, Western military capabilities have not declined relative to the capabilities of the Soviet bloc. However, the simple figures in Table 1-2 confirm perceptions of a decline in the American share of world military spending between 1960 and 1980. Increases in Soviet military spending, the rapid expansion of military spending and forces in the Third World, and increases in Western European military spending are reflected in the figures for world spending and personnel. The sharp decline in the American share of world spending and personnel between 1970 and 1980 reflects both the reallocation of American resources during the 1970s and the unusually high military effort in 1970 related to the Vietnam War.

What factors account for the clear relative American decline? The pattern of economic and military changes summarized in Tables 1-1 and 1-2 are partially the product of national choices that were, in turn, conditioned by the international distribution of power. Finite economic resource bases create a tradeoff among military spending, investment, and consumption. The priority that nations assign to guns, growth, and butter is the best single predictor of changes in economic and military strength. Table 1-3 summarizes the choices and growth rates of the United States, United Kingdom, West Germany, Japan, and the Soviet Union in the period 1960 through 1979. The Soviet Union financed very high investment and very high levels of military spending by repressing consumption and thereby attained military parity with the United States while sustaining a moderately high, but declining, growth rate. Japan opted for very high levels of investment and moderate levels of consumption while spending little on defense, and it achieved an astonishing growth rate of 8.5 percent per year. Germany balanced moderate investment, military spending, and consumption, and grew at 4.7 percent in the 1960s and 2.9 percent in the 1970s. Britain's high consumption, high military spending, and low investment strategy yielded an average 2.5 percent growth rate. The United States' high consumption, low investment, and moderately

TABLE 1-2. United States Share of World Military Spending and Personnel

	1960	*1970*	*1980*
US Military Spending as a Share of World Spending	51%	42%	28%
World Military Spending in billions 1978 $	$341	$469	$570
US Armed Forces Personnel as a Share of World Personnel	13%	14%	8.3%
World Armed Forces Personnel in thousands	18,550	21,484	24,435

SOURCES: Computed from *Department of Defense Annual Report for Fiscal Year 1983*, pages I-5 and C-3; Ruth Sivard, *World Military and Social Expenditures*, p. 24; and *Economic Report of the President*, Table B-3.

TABLE 1-3. Allocation of Gross Domestic Product — Average Percentages 1960-1979

	Annual Growth Rate	Fixed Capital Formation	Military Spending	Consumption Gov't +	Private =	Total
United States	3.6%	17.6	7.4	10.9	63.0	73.9
United Kingdom	2.5	18.4	5.4	13.0	62.8	75.8
West Germany	3.9	24.1	3.9	13.2	55.6	68.8
Japan	8.5	32.7	.9	7.7	55.4	63.1
Soviet Union*	4.1	28.7	14.0	–	–	54.1

SOURCES: For Western nations, see Robert DeGrasse, *The Costs and Consequences of Reagan's Military Buildup* (New York: Council on Economic Priorities, 1982). For the Soviet Union, see C.I.A., *Handbook of Economic Statistics 1981*, Table 37 on Fixed Capital Formation and Consumption, and Department of Defense, *Annual Report to Congress Fiscal Year 1983* for estimated military spending.

* The Soviet figures do not add to 100 because different sources were used for estimates of investment and consumption and of military spending. The C.I.A. estimate for "R&D, inventory change, net exports, outlays and defense" over this period comes to 17.25 percent of Soviet product.

high military spending approach yielded a growth rate of 3.6 percent. In summary, the United States did not match German and Japanese economic and Soviet military investments simultaneously.

These figures summarizing national allocation of resources to investment, defense, and consumption are clear and consequential, but they raise a difficult basic question. How can we explain these national choices? Robert Gilpin's important recent book, *War and Change in World Politics*, examines the decline of the Athenian, Roman, Dutch, British, and American empires, and develops a set of propositions to account for regularities in cycles of hegemonic decline. In each case, *external burdens of leadership, internal secular tendencies toward rising consumption,* and *the international diffusion of technology* appear to explain hegemonic recession. How well do these factors account for the American decline? Which factors bear on Soviet prospects?

Every strategy of dominance undercuts the economic bases of dominance. The United States' strategy of containment centers on the protection of Western Europe and Japan. Table 1-3 indicates clearly that the United States bears a disproportionate share of the burden of defense. In "An Economic Theory of Alliances," Mancur Olson and Richard Zeckhauser note that because the dominant state in an alliance has an absolute interest in offering protection, smaller allies have little incentive to contribute proportionately to their own defense.[3] Because the loss of the technologically advanced Western nations would have catastrophic effects on American interests, the United States cannot credibly threaten to retract American protection and therefore lacks leverage to coerce increases in allied defense spending. Lesser threats and jawboning by the Nixon, Ford, and Carter administrations did succeed in doubling the Europeans' share of the NATO burden, but the persistent tendency of the United States to devote a disproportionate share of national product to defense remains. American, Western European, and Japanese "choices" of guns, growth, and butter are conditioned by this elemental aspect of alliance relationships. Even with overt and covert coercive means, the Soviet Union bears an even more highly disproportionate share of military spending within the Warsaw Pact.

A second burden of leadership is at least partially self-imposed. During the 1950s and 1960s, the United States guaranteed the security of anti-communist governments in peripheral regions against internal and external threats. The globalization of containment rested on American willingness to intervene to forestall revolution under disadvantageous circumstances. The apotheosis of global containment — the American intervention in Indochina — entailed enormous costs in blood and treasure and triggered the Nixon's administration's search for less costly means of counter-revolution and the Carter administration's more tolerant attitude toward revolutionary nationalism. The diversion of resources into military consumption undercuts both military and economic investment. Prior to its invasion of Afghanistan, the Soviet Union avoided direct military interventions outside Eastern Europe. However, the recurrent costs of controlling Eastern Europe through invasion and occupation and the uncertain costs of the ongoing Afghan invasion must both be reckoned as substantial costs of dominance.

The costs of bidding for allegiances and bolstering the strength of allies are a third burden of leadership. American postwar promotion of European and Japanese recovery through direct financial assistance and tolerance of trade asymmetries, and security supporting assistance to many Third World states are not reflected in any of the figures in Table 1-3, but they clearly entail economic costs. The Soviet Union's strategy of alternating exploitation and subsidization of Eastern Europe and of providing more modest support for Third World clients lessens this cost of dominance. However, the continuing instability of Eastern Europe and defection of China follow, at least in part, from Soviet efforts to concentrate resources on Soviet economic and military growth.

The second major factor, a secular tendency toward increasing consumption, is directly reflected in Table 1-3. A former hegemonic power, Great Britain, and a declining hegemonic power, the United States, top the list in terms of proportion of national product devoted to consumption. Democratic governments may be incapable of cutting domestic consumption to maintain international position, and authoritarian governments may cut consumption only at the risk of increasing domestic political instability. Are the Soviets immune from this tendency toward rising consumption? Grumblings over the quality of life in the Soviet Union and Eastern Europe are endemic, and the recent rise of Solidarity in Poland was based on both economic and political discontent. Even if a totalitarian state can sustain extremely high levels of investment and military spending by suppressing consumption, the ends of economic growth and perhaps even greater military capabilities may be undercut by economic discontent and inefficiency. In the period 1960-1979, the Soviet Union devoted almost as great a share of national product to investment as did Japan, but it grew at less than half the rate. In the late 1970s and early 1980s, Soviet growth has been stagnant or negative.

The third major factor accounting for hegemonic decline — a tendency towards the international diffusion of technology — operates by eroding margins of technological superiority on which economic and military advantage may be based. Knowledge is intrinsically difficult to control, and the argument that technological superiority inevitably fades is substantiated by the narrowing or nonexistent margin of American technological superiority over Japan and Western Europe. If differences in rates of growth in Table 1-3 are explained by both levels of investment *and* technological borrowing, then more equal growth is likely to follow from technological equality. The Soviet Union can limit technological diffusion through controls over emigration and publication. However, this clear advantage is of less consequence to a nation whose power does not rest on broad-based technological superiority.

The programs and policies of the Reagan administration fail to address the first and third causes of hegemonic decline. The first factor, the burden of leadership, is likely to grow heavier under the Reagan administration. The Reagan administration's security strategy, discussed in Section II, expands American commitments, and the acceleration of defense spending may well assuage Japanese and Western European fears and trigger reductions in their defense spending. The third factor, technological diffusion, cannot be addressed without eliminating freedoms of communication that appear necessary for technological advance. In any event, the narrow or nonexistent gap between the United States and other advanced industrial states may have mooted the significance of this factor. The Reagan administration's program for reversing movement toward the international diffusion of power rests ultimately on managing the tradeoff among investment, military spending, and consumption.

The initial domestic economic program of the Reagan administration offered a remedy for headaches caused by the need to choose among guns, butter, and growth. The administration expected its package of tax and domestic spending cuts, investment incentives, regulatory reform, and monetary restraint to evoke a vigorous "supply-side" response and expand the capacity of the American economy. Reaganomics with the Laffer curve promised tax reductions without revenue reductions and rapid growth with declining inflation. A larger economic base would permit the administration to increase defense spending and investment without reducing consumption. By the autumn of 1982, continuing economic stagnation had demolished expectations of a quick and painless expansion of economic capacity.

Reaganomics without the Laffer curve is a program to reduce consumption to finance investment and military spending. The domestic spending cuts and regressive tax policies of the administration redistribute income away from the poor, with their tendency to devote resources to food and shelter, toward high-income groups with higher savings rates.[4] A tight monetary policy would further stimulate savings by sustaining high real interest rates. Taken together, these policies can repress consumption and spur savings, but they do not address the problem of managing the tradeoff between military spending and economic growth.

The Reagan Administration's Five Year Defense Plan projects a 7.4 percent annual real growth rate in defense spending over the period 1983-1987. The defense plan aims at building what Secretary Weinberger calls "the capital stock of the nation's defense establishment" by emphasizing procurement of defense durable goods.[5] James R. Capra, of the Federal Reserve Bank of New York, observes, "In procurement, the projected increase is larger, more rapid, and of longer duration than the Vietnam buildup." [6] The $1.7 trillion five year defense plan and the Reagan domestic package are the central elements of the administration's program to reverse trends towards the recession of American power. How are these two programs related?

In his FY 1983 Report to Congress, Secretary Weinberger declared:

> Fears that the defense budget of this Administration will strain the American economy are unfounded. In the 1950s and 1960s, when defense spending as a percentage of GNP was much larger than today, annual inflation rates ranged from about one to seven percent. Economic studies have found little difference in the effect of defense spending on inflation. Defense spending, like other Federal spending, produces something which contributes to the people's welfare.[7]

The relationship between military spending and economic performance is more complex than Secretary Weinberger suggests.

The nature of the tradeoff hinges on the extent of underutilization of the economy as a whole and defense sectors in particular, inflation rates, and monetary and fiscal policy. Consider two macroeconomic scenarios. If the Reagan domestic economic program succeeds in triggering growth in domestic fixed capital formation and production, then the Defense Plan would encounter serious bottlenecks and capacity limits. The defense sector and private sectors would be forced to bid against each other for scarce plant and engineering talent. The quality of volunteer enlistments would decline and the price of attracting and retaining skilled personnel would increase. With a domestic economy operating at or near capacity, the price of defense would increase, and price increases in the defense sector would spill over into the private sector. In the period 1975 through 1980, price increases in the defense sector averaged 2 percent more than general inflation as measured by the GNP deflator.[8] In a tight economy, the sharp Reagan defense spending increases would increase the spread even more. To date, the Reagan economic program has not stimulated capital formation or growth, and the American economy operates at far less than capacity. Industrial slack seems ample for defense production and the all-volunteer force is functioning as an employer of last resort. In Emma Rothschild's words, "Mr. Reagan, the first military Keynesian, may be spending his way out of the recession of 1982." [9] But all is not well.

With stagnation, financial/interest rate problems replace the capacity/ inflation problems of the first macroeconomic scenario. Federal revenues have run well below initial administration projections, and federal budgetary deficits are large. Although both domestic and defense spending contribute to deficits, in practical terms it is fair to speak of defense deficits. Under the Five Year Defense Plan, the military share of all federal spending is to increase from 25 to 38 percent, and the military share of the "disposable" federal budget — outlays excluding trust funds and interest on national debt — will increase from 50 to 75 percent.[10] With a substantial proportion of all lending projected to go to deficit financing, the Reagan administration effectively discourages private sector capital formation and thereby compromises its own long-term plans for stimulating productivity and growth. Furthermore, the shift from domestic spending to defense procurement may reduce employment for any given size budget. Defense durable goods are highly knowledge- and capital-intensive, and defense investment appears to compare unfavorably with other federal spending in terms of reducing unemployment.[11]

In short, if the Reagan domestic economic program begins to achieve its growth and investment targets, the ambitious defense procurement program is likely to produce capital goods bottlenecks and contribute to inflation. If the Reagan tax cuts fail to produce a strong supply-side response and growth, and the Federal Reserve Board restrains monetary growth, the defense increases will contribute to large budgetary deficits and high interest rates. Either a capacity/inflation or finance/interest rate problem is very likely to compel reductions in the growth of military spending. By developing defense and economic programs based on the assumption that no tradeoff exists, the administration may have inadvertently worsened the terms of the tradeoff. Secretary Weinberger notes that achieving defense savings in midstream has disproportionate effects on capabilities:

> Because of Defense spendout patterns, outlay reductions require program reductions about four times as large. This causes serious program disruptions and impacts heavily on faster spending readiness functions.[12]

The first installment of the defense program commits the government to multiple-year contracts with weapons producers and researchers. Because these future commitments can be abrogated only at substantial cost, reductions in the growth of the defense budget are likely to come at the expense of bread-and-butter operations and maintenance. Projecting massive increases in defense spending and then retrenching to a lower rate of growth produces *less* effective defense capability than planning and carrying out a far more modest defense program.

These short-term economic effects of the Reagan Defense Plan are of secondary importance. The administration's goals are long-term, and the administration's programs must be evaluated with respect to the long-term compatibility of defense and economic goals. Bruce Carter Jackson of Brown Brothers, Harriman & Company found that high levels of defense spending correlate with low economic growth for the seven advanced industrial states. He argues that military spending diverts resources and distorts their allocation, thereby hindering growth and contributing to inflation.[13] A recent study by the Council on Economic Priorities found that among advanced industrial states in the 1970s, economic growth, growth in productivity, and gross domestic fixed capital formation were strongly and negatively associated with military spending. The United States' position in international trade may be expected to erode as resources are drawn from commercial to military applications. Even without the Five Year Plan, the United States devotes a far higher share of national resources to defense than do other advanced industrial states. In the period 1960-1976, the United States devoted well over half of each research and development dollar to defense. Over the same period, 90 percent of German and 95 percent of Japanese research and development was devoted to nondefense purposes.[14] Any economy has finite resources, and spending on defense must come at the expense of consumption or investment. In practice, high rates of growth and capital formation are difficult to sustain in the face of high levels of military spending.

The Reagan administration can increase American near-term military capabilities at the expense of domestic economic welfare and international economic position. Ultimately, the tradeoff among military position, international economic position, and domestic economic welfare cannot be fudged; to argue otherwise is disingenuous. Even if the administration succeeds in repressing consumption to finance investment and military spending, it will not address other causes of the international diffusion of power. The international diffusion of technology appears irreversible, and economic burdens of leadership are increased by the administration's core security policy. American policy, alone, cannot arrest or reverse structural tendencies toward cyclical hegemonic decline. The goal of restoring American economic and military preeminence to what it was a generation ago is alluring and unattainable.

III: Configurations of Interest and Strategies of Adjustment

The international diffusion of power increases the analytic significance of a frequently neglected second aspect of international systems structure: the configuration of international interests. As direct control over the actions of other nations becomes difficult, the prosperity and security of a declining hegemonic power increasingly depends on how other nations define their interests and how it adjusts to its changing position in the international system. When the strong can impose their will on the weak, the interests of the weak are inconsequential. As power diffuses, international patterns of conflict and communality of interest often determine outcomes.

The initial security policy of the Reagan administration rested on the assumption that the scope and intensity of international conflict precluded resort to strategies of adjustment. The administration hoped that an assertive and focused security policy would weaken the position of the Soviet Union in the Third World, strengthen the anti-Soviet coalition, and ultimately force the Soviet Union to choose between external retrenchment and internal collapse. By contrast, the initial international economic policies of the administration were strangely indifferent to lines of international and domestic economic conflict. The administration adopted a minimalist foreign economic policy reflecting the administration's commitment to classical economic liberalism at home and abroad. Paradoxically, each core policy may ultimately operate to the detriment of its primary objective. Over the long term, the initial security policy may strengthen the Soviet position in the Third World, weaken the Western alliance system, and strengthen confrontationalist elements within the Soviet Union, and the initial foreign economic policy may destabilize the liberal international economic order that the administration seeks to strengthen. In both cases, the old strategies of adjustment explicitly repudiated by the Reagan administration appear to satisfy the administration's own goals better than the administration's own policies.

International Security Policy

The strategy of restoration rested, in part, on the view that a weakening America would find itself in an *increasingly* hostile world. Declining relative American military strength may cause international realignment toward the Soviet Union, as rising Soviet military strength evokes the twin spectres of a "Finlandized" Western Europe and Sino-Soviet entente. The effects of even marginal changes in the bilateral Soviet-American military balance are magnified if nations "bandwagon" and move from the weaker towards the stronger. The administration assigned a high priority to accelerating defense spending because it feared that international tendencies towards bandwagoning necessitated greater American military effort. By contrast, the familiar concept of the balance of power holds that tendencies toward the international concentration of power are offset by tendencies toward the formation of countervailing coalitions. International relations remain anarchic rather than imperial because the rise of a strong nation creates an incentive for other powers to align against the potential imperial power. The last four centuries of Western history support the view that *balancing* dominates *bandwagoning*. Again and again, rising powers seeking wider empire have conjured up opposing coalitions. Louis XIV, Napoleon, Kaiser Wilhelm, and Hitler reached for hegemony and ultimately mobilized opposing coalitions that contained or destroyed them. The strategy of adjustment in the 1970s sought to capitalize on this international tendency towards balancing to lessen the American burden of military leadership.[15]

The Reagan administration also saw important elements of the strategy of adjustment to declining power as contributing directly to the erosion of the United States' international position. Distasteful compromises and hard choices are inherent features of a strategy of adjustment. The Reagan administration differed from the administrations of the 1970s in viewing adjustments as potentially catastrophic and not merely distasteful.

A degree of retrenchment is the first element of a strategy of adjustment. Where the interests of the United States clash with the interests of other nations, declining American power will obviously have adverse effects on American interests. If power is insufficient to protect all threatened interests, damage may be limited by employing policies attuned to the distinction between vital and peripheral interests. During the 1970s, the United States altered first the means and then the ends of policy toward revolution in the periphery. Under President Nixon, the United States retained the goal of controlling revolutions but shifted from direct military intervention to the less expensive instruments of the Nixon Doctrine: security-supporting assistance, arms sales, military training programs, and covert action. By linking military and economic assistance to human rights, the Carter administration sought to force political and economic reforms that it believed would eventually stem revolutionary discontent while legitimizing American military aid for governments beset by revolution. Where reforms did not materialize, denial of military and economic assistance placed some distance between the United States and the anciens régimes and facilitated development of relations with possible successor regimes. Carter's policy rested ultimately on the assumption that the United States can live with revolutionary nationalist governments in the Third World and hence need not support authoritarian anticommunist governments that did not embrace programs of reform.

The Reagan administration viewed revolutionary change as both a direct threat to American security and economic interests and as a test of American resolve. In October of 1982, former Secretary of State Haig placed the administration's policy toward revolutionary change in a global context:

> We confronted a situation where strategic passivity during the Ford administration and the excessive piety of the Carter administration's human rights crusade had sapped the will of authoritarian anticommunist governments, eroded the confidence of Western allies, and encouraged risk taking by the Soviet Union and by Soviet manipulated totalitarian regimes. Since 1975, this bipartisan policy of failure had permitted the Soviet Union to inflict disastrous defeats on the United States at regular six month intervals.[16]

This global perspective rejected the notion of distinguishing between peripheral and vital interests. "Defeats" in the Third World were disastrous, in and of themselves, and also undercut the United States' global position by eroding confidence in the United States. By intent and in effect, the Reagan administration's reassertive policy on Third World revolution signaled a departure from the strategy of adjustment and policies of retrenchment. First, unconditional military and economic assistance to embattled authoritarian anticommunist regimes would stiffen the resolve of governing elites while bolstering counterinsurgency capabilities. Statutes linking aid to economic and political reform impeded full implementation of this strategy, but the administration increased the American commitment to many authoritarian governments after certifying progress on human rights. Second, covert paramilitary and overt political and economic pressure against Soviet clients and proxies would compel these regimes to loosen their ties to the Soviet bloc and to cease supporting neighboring insurgencies. The administration hoped that these two policies would check direct threats against perceived American interests in the Third World and would support the more general goal of restoring global confidence in the United States. Globalist policies tend to underestimate the significance of intraregional lines of conflict. The imperfect correspondence between the administration's globalist image and regional realities blunted the effectiveness of initial policies towards Latin America, Africa, and the Middle East.* Although the most telling criticisms of the administration's regional policies are regionally specific and idiosyncratic, the premises underlying Reagan policy towards revolutionary change merit further examination on a more general plane.

The primary extraregional American interest in stemming Third World revolution centers on the question of credibility. Does revolutionary change in the Third World undercut confidence in United States' core commitments to NATO and Japan? The European allies regarded the American intervention in Vietnam as a vastly disproportionate response to a peripheral concern. From their perspective, the American fixation on Third World revolution may weaken the West by diverting resources to a peripheral theater. At present, social democratic governments and parties in Western Europe are among the strongest opponents of administration policies toward Central America. A reversal of policy or successful revolution would be unlikely to create a crisis of confidence in Europe. The cost of controlling revolutionary change is potentially quite high. Suppressing strong revolutionary movements is expensive, and augmenting the capabilities of insurgents is cheap. The Soviets invested far less in Vietnam than did the United States, and a small covert investment of weapons and aid to the Afghan guerrillas requires a far larger offsetting Soviet investment. From a Soviet perspective, an American policy of offering unconditional support for authoritarian governments may create an ideal opportunity for accelerating the decline of the United States. By treating revolutionary change in the Third World as a central test of American credibility, the United States locks itself into a strategically unfavorable position.

How great a threat does revolution pose to the economic and security interests of the United States in the Third World?[17] Conflict between established governments and insurgents clearly disrupts economic relations and engenders international disputes over sanctuaries and arms flows. These consequences of ongoing revolutionary processes should be distinguished from the aftereffects of revolutionary change. Do the economic interests and policies of radical nationalist regimes differ from those of more traditional authoritarian regimes? Both revolutionary and nonrevolutionary regimes have on occasion sought to alter the terms of their relationship to the Western international economic system through complete or partial expropriation of multinational corporations, renegotiation or abrogation of contracts with foreign suppliers, renegotiation of mineral

---

* The evolution of American policy towards these regions is examined by Abraham Lowenthal in Chapter 10, "Ronald Reagan and Latin America: Coping With Hegemony in Decline"; Donald Rothchild and John Ravenhill in Chapter 11, "From Carter to Reagan: The Global Perspective on Africa Becomes Ascendant"; and Barry Rubin, Chapter 12, "The Reagan Administration and the Middle East."

leases, and threats of default on international financial obligations. Although, on balance, revolutionary states appear more likely to disrupt international economic ties, regimes of all ideological stripes appear to have an increasingly strong interest in maintaining access to Western markets, capital, and technology. To earn much-needed foreign exchange, the Marxist government of Angola uses Cuban troops to defend Gulf Oil operations from attack by nominally "pro-American" insurgents. Radical nationalist Guinea works in partnership with the Fria mining company. The Sandinist regime of Nicaragua renegotiated loans from foreign banks and actively seeks foreign investment. The relationship between external economic policy and internal political and economic ideology appears to be diminishing.

Do revolutionary nationalist regimes pose a threat to the security interests of the United States? When revolutionary regimes permit the Soviet Union to use their land for military bases and their armies for proxy interventions, their actions are clearly averse to the security interests of the United States. Soviet advisors, military training programs, military installations, and intelligence operations create opportunities for political penetration and control. The Reagan administration's policy of increasing pressure on regimes in the Third World is intended to intimidate these nations into loosening their ties to the Soviet Union and to impede Soviet consolidation of its Third World empire.

Confrontationist policies toward radical states may drive them closer to the Soviet Union. The Soviet Union's record of using close military relationships to penetrate and overthrow clients threatens the political autonomy of revolutionary nationalist regimes, and a number of clients have distanced themselves from the Soviet Union precisely to preserve their autonomy. The nationalism of revolutionary nationalist states is a centrifugal force that obstructs Soviet consolidation of its empire. The Reagan administration's policy of intimidation — whether through rhetoric, covert assistance to proxies, or overt assistance to regional adversaries of radical nationalist regimes — weakens this centrifugal tendency. These regimes confront a tradeoff between security and autonomy. By heightening their sense of insecurity, the confrontational policy of the Reagan administration increases these regimes' perceived need for Soviet military assistance and also provides an opening for the military instruments of Soviet political penetration. The administration's policy toward revolutionary states simplifies the Soviets' difficult task of manipulating Third World clients and abets Soviet consolidation of its empire.[18]

During the 1970s, American policy towards the Soviet Union was based on the existence of limited areas of mutual interest within the context of a larger competitive relationship. A confrontationist strategy rests on a largely zero-sum view of the Soviet-American relationship; the basic test of the appropriateness of individual actions centers on the comparison of the magnitude of *relative* gains and losses, and not the *mutuality* of gains. Where American benefits exceed Soviet benefits, and where American costs are less than Soviet costs, the United States can advance its position relative to the Soviet Union. From the perspective of most ranking members of the administration, Soviet conduct is constrained almost solely by Soviet military and economic resources. The administration's nuclear policy, East-West trade policy, Third World policy, and the previously discussed defense program are part of a coherent strategy to control Soviet conduct by reducing Soviet capabilities. Although the Soviet Union could offset any one or two elements of the strategy, the administration believed that the Soviets lacked the resources to respond to pressure on all fronts.

Starting from this perspective, many members of the administration reject the existence of "limited mutual interests" in a fundamentally conflictual relationship. In their view, strategic arms negotiations had strengthened the Soviet Union and weakened the United States. SALT I, the Vladivostok Agreement, and SALT II had reduced American will to modernize and expand strategic forces while permitting the Soviet Union to open a "window of vulnerability" against American land-based missiles. The administration's strategic programs and arms control policies were designed to place the United States into a position of "nuclear superiority" as defined from a counterforce escalation dominance perspective. This perspective defines nuclear superiority in terms of the ratio of counterforce capabilities remaining after exchanges of salvos of missiles targeted against strategic forces.[19] The administration argues that this form of nuclear superiority is necessary to deter a Soviet attack because Soviet civil defense and industrial dispersion programs have limited their vulnerability to countervalue and retaliation. The superiority in second-strike counterforce escalation dominance that the administration publicly seeks provides an even greater degree of first-strike superiority. As members of the administration have privately acknowledged, "A missile that can be fired second can be fired first. But that doesn't mean that we would." Other members of the administration argue that such an incidental first strike counterforce capability would permit the United States to use nuclear threats to deter conventional war.

To attain superiority, the administration followed a two-pronged approach. In their view, weapons such as the MX and Trident II directly increase counterforce capabilities and the threat to acquire such weapons would provide leverage to secure a strategic arms control agreement favorable to the United States. If such a favorable arms control agreement could not be negotiated, the United States — with its superior economic and technological base — would prevail in the ensuing arms race. This view of strategic arms negotiations as a possible path to strategic advantage conditioned the administration's position on related arms control issues. The administration announced that it would not renew negotiations on the Comprehensive Test Ban Treaty on the grounds that such a treaty would limit both Soviet and American modernization programs. In the autumn of 1982, the administration rejected negotiations over military competition in outer space and accelerated development of space warfare capabilities. Eugene Rostow, the Director of the Arms Control and Disarmament Agency, explained that the United States was not interested, because "Any space weapon limitation which limits the threat to United States satellites will necessarily protect threatening Soviet satellites as well." [20]

The administration's policy on strategic nuclear issues is grounded on several questionable assumptions. First, the administration assumes that Soviet civil defense and industrial dispersion programs have limited Soviet vulnerability to a second-strike countervalue attack. As Van Evera and Posen note in Chapter 3, 3,500 United States strategic warheads would survive a Soviet surprise attack, while only 141 large warheads could destroy over half of Soviet industrial capacity. Both the United States and the Soviet Union can destroy each other's civilizations many times over *after* absorbing an attack. Second, fear of the "window of vulnerability" and desire for the counterforce capabilities of the MX are based on the assumption that the ratio of surviving strategic forces under the escalation dominance scenario is a suitable measure of nuclear superiority or inferiority. The administration assumes that both sides have the capacity to fight a carefully controlled prolonged counterforce nuclear war. Even an undamaged organization with sensors and rationality intact would be challenged by the formidable tasks of distinguishing between a counterforce and countervalue attack, mounting retaliatory strikes against the strategic forces of the adversary, assessing the effectiveness of retaliatory strikes, retargeting remaining strategic forces, estimating the ratio of surviving forces, and negotiating an end to the nuclear war. Can badly damaged fragments of complex organizations perform these functions while under nuclear attack? The administration's definition of strategic superiority rests on this questionable foundation. By playing down the strategic significance of robust second-strike countervalue capabilities and exaggerating the importance of counterforce weapons and doctrines, the administration has contributed to an unrealistic image of American nuclear weakness. Whatever the demerits of escalation dominance as a basis for defining degrees of strategic superiority, both the Reagan administration and the Soviet leadership allocate resources and develop strategies consistent with the assumption that counterforce nuclear wars can be won or lost. The persistence of this common delusion jeopardizes the strongest of Soviet-American mutual interests — the avoidance of nuclear war. In his recent essay, "Fears of War, Programs for Peace," John Steinbrunner of the Brookings Institution makes a strong case for the strategic insignificance of attainable degrees of nuclear "superiority." He argues that this strategic reality provides a political opportunity for creating a stable *sense* of mutual restraint. The United States and the Soviet Union share an interest in balanced reductions of strategic forces and in a moratorium on strategic force modernization. By striving for negotiated unbalanced reductions and by foreclosing discussions on a comprehensive nuclear test ban, the Reagan administration effectively reinforces the common delusion in the significance of counterforce and precludes realization of the common interest in enhancing nuclear stability.

The second strand of the Reagan administration's Soviet strategy centers on the manipulation of international trade and finance to inflict costs on the Soviet Union, Eastern Europe, and Soviet clients in the Third World. The success of economic sanctions rests, ultimately, on the cooperation of third parties that can supply goods, technology, and credits and that can provide markets for target state exports. The Carter administration's post-Afghan sanctions were largely unilateral in scope, and inflicted minimal costs on the Soviet Union. Grain-producing nations such as Argentina, Canada, and Australia diverted grain exports from their traditional markets toward the Soviet Union even as the United States diverted grain shipments in the opposite direction. Beyond tightening existing restrictions on goods of military significance, the Western Europeans did not alter their East-West policies and replaced American contracts. Japan also tightened existing restrictions of goods of military significance, and canceled several large projects, which were picked up by France. In the absence of multilateral coordination, economic sanctions produce changes in trading partners without inflicting tangible costs on the target nation.

The Reagan administration bowed to domestic political pressure by lifting limits on grain exports, but it set about seeking to limit Soviet access to Western credits and nonagricultural goods. Although many in the Departments of State, Treasury, and Commerce regarded sanctions as little more than a form of symbolic speech, the Secretary of Defense and National Security Advisors believed that a strategy of economic warfare could reduce the capacity of the Soviet economy. Any transaction that the Soviet Union seeks alleviates, to a degree, the Soviet Union's guns-butter-growth tradeoff.[21] To the greatest extent possible, this second faction within the administration sought to reduce trade between the Soviet Union and the West in order to exacerbate the internal economic crisis within the Soviet Union.

Controlling alternative sources of goods, credits, and technology is crucial to the conduct of economic warfare, but the allies do not share the Weinberger-Clark view of the political and economic desirability of economic warfare. The European-American clash over the Siberian natural gas pipeline became a test of American will to execute the economic warfare strategy. The Clark-Weinberger faction hoped to delay or cancel a project that they saw as increasing Western European dependency on the Soviets and as providing the Soviets with hard currency that could be used to purchase additional goods. The Europeans were unwilling to give up exports of equipment and materials to be used in the pipeline project, to forgo an opportunity to reduce their dependency on Middle Eastern energy, or to ignore an opportunity to channel currency from the Middle East toward the heavily indebted Eastern bloc. Administration efforts to challenge Western European participation in the natural gas pipeline by invoking retroactive export controls against the Europeans imposed greater costs on the allies and the United States than on the Soviet Union. Although the pipeline policy was reversed in November of 1982, this dispute over East-West trade reflects a more general problem with the Reagan administration's foreign policy. In a world of declining American unilateral power, greater reliance on multilateral strategies becomes a necessity. Yet the Reagan administration's security strategy is not shared by any other major nation. Efforts to convince other nations of the merits of the Reagan approach have been notably unsuccessful. Where divergent interests exist, "leadership" may take the form of coercion or compensation. Administration efforts to control the actions of other nations through devices such as the extraterritorial application of American law have been counterproductive: The international diffusion of power increases the importance of coordination but lessens American leverage to coerce coordination. (Even during the 1950s and 1960s, at the peak of American preeminence in international affairs, the United States could not control the East-West trade policies of the Western Europeans.) Efforts to control the actions of other nations through compensation have run afoul of the expense of compensation. With reference to the pipeline case, the administration did not seriously develop proposals to create an attractive alternative to the Soviet-European package. The administration offered Norwegian natural gas to West Germany, but neglected to determine whether Norway was interested in accelerating its rate of production. Press reports to the contrary, the administration never presented a plan to West Germany for substituting American coal for Soviet gas. The basic fact that the Reagan administration's strategies are at variance with the strategies of other major states renders major elements of the Reagan approach to international affairs unworkable.

International Economic Policy

The extent and significance of international economic interdependence during the 1950s and 1960s is often exaggerated. During the 1970s, however, American integration into the international economic system proceeded at a startling pace. Table 1-4 presents United States' trade in

TABLE 1-4. United States Trade in Goods and
Services as a Percentage of GNP

	1950	*1960*	*1970*	*1980*
Exports/GNP	5.0	5.7	6.6	12.9
Imports/GNP	4.3	4.6	5.9	12.1

SOURCE: *Economic Report of the President, 1982,*
Table B-1.

goods and services as a percentage of the Gross National Product. Both
the import and export dependency of the United States *doubled* during
the 1970s. These developments in trade are paralleled in finance. In 1970,
foreign lending amounted to 7.6 percent of total bank lending. By 1980,
international lending amounted to 26 percent of total lending.[22] Even as
American international economic weight declined, the importance of the
international economy to the United States increased.

The administrations of the 1970s slowly broadened the scope of political multilateral management to address problems that arose as a consequence of increasing interdependence and declining American economic
power. Equally significantly, the administrations of the 1970s gradually
expanded the domain of United States governmental involvement at the
boundary between domestic and international economies. The federal
government's role in facilitating adjustment and in fostering export development expanded throughout the decade. The initial foreign economic
policies of the Reagan administration departed sharply from these trends.

The Reagan approach to economics, domestic or international, is
founded on the assumption that less government is better economics. The
administration's domestic economic program assumes that reducing regulations, taxes, and domestic public spending will trigger increased productivity and growth. By sheltering individuals and firms from the harsh
realities of the marketplace, government blunts incentives to work, save,
and innovate. By regulating and prohibiting economic transactions that
adversely affect the environment or the health of workers, government
decreases the efficiency of the private sector. By taxing, government distorts incentives and discourages work. Reagan's international economic
policy is firmly grounded on this marketist outlook.

The administration targeted international organizations with particular enthusiasm. One White House official summarized the views of his
colleagues: "If Federal government is bad, international government is
ten times worse." [23] The administration moved to reduce American
contributions to multilateral development banks and to shift the terms
of official development assistance from grants toward market-rate loans.
The administration rejected the Law of the Sea treaty on the ground that

the supranational authority created by the treaty would overregulate and overtax American firms engaged in seabed mining. The administration opposed a United Nations resolution discouraging the advertising and sale of infant formula in nations with unsanitary water on the ground that the United States should not countenance creation of a "global Federal Trade Commission." The administration opposed a World Bank program to fund energy conservation and exploration in the Third World on the ground that the World Bank program would create unfair competition for multinational oil companies. In each instance of the administration's opposition to an expansion of the scope of international political management, it believed that free market principles and particularistic corporate interests coincided. The administration quite naturally opposed regulations that appeared to operate to the detriment of individual American banks, seabed mining companies, formula producers, and oil companies.

The move away from international political management toward international deregulation undervalues the significance of political structures within which markets operate and ignores imperfections in markets. With respect to international finance, individual private banks acting rationally may seek to limit exposure when borrowers get into trouble. If all act to limit exposure, default may be assured. Multilateral international financial organizations serve the general interests of private international banks by providing distress funding and by pooling leverage over the economic policies of borrowing nations. Individual private firms acting rationally may hold back on seabed prospecting to secure a free ride on the exploration activities of other companies. Without internationally legitimized property rights, no firm can stake claims and no firm has a rational interest in investing heavily in seabed exploitation. Private dilemmas of collective action can give rise to a need for intergovernmental management.[24]

The administration also sought to bring the practices of foreign governments and the United States into line with its laissez-faire vision. In a 1981 speech before the annual meeting of the International Monetary Fund, President Reagan exhorted other nations to lessen the role of governments in economic management and to turn to multinational corporations and entrepreneurial drive as vehicles for development. To support this strand of policy, the administration linked treatment of foreign investment to aid and trade preferences in its Caribbean Basin Initiative. More fundamentally, the administration sought to limit the role of the American government in foreign economic transactions. To encourage American exporters and foreign importers to turn to commercial banks for trade finance, the administration initially reduced the lending authorization of the Export-Import bank. To permit the value of the dollar to be set by market forces, the administration opted for a policy of nonintervention in foreign exchange markets. To permit market forces to spur labor's adjustment to changing patterns of international trade, the administration eliminated income maintenance provisions of trade adjustment assistance. To permit private American manufacturers to compete more effectively in international markets, the administration sought to deregulate trade. A federal regulation discouraged American exporters from dumping unsafe toxic products onto world markets. The administration repealed the regulation one month after entering office. The Foreign Corrupt Practices Act barred American exporters and investors from bribing foreign governments. The administration favored repeal of the Act. Antitrust laws limited the ability of American corporations and banks to develop coordinated strategies for penetrating foreign markets. The administration secured repeal of antitrust regulations that had precluded development of coordinated export strategies. Regulations designed to limit exports of sensitive nuclear technology operated to the detriment of the American nuclear industry. The administration lifted many restrictions in an effort to assure potential purchasers of the reliability of American supplies. Specifically, the administration licensed the export of technology with nuclear applications to Argentina and South Africa, neither of which had signed the Nuclear Nonproliferation Treaty, and approved the export of reprocessing technology to advanced industrial states. Finally, the administration considered and rejected proposals to shift responsibility for domestic monetary management from the Federal Reserve Board to gold markets dominated by South Africa and the Soviet Union. In the realm of foreign economic policy, administration innovations aimed at reducing the role of government in international economic relations.

The administration's initial market-oriented economic policy did not squarely address international dilemmas of collective action in trade, finance, and monetary affairs. Benjamin Cohen's Chapter 4, on economic relations with other advanced industrial states; Richard Feinberg's Chapter 5, on economic relations with the Third World; and Robert Lieber's Chapter 6, on energy policy, identify areas in which the administration's policy departed from the managerial approach of the 1970s and evaluate the evolving policies of the administration.

Reagan's foreign economic policy and sanctions policy are at variance with domestic Reaganomics, and with each other. The imposition of economic sanctions, whether against nominal adversaries or nominal allies, always entails departing from market allocation of resources. Adversely affected groups invariably seek redress or a reversal of policy. The Carter administration promised to neutralize the price effects of its partial grain embargo, and encountered little initial resistance from American farmers. When the Carter administration dumped offsetting grain purchases back onto world markets, farm belt opposition mounted, and candidate Reagan committed his administration to ending the embargo. Domestic compensation schemes may be a practical political precondition of using sanctions as an instrument of diplomacy, but the substantial expense and intrinsic inefficiency of compensation runs directly contrary to the fundamental precepts of the domestic economic program.

Secondary sanctions aimed at bringing about Western compliance with American economic warfare programs directly disrupt the Western trading system and indirectly threaten the position of American exporters to Japan and Western Europe. By claiming retroactive extraterritorial jurisdiction of American law for American parts used by European companies, the administration created a powerful incentive for other nations to lessen their dependency on American goods and technologies. Diversification will operate to the detriment of the United States' export-oriented sectors.

Reagan's foreign economic policy and domestic Reaganomics are based on similar premises. Yet, paradoxically, domestic Reaganomics may prove to be incompatible with international liberalism. Unrestricted participation in international commerce and finance forces substantial domestic adjustments to shifting international trade and capital flows. Inevitable political pressures from sectors and groups that bear the domestic burden of adjustment constantly threaten to undermine liberal international economic policies. Free trade has uneven domestic distributional effects. The gains of consumers and growing export-oriented sectors come at the expense of import-competing sectors. The administrations of the 1970s gradually expanded federal programs to provide financial relief and retraining in import-competing sectors. The Carter administration added provisions for substantial relief payments over and above normal unemployment assistance in order to buy off political opposition to trade liberalization. When the Reagan administration slashed the expensive income maintenance provisions of the trade adjustment assistance program as part of its program of domestic fiscal austerity, it inadvertently increased domestic political pressures for protectionism. Beyond facilitating adjustment and buying off protectionist sectors, the government may have to play a more active role in supporting export-oriented sectors. The administration canceled its plans for reducing the lending authorization of the Export-Import Bank in order to secure leverage against foreign governments that provide their firms with export credit subsidies. Closer governmental involvement in export development and promotion, along the lines of the Japanese model, may be a requisite of successful modern international commercial success. A corporatist national industrial policy may be both a precondition for adherence to liberal international economic principles and antithetical to the precepts of Reagan's domestic economic program.[25] In short, a larger governmental role may be needed to defuse domestic illiberalism and to increase the effectiveness of liberal international economic policies.

IV: Conclusions

The foreign policies of the Nixon, Ford, and Carter administrations constituted a first round of adjustment to major changes in international circumstances. These administrations adapted to the emerging limits of American military power by narrowing the definition of American interests and commitments in peripheral regions, by shifting a greater share of the burdens of containment to China and Europe, and by acting on emerging areas of mutual interest with the Soviet Union. These administrations adapted to growing economic interdependence and declining American economic power by gradually increasing the scope of multilateral political management of the international economy. The Reagan administration challenged both the need to adjust and the methods of adjustment. It offered a strategy of restoration to stem the erosion of American power and a set of core security and economic policies that departed sharply from policies of the 1970s. Taken as a whole, the Reagan administration's experiment is proving impracticable.

The strategy of restoration relies on military and economic investment to reverse the diffusion of power. This largely domestic strategy does not lighten burdens of leadership, check technological diffusion, or address other international causes of hegemonic decline. The domestic political struggle over the allocation of American resources to guns, butter, and growth is ultimately a referendum on the desirability and feasibility of this approach to restoration. The administration garnered initial support for its military and economic programs by exaggerating Western military weakness and by ignoring the tension between military and economic aspects of its long-term strategy. This approach to implementing restoration may have purchased short-term political success at the expense of long-term American strength. The emergence of more balanced appraisals of the East-West military balance and the recognition of the substantial economic costs of the defense program will erode support for continued acceleration of defense spending. Inevitable modification of the five-year defense plan will leave the military with an excess of hard-to-cancel hardware and a shortage of easy-to-cancel operations and maintenance.[26] The administration's denial of the guns-butter-growth tradeoff also provides a spurious basis for economic planning and thereby damages American economic performance. By acting as if the tradeoff between economic and military strength were inconsequential, the administration has inadvertently worsened the terms of that tradeoff. Paradoxically, the administration's strategy of restoration appears likely to accelerate the erosion of American military and economic strength. Domestic and international limits circumscribe and vitiate the administration's quest for restoration of American power.

The Reagan administration's initial security and economic policies constituted an implicit indictment of the 1970s strategy of adjustment. The administration expanded American commitments in the periphery, developed regional policies that focused on the extraregional Soviet threat, redefined the American relationship with China and Western Europe, and accentuated conflicts of interest with the Soviet Union. These security policies were paired with a laissez-faire international economic policy that reduced the extent of governmental and intergovernmental management of international economic relations. The assumptions underlying the core security and economic policies did not accord well with international realities. During 1981 and 1982, international events compelled piecemeal modification of the initial core policies. The administration's predisposition toward alliance management by unilateral assertion contributed to the rapid deterioration of the Atlantic and Sino-American relationships. The Reagan administration eventually returned to the position of earlier administrations on Theater Nuclear Force negotiations, European participation in the Siberian pipeline project, and the Taiwan question. Initial regional policies in the Middle East and Africa were premised on the assumption that the United States could blunt intense intraregional conflicts by emphasizing the extraregional Soviet threat. The Arab-Israeli conflict and Namibian conflict forced the administration to adjust its globalist policies to mesh with local circumstances. The administration's confrontational rhetoric on strategic nuclear issues contributed to the growth of a transnational antinuclear movement. The administration entered into strategic arms control negotiations and softened its nuclear rhetoric. The administration's initial aversion to multilateral political management of international economic relations reduced the ability of the International Monetary Fund and the World Bank to function as lenders of last resort and thereby contributed to the international financial crisis in late 1982. The administration responded by supporting increased authorizations for these international organizations and by extending bilateral credits to individual debtor nations. To its credit, the administration has proved willing to grasp the nettles that it inadvertently cultivated. The core security and economic policies have been modified in response to crises. However, in the absence of crises the administration has adhered to its core policies. While softening its rhetoric on revolution in the periphery, the administration has continued to commit American credibility and resources to the maintenance of authoritarian regimes and to engage in covert action against revolutionary regimes. In international economic affairs, the administration continues to oppose the extension of multilateral management on issues such as the law of the sea and macroeconomic coordination.

Although the administration is shifting toward a strategy of adjustment, the ad hoc approach to adjustment is both dangerous and inefficient. By expanding commitments without regard to resources, the administration needlessly widens the gap between the means and ends of American foreign policy. By waiting for crises to compel policy changes, the administration needlessly risks exacerbating unavoidable problems and forgoes opportunities for preventive diplomacy. The task of developing a foreign policy attuned to the limits of American power and to the realities of economic interdependence is difficult under the best of circumstances. By persisting in its quest for restoration and by maintaining its core security and economic policies until compelled to change, the Reagan administration has lost an important measure of control over the form and extent of adjustment. The Reagan administration entered office committed to enlarging the capacity of the United States to control the international environment. Ironically, the evolution of Reagan administration foreign policy may appear, in retrospect, as a textbook example of how the international environment shapes foreign policy.

"International Systems Structure and American Foreign Policy" was written for this volume. Copyright © 1983 by Kenneth A. Oye.

Notes

1. Henry Kissinger, Address before the Annual Convention of the American Society of Newspaper Editors, Washington, D.C., April 10, 1980.
2. Alexander Haig, "A New Direction in U.S. Foreign Policy," Current Policy Number 275, Bureau of Public Affairs, Department of State.
3. Mancur Olson and Richard Zeckhauser, "An Economic Theory of Alliances," *The Review of Economics and Statistics* 48 (1966), pp. 266-279.
4. For Urban Institute estimates of the effects of tax and spending changes on groups of families stratified by income, see *The Economist*, September 25, 1982.
5. U.S. Department of Defense, *Annual Report to Congress Fiscal Year 1983* (Washington: U.S. Government Printing Office, 1982), p. I-6.
6. James R. Capra, "The National Defense Budget and Its Economic Effects," *Federal Reserve Bank of New York Quarterly Review* (Summer 1981), p. 21.
7. U.S. Department of Defense, *Annual Report to Congress Fiscal Year 1983*, p. I-9.
8. Capra, p. 25.
9. Emma Rothschild, "The Philosophy of Reaganism," *The New York Review of Books*, April 15, 1982.
10. Council on Economic Priorities, *Machinists and Aerospace Workers Report*, 1982.
11. *Ibid.*, p. 27.
12. U.S. Department of Defense, *Annual Report to Congress Fiscal Year 1983*, p. 1-44.
13. Bruce Carter Jackson, *Military Expenditures, Growth, and Inflation in Seven Leading Industrial Countries* (New York: Brown Brothers, Harriman & Co., 1981).
14. Council on Economic Priorities, p. 23.
15. Kenneth N. Waltz, *Theory of International Politics* (Reading, Mass.: Addison-Wesley, 1979) contains the best published discussion of balancing and bandwagoning.
16. Public Address, Princeton University, October 14, 1982.
17. For an extended discussion of interests and policies of radical nationalist Third

World nations and implications for United States foreign policy, see Richard Feinberg, *The Intemperate Zone: The Third World Challenge to U.S. Foreign Policy* (New York: Norton, 1983).

18. Robert Jervis provides a general analytic framework for assessing the appropriateness of strategies of confrontation and accommodation in his "Deterrence, the Spiral Model, and Intentions of the Adversary," in *Perception and Misperception in International Politics* (Princeton: Princeton University Press, 1976).

19. A Reagan administration arms negotiator, Paul Nitze, wrote the seminal essay on counterforce escalation dominance. See "Assuring Strategic Stability in an Era of Detente," *Foreign Affairs* (January 1976), for an extended discussion of this approach to defining nuclear superiority. For a critical review of Nitze's premises, see Gary Brewer and Bruce Blair, "War Games and National Security with a Grain of Salt," *The Bulletin of Atomic Scientists* (June 1979).

20. Eugene Rostow, Testimony before the Senate Foreign Relations Committee, Subcommittee on Arms Control (September 30, 1982).

21. Varied rationalizations have obscured the primary intent of the National Security Council and Department of Defense policy on East-West trade. Domestic politics compelled cancellation of the grain embargo. Efforts to distinguish between American grain sales and European natural gas purchases through mercantilist arguments on the effects of revenue absorbing and revenue producing transactions should be dismissed as political boilerplate.

22. Figures on international lending as a proportion of total lending were computed from Table B-63 (Total Bank Loans) and Table B-105 (Claims on Foreigners and Claims on Unaffiliated Foreigners Reported by United States Banks), *Economic Report of the President 1982* (Washington: U.S. Government Printing Office, 1982).

23. Background interview, Washington, D.C., July 1981.

24. For contrasting views on the extent to which dilemmas of collective action create a need for intergovernmental management, see John Conybeare, "International Organization and the Theory of Property Rights," *International Organization* (Summer 1980), and Robert O. Keohane, "The Demand for International Regimes," *International Organization* (Winter 1982).

25. The tension between the principles of domestic Reaganomics and international liberalism may be compounded by the short-term macroeconomic consequences of the domesttic economic program. Rapid noninflationary growth could render the Reagan foreign economic policy politically and economically viable. Growth would alleviate problems of adjustment and pressures for protection, while greater productivity would facilitate development and exploitation of foreign markets.

26. The administration may compound this problem if it resorts to a game of budgetary chicken to seek to preserve the original five-year defense plan. The administration could amplify the effects of budgetary changes on preparedness by locking an even higher proportion of its defense spending into long-term weapons procurement programs and thereby seek to deter budgetary changes.

2

Conservatism, Not Interventionism: Trends in Foreign Policy Opinion, 1974–1982

William Schneider

Foreign policy, it is often said, was an important factor in Ronald Reagan's election to the Presidency in 1980. After experiencing failure in Vietnam, blackmail at the hands of Arab oil powers, humiliation in Iran, and alarm over Soviet adventurism in Africa and Afghanistan, the electorate seemed determined to revive American military power and reassert U.S. leadership in the world. Some observers welcomed the prospect of this country's regaining its nerve after so much frustration and demoralization. Others feared that the nation was reverting to the paranoia that prevailed during the darkest days of the Cold War. But almost everyone expected a major change in the style and substance of American foreign policy.

What is surprising, then, is the modest extent of that change during the first two years of the Reagan administration. To be sure, the president pressed for and won a substantial buildup of the nation's military forces. Defiance and confrontationalism, however, were more evident in the administration's rhetoric than in its policies. By the middle of 1982, a number of staunch conservatives had become disillusioned and outspoken in their criticisms. "The Administration seems to be pursuing the same old policy of detente," neoconservative writer Midge Decter lamented to *The New York Times*, "and I think if Reagan were not in office now, he'd be leading the opposition." [1]

It can be argued that this outcome was inevitable. Ideology can

William Schneider is Resident Fellow at the American Enterprise Institute in Washington, D.C. He is also a political consultant to National Journal *and* The Los Angeles Times, *where his articles appear regularly, and coauthor of* The Confidence Gap: Business, Labor, and Government in the Public Mind (*Free Press, 1983*).

seldom stand the test of reality. The pressure of events and the complexity of the international situation necessitate a moderate and cautious approach to foreign policy for any administration. But, perhaps more to the point, this administration appeared to make a deliberate decision to place foreign policy, along with social issues, on the back burner for a while. Nothing was allowed to compete with the economy for preeminence on the national agenda — and there was certainly nothing moderate or cautious about the administration's approach to economic policy. In other words, there is reason to believe that the subdued foreign policy style of the Reagan Administration was very much a political decision.

If the decision was indeed political, it can be argued that it had a sound basis in public opinion. The public's views on foreign policy, like its views on many other issues, are complex and inconsistent. The electorate wanted boldness and self-assertion from the nation's leaders, but not risk or sacrifice. People favored a military buildup but no new foreign policy crusades. If conservative activists were dismayed, the public seemed to appreciate the administration's reluctance to become deeply involved in conflicts in Poland, El Salvador, the Falkland Islands, and the Middle East.

This essay will first examine the nature of the foreign policy "mandate" that emerged during the 1980 campaign. It will then review a model of public opinion and foreign policy that attempts to identify basic underlying foreign policy values and the mechanism behind the rapid shifts in the public's mood. The next section will describe the prevailing trend in foreign policy attitudes from 1974 to 1982, namely, a shift in a more conservative but not in a more interventionist direction. The final section will examine the domestic political constraints on the administration's initiatives in the areas of defense spending, arms control, and military intervention.

The 1980 Election: A New Consensus?

Ronald Reagan has advanced the view on many occasions that the 1980 election was a watershed event in American politics. It was indeed the culmination of many years of growing anti-government sentiment in the United States. Every two years since 1958, the Center for Political Studies (formerly the Survey Research Center) at the University of Michigan has been putting the following question to cross sections of the American electorate: "Do you think that people in the government waste a lot of the money we pay in taxes, waste some of it, or don't waste very much of it?" In 1958, 43 percent of the public felt that the government wastes "a lot" of tax money. In 1964, that figure had increased slightly, to 47 percent. It then shot up to 59 percent in 1968 and 69 percent in 1970. This antigovernment attitude continued to grow during the 1970s, reaching 77 percent in 1978, the year of the tax revolt. It was at an all-time high, 78 percent, in 1980, when Ronald Reagan was elected President.

At the same time, 1980 was the culmination of many years of growing conservatism in foreign affairs. Opinion on defense spending captures this trend quite well. The National Opinion Research Center at the University of Chicago regularly monitors public support for spending on "the military, armaments, and defense," as well as nine other areas of public spending. Table 2-1 reveals that support for higher defense spending was gradually increasing between 1973 and 1978. By the spring of 1980, a majority of Americans for the first time felt that this country should spend more on national defense. When President Reagan took office in January 1981, that figure had reached 65 percent, or almost two thirds of the electorate, according to the CBS News/*New York Times* poll. Table 2-1 also shows that over this same period, support for various domestic spending programs was tending to decline.

The 1980 campaign appeared to reflect this growing conservatism in foreign policy. The two traumatic events that marked the turn of the decade, the seizure of American hostages in Iran and the Soviet invasion of Afghanistan, seemed to shake the United States out of its post-Vietnam paralysis and revive the national will. The president, who had presided for three years over a foreign policy of passivity and strategic decline, proclaimed himself "born again" after a total immersion in Soviet treachery. His view of Soviet intentions, Jimmy Carter remarked, had "changed drastically" as a result of Afghanistan.

The president managed to use the newfound sense of national unity and determination to fend off a powerful challenge in his own party. Senator Edward M. Kennedy, recoiling from the ferocious backlash generated by his criticism of the Shah of Iran, realized that, under the circumstances of 1980, it would be impossible to oppose Jimmy Carter's foreign policy from the left. The Republicans nominated the most conservative candidate among their leading contenders, a man who had very nearly defeated an incumbent president four years earlier by attacking his own party's foreign policy from the right. Nevertheless, foreign policy did not play a major role in the 1980 primaries because the candidates often agreed on what needed to be done — or, if they did not, they tended to keep their reservations to themselves. Notably, Senator Kennedy did not once mention foreign policy in his much-acclaimed speech to the Democratic National Convention in New York City.

Both major party platforms in 1980 condemned Soviet aggression and decried the serious decline in U.S. military power and the danger to our national security. Even the incumbent Democrats admitted that "trends in the military balance have become increasingly adverse." According to the Democratic platform, "The Nixon-Ford administration presided over a steady decline of 33 percent in real U.S. military spending between 1968

TABLE 2-1. Support for Domestic and Defense Spending, 1973-1982

"We are faced with many problems in this country, none of which can be solved easily or inexpensively. I'm going to name some of these problems, and for each one I'd like you to tell me whether you think we're spending too much money, too little money, or about the right amount."

The percentages for "domestic spending" are the average of the responses for five items: "improving and protecting the environment," "improving and protecting the nation's health," "solving the problems of the big cities," "improving the nation's education system," and "welfare." The defense item was "the military, armaments, and defense."

Year	Too Little (Percent)	About the Right Amount (Percent)	Too Much (Percent)
Domestic Spending			
1973	48%	29%	17%
1974	49	30	15
1975	48	30	16
1976	44	30	21
1977	41	31	21
1978	42	31	21
1980	42	30	21
1982	45	29	19
Defense Spending			
1973	11	45	38
1974	17	45	31
1975	17	46	31
1976	24	42	27
1977	24	45	23
1978	27	44	22
1980	56	26	11
1982	29	36	30

SOURCE: National Opinion Research Center, University of Chicago, General Social Surveys. Number of respondents varies each year between 1,468 and 1,532.

and 1976." The Republicans countered with the charge that "in his first three years in the White House, Mr. Carter reduced defense spending by over $38 billion from President Ford's last Five-Year Defense Plan." Both parties pledged a real increase in defense spending and both promised a major effort to upgrade our strategic capabilities and our conventional forces. Even independent candidate John Anderson joined in the prevailing consensus. The platform issued by his "National Unity Campaign" resolved to enhance U.S. military power by modernizing and diversifying our strategic arsenal and improving our conventional forces. (Anderson did not, however, promise to increase defense spending. His platform said only, "We must spend what we need for defense.")

The general election campaign witnessed a sequence of charges and countercharges reminiscent of the fracas over "the missile gap" in 1960. The "outs" charged the "ins" with responsibility for growing Soviet strategic superiority. The "ins" tried to counter with evidence of major strategic advances, including a new nuclear targeting policy that was, in fact, specifically called for in the 1980 Republican platform. The parallel to the 1960 Cold War election was not coincidental. A sense of military weakness and insecurity was the prevailing public mood in 1980, and both major parties seemed to be proposing some version of a return to the Cold War doctrine of containment in response to perceptions of a decade of defeat and decline. In the end, the "tougher" candidate, Ronald Reagan, won the election with surprising ease, carrying a Republican majority with him into the Senate for the first time in twenty-eight years. The public seemed to be giving its enthusiastic endorsement to a new foreign policy of toughness and self-assertion.

That is how the Reagan administration has chosen to read the foreign policy mandate of 1980. In fact, however, significant cracks in this new consensus began to appear even during the 1980 campaign. For one thing, the data suggest that Ronald Reagan did not win the 1980 election because of his foreign policy stance; he won in spite of it. In a Gallup poll taken in September 1980 that rated the three major candidates on various issues, Reagan had a six-point advantage over Carter for handling domestic affairs, while Carter held a six-point advantage in foreign relations. To be sure, not all foreign policy issues worked to the Democrats' advantage. Peace certainly did. Carter led Reagan by twenty-five points as the best candidate for keeping the United States out of war. Reagan had an equally strong lead, however, as the best candidate for strengthening the national defense. Reagan was also felt to be more capable of increasing respect for the United States overseas. But Carter was preferred for dealing with the Arab-Israeli situation. Generally, peace issues benefited Carter, while Reagan held the advantage on defense issues.[2]

This ambiguity on foreign policy issues showed up in every campaign survey. NBC News and the Associated Press asked which candidate would do the best job of keeping the United States out of war. Carter was ahead of Reagan each time the question was asked. Reagan held the lead over Carter, however, when people were asked who would "do the best job in strengthening America's position in the world." In the ABC News/Harris poll, Reagan led Carter by thirty-five points as the candidate who "would keep U.S. military strength at least as strong as or stronger than the Russians.'" People also felt, by a margin of twenty-three points, that Reagan "would stand up most firmly if the U.S. were threatened by the Soviet Union." By a margin of twenty-eight points, however, the public felt that Reagan "might be most likely to get the U.S. into another war." The result was that Carter ended up ahead as the candidate who "would best handle foreign policy" — but by only two points.

The war-and-peace issue became the central thrust of Jimmy Carter's reelection campaign and, as the data show, he was successful in creating doubts about Ronald Reagan's inexperience and recklessness in foreign affairs.[3] In September 1980, according to the Gallup poll, the Democratic party's margin over the Republicans as the party "most likely to keep the United States out of World War III" was wider than it had been at any time since the Goldwater-Johnson contest in 1964. At the same time, however, the Democrats lost their historic advantage as the party "that will do the better job of keeping the country prosperous."[4] It was the economy, not foreign policy, that sealed the Democrats' fate in 1980. Indeed, preserving peace was Jimmy Carter's one substantial accomplishment in office, and the voters seemed to be aware of it. After the election, CBS News and *The New York Times* asked, "No matter how you feel in general about the job he's done, what do you think Jimmy Carter has done best during his four years as President?" The answers most frequently given were keeping the country out of war (15 percent), the Middle East peace agreement (11 percent), and foreign policy in general (7 percent) — as well as "nothing" (7 percent).

As will be seen below, Reagan's foreign policy ratings held up rather well during his first year in office, even while his economic ratings were rapidly deteriorating. At the end of 1981, however, a sequence of crises abroad, beginning with the declaration of martial law in Poland on December 13, brought foreign policy to the center of public attention. The result was that, once again, the public displayed substantial reservations about Reagan's tougher, more assertive approach. The polls showed that the public was concerned about the serious situations in Poland, El Salvador, the Falkland Islands, and the Middle East. But in every case, Americans revealed a strong preference for keeping the United States out of these conflicts — and a consistent fearfulness about President Reagan's desire to get us involved.

The most striking evidence of the weakness of Reagan's supposed new foreign policy consensus was the sudden emergence in 1982 of a popular movement in support of a nuclear freeze. The nuclear freeze campaign, which began at New England town meetings in the winter of 1981-1982 and spread quickly to a California ballot initiative, gained impetus with the proposal of a Senate resolution by Edward M. Kennedy, Mark O. Hatfield, and twenty-four other Senators calling for a nuclear freeze. One Representative called the nuclear freeze movement "the most powerful, spontaneous grass-roots movement I have seen since I was elected to Congress" in 1974. An aide to Senator Kennedy observed that the Senator was engaged, not in leading public opinion on the issue, but in "catching up with the country."

Poll after poll taken in the spring of 1982 showed enormous majorities in favor of a joint United States–Soviet agreement to ban the testing, production, and deployment of all nuclear weapons. For example, an ABC News/*Washington Post* poll taken in April showed an initial 76-to-20 percent majority favoring a nuclear freeze. The poll then reviewed fourteen separate arguments for and against the freeze, giving respondents the opportunity to evaluate each argument, one at a time. Afterwards, the respondents were once again asked whether they approved or disapproved of a nuclear freeze. Approval was still overwhelming, 72 to 25 percent.

Should one conclude, therefore, that the consensus in 1980 behind a new, more conservative foreign policy was more apparent than real? Are we simply observing a cyclical phenomenon whereby public opinion swings back and forth unpredictably between hawkish and dovish extremes? Are there any stable and enduring foreign policy values that the public endorses in a more or less consistent fashion?

A Model of Public Opinion and Foreign Policy

Political scientists often differentiate between "valence" and "position" issues.[5] Position issues involve legitimate alternative preferences or values — hawk versus dove, for or against a constitutional amendment to ban abortions, in favor of more or less government spending on social welfare programs, and so on. Valence issues entail only one position or value, which may have either a positive or negative "valence." Peace, prosperity, reform, and good government are all positively valued by the electorate, while unemployment, military weakness, incompetence, and corruption have negative valences. Position issues are inherently divisive, in the sense that candidates and voters can take sides on them. In the case of valence issues, however, everyone is on the same side. Salience is the most important characteristic of valence issues: How much demand is there for the desired quality, or how serious do people feel a problem has become?

Conflict over position issues takes the form of opposition between preferences staked out across a distribution of alternatives (more, less, or the same amount of military spending). Valence issues involve not so much opposition as competition to associate one's own side with the desired condition or value and the other side with its absence. Ronald Reagan asked in his acceptance speech to the Republican National Convention, "Who does not feel rising alarm when the question in any discussion of foreign policy is no longer, 'Should we do something?' but 'Do we have the capacity to do anything?'" Carter countered in New York by claiming that "we have reversed the Republican decline in defense. Every year since I have been President, we have made real increases in our commitment to a stronger defense.... There is no doubt that the United States can meet any threat from the Soviet Union." The issue in this case, military strength, is universally desired and essentially not divisive. The controversy centers on how badly our defenses have deteriorated, whether the Carter administration is responsible, and whether the Republicans can significantly improve the situation.

During the Nixon and Ford administrations, two foreign policy position issues became matters of intense disagreement — detente and antimilitarism. The first was, of course, the product of Nixon and Kissinger's dramatic decision to normalize relations with the People's Republic of China and to reach agreements with the Soviet Union to stabilize the international status quo. Antimilitarism was the left's interpretation of the lesson of Vietnam, to wit, that military power was no longer the most critical resource in the new world order and that the United States should think less in terms of national security and more in terms of global economic interdependence. The worldwide energy crisis was taken as further evidence for this position.

Detente and antimilitarism were issues that split the internationalist public and destroyed the Cold War consensus. In an earlier essay,[6] Mandelbaum and Schneider carried out a detailed analysis of data from a 1974 survey of American foreign policy attitudes sponsored by the Chicago Council on Foreign Relations. Our analysis revealed that certain "signals" or themes consistently divided internationalists, those generally better educated Americans who are attentive to foreign policy and supportive of an active United States role in world affairs. These polarizing themes included any reference to the military, such as military aid, troop commitments abroad, and defense spending; the notion of American hegemony or world leadership; the CIA, the military, and business as agents of or forces influencing American foreign policy; sympathy for Third World liberation movements; support for dictatorial regimes in countries otherwise friendly to the United States; and anti-Communism as a foreign policy priority. It was possible to differentiate conservative and liberal internationalists according to their views on these issues.

Conservative internationalists were found to picture the world primarily in East-West terms: democracy versus totalitarianism, capitalism versus communism, freedom versus repression. They were supportive of military power and gave high priority to national security as a foreign policy goal. They also showed a strong commitment to traditional anti-Communist containment and were suspicious of detente as a kind of cartel agreement whereby the two superpowers agreed to limit competition in order to stabilize the market and protect their interests.

Liberal internationalists emphasized economic and humanitarian problems over security issues and rejected a hegemonic role for the United States. They wanted leaders to think in global terms: the scarcity of natural resources, environmental and oceanic pollution, and international economic inequality. They tended to regard the common problems facing all of humanity as more urgent than the ideological differences between

East and West. Liberal internationalists approved of detente as a necessary first step toward a new world order based on global interdependence. The impact of Vietnam could be seen in this group's deep suspicion of military intervention and military power as instruments of foreign policy.

Both liberal and conservative internationalists perceive foreign policy in moralistic terms, and both attacked Henry Kissinger for the lack of moral commitment in his diplomacy. Conservative internationalists are antidetente and promilitary. They align ideologically with the international right, which is to say, their primary moral commitment is to the free world in its confrontation with Communism. Liberal internationalists are prodetente and antimilitary. They align ideologically with the forces of change in world affairs — not Communism, but the Third World left, including national liberation movements, oppressed minorities such as Palestinians and blacks in southern Africa, and, indeed, the Third World as a whole in its claim for economic justice against the industrialized North.

The basic assumption of Kissinger's balance-of-power approach was, of course, the superiority of the national interest over all other moral commitments. His policies were, in fact, prodetente and promilitary, and therefore ideologically confusing. For a while, conservatives were willing to go along with detente because Nixon and Kissinger were pursuing a tough military policy in Vietnam. Liberals expressed grudging approval of Nixon and Kissinger's overtures to China and Russia. But eventually, both sides turned against the secretary of state once the issues on which they differed with him became more salient than those where they agreed. The left attacked his preoccupation with military strength and big-power diplomacy, while the right passed a "Morality in Foreign Policy" amendment to the 1976 Republican party platform criticizing their own administration's policy of detente. Both sides seized upon the human rights theme as the perfect reproach to the cynicism and casuistry of the Kissinger style of diplomacy, although the left and the right had different notions of which specific forces in the world were the chief perpetrators of human rights violations. It was enough for Jimmy Carter to claim in 1976 that American foreign policy has paid too little attention to human rights and leave it at that.

Noninternationalists, who comprised almost half of the American public in the 1974 study, do not share this moralism. They are suspicious of international involvements of any kind. They tend to be poorer and less well educated and to know and care little about foreign affairs, which they see as remote from their daily concerns. This large, inattentive public is neither consistently liberal nor consistently conservative in its foreign policy beliefs. Nor is it ideologically isolationist in the sense that many Americans were between World Wars I and II. The inattentive public is simply not internationalist-minded. It is predisposed against American involvement in other countries' affairs unless a clear and compelling issue of national interest or national security is at stake. If we are directly threatened or if our interest *is* involved in any important way, this group wants swift, decisive action but not long-term involvement.

In the pretelevision era, social scientists spoke of an attentive audience for foreign affairs. This audience was better educated and followed foreign affairs regularly. It also tended to be more supportive of administration initiative and leadership in foreign affairs than the noninternationalist public was. When the attentive elite was asked about the Korean war, about American involvement in the rest of the world, about trade and treaties, it was consistently more supportive than the rest of the public.[7] Noninternationalists, on the other hand, showed a persistent strain of distrust and anti-involvement. But as a rule, noninternationalists got involved in foreign affairs debate only in election years. Between elections, the noninternationalist audience could generally be discounted.

This relationship broke down in the late 1960s when the attentive public split. As noted, one segment became liberal internationalists who dissented from the Cold War interventionism that had characterized the prevailing foreign policy consensus for almost twenty years. A different segment of the attentive public, also well-educated and heavily involved in foreign policy, took what has been described as a conservative internationalist line. This split in the attentive elite has created a far more unstable situation than was the case during the Cold War period of the 1950s and early 1960s, when there was an effective bipartisan consensus among the elite.

The foreign policy attitudes of the noninternationalist public are not primarily positional in nature. Noninternationalists do not consistently support either a liberal or a conservative U.S. world role. Instead, this group is strongly responsive to valence issues; that is, it swings left and right unpredictably in response to its current fears and concerns. The issue of detente, for example, has been deeply positional in that it has split liberal and conservative internationalists. But detente also comprises a powerful valence theme, namely, *peace.* The Nixon-Kissinger detente policy was extraordinarily popular during the 1970s because it was interpreted, not as a sellout to the Communists, but as a policy for keeping the peace. Peace, which liberal internationalists tend to regard as an ideological position and noninternationalists as a valence issue, draws these two constituencies together.

Similarly, liberal and conservative internationalists differ profoundly over military policy. But *strength* is a valence sentiment that appeals strongly to noninternationalists. The desire for military strength draws conservative internationalists and noninternationalists into a conservative coalition. Peace and strength are the valence issues of surpassing concern to noninternationalists. As the relative salience of these two issues changes, so does the coalition pattern and the dominant ideological complexion of foreign policy opinion.

Public opinion between 1964 and 1974 was totally preoccupied with the issue of peace. The result was to pull noninternationalists to the left. After 1968, for instance, the noninternationalist public turned against the American involvement in the Vietnam war as wasteful, pointless, and tragic. The antiwar coalition was a potent alliance between liberal internationalists and noninternationalists. The latter, however, never accepted the more extreme contentions of the antiwar activists that American purposes in Vietnam were essentially evil or corrupt.

Noninternationalists ally themselves with the left on questions of intervention because they see no point to American involvement in most of the world. They are against foreign aid, against troop involvement, against anything that smacks of foreign entanglement. Calling this viewpoint isolationist, however, is a bit too strong. Isolationism implies a principled opposition to American participation in world affairs. Noninternationalists are not so much opposed as they are nonsupportive. Being less well educated — that is the strongest demographic correlate of noninternationalism — this group has a limited understanding of the relevance of events that are complex and remote from their daily lives. They feel that most of what the United States does for the rest of the world is senseless, wasteful, and unappreciated. And sometimes they are right.

In cases like Vietnam and El Salvador, noninternationalists find a natural alliance with the left. But that alliance is neither automatic nor constant. The noninternationalist public is also oriented toward a strong military posture. After 1975, the mass public began to feel insecure about Soviet military strength and adventurism, and public opinion began to drift to the right. Noninternationalists were pulled into an alliance with conservative internationalists out of a shared concern over the nation's military security. Virtually every month from 1974 to 1981 saw greater public support for increasing the size of the defense budget. Noninternationalists voted heavily for Reagan, in part because of his promises of a defense buildup and a tougher line with the Soviet Union. This constituency likes strength and toughness in foreign affairs because that increases our independence and makes us less likely to become involved in the business of other countries. It protects the United States as long as we are the toughest kid on the block. The basic impulse is defensive; the public wants to see the United States beef up its military power in order to protect itself from a growing Soviet threat, not in order to assume an interventionist role in world affairs. Thus, noninternationalists support the conservative elite on many issues having to do with defense and toughness. They support the liberal elite when it becomes a question of direct American involvement.

The Foreign Policy Mood, 1974-1980

In *Eagle Entangled*,[8] Mandelbaum and Schneider used the data from the 1974 Chicago Council on Foreign Relations survey to create scales representing liberal and conservative internationalism. We did so by examining respondents' ratings of a list of foreign policy goals. One set of goals was considered liberal internationalist: "combatting world hunger," "helping to improve the standard of living in less developed countries," "fostering international cooperation to solve common problems such as food, inflation, and energy," "worldwide arms control," "strengthening the United Nations," "securing adequate supplies of energy," "keeping peace in the world," and "maintaining a balance of power among nations."

The second set of goals defined the conservative internationalist dimension: "containing communism," "protecting the interests of American business abroad," "strengthening countries who are friendly toward us," "defending our allies' security," "protecting weaker nations against foreign aggression," and "promoting the development of capitalism abroad." These goals are internationalist in a competitive rather than a cooperative sense. A factor analysis confirmed the empirical distinction between the two sets of goals. However, the two scales were positively correlated ($r = .29$), a relationship that we interpreted as showing their common internationalist content.

In 1978, the Chicago Council on Foreign Relations sponsored a second survey of American public opinion and foreign policy. Some fifty questions asked in 1974 were repeated in 1978. These two surveys, therefore, provide an excellent basis for examining trends over this four-year period.[9] Use of the two summary scales enables us to define separate trends for liberal and conservative internationalism.

Each of the fifty repeated questions was correlated with the two 1974 scales. The correlations revealed the degree to which each issue tapped liberal or conservative internationalist sentiment. For example, the goal of "containing communism" correlated .53 with conservative internationalism and .17 with liberal internationalism. The goal of "combatting world hunger" correlated .67 with liberal internationalism and .11 with conservative internationalism. The net change in public support from 1974 to 1978 was also measured for each question. In the case of "containing communism," for example, the net change was +4.5 percentage points. That is the average of the 6 percent increase in the proportion of the public calling it a "very important goal" and the 3 percent decrease in the proportion labeling this goal "not at all important." (The balance is accounted for by changes in the "somewhat important" and "not sure" categories.)

Across the fifty trend questions, the correlation between liberal internationalism and the net change in public support was negative ($r = -.30$, significant at p = .02). Liberal internationalism was associated with a negative shift in public opinion; the more liberal internationalist the position, the greater the loss (or the smaller the gain) in public support between 1974 and 1978.

The correlation between conservative internationalism and the net change in public support was a positive .25, which was barely significant at p = .05. It was pointed out above, however, that liberal and conservative internationalism were positively correlated. Internationalism affects them both. Regression analysis allows us to look at the trend in conservative internationalism controlling for liberal internationalism — that is, controlling for "internationalism" generally. The relationship now becomes stronger (partial r = .47) and statistically significant (p = .01).

The data summarized above show that conservative internationalism tended to gain public support between 1974 and 1978, but the gain becomes significant only when internationalism is partialed out. Conservative internationalism without internationalism is simply conservatism. The public appears to have become more favorable to such conservative symbols as the military, anti-communism, the CIA, business, and U.S. power. But that enthusiasm was tempered by a wariness of increasing U.S. commitments and involvements abroad. In sum, *foreign policy attitudes between 1974 and 1978 shifted in the direction of greater conservatism and less internationalism.*

Ten internationalist goals were rated by respondents in both the 1974 and 1978 Chicago Council on Foreign Relations surveys. Five were conservative goals, and of these, four increased in public support between 1974 and 1978:

— "defending our allies' security" (+10 percent),
— "protecting the interests of U.S. business" (+4.5 percent),
— "containing communism" (+4.5 percent), and
— "protecting weaker nations from foreign aggression" (+3.5 percent).

Note that the goal that gained the most support was explicitly defensive and security-oriented. The only conservative internationalist goal that did not gain support between 1974 and 1978 was "bringing democracy to other nations" (−0.5 percent), the most internationalist and non-self-regarding goal on the list.

Among liberal internationalist goals, four showed almost no change at all:

— "worldwide arms control" (0 percent),
— "combatting world hunger" (−0.5 percent),
— "securing adequate supplies of energy" (+1.0 percent), and
— "strengthening the United Nations" (+1.5 percent).

The fifth, "helping to improve the standard of living in less developed countries," declined in public support by 3.5 percent.

Many other conservative positions gained public support between 1974 and 1978. The single greatest increase was on the issue of defense spending (+17 percent), a conservative position that does not necessarily imply any greater internationalism. Support for NATO, which may be regarded as a defensive commitment, also rose between 1974 and 1978 (+9.5 percent). More Americans in 1978 said they wanted to increase our commitment to NATO or keep our commitment what it is now, while fewer said that we should decrease our NATO commitment or withdraw from the alliance altogether.

The dual trend toward greater conservatism and less internationalism is nowhere better illustrated than in the findings on foreign aid from the two surveys. The results show a seven-point *increase* in support for military aid to other nations between 1974 and 1978. At the same time, support for foreign economic aid "for purposes of economic development and technical assistance" *decreased* by 5.5 percent. Economic aid is an essentially pure internationalist issue, whereas military aid is associated with the countervailing conservative trend.

The two surveys asked whether various interests should play a more important role or a less important role in determining foreign policy. Congress and the United Nations, which were relatively high on the list in 1974, declined in public support in 1978. Congress appears to be a liberal symbol in foreign policy. In 1974 and 1978, despite the change in administrations, liberals were more likely than conservatives to feel that Congress was playing too weak a role in foreign policy relative to that of the president. But the shift on this question was also in a more conservative direction. The percentage of the public saying that Congress is playing too weak a foreign policy role declined from 38 percent in 1974 to 29 percent in 1978.

On the other hand, there was increased support for a more important foreign policy role for the military and for American business. Interestingly, there was no increase in support for greater foreign policy involvement by the CIA. The percentage who said the CIA should play a more important role increased by three points, but the percentage who said the CIA should play a less important role also increased by three points, producing a net change of zero. Support for the CIA did rise on another measure, however: "Do you feel the CIA should or should not work inside other countries to try to strengthen those elements that serve the interests of the U.S. and to weaken those forces that work against the interests of the U.S.?" The proportion in favor of such CIA activity (which is not necessarily subversive or illegal) increased from 43 percent in 1974 to 59 percent in 1978. This question showed no correlation with internationalism; indeed, the purpose of such a policy, as stated in the question, is entirely to protect the interests of the United States. Support for the CIA and support for defense spending were among the issues that showed the greatest increase in public support. Both are good examples of conservative but not internationalist ideology.

Support for sending American troops abroad — a conservative but decidedly internationalist policy — tended to increase. These increases were relatively small in 1978, however, and it could not be said that Americans had fundamentally altered their strong distaste for sending troops abroad — with one exception. The exception was a Soviet threat to Western Europe. When asked whether they favored the use of American troops "if the Russians took over West Berlin," the margin in 1974 was 44 to 33 percent opposed; in 1978, it had shifted to 48 to 38 percent in favor. Similarly, "if Western Europe were invaded," presumably by the Soviet Union, the public narrowly opposed sending American troops in 1974, 41 to 39 percent; in 1978, when asked what they would do "if Soviet troops invaded Western Europe," the use of American troops was now favored, 54 to 32 percent. Probably the public saw a Soviet attack on Western Europe not as an unnecessary international involvement but as a direct threat to American security.

Antipathy toward the Soviet Union may also explain the decline in support for "undertaking joint efforts with the Soviet Union to solve energy problems." This policy was favored by an overwhelming margin of 83 to 10 percent in 1974. In the 1978 survey, the margin of approval had fallen to 68 to 21 percent, the sharpest dropoff for any position tested. Unfortunately, no other questions on detente were repeated from the 1974 survey. But if this one question is typical, it indicates that while United States–Soviet detente remained basically popular, by 1978 it was beginning to lose the unreserved enthusiasm of the early 1970s.

Finally, several clearly internationalist positions lost support between 1974 and 1978. The question, "Do you think it would be better for the future of the country if we take an active part in world affairs or if we stay out of world affairs?" is almost a pure measure of internationalism. Support for the United States' taking an active part in world affairs dropped by 6 percent between 1974 and 1978. Indeed, the view that it would be best if we stayed out of world affairs was expressed by a larger percentage of the public in 1978 (29 percent) than in 1947 and 1956, when 25 percent felt this way.

Several human rights positions remained unchanged or actually lost popularity between 1974 and 1978, a trend that is consistent with the previous evidence but still surprising in light of the rise of Jimmy Carter and the promotion of his human rights campaign. The statement that "the U.S. should put pressure on countries that systematically violate basic human rights" received strong agreement from 35 percent of the public in 1974 and 31 percent in 1978; total agreement remained unchanged at 67 percent. In the case of a statement expressing the opposite point of view, "How the Soviet Union handles the treatment of Jews and other minority groups is a matter of internal Soviet politics and none of our business," strong agreement increased from 15 to 21 percent; in this case, total agreement also increased, from 41 to 50 percent. Public sympathy for Carter's human rights position apparently did not move the public to endorse any positive action that would run the risk of involving us in other countries' business.

Explaining the Shift

What caused this shift in the public mood?

Two trends parallel to those just reported appear to be relevant. One was the public's growing alarm over the military power of the Soviet Union and its perception of increasing American military inferiority. The other was the deterioration of the domestic economy and the predominance of economic concerns, especially inflation, in the public consciousness.

In December 1976, at the end of the Ford administration, the Harris poll asked people whether they felt that "the military defense system of the United States is stronger than that of the Russians, weaker, or about as strong as the Russian military defense system." The results indicated a close balance: 27 percent felt the Russians were stronger, 21 percent said that the United States was stronger, and 43 percent said we were about equal in military strength. The question was asked again in July 1978, when 31 percent said that the Russians were stronger and 18 percent said that the U.S. was stronger. By November 1978, the balance had shifted even more. Forty percent now said that Russia was stronger and only 14 percent that the United States was stronger. The figures were roughly the same in February 1980, 41 to 16 percent expressing the view that the Russians were stronger.

The CBS News/*New York Times* poll asked a similar question, whether the United States is "superior in military strength to the Soviet Union," about equal in strength, or not as strong. In June 1979, 43 percent said that the Soviet Union was superior and 11 percent felt that we were stronger. In January 1980, about the same margin prevailed — 42 to 14 percent claiming military superiority for the Soviet Union. Thus, both survey sources demonstrate that the perception of American military inferiority *antedated* the Iran and Afghanistan crises and had been growing for at least several years before 1980.

The trend away from internationalism began much earlier. It was well underway by the late 1960s, according to data collected by Potomac

Associates (see Table 2-2 on page 50). As American involvement in Vietnam ended in the early 1970s, the recession and the energy crisis immediately ensued and internationalism continued to decline. There are several plausible links between declining economic security and declining internationalism. One is that economic problems simply push all other issues aside. Foreign affairs become more remote and more irrelevant to most people in the face of economic decline, and international problems move down in their list of priorities. Second, the experience of the 1930s suggests that nationalist and isolationist policies become more popular during periods of economic downturn. For many people, a logical response to economic insecurity is to cut international commitments and erect protectionist barriers.

There may also have been a link between the antigovernment tax revolt of the late 1970s and the retreat from internationalism. In the 1978 Chicago Council survey, internationalism was very low among respondents who named taxes, big government, and excessive government spending as major national problems. Internationalist programs contribute to big government and certainly cost a lot of money. Those who want to reduce the size and power of the federal government would very likely put international programs like foreign aid at the top of their list of expendable government activities.

The period between 1978 and 1980 witnessed both a quantitative and a qualitative change in the earlier trends. The data on defense spending in Table 2-1 reveal that, while support for higher defense spending had been increasing gradually between 1973 and 1978, the dam literally burst in 1980. The critical events came at the end of 1979: the seizure of American hostages in Iran in November, followed by the Soviet invasion of Afghanistan in December. The result was a surge of nationalist sentiment in the polls, continuing the conservative trend of 1974-1978 but shifting it in a more interventionist direction.

Thus, surveys taken between December 1979 and February 1980 showed substantially greater support for American troop involvement in other parts of the world. According to the data in Table 2-2, the view that we should come to the defense of our major European allies "if any of them are attacked by the Soviet Union" reached an all-time high of 70 percent. Similarly, the feeling that we should use military force to defend Japan "if it is attacked by Soviet Russia or Communist China" rose to 57 percent, higher than at any point since this question was first asked by Potomac Associates in 1972.

Data reported by Alvin Richman[10] indicated sharp increases in the public's willingness to use American troops in response to Soviet invasions of Western Europe (43 percent in July 1978, 60 percent in February 1980), West Berlin (40 percent in July 1978, 54 percent in February 1980), and Yugoslavia (13 percent in March 1977, 36 percent in

TABLE 2-2. Potomac Associates Internationalism Scale, 1964-1980

A. Since the United States is the most powerful nation in the world, we should go our own way in international matters, not worrying too much about whether other countries agree with us or not.

	Agree	*Disagree*	*Don't Know*
1964	19%	70%	11%
1968	23	72	5
1972	22	72	6
1974	32	57	11
1975	23	67	10
1976	29	62	9
1980	26	66	8

B. The United States should mind its own business internationally and let other countries get along as best they can on their own.

	Agree	*Disagree*	*Don't Know*
1964	18%	70%	12%
1968	27	66	7
1972	35	56	9
1974	41	47	12
1975	36	52	12
1976	41	49	10
1980	30	61	9

C. We shouldn't think so much in international terms but concentrate more on our own national problems and building up our strength and prosperity here at home.

	Agree	*Disagree*	*Don't Know*
1964	55%	32%	13%
1968	60	31	9
1972	73	20	7
1974	77	14	9
1975	71	18	11
1976	73	22	5
1980	61	30	9

D. The United States should cooperate fully with the United Nations.

	Agree	*Disagree*	*Don't Know*
1964	72%	16%	12%
1968	72	21	7
1972	63	28	9
1974	66	20	14
1975	56	30	14
1976	46	41	13
1980	59	28	13

Table continues on following page.

TABLE 2-2. Continued

E. In deciding on its foreign policies, the United States should take into account the views of its major allies.

	Agree	*Disagree*	*Don't Know*
1964	81%	7%	12%
1968	84	9	7
1972	80	12	8
1974	69	16	15
1975	74	16	10
1976	72	18	10
1980	79	13	8

F. The United States should come to the defense of Japan with military force if it is attacked by Soviet Russia or Communist China.

	Agree	*Disagree*	*Don't Know*
1972	43%	40%	17%
1974	37	42	21
1975	42	39	19
1976	45	37	18
1978	50	35	15
1979	54	35	11
1980	57	24	19

G. The United States should come to the defense of its major European allies with military force if any of them are attacked by the Soviet Union.

	Agree	*Disagree*	*Don't Know*
1972	52%	32%	16%
1974	48	34	18
1975	48	34	18
1976	56	27	17
1978	62	26	12
1979	64	26	10
1980	70	17	13

SOURCE: Lloyd Free and William Watts, "Internationalism Comes of Age ... Again," *Public Opinion*, Vol. 3 (April/May 1980), pp. 46-50.

January 1980). Support for sending American troops to help defend Israel against an invasion by Arab forces rose from 21 percent in July 1978 to 35 percent in February 1980. Richman's data also help to pinpoint the exact time when support for a higher defense budget reached majority proportions. The NBC News/Associated Press poll showed 38 percent in favor of increasing defense spending in September 1979; three months later, in December 1979, that view characterized 51 percent of the public.

Table 2-2 reveals that the conservative tide of 1979-1980 was strong enough to cause a qualitative change in public opinion, namely, a marked increase in internationalism. Statements A through E in Table 2-2, which have been regularly tested in Potomac Associates polls since 1964, essentially measure unilateralist attitudes in the United States — whether we should "go our own way in international matters, not worrying too much about whether other countries agree with us or not," whether we should "mind our own business internationally and let other countries get along as best they can on their own," and whether we should cooperate fully with the United Nations or take into account the views of our major allies in making foreign policy decisions. In every case, the data reveal a decline in internationalism between 1964 and 1976. The figures for 1980, however, show a sharp reversal in this long-term trend, with more Americans suddenly favoring cooperation with allies and with the U.N. and rejecting go-it-alone sentiments.

It would be hasty, however, to reject the conclusions reached in our earlier analysis of the 1974 and 1978 Chicago Council surveys. For one thing, the Potomac Associates survey was taken in February 1980, at the very peak of the Iran hostage crisis, when the public was exceptionally mindful of the need for support and cooperation among allies. Moreover, the increase in support for military intervention between 1972 and 1980 (statements F and G) averaged 16 points, while the increase in support for nonmilitary internationalism (statements A through E) averaged less than one percentage point over this same period. These results suggest that conservatism was still the leading trend and internationalism a secondary development. Finally, statements A through E in the Potomac Associates survey include no clear indicators of liberal internationalism, such as foreign aid, arms control, human rights, or support for the Third World. All five statements are variations on a unilateralist theme and reveal a sudden increase in the view that the United States has to rely on its allies for help and cooperation, for reasons that were clearly understandable at the time. The point is, absent any evidence on a broader range of internationalist issues, the conclusion reached by Free and Watts in the title of their report, "Internationalism Comes of Age ... Again," seems premature.

Domestic Constraints on Foreign Policy, 1980-1982

Notwithstanding this conclusion, it is clear that the kinds of attitudes reported by Free and Watts in 1980 did have something to do with the election to the presidency of the best known conservative internationalist in American public life. As noted, the electorate displayed ambiguous feelings about Ronald Reagan's foreign policy views during the 1980 campaign, endorsing his call for a stronger national defense while fearing the

Republican candidate's reputation for recklessness and interventionism. The first 18 months of the Reagan administration demonstrate the degree to which this basic ambiguity in public opinion — conservative but not interventionist — has constrained the foreign policy initiatives of the new government.

Public opinion acts as a constraint by defining the limits of what is politically possible. In the economic area, those limits were very broad during the first year of the Reagan administration. Poll after poll showed that, while the public did not support most of the administration's specific spending cuts and deregulation policies, the electorate remained solidly supportive of the Reaganomics program as a whole. They felt that the end, resolving the nation's economic crisis, justified the means. The administration's principal foreign policy objective during the first year was to build up the nation's military defenses. That objective was strongly supported by public opinion and met with almost no political resistance.

Something of a turning point was reached early in 1982, however. Throughout most of 1981, while the president's economic ratings were declining sharply, his foreign policy ratings remained fairly high. From March 1981 through January 1982, according to the Harris survey, about equal numbers of people gave the administration positive and negative ratings on handling foreign policy matters. Those ratings took a sharp dip, however, in February 1982, when a majority of the public became negative for the first time. The excess of negative over positive ratings persisted through the spring of 1982.

This turning point coincided with the outbreak of a string of foreign policy crises, first in Poland (December 1981), and then in El Salvador (February 1982), the Falkland Islands (April), and Lebanon (June). Americans began to get jittery over possible American involvement in a war. During 1981, the percentage holding the view that the United States was likely to become involved in a war during the next few years rose from 59 percent in February to 68 percent in September (NBC News/ Associated Press poll). The fear that Ronald Reagan might get us into war, expressed by 32 percent in February 1981 and 37 percent in October, jumped to 48 percent in January and March 1982 (CBS News/ *New York Times* poll).

There are two mechanisms by which public opinion constrains public policy. First is the anticipatory effect of elections. Politicians are extraordinarily sensitive to the polls; they make careful estimates of what kinds of positions will be political assets or political liabilities at election time. Anticipation of a midterm election heightened this sensitivity among the president's political advisers and among members of Congress during 1982. Second is the splintering of the old bipartisan consensus on foreign policy, which has pulled the Democratic and Republican parties apart.

The Republican party has essentially accepted the conservative internationalist doctrine, while the Democratic party has moved closer to the liberal internationalist view.[12] Democrats are more willing than in the past to oppose a conservative foreign policy on grounds of principle and to seize such themes as human rights, arms control, and anti-interventionism as powerful issues to use against the opposition.

An analysis of 1981 roll-call votes by the *National Journal*[13] scored members of Congress on their degree of liberalism and conservatism on economic issues, foreign policy issues, and social issues. In the Senate, Democrats and Republicans averaged 147 points apart on economic issues in 1981, using the *National Journal's* index. The two parties were almost as polarized, 140 points apart, on foreign policy votes. In the House of Representatives, economic differences between the parties were somewhat greater (169 points), while foreign policy differences between Democrats and Republicans were notably weaker (86 points), though still strong. The Senate has traditionally been more deeply involved in foreign policy issues, while the House has greater influence over economic and budgetary matters. That may explain differences between the House and Senate in the degree of partisanship on domestic versus foreign issues.

The overall message, however, is that, by 1981, foreign policy had become a major area of partisan conflict. As in the past, the public remains strongly supportive of both peace and strength as foreign policy objectives. But more so than in the past, the Democrats have become the party of peace and the Republicans the party of strength, with each party trying to exploit the vulnerability of the other on one of these issues of common concern.

The trend toward conservatism but not interventionism has provided the Reagan administration with political opportunities and political constraints. During the second year of the administration, the constraints became increasingly evident in several areas of foreign policy.

One area was defense spending. As noted, support for higher defense spending reached majority proportions by the end of 1979 and almost two-thirds at the time of Reagan's inauguration in January 1981. After the first Reagan budget was announced, the Gallup poll asked people in May 1981 whether they approved of the president's proposal for "substantially increased defense spending, from 23.4 percent of the federal budget in 1980 to 27.2 percent of the federal budget in 1982." The public very strongly approved, 64 to 29 percent.

Four times between April 1981 and January 1982, the ABC News/ *Washington Post* poll asked people whether they thought Reagan's plans to increase military spending were going too far, not far enough, or were just about right. In every case, majorities of between 52 and 57 percent called the increases "just about right." Minorities of 13 to 19 percent felt they did not go far enough, and 18 to 28 percent felt they went too far.

The picture one gets is of general public satisfaction with Reagan's initial increases in defense spending; he did exactly what the public had elected him to do.

After the 1983 budget was announced, however, the public began to draw the line. In February 1982, the Harris survey told its respondents that "President Reagan has proposed an 18 percent increase in defense spending for 1983. This is $33 billion more than was spent on defense this year." Only 19 percent said they favored giving the president the full increase he asked for. Twenty percent felt that defense spending should be increased, but by less than the amount the president was requesting. The largest group, 36 percent, wanted to keep the 1983 defense budget at about the same level as it had been in 1982. On the other side of the issue, only 23 percent wanted to reduce defense spending below the 1982 level, that is, to undo the increase obtained in Reagan's first budget.

The basic picture was approval of Reagan's initial defense buildup, no desire to revert to the perceived weakness of the Carter period, but no desire to push the defense buildup any further. At the end of 1981, NBC News and the Associated Press reported that the proportion of Americans favoring an increase in defense spending had fallen by almost half, from 65 percent in January to 34 percent in November. For the first time in almost two years, a plurality of the public wanted to keep military spending at about the same level. This pattern is confirmed by the evidence in Table 2-1. In the 1982 National Opinion Research Center survey (taken in March) the proportion favoring higher defense spending dropped sharply, from 56 to 29 percent. For the first time since 1976, more people (30 percent) said we were spending too much than said we were spending too little on "the military, armaments, and defense," with a plurality of 36 percent expressing the opinion that military spending was just about right. On this issue, Reagan had essentially met the demands of the American public.

In February 1982, the Harris poll asked specifically about President Reagan's proposal to increase defense spending by 18 percent in the 1983 budget. Only 19 percent favored giving the president the full increase he was asking for. Twenty percent favored increasing military spending by less than the president wanted. A plurality, 36 percent, felt that defense spending should be kept at about the same level, while 23 percent wanted that level cut. When the March 1982 NBC News/Associated Press poll gave respondents only two choices — "Do you think that defense spending should be cut, or don't you think so?" — the sample split almost evenly, 44 percent for a cut and 48 percent against one. The February Harris poll asked respondents to choose between making "sharp cuts" in various social programs or "cuts in defense spending." In the case of eight out of the nine social programs tested — including social security, federal

aid to education, unemployment compensation, and federal aid to cities —
more people wanted to cut defense spending than to cut spending on the
program in question. The only social program less popular than defense
was food stamps.

Not surprisingly, in 1982 more members of Congress, particularly
Democrats, began to criticize the president's military spending program
as wasteful and excessive in light of the immense federal budget deficit
and the pressure to cut nonmilitary spending. The president's assertion
in July that he reserved the right to increase military spending in future
years beyond the limits agreed to by Congress met with vociferous criticism from both Democrats and Republicans. The president did in fact
get most of the increases in military spending he asked for, but the political atmosphere had clearly changed since 1981.

Interventionism is a second area in which domestic politics worked to
constrain the Reagan administration's foreign policy initiatives in 1982.
Support for interventionism crested during the Iran and Afghanistan
crises, as reported in Table 2-2, and began to subside shortly thereafter.
Gallup reported a 20 percentage point decline from February 1980 to
July 1981 in the public's willingness to employ American forces if Western Europe were invaded by the Soviet Union. Willingness to use American forces if our oil supply in the Middle East were disrupted fell by
fifteen points between October 1980 and July 1981. Support for sending
American troops to help defend Israel against an Arab invasion declined
seven points from February 1980 to July 1981. The Iran and Afghanistan
crises appear to have occasioned only a temporary surge of interventionist
sentiments. By 1982, the public had become more conscious of the risks
involved — and suspicious of the administration's interventionist rhetoric.

Thus, the public's reactions to the crises in Poland, El Salvador, the
Falklands, and Lebanon were decidedly noninterventionist. Survey after
survey in each of these situations revealed a strong public desire to avoid
direct American involvement, even though the public indicated definite
favoritism for one side over the other in each case. In the Polish situation, according to the Harris survey, the public supported sanctions
against the Soviet Union but not against Poland. When the *Los Angeles
Times* asked a national sample what, if anything, the United States
should do if Russia invaded Poland, the answer most often volunteered
by respondents was "nothing" (28 percent); only 5 percent suggested
the dispatch of U.S. troops. In the Falklands crisis, NBC News and the
Associated Press reported 53 to 35 percent approval of the United
States' "taking sides with Great Britain and against Argentina." But even
among those who favored taking the British side, sentiment was 85 to 12
percent against sending American troops to help the British. In June
1982, CBS News asked those who had heard or read about the crisis in
Lebanon what the United States should do in that conflict. Thirty-two

percent said "say or do nothing," while 20 percent wanted the United States to publicly support Israel, 7 percent wanted the United States to publicly criticize Israel, and 24 percent wanted the United States to reduce military aid to Israel.

The situation in El Salvador brought these noninterventionist sentiments into sharpest relief. ABC News and the *Washington Post* surveyed public opinion on El Salvador in March 1982. The public seemed to be quite conscious of American security interests in that part of the world. By the close margin of 46 to 44 percent, respondents felt that the war in El Salvador was "important to the security interests of the United States." By the more substantial margin of 64 to 27 percent, they felt that if the rebel forces took over El Salvador and set up a pro-Communist government there, it would endanger the security interests of the United States. Nevertheless, the interviewees disapproved of the United States' sending troops to fight in El Salvador, 79 to 18 percent. When the stipulation was added, "what if sending American soldiers seemed to be the only way of saving the current government in El Salvador from being defeated," the distaste for American troop involvement was almost unchanged (71 to 22 percent disapproval).

The public expressed a strong fear (64 to 27 percent) that if the government of El Salvador could not defeat the rebels, the United States eventually would send American troops to fight in that country. Americans were evenly split, 42 to 42 percent, over whether the Reagan administration was in fact telling the truth when it claimed that it had no intention of sending American soldiers to fight in El Salvador. As a result, the public disapproved, 45 to 40 percent, of the way the administration was handling the El Salvador situation. Perhaps the most telling response came when people were asked whether they felt that the war in El Salvador was "much like the war in Vietnam." By 65 to 28 percent, the public agreed that it was. Most strikingly, by 51 to 42 percent, a majority said they would support young men who refused to go to El Salvador if the United States were drafting soldiers and sending them to fight there.

Similarly, when the CBS News/*New York Times* poll asked, also in March, whether Central American countries were important to the defense interests of the United States, respondents agreed that they were, 57 to 27 percent. When asked what the United States should do now in El Salvador, however, an overwhelming 63 percent said "stay out"; only 10 percent endorsed economic aid, 6 percent endorsed military aid, and 6 percent favored sending American troops as "advisers to the government." Thus, in the strongest test case since Vietnam, and one much closer to home, the public evinced a powerful distaste for any form of direct American intervention, as well as considerable suspicion that the Reagan administration was contemplating just that. The polls show no evidence of any resurgence of crusading interventionism and substantial evidence that the public distrusted precisely that predilection in the current administration.

The public's distrust translated directly into congressional criticism of the administration's support for the government of El Salvador. Congress sent its own delegation to observe El Salvador's provisional elections on March 28 and required assurance of progress on human rights as a condition for sending additional aid to that country. The administration was pressured to reassure Congress and the public on several occasions that it did not intend to send American troops to fight in El Salvador. The president was apparently convinced that any direct American involvement in Central America would be politically costly, possibly jeopardizing support for his administration's primary commitment, namely, its economic program.

A third issue in which public opinion had a constraining influence on foreign policy was the nuclear freeze. The nuclear freeze issue was unusual in that the public was not reacting to a specific administration policy or proposal. Instead, the public took the initiative of pressuring for a United States–Soviet agreement "to achieve a mutual verifiable freeze on the testing, production, and further deployment of nuclear warheads, missiles, and other delivery systems," as the nuclear freeze resolution was officially worded. Every survey taken through July 1982 showed strong public support for such a proposal, usually by majorities of 70 percent or more. Public pressure was strong enough to get nuclear freeze proposals onto a quarter of the ballots cast nationwide in the 1982 midterm congressional elections. These proposals were passed by voters in eight out of nine states and twenty-eight out of thirty localities.

Did the push for a nuclear freeze amount to a repudiation of the Reagan administration's foreign policy?

The answer, generally speaking, is no. The public did not really backtrack in its desire for a stronger defense posture or a tougher line with the Russians. In these areas, as the evidence has shown, Reagan gave the public exactly what it asked for, and the public seemed to understand and appreciate that fact. Americans became increasingly aware, however, that the cost of a defense buildup and a tough anti-Soviet line was a greater risk of war. They did not want Reagan to abandon those policies. Rather, they wanted some assurance that he would not push those policies any further without making an equally strong commitment to pursue an effective arms control policy that would alleviate the threat of nuclear war.

The public is not convinced that building up our nuclear arsenal actually reinforces our national security. In a March 1982 *Time* Magazine/Yankelovich, Skelly, and White poll, the respondents were closely divided over whether "the nuclear arms race is so dangerous that spending more money on nuclear arms weakens our national security rather than strengthening it"; 45 percent agreed, 48 percent disagreed. A March 1982 *Los Angeles Times* poll asked, "If the United States manufactured more nuclear bombs, would that make you feel more secure or would that make you feel more vulnerable?" Put in those personal terms, 43 percent said "more vulnerable" and 34 percent said "more secure." The same poll asked whether "the United States needs more nuclear weapons for its defense" or whether "the United States now possesses enough nuclear weapons to destroy its enemies." By a decisive margin, 50 to 31 percent, the public felt that we did *not* need more nuclear weapons for our defense.

It turns out that the question just cited was strongly related to support for the nuclear freeze (see Table 2-3). People who said the United States had enough nuclear weapons strongly supported the freeze. Those who said America needed more nuclear weapons for its defense opposed the freeze. The same survey asked whether "the United States should get tougher with Russia, even if that means risking war," or whether "we should be more conciliatory, even if that invites Russia to become more aggressive." Pro-freeze sentiment notwithstanding, respondents endorsed the tougher stance by a decisive margin, 53 to 27 percent. Opinion on the nuclear freeze, however, was almost unrelated to the question of how we should deal with the Russians, as can be seen in Table 2-3. Those who wanted to get tougher and those who wanted to be more conciliatory both supported the freeze.

Thus, the nuclear freeze movement appeared to have little to do with toughness or anti-Soviet feeling, both of which remained very strong. It had to do with the growing sentiment that a nuclear arms race was dangerous and pointless. Nuclear weapons, to most Americans, do not signify greater strength, but greater risk.

On August 5, 1982, the House of Representatives voted to endorse an alternative nuclear weapons control policy backed by the Reagan administration. The vote was excruciatingly close, 204 to 202, and required the exercise of substantial pressure from the White House. Thus, on the nuclear freeze issue, as on defense spending and El Salvador, the administration essentially got its way. The point, however, is that the government had to adapt its policies to public and congressional demands by scaling down its defense spending proposals, by pledging to keep American forces out of Central America, and by coming up with an alternative policy for controlling nuclear weapons. In every case, public opinion forced the administration to face a major political test. Reagan won each test, but only after the expenditure of a considerable proportion of his administration's diminishing reserve of influence over Congress and the public.

TABLE 2-3. Opinion on a Nuclear Freeze Initiative by Attitudes Toward Nuclear Weapons and "Toughness"

Do you think the United States needs more nuclear weapons for its defense, or do you think the United States now possesses enough nuclear weapons to destroy its enemies?

	Percent in Favor of Nuclear Freeze Initiative*
U.S. needs more nuclear weapons	43
U.S. has enough nuclear weapons	69

Do you think the United States should get tougher with Russia, even if that means risking war, or do you think we should be more conciliatory, even if that invites Russia to become more aggressive?

	Percent in Favor of Nuclear Freeze Initiative
Get tougher with Russia	54
Be more conciliatory	59

SOURCE: *Los Angeles Times*/Cable News Network poll conducted March 14-18, 1982, with N = 1,504.

* Poll asked, "In some areas of the country, there is an effort to place a petition on the ballot that would urge the United States government to propose to the government of the Soviet Union that both countries agree to immediately halt the testing, production, and further deployment of all nuclear weapons, missiles, and delivery systems in a way that can be checked and verified by both sides.

"Supporters of this petition say our government needs to know that Americans do not want the development of more nuclear weapons. Opponents say it would halt production at a time when the United States is behind Russia.

"If such a nuclear freeze were being voted on today in your area, do you think you would vote for it or vote against it?"

The Public: An Unstable Audience

It was noted earlier that the general public is noninternationalist and shows a strong and persistent commitment to two basic values, peace and strength. What varies over time is not the commitment to these values but their relative salience. From 1964 to 1974, peace was the overriding concern to most Americans. From 1974 to 1981, military strength became paramount. But it cannot be said that the public really wavered in its commitment to peace. However strong the desire to increase defense spending and to adopt a tougher line with the Soviet Union, public support for arms control remained strong. Thus, polls from 1977 to 1979 revealed continuing approval of SALT II right up until the Soviet invasion of Afghanistan. Between September 1979 and October 1981, according to NBC News and the Associated Press, the proportion favoring "a new agreement between the United States and Russia which would limit nuclear weapons" increased from 62 to 70 percent. What appears to have happened is that public concern over military security reached a climax early in 1980 and helped Reagan win the presidential election. Public concern over peace, which was visible during the 1980 campaign, intensified after Reagan took office and materialized in the form of a major, spontaneous protest movement in 1982.

One additional factor contributes even greater instability to this inherently unstable pattern: the impact of the media, particularly television. The primacy of television has expanded the audience for news, especially foreign policy news. As print media reporters are painfully aware, the public now relies on television as its primary source of news and information. In polls conducted since the late 1950s by the Roper Organization for the Television Information Office, television surpassed newspapers as "the source of most news" in 1963. Today, 64 percent of Americans say they rely on television for news and information, compared to 44 percent who rely on newspapers.

The dominance of television has had a substantial impact on public opinion. Watching television is a different kind of activity from reading newspapers or magazines. When people read newspapers or magazines, they edit the material by selecting only those articles that interest them. If they are not interested in foreign affairs, and most Americans are not, they simply pass over the foreign affairs articles.

Television news, however, edits the information for the viewer. Few people turn off the television or walk away when they are confronted with news stories that do not particularly intrigue them. Television exposes its audience to a much wider range of information than the viewing public would normally select for itself.

Television thus encourages the forming of opinions where formerly there were none. Before the advent of television, much of the public was insulated from a great deal of political information. They edited it out of their lives. That was particularly true of foreign policy, since most Americans, then as now, did not choose to read about what was going on in the rest of the world. The majority of people probably would never have learned of El Salvador, must less cared about it. Today the sheer volume of exposure to new information created by television assures a more involved public. Television has created a vast, *inadvertent* audience for news about foreign policy.

Most media analysts agree that negative news makes good video. Consequently, television presents much of the news as conflict, criticism, and controversy. In a political debate or in a conflict between two countries, producers rarely show the two sides agreeing with one another. The public responds to this large volume of polarized information by becoming more cynical, more negative, and more critical of leadership and institutions. Researchers have found strong connections between political cynicism and exposure to negative information in the media. The increase in political distrust since the mid-1960s may have resulted from the increase in reports of conflict and controversy in our politics. Michael Robinson took this argument one step further and argued a theory of "videomalaise." Television news, he asserted, has an inherent bias toward reporting "interpretive, sensational, aggressive, and anti-institutional news items" — in other words, bad news.[14]

There is another dimension associated with the prominence of television. The television news audience is qualitatively different from the print media audience. People who regularly follow foreign affairs tend to have strong predispositions on the issues. People who are exposed to foreign policy news (or any other kind of news) irregularly or occasionally tend to have weakly held opinions about these issues, simply because they are not interested in them.

Social scientists have shown that when people with strongly held opinions are exposed to new information, they use that information to bolster their opinions. New information does not, as a rule, change their minds. On the other hand, when people with weak opinions are exposed to new information, the impact of that new information is very strong. They form new opinions, and if the information they receive is negative or critical, their opinions tend to develop in that direction.

The mass audience, which is not interested in foreign affairs, is non-internationalist in outlook and automatically suspicious of American involvement in the rest of the world. It is exposed inadvertently, through television, to more foreign policy information than ever before. This group is not converted by any specific editorial policy on the part of television news, but it is made aware of what is going on in the world and, in particular, of how deeply the United States is involved in world events. That information is brought home to these people in a very dramatic way on their television sets night after night, and it offends their noninternationalist sensibilities. They simply don't see the point of it.

As a result, the public has become less patient with foreign policy initiatives. The attentive elites compete for allies in the noninternationalist public, each on its own grounds. The net impact is a good deal more cynicism and distrust among people who find their leaders increasingly critical and deeply divided. There is no evidence that television changes the nature of the public's concerns in the area of foreign policy. Those concerns remain what they always have been, peace and strength. Television simply intensifies them and creates more negative and unstable public moods.

Recent trends, we have argued, have been in the direction of conservatism — greater concern for national security and military strength. Interventionism was temporarily buoyed by the conservative tide, but careful inspection of the evidence reveals no surge of internationalist feeling; just the reverse, in fact. The conservative trend worked to Ronald Reagan's advantage in 1980, and there is no reason why it should not continue to do so, as long as the president does not see a mandate for interventionism. Thus, the president's approval ratings on foreign policy showed a slight upturn in the late spring of 1982, prior to his trip to Europe, apparently because the public approved of his keeping the United States out of the El Salvador and Falkland Islands conflicts and of his support for the goals of the nuclear freeze movement, as stated in his speech at Eureka College on May 6. Polls taken as early as April (by ABC News and the *Washington Post*) and May (by CBS News and the *New York Times*) indicated that about one-third of the public was of the opinion that the president supported a nuclear freeze. In the CBS/ *Times* poll, more people thought he supported it than thought he opposed it.

If the rhetoric of this administration has been tough and aggressive, the substance of its foreign policy has been somewhat less so. Intellectuals and activists may be dismayed by this inconsistency, but the public does not seem to mind. Richard Nixon, the preeminent Cold Warrior of his time, was also the architect of detente. Today, according to the Harris survey,[15] the public rates Nixon as the best of the last nine presidents for handling foreign affairs. Lyndon Johnson, on the other hand, combined moderate rhetoric with incautious policies and is rated worst in foreign affairs. The problem for Reagan, as for any president, is to maintain a delicate balance between strong moral leadership and pragmatic policies. Already the president's overly strong rhetoric concerning nuclear war has frightened many people and produced a significant political backlash. On the other hand, the administration's confused and passive response to foreign policy crises has given rise to charges of ineptitude and drift. The point of this essay has been to argue that inconsistency is not, in and of itself, a political problem. Ineffectiveness, however, is potentially a very serious one.

Notes

1. *The New York Times*, January 21, 1982, quoted in *Conservative Digest*, Vol. 8 (July 1982), p. 15.
2. For complete data, see William Schneider, "The November 4 Vote for President: What Did It Mean?" Chapter 7 in Austin Ranney, ed., *The American Elections*

of 1980 (Washington, D.C.: American Enterprise Institute for Public Policy Research, 1981), p. 231.

3. Carter's 1980 campaign strategy is described by Patrick Caddell, "The Democratic Strategy and Its Electoral Consequences," Chapter 11 in Seymour Martin Lipset, ed., *Party Coalitions in the 1980s* (San Francisco: Institute for Contemporary Studies, 1981), especially pp. 279-282.

4. *Gallup Opinion Index*, Report No. 181 (September 1980), pp. 7-8.

5. The distinction was first made by Donald Stokes, "Spatial Models of Party Competition," in Angus Campbell, Philip E. Converse, Warren E. Miller, and Donald E. Stokes, *Elections and the Political Order* (New York: John Wiley and Sons, 1966), pp. 170-171.

6. Michael Mandelbaum and William Schneider, "The New Internationalisms: Public Opinion and Foreign Policy," Chapter 2 in Kenneth Oye, Donald Rothchild, and Robert Lieber, eds., *Eagle Entangled: U.S. Foreign Policy in a Complex World* (New York: Longman Inc., 1979), pp. 40-63.

7. John E. Mueller, *War, Presidents, and Public Opinion* (New York: John Wiley and Sons, 1973), pp. 122-140.

8. Mandelbaum and Schneider, pp. 40-43.

9. For complete descriptions of the two surveys, see John E. Rielly, ed., *American Public Opinion and U.S. Foreign Policy 1975* (Chicago: Chicago Council on Foreign Relations, 1975), and Rielly, ed., *American Public Opinion and U.S. Foreign Policy 1979* (Chicago: Chicago Council on Foreign Relations, 1979).

10. Alvin Richman, "Public Attitudes on Military Power, 1981," *Public Opinion*, Vol. 4 (December/January 1982), p. 45.

11. Lloyd Free and William Watts, "Internationalism Comes of Age...Again," *Public Opinion*, Vol. 3 (April/May 1980), pp. 46-50.

12. See discussion in William Schneider, "The Beleaguered Censensus," Chapter 11 in Joseph Nye, ed., *Managing U.S.-Soviet Relations* (New York: Council on Foreign Relations, forthcoming, 1983).

13. Richard E. Cohen, "Rating Congress — A Guide to Separating the Liberals from the Conservatives," *National Journal*, Vol. 14 (May 8, 1982), pp. 800-810.

14. Michael J. Robinson, "Public Affairs Television and the Growth of Political Malaise: The Case of 'The Selling of the Pentagon,'" *American Political Science Review*, Vol. 70 (March 1976), p. 426.

15. "Public Still Rates JFK as Best of Past Nine Presidents," *The Harris Survey*, 1982, No. 22 (March 18, 1982), p. 3.

II

Functional Problems

3

Reagan Administration Defense Policy: Departure from Containment

Barry R. Posen
Stephen W. Van Evera

The Reagan administration has proposed the biggest military buildup since the Korean War. The administration's five-year defense program requires an average real defense budget increase of 8.1 percent per year from 1981 to 1987, for a net real increase of 59 percent. Under this five-year plan, United States defense spending would rise from 5.6 percent of gross national product (GNP) in 1981 to 7.4 percent of GNP in 1987.[1] Federal budget deficits and congressional opposition doubtless will prevent the administration from enacting all the defense increases it has proposed; nevertheless, the general direction of the Reagan defense budget will be sharply upward.

Is this buildup necessary? Is the money being well spent? To answer, we must first clarify the United States' grand strategy. What are America's basic aims? What missions must the United States military perform to achieve these aims? Can current United States forces already perform these missions, or do they fall short?

Defense policy cannot be evaluated unless national strategy and national military capabilities are specified first. Otherwise, planners lack goals and guidelines to measure national defense requirements, foreign and defense policies are bound to be mismatched, and planners risk

Barry R. Posen is a Council on Foreign Relations International Affairs Fellow. He holds a Ph.D. in political science from the University of California, Berkeley. This essay was written while he was a postdoctoral fellow at the Center for International Affairs, Harvard University, and the views expressed are his own. Mr. Posen is the author of "Inadvertent Nuclear War? Escalation and NATO's Northern Flank," International Security, *Vol. 7, No. 2 (Fall, 1982) and* Israel's Strategic Doctrine *(Santa Monica: Rand R-2845NA, Sept. 1981) with Yoav Ben Horin.*

Stephen W. Van Evera is a lecturer in Politics at Princeton University.

wasting money on areas in which their forces are already strong, while failing to correct weaknesses. Defense budget cuts make sense only if a leaner force can still carry out national strategy. Increases make sense only if current forces cannot carry out assigned missions and military reforms cannot make up the shortfall. In short, defense planners should ask the big questions first — they should clarify basic aims and basic strategy before choosing forces and tactics — or their programs and policies will not be coherent or economical.

Disputes about American defense needs often spring from hidden disputes about strategy. People differ on how much to spend on defense because they differ on whether the United States should adopt a more or less demanding strategy; it costs more to perform many missions than to perform fewer, so deciding how much is enough depends on first deciding "enough to do what?" People also differ on the merits of specific weapons systems because they differ on what missions the military must perform; different missions require different forces, so debates about hardware often grow from unacknowledged disputes about which strategy is best. Likewise, disputes about the East-West military balance often spring from hidden disagreements about how many missions we expect the military to achieve. We appear strong if the requirements are few and weak if they are many. Pessimists and optimists often differ less on what American forces *can* do than on what they should be *asked* to do. In short, the defense debate is largely about strategy.

Yet the Reagan administration has failed to explain what strategy it pursues and neglected to detail the capabilities and weaknesses of current American forces, leaving defense analysts and the public without yardsticks by which to judge whether the proposed buildup is necessary or appropriate. Reagan administration statements do suggest the outline of a strategy, but important questions are left unanswered. Secretary of Defense Caspar Weinberger's first *Annual Report to the Congress*, the main public document explaining the buildup, leaves roles and missions undefined and fails to specify shortfalls between current American capabilities and required missions. The secretary rejects "arbitrary and facile" estimates of the number of contingencies for which American forces must prepare.[2] He believes that the United States should "discard artificial definitions and contrived categories," and avoid "the mistaken argument as to whether we should prepare to fight 'two wars,' 'one and a half wars,' or some other such tally of war."[3] He demands a "necessary recasting of our strategy"[4] without explaining what the old strategy was, or what the new strategy will be. He points to "serious deficiencies in our military forces"[5] without explaining which missions cannot be met. The administration, in short, does not publicly explain its proposed military buildup in concrete terms that allow us to measure its benefits against its costs. Thus, the first fault with President Reagan's defense program lies with its lack of a clearly articulated defense strategy.

Second, insofar as the administration does have a strategy, it seems extravagant and dangerous. Fragmentary statements and administration procurement programs suggest that the administration has adopted a more demanding strategy than any since the Eisenhower administration, or perhaps earlier. The Reagan administration appears to have embraced more and harder missions than the original Cold War "containment" strategy would require, and it puts more emphasis on offensive missions and tactics. All administrations since Truman have adopted defense strategies that included more missions than a pure containment strategy would seem to require, but the implicit Reagan administration strategy departs further from containment than its predecessors.

This demanding new strategy is what drives the Reagan defense budget upward, but the extra missions it requires have not been explained or debated, and the prima facie case that they protect vital American interests seems weak. On the whole, then, when we do catch a glimpse of the administration's grand strategy, it appears to depart from original cold war strategic ideas and toward a more ambitious and more dangerous grand strategy.

The following describes the original Cold War strategy of containment and the four essential military missions that follow from it. Then NATO forces are measured against these missions to assess current NATO military strength. Section II outlines which additional missions are implicit in Reagan administration statements and programs, while sections III and IV discuss the causes of current public alarm about Western military strength, and suggest reforms which could strengthen NATO forces without a major defense budget increase.

I: United States Strategy and Capabilities

Containment and United States Strategy

To assess the current defense debate, we begin by measuring current American military strength. First, we need a set of missions against which to measure American forces. Past consensus held that American force had four main missions. First, American strategic nuclear forces must be able to inflict unacceptable damage on the Soviet Union even after a Soviet nuclear first strike against our forces. Second, American forces must be strong enough to check a Soviet invasion of Western Europe for several weeks, against whatever weapons Soviet invaders choose to use — conventional, chemical, or tactical nuclear.[6] A third mission was added once the West became dependent on Middle East Oil: to defeat a Soviet seizure of the Persian Gulf oil fields. Finally, most strategists agree that the United States requires the capacity to fight an extra "half war" against another country, even while fighting a major war against the Soviet Union, thus creating a total "one-and-a-half war" requirement. For planning purposes an attack by North Korea on South Korea was taken as the "half war," but the half war mission had no defined adversary, and might be fought anywhere against anyone.

These four missions reflect the basic aims of containment, as framed by George F. Kennan, Walter Lippmann, and other strategists in the 1940s:[7] to prevent the industrial power of Eurasia[8] from falling under the control of any single state. They warned that any state controlling all Eurasia could threaten the United States, since the total industrial power of Europe and Asia (64% of gross world product in 1978) far exceeds that of the United States (24% of GWP in 1978).[9] A hegemonic Eurasian superstate could convert this superior economy into a stronger war machine: Hence the United States must prevent such a superstate from arising. In short, containment was a geopolitical security strategy; its purpose was to maintain the political division of industrial Eurasia, to protect the United States from a hostile Eurasian power concentration.

After World War II, containment was directed against the Soviet Union because the Soviets became the biggest threat for dominating Europe once Nazi German power had been destroyed. According to Kennan (see Note 7), the stakes in this Soviet-American competition were centers of military-industrial production — places where military power could be created. The purpose of containment was to keep the Soviets from seizing these industrial regions and mobilizing them against the United States. This would be achieved by cooperative effort among the states threatened by Soviet expansion, not by solitary action on the part of the United States. The final goal was to limit Soviet power but not to destroy it, since this would be too difficult and might create a new potential hegemony, just as the destruction of German power created the Soviet threat to Europe in 1945. Containment did not seek a decisive result: It succeeded if Soviet hegemony was prevented.

As it was originally conceived, containment thus was more a geopolitical than an ideological strategy. It opposed the Soviet state, not communism per se (although American leaders often explained containment with simplistic anti-Communist rhetoric). The logic of containment would have defined the Soviet Union as the American adversary even if it had abandoned communism for democracy, as long as it remained strong and aggressive. Containment also was fundamentally defensive: Eurasia was to be divided, not dominated or policed. Containment was directed toward the industrial world, not the Third World, since industrial warmaking power was the prize. And it assumed the defense of the West was a joint effort, not an exclusive American operation. The basic purpose of containment was the same basic purpose that led the United States to ally with the Soviets against Hitler: namely, to keep the rest of Europe free from being overrun by the strongest European state. Kennan summarized the logic of containment in these terms:

It [is] essential to us, as it was to Britain, that no single Continental land power should come to dominate the entire Eurasian land mass. Our interest has lain rather in the maintenance of some sort of stable balance among the powers of the interior, in order that none of them should effect the subjugation of the others, conquer the seafaring fringes of the land mass, become a great sea power as well as land power, shatter the position of England, and enter — as in these circumstances it certainly would — on an overseas expansion hostile to ourselves and supported by the immense resources of the interior of Europe and Asia.[10]

Kennan identified five important military-industrial regions: the Soviet Union, the Rhine valley, the British isles, Japan, and the United States.[11] Today the Persian Gulf is a sixth important region, since Europe and Japan depend on Persian Gulf oil. In Kennan's terms, the task of the United States is to contain the Soviets within their military-industrial region, which in practical terms means defending Western Europe, Japan, and now the Persian Gulf. The direct Soviet threat to Japan is minimal, so the defense of Europe and the Gulf are the main military missions.

Besides containing the Soviets, the United States has a second basic aim: to keep America out of a nuclear war. This aim involves two objectives: to keep any war conventional, avoiding the use of nuclear weapons as long as possible; and to keep any nuclear war off American territory if possible, confining it to the theater where it breaks out. These goals are not required by containment per se, but rather by the invention of nuclear weapons, which demand more careful tactics of containment.

These general aims — containing the Soviet Union and keeping the United States out of a nuclear war — engender the specific requirements for American conventional and tactical nuclear forces. Hypothetically, the United States could defend Europe and the Gulf simply by threatening to attack Soviet cities with strategic nuclear weapons if the Soviets invaded. But the Soviets could retaliate against American cities, and American strategists do not want to "trade Boston to defend Bonn." Moreover, the Soviets might not be convinced that American leaders would carry out such a threat. This fear led to the requirement that American theater forces in Europe and the Gulf should be strong enough to halt Soviet invaders. The hope is to keep the war away from American soil, confining it to the theater of action.

The United States would try to defend Europe and Japan conventionally, if the Soviets attacked conventionally, to lower the risk of nuclear escalation. American conventional forces are intended to form a buffer between peace and nuclear war — to give us a choice, in other words, between all or nothing. In official thinking, such a buffer lowers the risk of a holocaust by widening Western options: The United States can defend conventionally if the Soviets attack conventionally.[12] Before

1967 the United States had planned to defend Europe chiefly with tactical and strategic nuclear weapons, but then NATO endorsed a new plan to fight conventionally for at least several weeks, to give statesmen time to seek peace through negotiation. This plan, of course, does not guarantee a nuclear war would not happen anyway. Any major East-West conventional war may escalate against the wishes of both sides.[13] Moreover, Soviet military writing indicates that the Soviets might use nuclear weapons from the outset of the war.[14] But conventional forces are intended to reduce this risk.

Past administrations have often added a fifth or a sixth mission to these four — most notably, an anti-China mission, a "counterforce" mission,[15] or a Third World intervention mission. Before 1969, American strategists planned for a simultaneous war against Russia, China and a third enemy, creating a total "two-and-a-half war" requirement, in contrast with the "one-and-a-half war" strategy adopted by the Nixon, Ford, and Carter administrations. Before 1964, and again after 1974, official policy included an ambiguous counterforce requirement. During the 1960s, American planners assumed that we must be capable of intervening against Third World insurgencies. Kennan, Lippmann, and others often pointed out that American foreign policy goals were expanding beyond the original aims of containment; likewise, American defense policy incorporated more missions than pure containment would seem to require. But the four missions outlined above are the only missions to receive continuous consensus support. They are also the only four that follow unambiguously from a containment grand strategy[16] so these are the missions against which we measure American forces.

American strategists have traditionally assumed that our allies would help carry out these missions; the United States would not shoulder the full burden alone. Eurasian states on the Soviet periphery have at least as much at stake in containment as the United States, since Soviet expansion threatens their freedom more directly. American strategists have therefore assumed these states will contribute a major share to NATO defenses. A chief purpose of the Marshall Plan and postwar military assistance programs was to strengthen Western Europe so it could defend itself against the Soviets. The notion was always that the United States would stand with those who were attacked, and with others whose interests were threatened by Soviet expansion; but the United States would not perform solo, since containment served a general Western interest. The proper comparison, then, is between NATO and Warsaw Pact forces, not between the United States and the Soviet Union.

Depending on whether we add or subtract missions from this list of four, American defense costs will vary sharply. A strictly bare-bones containment strategy might require only the three anti-Soviet missions — a nuclear retaliatory capability and denial capabilities in Europe and the

Persian Gulf, with no extra "half-war" mission — because, as a containment purist might argue, only Soviet expansion poses a threat, and the Soviets can threaten only Europe and the Gulf. On the other hand, Reagan administration defense requirements are exceptionally high because this administration, even more than past administrations, assumes a longer list of missions than a pure containment strategy would require.

United States Military Capabilities

Administration statements and press accounts paint a picture of serious American military weakness. Defense Secretary Weinberger, for example, points to "serious deficiencies" and "major weaknesses" in American defenses and warns of "our collective failure to pursue an adequate balance of military strength" while the Soviets have pursued "the greatest buildup of military power seen in modern times." [17] The *Wall Street Journal* declares that the Soviet Union "now is superior to the U.S. in almost every category of strategic and conventional force." [18]

Yet American forces seem capable of carrying out their four basic missions today. The United States looks weak only when American capabilities are measured against a more demanding strategy. American forces suffer some deficiencies, and a higher level of confidence in their capabilities would be prudent; but these problems can be addressed by modest reforms and/or a modest spending increase. More pessimistic views of American capabilities often rest on hidden assumption that more missions are demanded or that American allies do not help.

NATO forces *should* be capable of achieving their basic missions, given the total size of the NATO defense effort. NATO states have more men under arms than the Warsaw Pact (5.0 v. 4.8 million men)[19] and spend more money on defense than do the Pact states. Latest United States government figures show NATO narrowly outspending the Pact ($215 to $211 billion in 1979, a 2 percent difference),[20] while figures from the London-based International Institute for Strategic Studies (IISS) give NATO a wider margin ($180 to $160 billion in 1978, a difference of 12½ percent).[21] Moreover, about 15 percent of the Soviet defense effort is directed toward China. If we deduct these Soviet forces, United States government figures show a NATO spending lead of 17 percent, and IISS figures show NATO leading by 30 percent. These numbers are based on guesswork rather than precise estimates, but they suggest the rough balance of total assets invested on both sides.

In fact, some analysts claim that official American figures exaggerate Soviet spending. One expert recently guessed that the CIA may exaggerate Soviet spending by perhaps 25-30 percent, and that the Soviets only outspend the Americans by 15-20 percent.[22] If we adjust United States government figures accordingly, NATO actually outspends the Pact by 25 percent. If Soviet forces facing China are then deducted, NATO outspends the Pact by 42 percent. Another expert suggests that government figures underestimate Western European NATO spending by perhaps 22 percent.[23] If so, NATO outspends the Pact by 12 percent using official figures, or by 29 percent if Soviet forces facing China are deducted.

In short, NATO has the personnel and the resources needed to defend successfully. If NATO forces are weak, this reflects mistaken force posture, doctrine, and choice of weapons, not inadequate defense spending. Moreover, as argued below, NATO forces probably can achieve their basic missions even today.

United States Strategic Nuclear Capabilities. United States strategic nuclear forces consist of a triad of 1,051 intercontinental ballistic missiles (ICBMs) based in the U.S.; 520 submarine-launched ballistic missiles (SLBMs) carried in 32 nuclear-powered submarines; and 376 strategic bombers, which carry nuclear gravity bombs and nuclear-tipped short-range missiles. These strategic forces consume only 15 percent of the U.S. defense budget, the rest going to conventional forces,[24] but they are the most important and powerful of the American military forces.

The Soviets also have a triad of 1,398 ICBMs, 989 SLBMs, and 150 bombers. Because more American missiles are "MIRVed" — carry more than one warhead [25] — American strategic forces carry more warheads (9,268 to the Soviets' 7,300); however, Soviet warheads are bigger, so the Soviet force carries more total explosive power.[26]

The administration warns that these American strategic forces are dangerously weak. President Reagan declares that Soviet strategic forces have a "definite margin of superiority" over American forces,[27] while Defense Secretary Weinberger warns that the Soviets hold a "degree of superiority and strategic edge" in strategic nuclear capability that "will last for some years through the decade even if we pursue all the programs the President has sought." [28]

In fact, American strategic nuclear capability depends on which missions American forces are measured against. American strategic forces have much more than a "second-strike capability" (the capacity to inflict "unacceptable damage" [29] on Soviet population and industry even after absorbing a Soviet nuclear first strike), and far less than a "first-strike capability" (the capacity to render Soviet forces incapable of inflicting "unacceptable damage" on American population and industry). Nor do American forces have a "second strike-counterforce" capability (the capacity to absorb a Soviet first strike and then render remaining Soviet nuclear forces incapable of inflicting unacceptable damage on remaining American population and industry). In short, American forces could not prevent the Soviets from devastating our population and industry after an American first strike or after an American mid-war strike against Soviet reserve nuclear forces; but they could destroy most of the Soviet Union in retaliation after a Soviet first strike.

Thus, overall, American "counterforce" capability — the ability to destroy Soviet retaliatory capability — is minimal, while American retaliatory capability is enormous. Neither side can disarm the other, and both sides can retaliate. An estimated 3,500 American strategic nuclear warheads could survive a Soviet surprise attack,[30] enough to destroy Soviet society several times over. Just seventy-three U.S. warheads could destroy over 70 percent of Soviet petroleum production capacity.[31] Just 631 small (50 kiloton) American warheads or 141 big (1 megaton) American warheads could destroy over 50 percent of total Soviet industrial capacity.[32] Some doubts surround the survivability of the American strategic command, control, communications, and intelligence apparatus ("C³I"), but public information on strategic C³I is not adequate to judge the extent of the deficiency, or what is needed to correct it.[33] Assuming sufficient C³I survives, the United States now has many more than enough survivable warheads to retaliate effectively.

This does not mean the United States can stand still. The Soviets invest heavily in counterforce nuclear forces, and American strategic forces must be continuously modernized to cope with these Soviet threats to United States second-strike capabilities as they emerge. Improved high-accuracy Soviet ICBMs are now threatening American ICBMs, and improving Soviet air defense capabilities may eventually threaten the penetration capability of American strategic bombers; hence some improvement or replacement of current ICBMs and bombers will be required to keep our second-strike capability at current levels.[34] But certainly current American forces can retaliate effectively today.

In short, American strategic forces are strong or weak depending on the mission required: The United States is a long way from a meaningful counterforce capability, but American second-strike capability is robust. This reflects the nuclear facts of life: Nuclear weapons are very powerful, cheap, small, light, easily hidden, easily protected, and easily delivered. As a result, a second-strike capability is very cheap and easy to maintain, while a first-strike capability is virtually impossible under any known technology. It is much harder to find new ways to destroy enemy warheads than it is for the enemy to find new ways to protect them. The "cost-exchange ratio" — the ratio of the cost of producing a capability to the cost of neutralizing it — lies very heavily in favor of the second-strike capability. As a result *neither* superpower can deny the other a second-strike capability, because technology simply will not allow it. The notion that either superpower could gain a militarily meaningful "margin of superiority" is an illusion.

Western Europe. The common assumption holds that Warsaw Pact conventional forces could quickly overrun Western Europe in a conventional war. Then-Secretary of State Alexander Haig warned that the United States must "triple the size of its armed forces and put its economy on a war footing" before NATO could defend Europe success-fully.[35] The Committee on the Present Danger notes "a near consensus on the inadequacy of present NATO forces to defend Western Europe suc-cessfully with conventional arms." [36]

In fact, NATO conventional forces in Europe are substantially stronger than these gloomy views suggest, although they remain weaker than prudence requires.[37] If Warsaw Pact forces perform a little better than best evidence suggests they will, or if NATO forces perform worse than expected, or if NATO leaders fail to mobilize NATO forces promptly after they receive warning of a Pact mobilization, then Pact forces *can* win the battle. But overall the odds favor NATO, if NATO leaders mobilize their forces quickly once they receive warning[38] and if Pact forces demonstrate no surprising margin of strength over NATO forces. Although NATO forces could not crush Pact attackers deci-sively, they probably could deny the Soviets a quick victory and thereby turn the conflict into a long war of attrition.

In short, NATO forces cannot promise victory with the level of con-fidence that NATO leaders should demand, but they seem more likely to win than to lose. Moreover, NATO could be substantially strengthened without a major military buildup, if NATO forces are reformed along the lines we outline below (see Section IV). NATO forces are now close to speed, and could be brought up to speed, without a large spending increase, by improving NATO force structure and procurement practices.

A Warsaw Pact attack will probably fail because Pact forces prob-ably lack the superiority in firepower and manpower they would need to overcome the natural advantage held by the defender, and to compensate for the obstacles that West German geography would pose to an ag-gressor. The Pact has only a slender manpower and material advantage in Central Europe — between 15 and 20 percent in total manpower, and 20 percent in total ground firepower (i.e., firepower in all NATO and Pact army formations available in Central Europe).[39] Moreover, this fire-power ratio may undercount NATO firepower because it omits some NATO weapons held as replacements for combat losses, leaves out some German reserve units, and ignores NATO's greater investment in divi-sional command, control, and intelligence hardware and staff, which increase the effectiveness of NATO firepower. If these factors were in-cluded, the Pact advantage might disappear.

The Pact also trails NATO in tactical airpower. Total NATO tacti-cal aircraft in Europe have triple the aggregate payload of Pact aircraft at distances of 100 miles, and seven times the payload of Pact aircraft at distances of 200 miles, according to the latest available data.[40] This reflects the much greater carrying power of NATO aircraft: A NATO F-4 Phantom carries 16,000 pounds, while a MiG 27 carries only 6,600 pounds.

NATO planes should also be superior in air-to-air combat. NATO fighters are more sophisticated, NATO has better "battle-management" systems (the AWACs aircraft), and NATO pilots are better than Pact pilots. American pilots have more combat experience, they fly more hours, and their training is more realistic.[41] Overall, as Air Force Director of Plans General James Ahmann has testified, NATO fighter forces are "superior to the Warsaw Pact" and could achieve "very favorable aircraft exchange ratios" against Pact fighters.[42]

These facts are often overlooked because press accounts stress Pact advantages in unrepresentative subcategories, such as numbers of tanks or artillery or planes, where the Pact does have an advantage (150, 180, and 15 percent respectively).[43] Such comparisons ignore NATO quality advantages (NATO planes, artillery, and antitank weapons and ordnance are better than those of the Pact), and categories where NATO leads (major warships, helicopters). In general, NATO forces in Europe are not significantly outnumbered and may even hold the advantage in overall military capability.

Geography and the advantage of the defender also favor NATO. As a rule, attackers require substantial material superiority for success — between three- and six-to-one at the point of attack, and between one-and-one-half-to-one and two-to-one in the theater of war.[44] But the Pact probably cannot gain enough superiority unless NATO mobilizes late. In fact, NATO can maintain force ratios close to the premobilization ratio if NATO mobilizes simultaneously with the Pact.[45] If NATO waits several days and then mobilizes, the balance in favor of the Pact would briefly exceed one-and-one-half-to-one but still would not reach two-to-one in favor of the Pact. Then it would fall back to a level close to the pre-mobilization ratio. The odds clearly favor the Pact only if NATO delays mobilization more than a week after receiving warning.[46]

German terrain further complicates a Pact attack. German forests, mountains, and other obstacles limit the Pact to four possible attack routes: the North German plain, the Hof Corridor (toward Stuttgart), the Fulda Gap (toward Frankfurt), and the Gottingen Corridor (toward the Ruhr). Because the Pact attack is canalized by this geography, NATO can focus its defensive efforts, and Pact forces are compressed to the point where they cannot fight efficiently. NATO troops can "cross the T" — chew up forward Pact units serially — while other Pact units sit idly in the rear, since the Pact will not have room in these narrow channels to bring all its units forward at once.[47] Moreover, three of these channels run the width of Germany, so attacking Soviet forces cannot spread out even if they break through NATO front-line defenses. The war wouldn't unfold like the German attack on France in 1940, when the Germans burst into open plains, ideal tank country, after crossing the Meuse. Instead, Pact forces would be confined by geography to a narrow area until they penetrated deep into Germany.[48]

NATO suffers some unique weaknesses, but these are roughly counterbalanced by unique Pact handicaps. NATO's seven European armies have not standardized their weapons, so ammunition, spare parts, and communications gear are not fully interchangeable. As a result NATO armies cannot easily feed on one another's supplies, a limitation that undercuts their wartime flexibility. In contrast, the Soviets have imposed Soviet arms on all their Pact vassals. But this advantage is offset by the fact that Pact forces are less reliable than NATO forces; in wartime the Soviets cannot be sure whether the Poles and Czechs will fight with them, sit the war out, or even fight against them. Some 45 percent of Pact standing ground forces in Europe are East European, a circumstance that greatly complicates Soviet planning.

Most published estimates of the European balance are admittedly more pessimistic than ours,[49] but they fail to fully utilize available information. Key data required for a thorough assessment are missing from their analyses: aggregate firepower estimates for the forces on both sides,[50] terrain factors, and estimates of troop movement and interdiction rates. Instead, their judgment of NATO's weakness is supported by unrepresentative statistics and by conclusions based on unduly pessimistic political and factual assumptions. An overwhelming Pact firepower advantage, for example, is suggested by focusing on subcategories of weapons in which the Pact has the lead. Sometimes the number of Soviet divisions promptly available is exaggerated. Other estimates overlook Soviet weaknesses, such as the unreliability of East European armies. Still others neglect the advantage of fighting on the defense. In short, pessimistic estimates are more common, but they are based on sketchier information and less comprehensive analysis.[51]

The Persian Gulf. Conventional wisdom holds that American forces could not block a Soviet seizure of the Iranian oil fields, or even the Saudi Arabian oil fields, without using nuclear weapons. One columnist suggested that American forces "could never be a match for the Soviet juggernaut across the Iranian border."[52] Defense Secretary Weinberger warned that American forces were "incapable of stopping an assault on Western oil supplies,"[53] while one prominent defense analyst proclaimed that Iran "may be inherently indefensible."[54] But these predictions, like those pessimistic predictions concerning Europe, do not make full use of available information. In fact, American forces could probably halt the Soviets short of the oilfields, chiefly because a Soviet attack would require an enormous transportation and logistics effort, which probably lies beyond Soviet capabilities.

The United States stands a good chance in the Gulf because Soviet forces could not gain decisive materiel superiority in the battle area. Even though the Soviets are much nearer, the United States can probably bring as much firepower to bear in the Persian Gulf theater as can the Soviets.[55]

Proximity would seem to give the Soviets the upper hand; but appearances are misleading, for three reasons.

First, the United States has invested more money in mobility equipment (transport aircraft and amphibious assault ships, aircraft carriers, airmobile and seamobile forces), which partially offsets greater Soviet proximity.

Second, the Soviets have not tailored their military to invade the Persian Gulf, so their forces are not ready to attack on short notice. As a result NATO would gain valuable advance warning if the Soviets chose to invade. Before the Soviets attack, they must assemble and test a command and control apparatus in Transcaucasia, which would make telltale radio noises. They must amass tens of thousands of trucks in the Caucasus, to supply Soviet divisions advancing into Iran, because Soviet forces near Iran do not have enough trucks. Soviet army divisions are structured for war in Europe, with its many railroads. As a result, these divisions are designed to operate no farther than 100 miles from a railhead, so they normally include relatively few trucks. Soviet forces invading the Gulf would be fighting hundreds of miles from any functioning railroad, requiring an enormous additional complement of trucks to ferry supplies on Iranian roads. By one estimate all the trucks from more than fifty-five Soviet army divisions (one-third of the *mobilized* Soviet army) would be required to support a Soviet invasion force of seven divisions in Iran, assuming no trucks break down or are destroyed in fighting.[56] By another estimate almost all the trucks in the Soviet army might be required.[57] This armada could not be assembled quickly or discreetly.

These preparations would give NATO at least one month's warning.[58] In the meantime, the United States could move substantial forces into the Gulf to greet Soviet attackers — perhaps 500 land- and sea-based tactical fighters, the 82nd Airborne Division, and two Marine brigades within two or three weeks. Later the United States could bring in much bigger forces by sea.

Third, although the Soviets are much closer to the Gulf oilfields than is the United States, each mile the Soviets must travel is much harder to traverse. Soviet invasion forces must move 850 miles overland to reach the Iranian oil fields in Khuzestan province in Southwest Iran. If they attack from the Soviet Union, they must cross two formidable mountain ranges: those along the Iranian northern tier, and the Zagros Mountains, which separate Khuzestan from central Iran. If they attack from Afghanistan they must pass over the fierce, desolate Khorassan desert and the Zagros. Only a handful of roads cross the northern mountains, and only four roads and one railroad span the Zagros.[59] In the mountains these roads cross bridges, run through tunnels, cling to the sides of countless gorges, and wind beneath overhanging cliffs. As a result Soviet supply arteries would be dotted with scores of choke points — places where the artery could be destroyed or blocked. The blockage could not be by-passed or easily repaired.

With all the geographical barriers, Soviet movements in Iran would be exceptionally vulnerable to delaying action by American airstrikes, commando raids, or attacks by Iranian guerrillas on the scores of choke points between Khuzestan and Russia. This distance is too great for the Soviets to erect solid air defenses along their entire groundline of communication, so American airpower could probably continue striking these choke points even if they were overrun by advancing Soviet forces. These air strikes could be flown from aircraft carriers, by land-based aircraft that could be moved to the Mideast after warning is received, or by B-52s based on Diego Garcia in the Indian Ocean, on Guam in the Pacific, or even in the United States.[60] Iranian forces could also slow down Soviet forces and disrupt Soviet supply lines, especially if they organized in advance for guerrilla war.

By one estimate, American air strikes and helicopter infantry teams working in the Zagros could slow the Soviet advance toward Khuzistan by 60 days.[61] If we assume the United States receives and uses thirty days of warning, then American forces have ninety days to prepare the defense of Khuzistan. In this time the United States can move enough ground forces to Khuzistan to equal the firepower of Soviet divisions coming through the Zagros.[62] Moreover, the United States can probably bring more airpower to bear in Khuzestan than can the Soviets,[63] giving the United States a net firepower advantage. If so, American forces have more than enough firepower to win.

Some Westerners suggest that the Soviets might mount a surprise airborne attack on Iran, seizing key air fields and other facilities with airborne units and holding them until Soviet ground forces could follow up, instead of mounting a prepared ground assault. But such an airborne strike seems even more likely to fail than a ground assault, because the Soviets could not assemble the trucks their ground forces require without giving away the surprise which an "airborne grab" would demand. As a result, any airborne divisions dropped into southern Iran would have to hold off American and Iranian counterattacks for weeks while the Soviets readied their ground invasion force in the southern Soviet Union. Moreover, these airborne units could not be easily resupplied by air in the meantime, because Soviet fighter aircraft probably lack the range to provide adequate air cover over southern Iran from bases in the Soviet Union or Afghanistan, and the Soviets probably could not quickly seize, secure, and prepare enough air bases in Iran suitable for modern fighter aircraft. As a result, the Soviets probably could not defend their transport aircraft over southern Iran against American fighters, leaving their airborne units stranded. In sum, a Soviet "airborne grab" against southern Iran seems even harder than a Soviet ground attack.

Lord Salisbury once remarked, concerning British fears that Russia would sweep through Afghanistan into India: "A great deal of misapprehension arises from the popular use of maps on a small scale." [64] Likewise, American fears that the Soviets could sweep through Iran spring from dismissal of geographic and military realities. Overall, as one analyst notes, "the invasion of Iran would be an exceedingly low confidence affair for the Soviets." [65]

As with the European balance, pessimistic estimates of the Gulf conventional balance do not fully utilize available data, or they rest on dubious factual or political assumptions.[66] Again, aggregate firepower estimates, geographic factors, movement tables, interdiction rates, and warning estimates are usually missing. Instead, misleading statistics are combined with unduly pessimistic political assumptions: e.g., that the Gulf states refuse American help or cooperate with Soviet invaders, or that the United States loses simply because it lacks the will to fight, or that the American mission is to defend only *northern* Iran, which would be much harder than defending the southern oilfields, or that American leaders would simply fail to heed the warning they receive.[67]

In short, public alarm about American capabilities to achieve basic missions seems exaggerated. Publicly available information on American capabilities is spotty, so estimates of our current capabilities must be tentative — partly because the government has not published much useful information about military balances. Still, the best evidence indicates that these missions are not beyond the capacity of current U.S./NATO forces.

II: The Implicit Reagan Military Strategy

The Reagan defense buildup is driven by the tacit assumption that, in addition to the four traditional containment missions outlined above, American forces must perform five extra missions, which in most cases were not publicly accepted elements of American strategy a decade ago.[68] Moreover, the case made against these missions in the past — that they do not serve traditional containment aims — still seems sound. In short, the Reagan defense buildup is predicated largely on an unacknowledged and undebated shift from a cheaper to a more expensive strategy. In this section we enumerate these five missions and the arguments about them.

Counterforce

The counterforce debate has continued nonstop since the 1940s. Policy analysts agree that the United States requires a second-strike capability, but America's need for a counterforce capability (either a first-strike or a second-strike counterforce capability) has always been controversial.[69] The size and shape of American strategic forces depend on how this argument is resolved, since a meaningful counterforce capability requires much bigger and rather different nuclear forces from those deployed today.

A successful disarming counterforce attack against the Soviet Union would require two operations: a strike against Soviet nuclear forces and a battle to limit the damage done to American cities by surviving Soviet nuclear warheads launched in retaliation. Accordingly, counterforce weapons include those that can preemptively destroy Soviet nuclear warheads before they are launched against the United States *and* those that destroy retaliating Soviet warheads in flight toward American cities or at least limit the damage these warheads do to American cities. Thus, counterforce weapons include highly accurate ICBMs and SLBMs (which can preempt enemy ICBMs and bombers), antisubmarine ("killer") submarines and other antisubmarine warfare forces (which can destroy Soviet ballistic missile submarines), air defense systems (which can shoot down retaliating Soviet bombers), area-wide antiballistic missile systems (ABM) (which can defend cities against retaliating ICBMs and SLBMs), and civil defense (which limits the damage inflicted by Soviet retaliation). Such "defensive" systems as air defense, area-wide ABM, and civil defense are really "offensive" in the nuclear context, because they are a vital part of an offensive first-strike system. Second-strike weapons are those that can ride out an enemy attack and retaliate against enemy cities or other "value" (industrial or economic) targets; they include, for example, U.S. Poseidon SLBMs. They need *not* be able to destroy enemy strategic nuclear forces.

In the late 1960s and early 1970s a public consensus formed against counterforce, reflected in the congressional decision to constrain American ICBM accuracy improvements and in congressional hostility toward the proposed ABM system. Some people opposed counterforce on grounds that it increased the risk of war and the risk of wartime escalation. First-strike capabilities on both sides would create a hair-trigger dilemma: Whichever side fired first would win, so both sides would be quick to shoot in a crisis.[70] Moreover, conventional war would be much harder to control, since the first side to use nuclear weapons would hold the upper hand, creating a strong temptation to escalate if conventional war broke out.

But the clinching argument was that a counterforce capability simply could not be achieved. According to this view the Soviets, like ourselves, could always take steps — implement countermeasures — to preserve their second-strike capability, because a second-strike capability is so much cheaper to maintain than a counterforce capability. Moreover, the Soviets could not tolerate an American first-strike capability, so they would make sure we never got one, whatever this cost. A second-strike capability is essentially defensive, but a counterforce capability is offensive: A state that can disarm the other side can demand its surrender. Neither superpower could ever let the other get such a capability. Hence, the argument went, American spending on counterforce is futile, because the Soviets will always counter the counterforce we build.

Counterforce came back in fashion in the mid-1970s, with Ford and Carter administration decisions to build major new counterforce systems, chiefly the high-accuracy MX and Trident D5 ("Trident II") missiles. The Reagan administration has accelerated the Trident D5 program and added new counterforce programs: a modernized continental air defense system, including new F-15 interceptors and AWACs early-warning aircraft; an enlarged civil defense program; and increased research on ABM systems.[71] Administration planning documents suggest a requirement for a second-strike counterforce capability, which could disarm the Soviet Union even after absorbing a Soviet first strike. Presumably a force with this capability could disarm the Soviets more reliably if the United States struck first. A secret administration "Defense Guidance" paper calls for nuclear forces that "can render ineffective the total Soviet (and Soviet allied) military and political power structure," even if American forces struck second.[72] The administration envisions attacks on the whole Soviet force structure, including "decapitation" strikes against Soviet political and military leadership: Targets would include Soviet "political and military leadership and associated control facilities, nuclear and conventional military forces, and industry critical to military power." [73]

Yet a counterforce capability is much harder to build today, because American forces must destroy a much bigger set of Soviet targets. In 1970 the Soviets had 1,800 strategic nuclear warheads, in 1982 there were 7,300.[74] The number of Soviet strategic delivery vehicles (missiles and bombers) has not gone up substantially, but the number of warheads these launchers carry has gone up dramatically (because the Soviets have "MIRVed" their missiles), so an American first strike must be much more effective to contain the Soviet retaliation to acceptable size. In fact, the administration's own warning that this Soviet buildup threatens American second-strike capability conflicts with arguments for counterforce: If American second-strike capability is precarious, then a counterforce capability would not seem feasible, since counterforce is much more demanding. Moreover, top priority should go to enhancing American second-strike capability if our retaliatory forces really are not secure, since second-strike capability is the backbone of our defenses.

Hence, the case against the feasibility of counterforce seems even more persuasive than it was when counterforce was unpopular. Moreover, no new information has appeared to discredit the now-forgotten fear that a first-strike capability on either side would raise the risk of war and escalation. The administration's commitment to decapitation strikes also seems dangerous, since decapitating the Soviets would leave the United States with no negotiating partner while turning Soviet forces over to

Soviet generals and colonels imbued with nuclear warfighting ideas.[75] In such an event, how could the war be stopped?

In the late 1970s the notion arose that counterforce made more sense, both because new technology (ICBM accuracy improvements, for example) allegedly made counterforce easier, and because the Soviet counterforce buildup required a symmetrical American response, to retain American "essential equivalence." But by any measure, counterforce is much harder now than fifteen years ago, because the Soviet arsenal is much bigger and better protected. The fallacy lies in counting how many warheads American forces hypothetically could destroy (which has increased), instead of counting how many could not be destroyed (which has also increased), and how much damage these remaining warheads could do to the United States.

The Soviets devote even more effort to strategic nuclear counterforce programs than does the United States, and the Soviet strategic nuclear buildup in the 1970s heavily stressed counterforce. But this does not argue for a simpleminded American imitation of Soviet programs. Rather, the Soviet buildup should have signaled the end of any dreams for a useful American counterforce capability, since this buildup also greatly enhanced Soviet second-strike capability by multiplying the number of protected warheads the United States would have to attack successfully. The most effective response to Soviet counterforce capability is to remove it by enhancing the survivability of American forces. This negates the enormous Soviet counterforce investment, at much smaller cost to the United States.

The administration's emphasis on counterforce conflicts with its efforts to control the strategic nuclear arms race. Counterforce drives the arms race: Neither side can allow the other to gain a meaningful counterforce capability, so counterforce programs on both sides generate answering second-strike programs on both sides, and vice versa. Forces must modernize and arsenals must expand, because neither side can let the other reach its goal. Nuclear arsenals on both sides vastly exceed overkill because both sides sought counterforce capabilities, which bred ever-larger forces, which then created a larger counterforce target set for the other side, which bred still larger forces on the other side.

The nuclear arms race is best controlled by first controlling counterforce. If the superpowers forswore counterforce, the rationale for nuclear arms-racing would largely disappear, since programs on both sides would no longer create new requirements for the other. Conversely, meaningful arms control is very difficult if the superpowers pursue counterforce seriously, because counterforce programs on both sides force both sides to keep building up. Under these circumstances, arms control agreements merely ratify decisions to build ever-larger arsenals. In short, the administration emphasis on counterforce lessens the possibility that meaningful arms control can be achieved.

What direction should American strategic programs take? Three problems should take priority. First, American second-strike capability requires reliable, survivable strategic C³I, so weaknesses in strategic C³I must be corrected. Second, American force improvements should emphasize long-term survivable ("enduring") new systems, since the United States now lacks a satisfactory nuclear delivery system that could survive months of nuclear combat. Third, our Minuteman ICBMs eventually must be replaced if we are to maintain a triad of diverse, secure retaliatory forces at current levels of second-strike capability. An ICBM replacement could perhaps be found more easily if the ICBM force were relieved of its counterforce mission, since this mission reduces the number of ways the missiles can be based. Basing modes might exist that diminish the ICBM "time-urgent, hard-target kill" capability, but that do secure the ICBMs from Soviet preemptive attack (for example, deep burial arrangements[76] or "mini-man" road-mobile small ICBMs). Hence the vulnerability of American forces might be cured more easily if planners put less emphasis on making Soviet forces vulnerable. As a general matter, resources should be shifted from counterforce programs to meet these needs.

Offensive Conventional Forces and Operations

The overall cast of Reagan administration strategic thought is more offensive than in the past. Reagan adviser Thomas Reed dismisses the old policy of containment and declares that the United States now focuses on prevailing over the Soviets.[77] Defense Secretary Weinberger warns against "the transposition of the defensive orientation of our peacetime strategy onto the strategy and tactics that guide us in the event of war." [78]

In the nuclear area the administration stresses counterforce, and in the conventional area the administration has adopted a new, more offensive warfighting strategy. Defense Department documents declare that American conventional forces should be "capable of putting at risk Soviet interests, including the Soviet homeland," and emphasize "offensive moves against Warsaw Pact flanks." [79] Navy Secretary John Lehman advocates "getting at the Soviet naval threat at its source." [80] Defense Secretary Weinberger would destroy Soviet bombers "by striking their bases" and attack Soviet "naval targets ashore." [81] He speaks of a "counteroffensive against [Soviet] vulnerable points ... directed at places where we can affect the outcome of the war." [82] Most discussion surrounds possible strikes against Soviet naval and air bases on the Kola peninsula (northeast of Finland, on the Barents Sea) or at Vladivostok and Petropavlovsk, in East Asia. These bases would be hit by carrier based aircraft, or possibly by long-range strategic bombers. The administration has programmed new conventional forces to match this offensive strategy, chiefly two new nuclear powered aircraft carrier task forces.

Two criticisms can be leveled against this strategy. First, only a huge fleet of carriers could safely attack the Soviet homeland, because Soviet land based aircraft could destroy a smaller American fleet as it approached. Even with two new carriers, American carrier forces would probably be too weak to mount such a strike. Overall, a counteroffensive strategy is a bottomless pit, since it generates very demanding missions that cannot be achieved without huge expenses, if they can be achieved at all. Indeed, the notion of an offensive conventional strategy does not square with administration warnings of American weakness: If we are so weak, how can we think of taking on such ambitious new missions?

Second, a counteroffensive strategy defeats the basic purpose of American conventional forces — the control of escalation. If it succeeds, a counteroffensive would jeopardize assets essential to Soviet sovereignty, or appear to do so, raising the prospect of a Soviet decision to escalate from conventional to nuclear war. For instance, the Soviets base vital elements of their second-strike capability at Murmansk — over half their ballistic missile submarine force, and its command apparatus. American strikes against nearby Soviet naval bases and forces could threaten the submarines and provoke desperate Soviet decisions — nuclear strikes against American carriers, for example — if the base could not be defended any other way.[83] The chief purpose of American conventional forces is to provide a buffer between conventional and nuclear war, but an offensive operational strategy would use this force in a way that defeats this fundamental aim.

Intervention Forces

A significant portion of the American defense effort is now allocated to forces best suited for Vietnam-style or Dominican Republic-style interventions in Third World countries. These forces could be used against the Soviet Union, but they are not ideally suited for that purpose.

Two attributes distinguish intervention forces from others. First, they are highly mobile. Anti-Soviet forces usually need not be highly mobile, since the locations of possible Soviet threats are known, and defending forces usually can be put there in peacetime, as in Western Europe. Clearly the United States needs some mobile forces to deal with the Soviets, especially in the Persian Gulf. The question is, how many? Today the United States has more mobility forces than anti-Soviet contingencies demand, especially more aircraft carriers (unless these are used offensively, in which case we probably do not have enough; see above). Second, intervention forces are lightly armed. Light forces are useful for some anti-Soviet contingencies, for instance, operations against Soviet supply lines in the Iranian mountains. But generally this type of force, best suited for fighting lightly armed opponents (guerrillas, for example), isn't appropriate for fighting Soviet forces, which are heavily armed. Again the question is: How many light forces do we need?

Total American mobility forces and unarmored ground forces include the thirteen Navy aircraft carriers, one airborne and one air-mobile army division, one air cavalry brigade, four regular army light infantry divisions, Special Forces units, three Marine divisions and associated ships and air wings, airlift and sealift forces, and CIA covert operatives. A war against the Soviets in Europe or the Persian Gulf would productively engage most of these forces, but not all. Some American aircraft carriers (perhaps ten, including those in overhaul) would be required to attack Soviet forces in Iran and guard the Atlantic and Pacific sea lanes, but some carriers would be left over (perhaps three; five with the Reagan program).[84] Possibly six of the nine American light ground divisions would be engaged in Iran or tied down in Norway or Korea, with three left over.

Thus, overall, the United States appears to have substantial superfluous intervention capability, to which the Reagan administration plans to add even more, with new carriers, new "forcible-entry" amphibious assault ships, and new airlift. The administration also indicates a revived interest in intervention by rejecting a "one-and-a-half war" strategy, instead suggesting the United States prepare to fight on several fronts simultaneously.[85] This represents a shift toward intervention, since more "half wars" in addition to Korea would probably be fought in the Third World.

How should the American requirement for intervention forces be assessed? If containment criteria are applied, two questions are paramount: (1) How much would potential Soviet conquests in the Third World enhance Soviet power? (2) How much would Soviet influence in the Third World increase if the United States were not prepared to intervene? The answers to these questions rest chiefly on three factors: Western dependence on Third World raw materials, the military value of basing rights in Third World states, and the degree of cohesion in the world Communist movement. Feasibility should also be kept in mind. At what cost, in dollars and army morale, can American forces suppress guerrilla insurgencies in foreign cultures?

First, Western dependence on Third World raw materials should be restudied carefully, not assumed. The West should ask how much economic damage Western economies would suffer if they lost access to given supplies from given countries, measuring damage in terms of declining economic growth rates, rising unemployment, higher rates of inflation, and the cost of measures — such as domestic production, product substitution, conservation, stockpiling, or purchase from other foreign suppliers — that would have to be initiated if supplies were lost.[86] Instead, dependence is usually proven by listing raw materials that the West imports, as if trade and dependence were one and the same thing. It is not the volume of trade but rather the cost of halting trade that matters. American dependence on a given country or commodity equals the damage the American economy would suffer if trade in that commodity or with that country were cut off.

In fact, the claim that Western states are dangerously vulnerable to Third World raw material embargoes is quite weak. The United States and its allies depend heavily on foreign oil, but oil is the exception. The Organization of Petroleum Exporting Countries (OPEC) remains the only successful international cartel — a telltale sign that Western dependence on other products is low. The West imports many other products from Third World countries, but most of these materials can be synthesized, replaced by substitutes, or acquired from alternate sources. Otherwise, successful cartels would exist already in those materials as well.

Second, the value of Third World military bases cannot be assessed unless American strategy is spelled out clearly; therefore, the vagueness of current American strategy makes judgment hard. Bases matter if Soviet or Western bases in the Third World can affect the United States' ability to execute its overall military strategy. Thus the danger posed by Soviet bases in Third World areas cannot be assessed without knowing how much harder they make American strategy to execute, and this cannot be assessed without knowing what that strategy is.

The effect of the nuclear revolution should be remembered when the strategic importance of the Third World is assessed. The notion that events in Southeast Asia, Southern Africa, or other jungle areas could tip the world balance of power is even more doubtful in a world of second-strike capabilities. Nuclear weapons make conquest much harder, and vastly enhance the self-defense capabilities of the superpowers. This should allow the superpower to take a more relaxed attitude toward events in third areas, including the Third World, since it now requires much more cataclysmic events to shake their defensive capabilities. Whatever had been the strategic importance of the Third World in a non-nuclear world, nuclear weapons have vastly reduced it.

Finally, the United States should carefully assess how formidable the Soviet threat to the Third World really is. Direct Soviet threats are often exaggerated because Soviet intervention capabilities are deemed larger than they actually are. Likewise, indirect Soviet threats via Soviet revolutionary "proxies" are measured in simplistic fashion.

Cold War experience teaches that the Soviets do not expand via national revolution, but by the jackboot of the Soviet army. Time and again, Soviet influence has proven ephemeral wherever that jackboot was not planted, even where Soviet "proxies" won control. The notion that Third World leftists are loyal Soviet vassals seldom proves correct, except when American policies help make it true, as with Vietnam, Cuba, Nicaragua, and earlier with China.[87]

The bitter nationalisms that tear the Third World make it harder for both the Soviets and the United States to establish durable influence. In the end this actually serves American interests, since our chief purpose is to keep the world free from Soviet control, not to rule it ourselves. This means the United States should view Third World nationalism as an American asset rather than a danger, and that the United States can usually contain the Soviets in the Third World simply by leaving well enough alone.

Advocates of intervention forces often suggest that we need them to halt Soviet "geopolitical momentum," a tide of Soviet influence supposedly sweeping the Third World. In fact Soviet "geopolitical momentum" is a myth; over the past two decades the Soviets have barely held their own ground, or perhaps lost ground.[88] While in the last decade the Soviets gained influence in Afghanistan, Vietnam, Laos, Cambodia, Ethiopia, Angola, Mozambique, Grenada, Nicaragua, Libya, Cape Verde, and the People's Democratic Republic of Yemen, they lost influence in Egypt, Indonesia, Sudan, Somalia, Iraq, Guinea, and Equatorial Guinea. More important, the Sino-Soviet dispute also deepened and Japanese-Soviet relations deteriorated. Overall, Soviet losses since 1960 probably outweigh Soviet gains.

The debate on U.S. military intervention should not be a matter of hawks versus doves, but of clear strategy. Soviet military power is the principal danger the West faces. American forces should confront this power directly. The United States should realize that it weakens itself and indirectly strengthens the Soviets if it diverts its energy toward less relevant Third World contingencies.

The Long Conventional War

The Reagan administration has removed the limit on the time American conventional forces must be able to hold a Soviet conventional attack in Europe or the Gulf. Secretary Weinberger warns against the "short war fallacy," [89] and explains that the United States must prepare to mobilize for a long World War II-style conventional war.[90] This revises the assumption of the 1960s that American conventional forces would only provide a "pause" for negotiation, after which the West would escalate, and puts a bigger demand on American conventional forces.

This shift in strategy may be a reasonable move, but the change must be carried out carefully. First, a long conventional war strategy will not succeed if our allies do not accept it and design their forces accordingly. Otherwise allied forces in Europe will collapse in a few weeks which would collapse the whole NATO defense, even if American forces could fight on. But Western Europe has not accepted the new long-war strategy, nor bought the stocks of ammunition and spare parts necessary to support extended combat. We cannot make this new strategy work simply by spending more; we also must sell it to our European allies.

Second, American planners should not confuse a requirement for a conventional long-war capability with a prediction that a Third World War would actually be either long or conventional. Today there is a dangerous tendency to speak as if World War III would resemble World War II, on the hopeful assumption that efforts to control the war will succeed. This is a dangerous delusion: We cannot eliminate the risk of nuclear escalation from any East-West conventional war. A global conventional war would present enormous problems of management and coordination. Even during the Cuban Missile Crisis, American leaders couldn't fully control, or even understand, all the operations in which American forces were engaged.[91] An East-West conventional war would be vastly harder to manage. We should take every step we can to lower the risk of escalation, but we should never believe that these steps make a conventional war easy to control. If we underestimate the risks of nuclear war we invite a frivolous attitude toward war. Moreover, we lose the deterrent benefits of the danger of nuclear war if our declaratory policy leads the Soviets to think they can safely use conventional force without risking nuclear escalation. If the risk of escalation is real, American declaratory policy should communicate this clearly.

Third, if American planners take long conventional war seriously, the rest of American strategy should be consistent. Strategies and forces which raise the risk of nuclear escalation should be kept to a minimum. Instead the Reagan defense program emphasizes counterforce and offensive conventional forces and operations, which heighten the risk of nuclear escalation. Thus the administration plans a long conventional war but then defeats this effort with steps that diminish the odds that any war could be kept conventional.

Less Allied Contribution

The United States now carries a disproportionate share of the NATO defense spending burden, yet the Reagan defense program would shift the burden further toward the U.S. In 1980 the United States spent 5.5 percent of its gross national product on defense, while its thirteen NATO allies only spent an average of 3.4 percent of GNP.[92] Among major American allies, only Britain spends nearly as much, 5.1 percent, as the United States. These figures understate the European defense effort by failing to correct for the low salaries that the Europeans pay their conscripted manpower; but even if we eliminate this bias by pricing NATO manpower at American pay scales (which adds 22 percent to European budgets),[93] average European spending comes to only 4.1 percent of GNP, or 75 percent the size of the burden carried by the United States in 1980.

This unequal arrangement arose after World War II, when the United States guarded against the Soviets while the Europeans repaired war damage. Americans assumed that the Europeans eventually would take on the main share of the burden once their economies recovered. No one expected the United States to carry the main burden indefinitely.

Yet Europe still carries a lighter load today, even though West Europeans have a combined GNP larger than the United States, their economies grow at a faster rate, and their standard of living is almost as high.

The Reagan defense plan will widen the gap between American and allied defense spending even further. Properly speaking, this decision doesn't mean the United States takes on a new "mission" — rather, the United States would carry a bigger share of responsibility for existing joint NATO missions — but it adds up to the same thing. In taking on a bigger share of the NATO defense burden the United States asks its forces to perform traditional missions with less allied assistance, which is a more difficult overall task.

If, as planned, the administration increases American spending to 7.4 percent of GNP, non-United States NATO military spending will dwindle to 56 percent the size of the burden carried by the United States, even if non-United States NATO manpower is priced at American rates (46 percent if it is not). Moreover, American willingness to carry such a heavy share of the NATO burden gives other NATO states even less incentive to spend more, so the American share of the NATO burden may grow still heavier if European defense programs stagnate or decline in response to the Reagan program. Because we will do more of the work, we will give Europe even more reason to take a free ride on us.

In Europe's defense it might be argued that the United States outspends her allies because it spends more extravagantly, or spends on missions not vital to containment, such as Third World intervention. If the main trouble is American wastefulness, not European lassitude, then the solution is a leaner American defense policy, focused more clearly on the Soviets, like European defense policies. But there is no legitimate reason why the American share of NATO burdens should substantially exceed allied spending in the long run.

III: Why Do We Think We Are Weak?

The administration's defense program has won public approval largely because the administration could draw upon the widespread myth of American military weakness. If Western forces can in fact achieve their main missions today, what explains this American sense of impotence? Three causes contribute.

First, statistical games substitute for proper measures of national military strength in the public debate about defense. Congressman Les Aspin once described the "Games the Pentagon Plays" — false measures that support Pentagon arguments for preferred policies.[94] These games still confuse and mislead the public on both the size of the Soviet threat, and the best solution to defense problems.

In the "numbers game," the sizes of selected Soviet and American forces are compared, always showing the United States lagging. Areas of Western numerical or qualitative superiority are ignored, and differences in the needs of each side are obscured. Thus, we often hear that the Soviets have more tactical aircraft (although American aircraft are much better, and total American tactical air capability is probably greater); more attack submarines (although American submarines are much more capable); more naval warships (although American ships are much bigger, more expensive, and more capable); and so forth. The only question that really matters — "Can we carry out our strategy?" — is not asked. Yet such misleading analysis is abundant in Secretary Weinberger's *Report to the Congress*, in the Joint Chiefs' *Military Posture* statement,[95] and in newspaper and magazine reporting on defense matters.

In the "trend game," alarming trends are presented without baseline figures or explanations. Thus we often hear that the U.S. Navy has fallen from 1,000 ships to fewer than 500; it is not explained that the Navy shrank because many ships built for World War II were finally scrapped in the 1960s and 1970s and because the Navy shifted from smaller to larger ships, so it now builds fewer ships of greater tonnage. In fact, the United States has outbuilt the Soviet Union by three to one in warship tonnage since 1960, while NATO as a whole outbuilt the Soviets by nine to two.[96]

In the "go it alone game," Soviet and American forces are compared head to head, as though the United States had no allies and the Soviets no other enemies. Thus we often hear of Soviet advantages over the United States in categories where NATO holds the lead over the Warsaw Pact, such as military manpower or defense spending. Such comparisons dismiss the success of the entire postwar European and Japanese economic recovery programs, the express purpose of which was to build up American allies so they could defend themselves.

Instead, a proper assessment measures forces against missions, under politically realistic scenarios. Strategic nuclear capabilities on each side are measured by asking: how many warheads *can't* each side destroy, and what damage can these warheads wreak on the enemy society? American second-strike capability equals the damage surviving American warheads can inflict on Soviet society, while American counterforce capability is the inverse of the damage that surviving Soviet warheads could inflict on American society. Comparing warheads, megatons, throwweights, missiles, and bombers tells us very little if these are not converted into measures of capacity to destroy people and industry. We seldom see such measures, partly because they undercut arguments for counterforce by demonstrating the futility of building more counterforce.

A conventional theater balance cannot be measured without a thorough campaign analysis. At a minimum such an analysis should incorporate data measuring (1) the total firepower available to both sides, (2) the rate at which both sides can mobilize this firepower and move it into the theater of action, (3) the ability of each side to interdict the other's movement, (4) the advantage that geography gives the attacker or defender, and (5) the amount of warning both sides can expect. Yet defense analyses in the press and popular journals almost never discuss defense problems in these terms.

Second, our defense debate often confuses political and military factors and too quickly suggests military solutions for political or diplomatic problems. Debates on hardware often turn on differences over the quality of American statesmanship and diplomacy. Thus pessimists often base arguments for more defense spending on scenarios that assume Western statesmen will not use the warning they receive of a Warsaw Pact attack, or that assume the United States cannot persuade allies to cooperate in their own defense. Pessimistic scenarios for war in the Persian Gulf, for instance, sometimes assume the European states will not permit American aircraft to refuel in European countries, although vital European interests will be at stake. A better answer, though, is for American leaders to provide the leadership that these scenarios assume is missing. Moreover, it often turns out that no amount of spending can cure the problems created by weak leadership. American defense requirements are enormous if we assume our leaders are fools and our allies are malicious or self-destructive. These are problems that more spending cannot easily solve.

Third, American assumptions have shifted from a less demanding to a more demanding grand strategy during the past decade, as outlined above. The drift toward counterforce, intervention, multiple simultaneous contingencies, long conventional war, and offensive conventional operations creates much more demanding military requirements. In the authors' judgment, Western military forces have maintained or even increased their capability to pursue their basic missions over the past decade, but American forces are now measured against harder missions, which makes us *feel* weaker because the proposed jobs are harder.

IV: What Reforms Make Sense?

Although American capabilities are widely underestimated, American forces nevertheless suffer some real shortcomings. These weaknesses are best alleviated by reforming current forces rather than spending more across the board. Emphasis should fall on selective spending increases, aimed at solving defined problems, or on structural adjustments. In both Europe and the Persian Gulf, relatively inexpensive reforms can make current forces more capable.

With regard to American forces for Europe, five reforms should take priority. First, American weapons design practices need correction. The United States still "gold plates" too much equipment: It passes over cheaper, simpler designs in favor of expensive, complex ones that are only marginally more capable. This happens because the military often demands state-of-the-art in the technology it buys — for instance, the world's first gas turbine engine to make the new M1 tank the fastest in the world. Frequently the military also demands that one weapon be capable of performing several missions; so the Navy's new F18 fighter must be a superior air-to-air fighter *and* a superior ground attack aircraft. These requirements can drive up costs dramatically. Some analysts estimate that the last 5 percent of performance in American equipment often results in a 50 percent cost increase.[97] This gold plating leaves the United States without enough equipment in areas where quantity matters more than quality. Gold plating also makes the readiness problem worse, because its use and maintenance requires scarce, expensive, highly skilled manpower and greater quantities of more costly spare parts.

Instead, the Reagan defense program moves in the direction of more, rather than fewer gold plated systems — more fancy F-14 and F-15 aircraft, more elaborate SSN688 "Los Angeles" class nuclear attack submarines, and more nuclear aircraft carrier task forces and their complex Aegis air defense cruisers.[98] Overall the administration is moving toward a force that is too complex.

Second, efforts now underway to improve overall combat readiness should be continued. Congress likes to fund glamorous new weapons systems but neglects maintenance for older systems. As a result, much American military equipment is not ready for action on short notice.

In the short run, Reagan programs will improve this situation by increasing fuel and ammunition stocks and improving training and maintenance. These efforts should continue. But in the long run, Reagan programs will make the readiness problem worse, since Reagan forces are so gold plated they will be even harder to maintain. One result of the Reagan buildup, in fact, may eventually be a new readiness crisis.

Third, more military equipment should be pre-positioned in Europe. Pre-positioning permits the United States to send reinforcements to Europe more quickly, since less equipment must be moved across the Atlantic. This strengthens the United States in Europe and the Persian Gulf because American airlift and sealift forces are freed for use in the Middle East. The same concept applies to fighter aircraft: The more basing facilities are built in Europe in peacetime, the less equipment must be moved in wartime.

Fourth, the United States should move faster to ready its civilian airliners to transport military equipment and supplies in wartime. Civilian wide-body passenger jets can be modified at modest cost to serve as military cargo planes in wartime. A cargo-convertible "CRAF" (civilian reserve air fleet) is much cheaper than buying a purpose-built military transport aircraft. The Reagan administration is trying to move forward

with CRAF modifications, but the airline industry has not been cooperative. At the same time, however, the administration plans an expensive
new air transport, the C5N. Pressing ahead with CRAF is a better idea.

Finally, Washington should consider shifting more Army manpower
from support to combat roles. The "teeth-to-tail" ratio still seems too
low. An American combat division with all its support personnel includes
roughly 48,000 troops. To deploy comparable numbers of weapons, the
Israelis and West Europeans use only 30,000–35,000 soldiers and the Soviet
Union only 22,000–25,000. The Soviets probably lack sufficient logistics
and support, while we have too much.

Allied reforms and improvements would do even more to strengthen
European defenses than would American reforms. Four programs should
take priority.

First, trained West European military reserve manpower should be
organized into reserve units to fill the need for extra forces that can be
held back from the front to cope with a possible Warsaw Pact armored
breakthrough. Today many of these reserves are used inefficiently, as
individual replacements for casualties in units already in action. Restructuring West European reserves should be at the top of the NATO agenda.

Second, the allies' war reserve stocks — ammunition, parts, and replacement equipment — are much lower than those maintained by the
United States. They should be increased. Otherwise European forces will
collapse early in the war, nullifying the purpose of American stocks.

Third, West European ground forces should be armed more heavily.
Latest figures indicate they have only half as many major weapons per
thousand men as Soviet and American units.[99]

Fourth, NATO and Japan should also pay their airlines to develop
cargo-convertible CRAFs. This would increase the potential speed of
American reinforcement in Europe and also free American military aircraft
capabilities if a simultaneous crisis arose, for example, in the Persian Gulf.

Western capabilities in the Persian Gulf could also be increased at
relatively low cost. American intervention forces should be tailored more
specifically for Persian Gulf contingencies. The Marines and Army airborne and airmobile units should be better equipped for armored war,
with light armored vehicles. More American equipment should be pre-
positioned on ships, in Australia, or at the American Diego Garcia base
in the Indian Ocean. The NATO allies and Japan should be better prepared to defend themselves, since this frees American military power for
the Persian Gulf. American allies should also be prepared to move their
own forces into the Gulf if the need arises. The defense of the Gulf is an
allied problem: Washington should demand an allied effort. Finally,
Washington should quietly discuss prepositioning equipment in the Persian Gulf states. If Gulf governments do not want a visible American
presence, "prepositioning" could take the form of extra stocks and equip-

ment for the Gulf states' armies, which Western forces could use in an emergency.

V: Conclusion

The Reagan administration proposes needed new measures, but the overall direction of its defense policy has not been adequately explained, and the scope of administration defense programs seems excessive and ill-directed. The administration report card on defense isn't all bad. It deserves credit for its efforts to increase short-term readiness, to rationalize procurement with multi-year contracts, to restructure American forces for Persian Gulf defense; and to improve strategic C^{3}I. But the basic direction of administration defense policy seems mistaken.

The strategy implicit in administration programs and statements is unrealistically demanding. Insofar as the administration has a strategy, it appears to incorporate requirements for fighting wars of every kind, all at once — global conventional war against an unspecified range of adversaries, offensive conventional operations against the Soviet homeland, and a victorious nuclear war against the Soviets. This is quite a tall order. Both counterforce operations and offensive conventional operations generate open-ended requirements that simply cannot be met.

In fact, press accounts suggest Reagan defense planners believe they cannot achieve their strategy without another enormous military buildup once the current one is completed. The Joint Chiefs of Staff have reportedly warned they would need an additional $750 billion to carry out the missions specified by the administration, beyond the $1.6 trillion budgeted for defense in the administration five-year plan.[100] In short, the administration strategy simply costs too much.

Moreover, the Reagan emphasis on counterforce, conventional offense, and intervention seems inconsistent with containment and with the U.S. interest in controlling any war that might break out. Containment suggests a military strategy focused on Eurasia and emphasizing defense, not the global, offense-oriented strategy of the Reagan administration. Escalation control calls for capable defensive forces and a defensive operational strategy rather than the Reagan strategy. The Reagan emphasis on conventional offense, counterforce, and nuclear war fighting raises the risk that a conventional conflict will escalate to a general thermonuclear war.

Eventually the public may wonder whether NATO really needs such vast new investments, or why the United States should bear such a heavy share of the NATO burden. Then we may be caught with half-completed programs and a Congress unwilling to fund full readiness for a force that is both too big and too complex. A steady defense policy that avoids boom-and-bust spending cycles, but that will stand up to scrutiny in the long run, is a better idea. A spending spree to exploit a fleeting public panic will not strengthen the country in the end.[101]

Moreover, wasteful military spending is itself a national security threat, because it contributes to our national economic decline. This decline in turn narrows the economic base from which we distill our military power and curtails our worldwide economic power. The American share of gross world product has fallen steadily since World War II and seems likely to keep falling in the future. Halting this national economic decline is a vital national security goal for the United States. We subvert this goal by damaging the American economy with excessive defense spending.

On the arms control front, the administration's commitment to counterforce works at cross-purposes with efforts to negotiate new limits with the Soviets. Moreover, the initial administration START [102] proposal does not seem to constrain counterforce capabilities on either side, so even if the Soviets accepted the Reagan proposal, the risk of war would not be reduced. Arsenals on both sides would be smaller, but they might be more vulnerable, so in a sense the administration's START proposal is a step backwards, since second strike capabilities on both sides might be weakened. Instead, the administration would be better off to pursue an agreement that focused on controlling counterforce systems, as Congressman Albert Gore suggests.[103] Qualitative arms control is the best route to quantitative arms control: The size of nuclear arsenals is best controlled by limiting the counterforce programs that drive the arms race.

Finally, the administration deserves criticism for sowing the defense debate with confusion. The administration's refusal to specify the strategy that requires the Reagan buildup deprives Congress and the public of the tools they need to analyze defense policy. As a result, the whole buildup proceeds with no clear definition of its purpose, no way to judge its necessity, no criteria to judge whether new forces are meeting real needs or leaving real needs unmet, and no logical stopping point. Moreover, those fragments of strategy that the administration offers often conflict with one another, creating an overall incoherence. Mutually contradictory notions appear in the same statements; for example, in claims that Soviet forces are so strong that the United States requires a major buildup, but so weak that an offensive American strategy is possible.[104]

In addition, this administration has done even less than its predecessors to make basic defense information available to the public, and its publications have been even more misleading. The Defense Department *Annual Report to the Congress* no longer contains such basic data as the relative spending of NATO and the Warsaw Pact, the aggregate tonnages of Pact and NATO fleets, strategic nuclear warhead inventories on both sides, and so forth. Instead, it is filled with alarming charts that imply American weakness but do not clarify where weaknesses really lie.

Public confusion about the basic facts of defense is a principal American national security problem. To rationalize our defense debate, better basic public information on defense is essential. Neither the government nor the major academic institutions are doing enough to make basic information available to news reporters, students, members of Congress, or other citizens who are concerned about defense policy. Adequate reference books do not exist. Most writing on defense policy is written by experts, to experts. Defense matters are not too complex for lay persons to understand. They merely seem too complex because academic experts and government agencies do so little to explain defense issues in simple terms and make basic facts available in convenient form. The mistakes made by the Reagan administration began with public confusion about facts of history, hardware, and strategy. Clearing up this confusion is the first step toward better defense policy.

Notes

1. William W. Kaufmann, "The Defense Budget," in Joseph A. Pechman, ed., *Setting National Priorities: The 1983 Budget* (Washington, D.C.: Brookings, 1982) (hereafter "Kaufmann SNP 1983"), p. 53; and William W. Kaufmann, "The Defense Budget," in Joseph A. Pechman, ed., *Setting National Priorities: The 1982 Budget* (Washington, D.C.: Brookings, 1981) (hereafter "Kaufmann SNP 1982"), p. 135, The 1981 essay is also published as a booklet: William W. Kaufmann, *Defense in the 1980's* (Washington: Brookings, 1981).

2. Caspar W. Weinberger, *Annual Report to the Congress: Fiscal Year 1983* (Washington: U.S. Government Printing Office, 1982; also available free on request from the Defense Department Public Affairs office) (hereafter *Annual Report* 1983), p. I-15.

3. *Annual Report 1983*, p. I-15.

4. *Annual Report 1983*, p. I-11.

5. *Annual Report 1983*, p. I-3.

6. "Strategic nuclear" forces are those that would strike the enemy homeland, while "tactical nuclear" or "theater nuclear" forces are those that would be used in a theater battle, in neither homeland.

7. An excellent summary of early containment thinking is John Lewis Gaddis, *Strategies of Containment* (New York: Oxford University Press, 1982), pp. 25-88. See also Gaddis, "Containment: A Reassessment," *Foreign Affairs*, Vol. 55, no. 4 (July 1977), pp. 873-887; George F. Kennan, *Realities of American Foreign Policy* (New York: W. W. Norton, 1966); and Walter Lippmann, *The Cold War: A Study in U.S. Foreign Policy* (New York: Harper & Brothers, 1947). For an earlier discussion of American grand strategy from the Kennan/Lippmann perspective, see Nicholas John Spykman, *America's Strategy in World Politics: The United States and the Balance of Power* (Harcourt, Brace & World, Inc., 1942; reprint ed., n.p.: Archon, 1970), pp. 3-199.

8. Eurasia = all of Europe and Asia.

9. Ruth Leger Sivard, *World Military and Social Expenditures 1981* (Leesburg, Va.: World Priorities, 1981), pp. 25-26.

10. George F. Kennan, *American Diplomacy 1900-1950* (New York: New American Library, 1951), p. 10.

11. Kennan, *Realities*, pp. 63-64; and Kennan, *Memoirs 1925-1950* (Boston: Little, Brown, 1967), p. 359.

12. For a critique of this thinking, see Bernard Brodie, *Escalation and the Nuclear Option* (Princeton: Princeton University Press, 1966).

13. For escalation scenarios see Barry R. Posen, "Inadvertent Nuclear War? Escalation and NATO's Northern Flank," *International Security*, Vol. 7, No. 2 (Fall 1982), pp. 28-54.

14. A useful short summary of Soviet military thought is Benjamin S. Lambeth, "How To Think About Soviet Military Doctrine," in John Baylis and Gerald Segal, eds., *Soviet Strategy* (Montclair, N.J.: Allenheld, Osmun, 1981), pp. 105-123. A typical Soviet military view on European war is Col. A. A. Sidorenko, *The Offensive* (Washington: U.S. Government Printing Office, 1970).

15. On "counterforce," see below, pp. 74-75, 81-84.

16. The "half-war" mission is a possible exception, since some might argue that it doesn't protect important interests from the Soviets, as we note below.

17. *Annual Report 1983*, pp. I-3, I-4.

18. "The Wrong Defense," (editorial), *Wall Street Journal*, March 25, 1982.

19. International Institute for Strategic Studies (IISS), *The Military Balance 1982-1983* (London: IISS, 1982), p. 132.

20. U.S. Arms Control and Disarmament Agency, *World Military Expenditures and Arms Transfers 1970-1979* (Washington: ACDA, 1982), Spain included.

21. IISS, *The Military Balance 1979-1980* (London: IISS, 1979), p. 94.

22. Franklyn D. Holzman, "Is There a Military Spending Gap?" (mimeo; March 16, 1982), p. 6. See also Franklyn D. Holzman, "Are the Soviets Really Outspending the U.S. on Defense?" *International Security*, Vol. 4, No. 4 (Spring 1980), pp. 86-105. For a summary of Professor Holzman's views see Holzman, "Dollars or Rubles: The CIA's Military Estimates," *Bulletin of the Atomic Scientists*, June 1980, pp. 23-27.

23. Ruth Sivard, *World Military and Social Expenditures, 1981*, p. 37, col. 3.

24. *Annual Report 1983*, p. I-17.

25. "MIRV" = "Multiple Independently targeted Re-entry Vehicle."

26. IISS, *The Military Balance 1982-1983*, pp. 140-141.

27. "President's News Conference on Foreign and Domestic Matters," *New York Times*, April 1, 1982, p. A22.

28. Theodore Draper, "How Not To Think About Nuclear War," *New York Review of Books*, Vol. 29, No. 12 (July 15, 1982), p. 38.

29. What damage is "unacceptable" to either side depends on the intentions of the parties and the nature of the dispute: What damage is each side willing to suffer to achieve its aims?

30. Kaufmann, SNP 1982, p. 63.

31. Office of Technology Assessment, *The Effects of Nuclear War* (Washington: U.S. Government Printing Office, 1979), p. 76.

32. Arthur M. Katz, *Life After Nuclear War: The Economic and Social Impacts of Nuclear Attacks on the United States* (Cambridge, Mass.: Ballinger, 1982), p. 316.

33. On U.S. strategic C³I, see John D. Steinbruner, "Nuclear Decapitation," *Foreign Policy*, No. 45 (Winter 1981-1982), pp. 16-29; Desmond Ball, *Can Nuclear War Be Controlled?* (London: International Institute for Strategic Studies, Adelphi Paper #169, 1981); and Congressional Budget Office, *Strategic Command, Control and Communications: Alternative Approaches for Modernization* (Washington: CBO, 1981).

34. A good analysis of current options to enhance the survivability of American ICBMs is Albert Carnesale and Charles Glaser, "ICBM Vulnerability: The Cures Are Worse than the Disease," *International Security* Vol. 7, No. 1 (Summer 1982), pp. 70-85.

35. *New York Times*, April 7, 1982, p. A8.
36. Committee on the Present Danger, *Is America Becoming Number 2? Current Trends on the U.S.-Soviet Military Balance* (Washington, D.C.: CPD, 1978), p. 31.
37. An excellent essay on the NATO conventional balance is John J. Mearsheimer, "Why the Soviets Can't Win Quickly in Central Europe," *International Security*, Vol. 7, No. 1 (Summer 1982), pp. 3-39, also reprinted in Mearsheimer, *Conventional Deterrence* (Ithaca, N.Y.: Cornell University Press, 1983). Also useful are Robert Lucas Fischer, *Defending the Central Front: The Balance of Forces* (London: IISS, Adelphi Paper #127, 1976); and Congressional Budget Office, *Assessing the NATO/Warsaw Pact Military Balance* (Washington: CBO and U.S. Government Printing Office, December 1977).

    In addition to these and other sources, we base our discussion of U.S. conventional capabilities on interviews with Defense Department officials and other members of the American defense community.
38. A substantial percentage of both NATO and Warsaw Pact military capability becomes battle-ready only after several days of preparation, so it is critically important that NATO not allow the Pact a large head start in mobilization. NATO leaders must respond quickly when they receive warning of Pact mobilization measures. Failure to keep up with Pact mobilization would soon allow the Pact to muster sufficiently favorable force ratios to achieve a breakthrough against NATO.
39. Mearsheimer, "Why the Soviets Can't Win Quickly," pp. 7-8. This "firepower" score is a composite index that includes the killing power of all tanks, antitank weapons, artillery, and so on — all the killing instruments in the division.
40. Carnegie Endowment for International Peace, *Challenges for U.S. National Security: Assessing the Balance: Defense Spending and Conventional Forces* Part II (Washington: Carnegie Endowment, 1981), p. 71. A similar qualitative advantage for NATO tactical air forces may be construed from figures offered by Alain C. Enthoven and K. Wayne Smith, *How Much Is Enough?* (New York: Harper Colophon, 1971), p. 145, and *Annual Report 1983*, p. II-18.
41. Joshua M. Epstein, "Soviet Vulnerabilities in Iran and the RDF Deterrent," *International Security*, Vol. 6, No. 2 (Fall 1981), pp. 149-150.
42. U.S. House of Representatives, *Hearings Before a Subcommittee of the Committee on Appropriations, Subcommittee on the Department of Defense*, Part 4, 95th Congress, 2nd session (Washington: U.S. Government Printing Office, 1978), p. 347. On deficiencies in Soviet pilot training, see also Joshua M. Epstein, "On Conventional Deterrence in Europe: Questions of Soviet Confidence," *Orbis*, Vol. 26, No. 1 (Spring 1982), pp. 71-88.
43. Mearsheimer, "Why the Soviets Can't Win Quickly," p. 4; Carnegie Endowment, *Challenges for U.S. National Security*, p. 71.
44. These ratios represent a best estimate for average situations. There are, however, some historical cases of successful armored assaults by attackers who enjoyed less than a three-to-one force ratio. It is possible, though not likely, that the Pact could achieve local successes against some NATO forces with less than a three-to-one advantage at the point of attack. If so, NATO might find itself without enough ground forces. This possibility is one of the uncertainties that the reforms suggested in Section IV (below) are designed to buffer against.
45. Mearsheimer, "Why the Soviets Can't Win Quickly," p. 9.
46. *Ibid.*
47. *Ibid.*, pp 28-29.
48. *Ibid.*, p. 22.
49. Pessimistic estimates include those of John M. Collins, *U.S. Soviet Military Bal-*

ance: Concepts and Capabilities 1960-1980 (New York: McGraw-Hill, 1980), pp. 291-330 and pp. 539-549; Jeffrey Record, *Force Reductions in Europe: Starting Over* (Cambridge, Mass.: Institute for Foreign Policy Analysis, Inc., 1980), pp. 5-33; Joseph M. A. H. Luns, *NATO and the Warsaw Pact: Force Comparisons* (n.p.: NATO, 1982); Phillip A. Karber, "The Growing Armor/Anti-Armor Imbalance in Central Europe," *Armed Forces Journal International* (July 1981), pp. 37-48; and Congressional Budget Office, *U.S. Ground Forces: Design and Cost Alternatives for NATO and Non-NATO Contingencies* (Washington: CBO, 1980).

50. Congressional Budget Office, *U.S. Ground Forces,* is an exception.
51. See, for instance, the 1980 Congressional Budget Office study *U.S. Ground Forces,* which is perhaps the most thorough pessimistic assessment, but which exaggerates the number of Soviet divisions available to attack Western Europe, undercounts forces available to NATO, and plays down terrain factors favoring NATO.

The CBO assumes that Soviet "Category III" cadre divisions can be readied and moved from the Soviet Union to Germany in thirty-five days, although other analysts estimate this would require three to four months. (For instance, see Jeffrey Record, *Sizing Up the Soviet Army* (Washington, D.C.: Brookings, 1975), pp. 21-22, estimating that Soviet Category III divisions cannot be ready before ninety to one hundred and twenty days.)

For an assessment of the readiness of Soviet Category III divisions which suggests that they mobilize slowly, see testimony by the Defense Intelligence Agency to the Joint Economic Committee, published in "Allocation of Resources to the Soviet Union and China — 1981," Hearings before the Subcommittee on International Trade, Finance, and Security Economics of the Joint Economic Committee, Congress of the United States, 97th Congress, 1st session, Part 7 (Washington: U.S. Government Printing Office, 1982), p. 199. As a result, the CBO credits the Pact with a 120-division force instead of the 90-division force that most NATO plans assume the Soviets can field, or the 71-division force the Soviets could field if they failed to field any Category III divisions, relying exclusively on Category I and Category II divisions (Robert Shishko, *The European Conventional Balance: A Primer* (Santa Monica: Rand Corp., P-67-7, 1981), p. 8). The CBO's pessimistic conclusions depend on this unexplained assumption, since the CBO grants that NATO could halt a 90-division Pact assault (p. xiii).

Second, the CBO understates the capability of the German territorial forces. The German territorials are trained reserves that can be mobilized at least as fast as Soviet Category III divisions, to a total 750,000 men. By simply mobilizing the German territorials, NATO almost doubles the size of total NATO European forces, which would grow from 780,000 to 1,530,000 men. Yet the CBO credits the territorials with only six mechanized brigades — roughly two divisions, or about 70,000 men, a fraction of the total German territorial forces actually available to NATO.

Third, the CBO understates the advantage conferred on the defender by terrain in the North German Plain, instead repeating the conventional wisdom that the plain is an easy invasion route for Soviet forces. In fact this area is crossed by rivers, bogs, and urban sprawl, which make defense easier.

52. Jack Anderson, "Frightening Facts on the Persian Gulf," *The Washington Post,* February 3, 1981, p. 18, quoting "top military hands."
53. Robert S. Dudney, "The Defense Gap that Worries the President," *U.S. News and World Report,* February 16, 1981.
54. Jeffrey Record, "Disneyland Planning for Persian Gulf Oil Defense," *The Washington Star,* March 20, 1981, p. 17.
55. The best assessment of the East-West balance in the Gulf is Epstein, "Soviet

Vulnerabilities." For briefer assessments see Kaufmann, SNP 1981, pp. 304-305, and SNP 1982, p. 160. Also useful is Keith A. Dunn, "Constraints on the USSR in Southwest Asia: A Military Analysis," *Orbis*, Vol. 25, No. 3 (Fall 1981), pp. 607-631.

56. Epstein, "Soviet Vulnerabilities," p. 144.
57. Andrew Krepinevich, *The U.S. Rapid Deployment Force and Protection of Persian Gulf Oil Supplies* (unpublished paper, Kennedy School of Government, 1980).
58. Epstein, "Soviet Vulnerabilities," pp. 139-140; and Kaufmann, SNP 1981, p. 305.
59. Epstein, "Soviet Vulnerabilities," p. 139.
60. *Ibid.*, p. 136.
61. *Ibid.*, p. 140.
62. *Ibid.*, pp. 145-148.
63. *Ibid.*, p. 146.
64. Quoted in Bernard Brodie, *War and Politics* (New York: Macmillan, 1973), p. 356.
65. Epstein, "Soviet Vulnerabilities," p. 157.
66. Pessimistic estimates include Jeffrey Record, *The Rapid Deployment Force and U.S. Military Intervention in the Persian Gulf* (Cambridge, Mass.: Institute for Foreign Policy Analysis, 1981), pp. 8-42, 61-68; John Collins, *U.S. Soviet Military Balance*, pp. 367-394; Albert Wohlstetter, "Meeting the Threat in the Persian Gulf," *Survey*, Vol. 25, No. 2 (Spring 1980), pp. 128-188; and W. Scott Thompson, "The Persian Gulf Correlation of Forces," *International Security*, Vol. 7, No. 1 (Summer 1982), pp. 157-180.
67. Regarding the "half-war" balance, published information on U.S. capacity to fight a Korean "half war" is so scanty we cannot supply a detailed analysis of American capabilities. However, most public sources indicate American forces can perform the Korean "half war" mission they are sized against. (See Kaufmann, SNP 1983, pp. 89-90; and Congressional Budget Office, *U.S. Ground Forces*, p. 67.)
68. For Reagan strategy ideas see Thomas C. Reed, "Details of National Security Strategy," speech delivered to the Armed Forces Communications and Electronics Association, June 16, 1982 (mimeo, available from the White House, Office of the National Security Advisor); *The New York Times*, "Revised U.S. Policy Said to Focus on 'Prevailing' Over Russians," June 17, 1982, p. B17, summarizing Reed; Richard Halloran, "Pentagon Draws Up First Strategy for Fighting a Long Nuclear War," *New York Times*, May 30, 1982, p. A1, summarizing the secret Administration 5-year defense guidance document; Richard Halloran, "Weinberger Denies U.S. Plans for 'Protracted Nuclear War,'" *New York Times*, June 21, 1982, p. A5; "Lehman Seeks Superiority," *International Defense Review*, May 1982, pp. 547-548; and *Annual Report 1983*.
69. For the difference between a "second-strike capability," a "first-strike capability," and a "second-strike counterforce capability," see p. 74 of this chapter.
70. On preemptive war, see Thomas C. Schelling, *Arms and Influence* (New Haven: Yale University Press, 1966), pp. 221-259; and Schelling, *The Strategy of Conflict* (New York: Oxford University Press, 1963), pp. 207-254. For another important argument why counterforce is dangerous, see Robert Jervis, "Cooperation Under the Security Dilemma," *World Politics*, Vol. 30, No. 2 (January 1978), pp. 186-214, also excerpted in Robert J. Art and Kenneth N. Waltz, *The Use of Force*, 2nd. ed. (University Press of America, 1983).
71. See Kaufmann, SNP 1983, pp. 65-66. Other administration programs also enhance U.S. counterforce capability, including enhanced nuclear "battle-management" C^3I, and new nuclear killer submarines.
72. Halloran, "Weinberger Denies U.S. Plan," p. A5.

73. *Ibid.*
74. Ground Zero, *Nuclear War: What's in It for You?* (New York: Pocket Books, 1982), p. 267, and IISS, *The Military Balance 1982-1983*, p. 140.
75. For Soviet military thinking about intercontinental thermonuclear war see Joseph D. Douglass, Jr., and Amoretta M. Hoeber, *Soviet Strategy for Nuclear War* (Stanford, Calif.: Hoover Institution Press, 1979).
76. On deep burial see Congress of the United States, Office of Technology Assessment, *MX Missile Basing* (Washington, D.C.: U.S. Government Printing Office, 1981), pp. 269-274.
77. *New York Times*, "Revised U.S. Policy Said to Focus on 'Prevailing' Over the Russians"; and Reed, "Details of National Strategy," p. 17.
78. *Annual Report 1983*, p. I-16.
79. Halloran, "Pentagon Draws Up First Strategy," p. 12.
80. *International Defense Review*, "Lehman Seeks Superiority," p. 547.
81. *Annual Report 1983*, p. III-21.
82. *Annual Report 1983*, p. I-16. See also p. III-21.
83. On the risk of escalation raised by offensive conventional operations see Posen, "Inadvertent Nuclear War."
84. A force of ten carriers would give the United States eight carriers for combat missions in wartime, since two carriers would normally be in overhaul. By one estimate, two carriers are required to defend the sea lanes in the Atlantic and two to defend the Pacific sea lane. (See Congressional Budget Office, *Navy Budget Issues for Fiscal Year 1980* (Washington: CBO, March 1979), pp. 41-42.) This would leave four carriers for anti-Soviet missions in the Persian Gulf or the Mediterranean. The wartime requirement for carrier battle groups in the Mediterranean seems questionable, since NATO land based reconnaisance and fighter aircraft based in Spain, Italy and Turkey — all NATO members — are capable of covering most of the Mediterranean. This leaves four carriers available for the Persian Gulf area.
85. *Annual Report 1983*, p. I-15.
86. On measuring interdependence, see Kenneth N. Waltz, "The Myth of National Interdependence," in Charles P. Kindleberger, ed., *The International Corporation* (Cambridge, Mass.: MIT Press, 1970), pp. 205-223; and Waltz, *Theory of International Relations* (Reading, Mass.: Addison-Wesley, 1979), pp. 138-160.
87. On the effects of U.S. policies on relations between radical nationalist regimes and the Soviet Union, see Chapter 1 in this volume by Kenneth A. Oye, p. 20.
88. "Soviet Geopolitical Momentum: Myth or Menace? Trends of Soviet Influence Around the World From 1945 to 1980," *Defense Monitor* Vol. 11, No. 1 (January 1980).
89. *Annual Report 1983*, pp. I-16, I-17.
90. *Annual Report 1983*, pp. I-13, I-14.
91. See John Steinbruner, "An Assessment of Nuclear Crises," in Franklyn Griffiths and John C. Polanyi, eds., *The Dangers of Nuclear War* (Toronto: University of Toronto Press, 1979), pp. 35-40; and Graham T. Allison, *Essence of Decision: Explaining the Cuban Missile Crisis* (Boston: Little, Brown, 1971), pp. 130, 136-143.
92. IISS, *The Military Balance 1981-1982*, pp. 27-39, 112. Spain, which joined NATO in 1982, is excluded.
93. Sivard, *World Military and Social Expenditures 1981*, p. 37, col. 3.
94. "Games the Pentagon Plays," *Foreign Policy* No. 11 (Summer 1973), pp. 80-92.
95. Organization of the Joint Chiefs of Staff, *United States Military Posture for FY 1983* (Washington, D.C.: U.S. Government Printing Office, 1982).

96. Congressional Budget Office, *Shaping the General Purpose Navy of the Eighties: Issues for Fiscal Years 1981-1985* (Washington, D.C.: CBO, 1980), p. 44.
97. Jaques Gansler, *The Defense Industry* (Cambridge, Mass.: MIT Press, 1980), p. 279. For more on gold plating see Jack N. Merritt and Pierre M. Sprey, "Negative Marginal Returns in Weapons Acquisition," in Richard G. Head and Ervin J. Rokke, *American Defense Policy*, 3rd ed. (Baltimore: Johns Hopkins University Press, 1973), pp. 486-495.
98. Reagan programs are summarized in *Aviation Week*, April 12, 1982, p. 64.
99. Congressional Budget Office, *U.S. Air and Ground Conventional Forces for NATO: Firepower Issues* (Washington, D.C.: CBO, March 1978), p. 14.
100. George C. Wilson, "Pentagon: $1.6 trillion will not do job," *Boston Globe*, March 8, 1982, p. 1.
101. For a list of possible cuts that might be made in the Reagan program, see Kaufmann, SNP 1983, pp. 86-95.
102. "Strategic Arms Reduction Talks," the Administration's new name for the SALT talks.
103. Albert Gore, Jr., "The Fork in the Road: A New Plan for Nuclear Peace," *The New Republic*, Vol. 186, No. 18 (May 5, 1982), pp. 13-16.
104. See, e.g., Reed, "Details of National Security Strategy."

4

An Explosion in the Kitchen?
Economic Relations with
Other Advanced Industrial States

Benjamin J. Cohen

> In the 1980's, the United States will continue to be subject to adverse foreign economic pressures. These pressures...will lead to conflict. American foreign economic policy under President Carter and his successors will be judged according to its success in keeping international conflict manageable while retaining domestic political support and maintaining U.S. influence as well as fostering prosperity at home and abroad. The foreign economic policy kitchen will be hot; success will come to those who can turn out the goodies without setting off an explosion.
>
> — Robert O. Keohane[1]

Robert Keohane's closing words in his contribution to *Eagle Entangled* provide a useful starting point for an analysis of the foreign economic policy of the Reagan administration during its first eighteen months in office. The test, as Keohane stresses, is not whether conflict has been absent — conflict is virtually inevitable in international economic relations — but rather whether conflict has been kept manageable. Has the United States used its resources wisely, given existing policy constraints, to promote national interests and objectives? Has prosperity been promoted? Have domestic support and foreign influence been retained?

We know that the Reagan administration has so far avoided an outright explosion. But that is no more than a *de minimus* test of success. Judged by the more discriminate criteria suggested by Keohane, the

Benjamin J. Cohen is William L. Clayton Professor of International Economic Affairs at The Fletcher School of Law and Diplomacy, Tufts University. Educated at Columbia University, he previously taught at Princeton University and is a frequent consultant to United States government and international agencies. He has written six books, including Organizing the World's Money *(1977) and* Banks and the Balance of Payments *(1981).*

administration's record can be described as dismal at best. The purpose of this chapter is to evaluate that record in greater detail, focusing on our relations with other advanced industrial states. Relations with developing nations are discussed separately by Richard Feinberg in Chapter 6.

Traditional Objectives of Policy

Analysis of decision making in foreign economic policy may be approached in a variety of ways. For an economist, the most congenial approach views policy as a problem of "maximization under constraint." Conventional economic analysis begins with the assumption of scarcity: The things that people and societies value are limited in supply; Tin Pan Alley notwithstanding, the best things in life are *not* all free. Choices therefore are necessary. The task for economic decision makers (assuming they are rational) is to do the best they can to maximize some value or other — or several values simultaneously — under the constraint of scarcity. The task for the analyst seeking insight into such behavior is to focus on this problem of choice, to understand the tradeoffs among objectives. As Walter Heller has written of the political economist: "Problems of choice are his meat and drink. His method is to factor out the costs, the benefits, and the net advantage or disadvantage of alternative courses of action." [2]

In United States foreign economic policy, the choices of decision makers have traditionally focused on four main objectives: (1) national economic welfare, (2) distribution, (3) national security, and (4) system preservation. All four "target variables" reflect fundamental political and economic interests.

The first target, national economic welfare, stands for real income, that is, the quantity of real goods and services available to the nation for final use. Although this is the traditional objective identified in conventional economic analysis, it is not a simple concept. Indeed, despite more than two centuries of development of modern economic theory, we still do not know precisely how to go about maximizing economic welfare, in good part because the target is decomposable — at the micro level identified with efficiency of resource allocation; at the macro level, with both full employment and price stability. As these three dimensions may not always be mutually compatible, policy choices necessarily involve value judgments regarding the relative weights to be attached to each and the tradeoffs to be made among them. On such matters, clearly, reasonable people may reasonably disagree.

The second target variable, distribution, stands as a proxy for the set of relevant domestic political goals of policy. Being politicians and not disinterested statesmen or philosopher-kings, policy makers may be assumed to concern themselves not only (if at all) with the general interests of the nation as a whole, but also with the specific interests of certain narrower constituencies within the nation, and to seek through policy decisions to maximize the gains of such domestic groups or minimize their losses. In other words, they may be assumed to aim at some particular distribution of the costs and benefits of policy. This of course is the traditional objective identified in political analysis, the meat and drink of the political scientist: Whose ox is gored if one policy is chosen rather than another? It is also, like economic welfare, not a simple concept. As with economic welfare, we still do not know precisely how to go about achieving some particular distribution of the costs and benefits of policy, again in good part because the objective is decomposable. Distribution implies not only gains or losses of real income but also of relative rank, prestige, privileges, and the like; and since here too value judgments and tradeoffs are necessarily involved, here too disagreements among reasonable people are possible.

The two remaining variables, national security and system preservation, embody the principal objectives that must be added when we move from purely domestic considerations to the foreign dimension of economic policy. National security is mainly concerned with such issues as political independence and territorial integrity, and it can logically be translated into an imperative to maximize, insofar as is possible, influence abroad and autonomy of decision making at home. System preservation reflects the interest that the United States has in common with other countries to avoid disruption of the international economic relations from which we all presumably benefit, even if unevenly. Many observers have called attention to the similarity of the system of international economic relations to a "nonzero-sum game" in which, because the interests of the players are neither entirely harmonious nor completely irreconcilable, state policies inevitably mix elements of competition and cooperation.[3] The targets of national security and system preservation express, respectively, these two elements of policy (although they may, of course, receive quite different relative weights in the policies of different governments).

Of the four objectives of American policy, national economic welfare always seems to take precedence at the level of rhetoric. Upon assuming office, every new administration declares America's prosperity to be its fundamental goal, defined in terms of such desiderata as full employment, price stability, and rapid growth. But then, at the level of action, every administration eventually compromises its welfare objective in some degree for the sake of the other three. Ultimately, all four targets come into play in practice. Successive administrations differ only in the nature of the compromises they regard as acceptable or are willing to admit.

For example, every American administration since World War II has emphasized this nation's commitment to an open and liberal (that is, market oriented and nondiscriminatory) world trading system. Yet, repeatedly, administrations undertake to protect specific domestic constituencies against "injury" from foreign imports, even at the expense of perpetuating an inefficient resource allocation and potentially retarding domestic growth. Likewise, all administrations have seemed prepared to pay an economic price for the sake of extending American influence overseas or preserving the international system that we were so instrumental in constructing after 1945. In postwar Europe the United States tolerated, even promoted, preferential regional trade and payments arrangements despite their inherent and obvious discrimination against American export sales, because it was thought essential to restore the health of key economic allies; similarly, America's internal market was opened to Japanese exports even when markets elsewhere remained tightly closed to goods labelled "Made in Japan." It must be assumed that policy makers are not unaware of the potential welfare costs of the compromises they make.

The reasons for such compromises are familiar. Measures to protect the interests of specific domestic constituencies have their roots in our internal politics — our fragmented and pluralistic Federal system in which disproportionate influence can be wielded by relatively narrow pressure groups. Similarly, measures to extend American influence or autonomy of decision making have their roots in our external politics — our anarchic and insecure international system in which national interests are never entirely safe from overt or covert threat. As a major power, the United States has long enjoyed a high degree of influence over global economic events as well as comparative freedom from external constraint on internal decision making — for so long, in fact, that what in other countries would be regarded as a privilege has come to be treated here, by many, as a right. One need only think of Washington's continued reluctance to give up the international reserve-asset role of the dollar, which gives this country the extraordinary privilege (what Charles de Gaulle used to call the "exorbitant privilege") to finance balance of payments deficits, in effect, with IOUs rather than with reserve assets of our own. Few other countries enjoy a similar privilege, and none, certainly, to the same extent.

System preservation has also long figured prominently among our policy targets because of our continuing position of leadership in international economic affairs. The story of our "hegemonic" role in shaping the institutions and structures of the postwar world economy needs no retelling here.[4] Once having fashioned an external environment largely favorable to American objectives, we thereby gained a vested interest in maintaining it. Other countries might act as "free riders," enjoying the benefits of a system of growing economic interdependence without contributing significantly to its preservation, but not the United States, whose support continued to be a necessary (even if now no longer a sufficient) condition of systemic survival. American policy makers have often felt obliged to make concessions to keep the system functioning without undue discord or disruption.

Thus while national prosperity may be described as the most enduring interest served by American foreign economic policy, it is by no means either exclusive or absolute. It is not exclusive because other interests are also felt to be vital, most notably the compulsion of a great power to maintain a maximum of influence abroad and autonomy of decision making at home. It is not absolute because in order to promote economic welfare in the long term, concessions in the short term have often been felt to be necessary, most notably to safeguard the interdependent international system whose coherence and viability continued to be identified with our own national self-interest. In addition, since every administration feels the need to cultivate and retain domestic political support, the particular interests of key domestic constituencies are also factored into policy calculations of the interests of the nation as a whole.

For our purposes, what is most significant about these compromises is the extent to which, over time, their costs in terms of welfare have risen as a result of the evolution of objective conditions, both domestically and internationally. At home, our political system has grown ever more fragmented and stalemated as a result of the historic ebb of power in recent years from the "Imperial Presidency" toward Congress, where particular regional or sectoral interests can more easily exercise effective policy influence. Today even relatively small private groups, if well organized, can have a significant impact on public decision making. Accordingly, the price required to accommodate them seems to have steadily increased.

Abroad, too, the system has grown ever more fragmented and stalemated, as a result of the historic ebb of power away from the "imperial" United States. At the end of World War II, America could truly be described as a hegemonic world power. In international trade and finance our dominance was unquestioned; we could well afford the cost of aid programs and trade concessions designed to maintain our foreign influence and shore up the newly erected international economic order. But as time has passed and, as is well known, our economic position has declined relative to that of our allies in Europe and Japan and, more recently, in relation to others (such as OPEC) as well, our leadership role has come under increasing challenge from other countries. Still preeminent but no longer predominant, we are no longer able to determine the course of events on our own at comparatively low cost to ourselves. As in the domestic arena, power has become more diffused. Hence in the international arena too the price of accommodation has increased.

Finally, the costs of compromise have risen owing to the sheer complexity of international economic relations today. The proliferation of issues and multiplying linkages among them have greatly magnified the uncertainties inherent in the decision-making process and limited even further the government's ability to develop an effective and coherent set of policies.

Not that we have therefore become a pitiful, helpless giant. Quite the contrary, as is also well known, the United States still commands impressive resources in international economic relations, based on an economy that is still the largest, most diversified, and most technologically advanced in the world. Our foreign trade is still greater than that of any other single country, our overseas investment the most extensive, our financial markets the most attractive, our currency the most widely used for international purposes. But conditions *have* changed, and as a result our ability to achieve traditional policy goals, while still considerable, is no longer what it used to be. Decision makers find their range of choice increasingly hemmed in by pressures of interest groups at home, by the growing assertiveness of governments abroad, and by the ever greater complexity of the issues with which they have to deal. The constraints are real. How to come to terms with them has been the central dilemma of foreign economic policy making for all recent administrations.

From Carter to Reagan

How have successive administrations tried to cope with this dilemma? At first glance, little continuity seems apparent in the historical record. As the constraints on American policy have grown, decision makers have veered often, and sharply, between efforts to adjust to the new limits of power and efforts to reassert the primacy of American interests. When Richard Nixon became president, for instance, the first inclination of his administration seemed to be to accommodate our economic allies in Europe and Japan with macroeconomic policies that would help bring the burgeoning American balance of payments deficit under control. But when appeals for complementary initiatives from the Europeans and Japanese, particularly with respect to exchange rates, seemed to fall on deaf ears, policy soon shifted to a more confrontational stance, culminating in August 1971 with a 10 percent import surcharge and suspension of the dollar's convertibility into gold. The purpose of these moves, Washington made clear, was to pressure other countries into accepting an exchange rate realignment that would improve America's competitive position, whether others liked it or not: "economic gunboat diplomacy" at its most naked. Under the influence of his blunt and impatient Treasury Secretary, John Connally, President Nixon was not above destroying one of the key foundations of the postwar Bretton Woods system for the sake of promoting American exports.

Not that such policy swings are anything new. One need only recall the Smoot-Hawley tariff of 1930, followed four years later by the first Reciprocal Trade Agreements Act; or the generosity of our early post-war policies in Europe and Japan, followed shortly by a reversion to the narrowest sort of protection of domestic clothespin manufacturers and the like. Nor are such swings confined only to economic policy. Other dimensions of foreign policy manifest the same "oscillations," as Robert Osgood calls them, "between assertion and retrenchment, between the affirmation and restraint of national power." [5] These oscillations have deep roots in America's historic approach to the outside world, which has always reflected an uncertain tension between pretensions to America's leadership in international affairs and a gut urge to be rid of all foreign entanglements, with policy preferences switching frequently between the two. The apparent discontinuities in the historical record really constitute one of the more notable continuities in the rhythm of our external relations, political no less than economic. It is hardly surprising that other countries often accuse us of "incoherence" in our foreign policies, of "insensitivity," "indifference," or "lack of finesse."

In this respect, the administration of Jimmy Carter was no exception. Initially inclined toward an activist reaffirmation of America's influence over economic events, it ended by stressing most the advantages of compromise and collaboration with our key allies in Europe and Japan. This trend, despite criticisms of inconsistency (or worse), was evident in both the main dimensions of our economic relations with the other industrial states, macroeconomics and trade.

In macroeconomic relations, the administration began by promoting a grand strategy of reflation by the strongest industrial states — quickly dubbed the "locomotive" strategy — to pull the world economy out of recession. When the other main locomotives, Germany and Japan, balked at introducing new expansionary measures, primarily for fear of renewing rampant inflationary pressures, the United States pressed ahead anyway. The new administration felt a heavy responsibility for renewed growth not only at home but in the world economy as a whole, which seemed gravely threatened by slow growth, rising unemployment, and severe balance of payments problems; and it was determined to take the lead in fostering global recovery — on its own, if need be. [6]

The outcome is well known. [7] Inflation began to accelerate again in in the United States. In addition, owing to the absence of parallel stimulus elsewhere, very large deficits reemerged in the American balance of payments, in turn leading to severe selling pressures on the dollar and uncertainty in the exchange markets. At first, Washington tended to view the dollar's decline with equanimity: "[T]he Administration does not believe it is appropriate to maintain any particular value for the dollar," President Carter's Council of Economic Advisers asserted in its first *Annual Report*. [8] But as exchange-market conditions grew more chaotic, criticisms of our policy mounted, and in Europe plans began for construction of a new "zone of monetary stability" — the European Monetary System — to insulate currencies on the other side of the Atlantic from the vagaries of the dollar.[9] Increasingly isolated, the administration eventually shifted toward greater demand restraint at home, more active exchange intervention abroad, and closer coordination of both macroeconomic and intervention policies with other major industrial countries. The turning point came with the Bonn economic summit in July 1978, when the United States pledged to ease up on its domestic expansionary policies, and it was confirmed on November 1, 1978, when the administration announced a decisive new commitment to support the dollar in exchange markets (backed by a $30 billion "rescue package" arranged with allied governments and the International Monetary Fund). By mid-1979 it could accurately be said that "[t]he Carter Administration had conceded defeat."[10] In its last two years the administration's emphasis was placed not on unilateral initiatives but, rather, on the need for greater international collaboration and cooperation to sustain macroeconomic and intervention policies consistent with both internal and external balance. In its last *Annual Report*, the very same Council of Economic Advisers could now speak of the merits of "consistency in economic policy objectives and cooperation in exchange-market policies ... to ensure the smooth functioning of the international monetary system."[11]

Similarly, in the trade area the administration began — ritual declarations of adherence to traditional liberal principles notwithstanding — by reasserting the primacy of American commercial interests. Our policy was now to be "free but fair trade," according to President Carter's Special Trade Representative, Robert Strauss. In practice, this translated into a series of measures designed to protect sensitive domestic industries from the competition of lower-cost imports. During 1977, so-called orderly marketing agreements (negotiated quotas) were established to restrict, *inter alia*, imports of footwear from Korea and Taiwan and color television sets from Japan. And in early 1978 the so-called triggerprice mechanism was instituted to discourage steel imports into the United States, by assuring that any imports below the specified reference price (based on the production costs of the most efficient producer, Japan) would trigger an accelerated antidumping investigation. In effect, the device fixed a minimum price for imported steel. In addition, the administration significantly tightened application of provisions of the 1974 Trade Act involving countervailing duties (intended to offset the price reducing effects of foreign export subsidies) and escape clause actions.[12]

However, here too the tide shifted in 1978, again in good part because of mounting criticisms from abroad. The Carter administration was never mercantilist in an ideological sense. Most of its protectionist initiatives were apparently taken reluctantly, and only under strong domestic pressures. Not surprisingly, therefore, when similar tendencies toward increased restrictiveness became manifest in Europe and Japan,[13] threatening a snowballing of retaliatory measures that could bring down the whole edifice of international trade, the thrust of policy eventually became more conciliatory, shifting toward mutual accommodation with our principal trading partners. In late 1978 a new National Export Policy was announced, switching the emphasis in trade relations from import restraint to export promotion. And in April 1979 the so-called Tokyo Round of multilateral trade negotiations was brought to a conclusion, with the United States making crucial concessions on such matters as countervailing duties, agricultural subsidies, and customs valuation procedures.[14] During the administration's last two years, not a single new restriction was imposed on imports from other industrial countries, despite persistent protectionist sentiment at home (aggravated, especially, by the recession of 1980).

In effect, in both macroeconomics and trade the Carter administration went through a kind of difficult learning process, first reasserting traditional policy goals and then gradually becoming educated to the new limits of American power. To its credit, the administration seemed to learn the lesson well. In its second two years, unilateral foreign economic policy initiatives were infrequent and then taken only in response to what seemed extreme provocation; for example, the 1979 freeze of Iranian assets following the seizure of American hostages in Teheran or the 1980 grain embargo on the Soviet Union following Russian intervention in Afghanistan.[15] For the most part, policy emphasis shifted instead to closer collaboration with our allies, in a groping attempt to find some way to manage jointly what, it was now recognized, the United States could no longer control entirely on its own. Given the evolution of objective conditions, there seemed little realistic alternative to a stance of mutual accommodation and compromise. But to a nation long accustomed to a high degree of autonomy and influence in international economic affairs, it was a frustrating if not alarming experience; and it no doubt contributed to Jimmy Carter's defeat in November 1980.

With the arrival of Ronald Reagan, the pendulum swiftly swung back again, almost as if the Carter learning process had never occurred. For the new Republican administration, elected in part precisely because of the frustrations and alarms of the preceding years, it was simply inconceivable that the United States could not reclaim its accustomed autonomy and influence over economic events. President Reagan's reading of history was far different: Objective conditions had *not* fundamentally changed; American power *could* be reaffirmed. All that was needed was renewed vigor and incisive action in support of American interests. At home, a new macroeconomic policy had to be initiated unencumbered by troublesome accommodation of governments elsewhere. Abroad, trade policy had to be used forcefully to promote the market position of American producers. In such initiatives, it was felt, lay the real alternative to the compromises of the Carter years.

The key, according to the Reagan administration, was to be found in the "magic of the marketplace." If markets would be allowed to work, America's natural leadership would swiftly reemerge. In this respect, there was no distinction at all between the administration's faith in private economic activity and its faith in the country: The two were intertwined. In the words of President Reagan's Council of Economic Advisers:

> The successful implementation of policies to control inflation and restore vigorous real growth in the United States will have a profound and favorable impact on the rest of the world.... More generally, the Administration's approach to international economic issues is based on the same principles which underlie its domestic programs: a belief in the superiority of market solutions to economic problems and an emphasis on private economic activity as the engine of non-inflationary growth.[16]

How well did this market-oriented approach fare during the administration's first eighteen months?

Macroeconomic Policy: Reaganomics Rampant

Like so many before it, the Reagan administration came to office proclaiming America's prosperity to be its fundamental goal. The country was to have a "New Beginning." The first order of business was to be a "Program for Economic Recovery," announced with great fanfare by President Reagan himself before Congress and a prime-time television audience on February 18, less than a month after his inauguration. The program embodied the four main pillars of Reaganomics: (1) noninflationary (tight) monetary policy, (2) slower growth of government spending, (3) reduction of federal tax rates, and (4) regulatory reform. Together, the president promised, these four steps would achieve "a full and vigorous recovery of our economy...and a brighter future for all our citizens."[17]

Of course, neither monetary nor fiscal policy was entirely under the president's own control. Monetary policy was still the province of the independent Federal Reserve System; tax and spending policies still had to be vetted by the Congress. Yet to a remarkable degree President Reagan was able to work his will with both institutions. Monetary growth (as measured by M1B) was slowed by a willing Federal Reserve from an annual rate of 13 percent in the last quarter of 1980 to under

4 percent in the second half of 1981. In the summer, the president got his tax cuts, reducing personal income tax rates by a full 25 percent over three years. And in the fall Congress voted his spending cuts as well, eliminating overall $95 billion from the next two fiscal years (as measured against previous spending trends) while greatly raising military expenditures. At year's end the president felt satisfied to look back on what he described as a "substantial beginning." [18]

But what a beginning! In his February program, President Reagan predicted that economic growth would recover from the 1980 recession to a 4-5 percent annual growth path through 1986; inflation would decline from double-digit figures to less than 5 percent; and unemployment would drop under 6 percent.[19] Privately, in his celebrated *Atlantic Monthly* interviews, David Stockman, the president's director of the Office of Management and Budget, forecast a "bull market . . . of historic proportions." [20] Yet in fact conditions mostly grew worse, not better. After a strong first quarter the economy began by summer to sink into a new recession, with GNP dropping at an annual rate in excess of 5 percent in the last quarter of 1981 and unemployment rising to near 9 percent. Only the inflation picture improved, and even that in part was caused by exceptional declines in food and energy costs. A bull market was nowhere to be found.

The reason was obvious. Reaganomics, it soon came to be recognized, was threatening to produce the biggest budget deficits in the history of the United States; and in turn the expectation of those, in conjunction with the Federal Reserve's tight monetary policy, was generating record high interest rates. Economic growth, in effect, was being crowded out by anticipated Treasury borrowing. In February the administration had predicted a budget deficit of only some $45 billion in FY 1982, shrinking to near balance by FY 1984.[21] But the unfounded optimism of these numbers — even David Stockman admitted in private that they were based on "shaky premises" [22] — gradually became too evident even for the administration to deny. In December new estimates were released projecting a deficit of $109 billion in FY 1982, rising to $162 billion in FY 1984.

How could the administration have been so wrong? The answer was provided by David Stockman: "The whole thing is premised on faith . . . on a belief about how the world works." [23] The belief was supply-side economics, the new religion of the Grand Old Party. Administration supply-siders, above all the president himself, assumed that the key to national prosperity lay in increasing incentives for saving and investment. If taxes could be cut, the role of the government rolled back, and money kept tight, investor confidence in the future value of money would be restored, leading to a rise of productive employment that would, in turn, help balance the Federal budget. Of little concern were charges of "voodoo economics." Disciples of the new faith were confident that taxes could be shrunk, military expenditures raised, and the budget balanced all at the same time. It took months of depressing economic statistics — and the publication of David Stockman's confessions — to demonstrate what a false doctrine this really was. As one commentator put it, "After a year's trial, Reaganomics proves only one thing — you *can't* do it with mirrors." [24]

In 1982 the chickens came home to roost. Hoisted on the petard of his own policies, President Reagan submitted a budget in February projecting a deficit of $91.5 billion in FY 1983, declining to $82.9 billion in FY 1984, which was almost immediately dismissed by Congress as unrealistic.[25] Domestic political support for Reaganomics began to splinter, and soon one budget plan succeeded another as congressional leaders and administration officials sought to regain control over fiscal policy. Yet by midyear there was still no final agreement, while in the meantime the recession persisted, unemployment continued to climb, and interest rates remained near the record highs established in 1981. The economy seemed further than ever from the "full and vigorous recovery" promised by President Reagan, although administration spokesmen continued to predict an end to the recession and lower interest rates in the second half of the year.

From an international perspective, what was most striking during this period was the way in which policy was determined in almost total disregard for the outside world. At no time during the administration's first eighteen months was there any serious attempt to moderate the external impacts of our fiscal dilemma, via either collaboration with our industrial allies or intervention in the exchange market. On the contrary, being convinced of its own rectitude, the administration accepted no responsibility at all for problems that might crop up elsewhere. Early in 1981, consistent with its belief in the superiority of market solutions, the Treasury scaled back foreign exchange operations dramatically. Henceforth, according to Treasury Under Secretary Beryl Sprinkel, the United States would intervene in the exchange market only at times of extreme disturbance (for example, in the event of an attempted presidential assassination). Otherwise, the dollar would be free to seek its own value. The best way to stabilize exchange rates, it was said, was for each country to restore price stability domestically. America was doing its part. If others were experiencing difficulties, they might profitably follow our example. As President Reagan said at the 1981 Annual Meetings of the International Monetary Fund and World Bank: "The most important contribution any country can make to world development is to pursue sound economic policies at home." [26]

But that was just the point. Many felt that the United States was not, in fact, pursuing sound economic policies at home. Criticisms focused on two issues: (1) our fiscal-monetary "mix" and (2) the emphasis of our monetary policy on monetary aggregates. Our mix of tight money and large budget deficits could not help but keep interest rates high; the concentration of our monetary policy on money supply targets rather than on interest rates could not help but increase their variability. Historically, the Federal Reserve had judged the appropriateness of monetary policy primarily by looking at credit conditions. But in October 1979, under the influence of Federal Reserve Board Chairman Paul Volker, the system converted to a "monetarist" focus on the quantity of money rather than its price. Primary emphasis was now placed on the overall amount of bank reserves as an operating target: Interest rates were to be allowed to respond more freely to market forces. Not surprisingly, therefore, the volatility of rates increased sharply. The commercial bank prime lending rate was representative, roller-coasting from a low of 11 percent in mid-1980 to 21 percent at year's end, 17½ percent in April 1981, 20½ percent in the summer, 16 percent in the fall, 21 percent in the winter, and 16 percent in the spring of 1982.

Such high and variable interest rates were bound to wreak havoc in exchange markets. With each ratcheting up of yields on United States assets, short-term capital poured into the country, pushing the dollar to heights not seen since the start of generalized floating in 1973. In the twelve months from August 1980 to August 1981 the average value of the dollar in terms of the currencies of the ten major industrial countries (as measured by the Federal Reserve) rose by 30 percent; in relation to the currencies of the European Monetary System, the increase was more than 40 percent. Throughout the period, exchange rate movements closely paralleled the gyrations of interest rates in the United States.[27]

For our industrial allies, these developments compounded an already unpleasant policy dilemma.[28] Following the run-up of oil prices in 1978–1979, inflation had once again accelerated even as growth slowed and unemployment continued to rise. In most of the industrial countries, the desire to reverse price trends in 1981 kept central banks from easing up on monetary policy, despite the sluggishness of domestic output and employment. The appreciation of the dollar, which meant of course depreciation of their own currencies, only added to the inflationary pressures in their economies by raising import costs. The volatility of exchange rates only added to the uncertainties impeding economic revival. Europeans, in particular, were vocal in their criticism of American policy, resurrecting charges of benign neglect not heard since the first two years of the Carter administration. America, they knew, was not the sole — or perhaps, even the principal — cause of their troubles. But they were understandably aggrieved by the Reagan administration's unwillingness to do anything at all to help, either in terms of domestic policy or in the exchange market. As Flora Lewis has perceptively explained:

Successive U.S. governments have insisted on their sovereign right to run the economy as they think best. But it adds to Europe's sense of impotence, and resentment, when changes of policy it cannot influence aggravate its own less than satisfying attempts at economic management.[29]

Nor were the criticisms exclusively foreign. In the United States, too, questions began to be raised about the administration's neglect of the external dimension of domestic policy. Exporters, in particular, grew concerned about the impact of a rising dollar on their foreign sales. Within a month of President Reagan's inauguration, *The Economist* reported that "The implications of a strong dollar are . . . slowly dawning." [30] By midyear, apprehensions were widespread. C. Fred Bergsten, formerly Assistant Secretary of the Treasury under President Carter, proved prescient in predicting that "the unprecedented overvaluation of the dollar caused by the policy mix will produce huge U.S. trade deficits and retard U.S. economic growth." [31] In fact, much of the blame for the recession that began in the summer could be laid to our balance of trade, which deteriorated steadily throughout 1981. Fully one-third of the decline of GNP between the first quarter of 1981 and the first quarter of 1982 was attributable to falling net exports. By the spring of 1982, it was clear that the administration's benign neglect policy in exchange markets had become another barrier to recovery. As Lawrence Krause of the Brookings Institution explained pointedly. "The dollar is one of the elements in our international competitiveness, but we ignore it as a matter of principle." [32]

Nevertheless, the administration stubbornly defended its policies. At his first economic summit, in Ottawa in July 1981, President Reagan successfully deflected complaints, such as Helmut Schmidt's, that interest rates were at their highest level "since the birth of Christ." Although only Britain's conservative Prime Minister Margaret Thatcher expressed support for his program, the other leaders present, recognizing that the president had no intention of yielding so soon after his electoral mandate, were prepared to accept the assurances of Treasury Secretary Donald Regan that rates would be several points lower by the end of the year.[33] According to the *Financial Times*, "by implication they appear reluctantly to have conceded defeat, and will give the U.S. another six months before returning to the attack." [34]

However, when rates did not in fact come down, return to the attack they did. Shortly after the New Year, the German government went public with its view that "mistaken" American policies were a prime cause of sluggish growth and rising joblessness throughout the industrial world. Chancellor Schmidt and his Economics Minister, Count Otto Lambsdorff, were reported to have described the Reagan administration's approach as simplisitic and brutal, both toward American workers and toward the Western political and economic alliance.[35] And later in January, the French Finance Minister, Jacques Delors, argued at a private meeting with his counterparts from the United States, Britain, Germany, and Japan that America was straining the alliance and encouraging neutralism in Europe with its economic policies.[36] By February, European officials were talking openly of a "complete breakdown" in monetary cooperation between America and Europe, describing Atlantic economic relations as now at their lowest point since President Nixon's suspension of the dollar's convertibility into gold in 1971. According to one senior official, "We have simply never before seen a United States Administration that displayed this degree of indifference to the effects of its actions on its allies." [37] This was not benign neglect, wrote one British commentator: This was "an almost malign rejection of the need for a 'good neighbor' policy." [38]

Yet the indifference persisted, despite repeated entreaties by European leaders through the winter and spring. More active exchange intervention or revised domestic policy priorities were not the solution, they were told. What we needed, simply, was time to let the president's economic program work. Administration spokesmen stuck by their prediction of recovery and lower interest rates in the second half of the year. As alliance leaders gathered for President Reagan's second economic summit, at Versailles in June, the dilemma was astutely summarized by an American commentator:

> The Europeans believe that, without greater United States cooperation, the world economy may be facing extreme currency instability, high interest rates, painfully slow growth and high unemployment for years to come.
>
> The United States is not in fundamental disagreement with the objectives of its allies. But the American approach is far more noninterventionist, far more free-market oriented than the Europeans would prefer.... The Reagan Administration wishes to keep a free hand, since it considers the success of its domestic economic policy far more important than what happens in the foreign-exchange market or even to America's foreign trade.
>
> Furthermore, the Reagan Administration still appears dominated by a monetarist economic theory. This theory implies that it is unnecessary to worry about foreign economic relationships, provided that one maintains a slow and steady growth of the money supply, thus keeping inflation under control. To the Europeans, this seems like a counsel of perfection that has not worked.[39]

What *would* work? Clearly what was needed was a renewal of the spirit of mutual accommodation and compromise that had characterized the Carter administration in its latter years — a realistic appraisal of the constraints on policy and a willingness to cooperate in pursuit of common objectives. In concrete terms, this would mean (1) a revised fiscal-monetary mix (smaller budget deficits and somewhat less restrictive monetary policy) that would permit a gradual reduction of interest rates; (2) return by the Federal Reserve to a greater emphasis on credit conditions to dampen the variability of interest rates; and (3) resumption of coordinated intervention to smooth the movements of exchange rates. At Versailles most of the other leaders present (again, Margaret Thatcher excepted) continued to press President Reagan to reconsider his policies. But, in fact, no concessions of substance were achieved. Instead, apart from some rhetorical support for "greater control of budget deficits," only procedural decisions were included in the final communiqué: a commitment to a joint study of the feasibility of exchange intervention and an agreement to consult regularly in the future to promote "convergence" of economic policies. Administration officials went out of their way to deny that either decision implied any major shift of American policy and insisted that the United States would retain its traditional autonomy of action.[40] In effect, the president simply managed to buy yet a bit more time for his program.

Thus as the administration rounded out its first eighteen months, prospects for macroeconomic relations with our economic allies were the bleakest in years. Effectively placing autonomy of decision making above all other objectives of policy, the administration had succeeded neither in promoting economic prosperity nor in fully retaining domestic political support, and it had managed only to alienate most of the other industrial states. An unnecessary — and potentially perilous — strain had been placed on the Western alliance by our exercise in unilateralism. The general atmosphere was best summarized by a cartoon published in *The Times* of London just as the Versailles summit was getting under way. It pictured a mob surrounding the palace and demanding jobs, with a voice from within responding, "Let them eat monetarism." The last time something like that happened, there was a revolution.

Trade Policy: Reciprocity Redolent

Nor was administration performance much better in the area of trade relations with our allies. Here, too, unnecessary and potentially perilous strains were produced by a shift away from the generally conciliatory attitude of the latter Carter years. Once again the primacy of American commercial interests was asserted. Ritual declarations of adherence to traditional liberal principles notwithstanding, domestic distributional goals were effectively placed above all other objectives of policy. And once again, this led to the threat of a snowballing of retaliatory measures that appeared to place the whole edifice of international trade in jeopardy. After the Reagan administration's first eighteen months, the trade outlook too looked bleak.

The new administration's attitude was best summarized by President Reagan's Trade Representative, William Brock, in a carefully crafted white paper on American trade policy released in July 1981.[41] Although free trade was pronounced essential, the white paper also contained warnings that free trade must be a two-way street and that the American market would not necessarily remain open to countries that in the administration's view fail to play by commonly agreed rules. "We will *insist* that our trading partners live up to the spirit and the letter of international trade agreements, and that they recognize that trade is a two-way street ... and we *will make full use of all available channels for assuring compliance*" [emphasis supplied]. These would include both (1) strict enforcement of existing import regulations (for example, antidumping and countervailing-duty laws) designed to neutralize or eliminate "trade distortive practices which injure U.S. industry and agriculture," and (2) active pursuit of satisfactory market access for American business abroad "in a manner consistent with the goal of reducing trade barriers and trade-distorting measures." The guiding light for our policy would be the principle of "reciprocity." The objective would be to "promote positive adjustment of economies by permitting market forces to operate."

Underlying the administration's policy was a perception, common in Washington, that the United States was not getting a fair shake in international trade. In part this was, supposedly, because in past multilateral bargaining, including the Tokyo Round, the United States had failed to negotiate trade rules that adequately served American interests. The American market, it was thought, had been opened up to a far greater extent than markets elsewhere. And in part this was because other industrial states were believed to systematically ignore or violate the framework of understandings historically championed by this country in the General Agreement on Tariffs and Trade. American manufactured and agricultural trade was handicapped by a myriad of foreign nontariff distortions; service industries and direct investments fell victim to subsidized competition or trade-related performance requirements. Hence the spotlight on reciprocity, generally understood to stand for "substantially equivalent market access." From now on it would be necessary not only to monitor foreign access here but also to seek unilateral concessions from other governments to provide American business with "fair and equitable" opportunities abroad. Otherwise, retaliatory measures would have to be contemplated.

This was not simply protectionism in disguise. Most officials of the administration, from President Reagan on down, genuinely believe in the desirability of free trade. At the Ottawa summit the president gave his full support to a call for a ministerial-level meeting of the GATT in 1982, to maintain the momentum of global liberalization. But it was, as *The Economist* suggested, "free-trade-tempered-by-nationalism," [42] reminiscent of the assertiveness of Robert Strauss's "free-but-fair-trade" campaign of the early Carter years. Throughout the Reagan administration's first eighteen months, Trade Representative Brock sought to focus the upcoming GATT meeting (scheduled for November 1982) on plans for a new round of multilateral negotiations aimed at liberalizing the movement of capital and services such as banking, insurance, data processing, engineering, shipping, and telecommunications — all areas in which the United States, as the world's leading service-industry economy, could be expected to benefit disproportionately. And to back up this approach, Brock also formally asked Congress to strengthen his bargaining hand by authorizing retaliation against countries that discriminate against imports of "invisibles" or investments from this country. In these areas, Mr. Brock said in a speech, no less than in the traditional area of visible trade, America will no longer "tolerate unfair trading practices that adversely affect either our domestic market or our opportunity to trade elsewhere." [43]

The belligerence of the administration's tone could not be explained solely by domestic political pressures — though such pressures were clearly important, just as they had been during the Carter years. In fact, protectionist sentiment continued to build after the recession of 1980, and was further aggravated by the remorseless climb of the dollar in exchange markets. A host of industries, from automobiles and steel to textiles and electronics, were petitioning for import relief or export support. In Congress, within months of the new administration's arrival in Washington, more than thirty bills had been introduced embodying some kind of reciprocity clause. But there was more to the administration's attitude than merely the narrow interests of specific domestic constituencies. For many of President Reagan's officials, what was even more importantly at stake was the general interest of the nation as a whole in a system that seemed to them increasingly discriminatory against American industry and agriculture. As Trade Representative Brock explained, "I am confident that, under this President, reciprocity will not become a code word for protectionism, but it will be used to state clearly our insistence on equity." [44]

Unfortunately, equity is a subjective matter. What looks like getting a fair shake to some may well appear as protectionism in the eyes of others. Hence there was a danger that in adopting the tone it did, the administration risked provoking the very trade-distorting measures it was pledged to reduce. Many foreign governments questioned the perception that in trade relations, the United States was more sinned against than sinning. What about our own unfair trade practices, they asked, such as the many "Buy American" regulations at federal and state levels? What about our import restrictions on such agricultural commodities as sugar, meat, and cheese? What about our tax incentives, amounting to subsidies, given to exporters through our system of Domestic International Sales

Corporations (DISC)? Most governments seemed prepared to resist administration efforts to wring unilateral concessions from them, and some made quite clear that they would respond in kind to retaliatory measures from the United States.

Furthermore, many complained, the very concept of reciprocity could signal a retreat from the postwar system of multilateral trade relationships, a step toward bilateralism. The charge was denied by the administration, which lost no opportunity to reaffirm this country's commitment to the fundamental rule of the GATT, embodied in the most-favored nation clause, that trade should be conducted on the basis of nondiscrimination. Critics warned, however, that in practice the concept could easily degenerate into a rigid insistence on "equivalence" market by market and product by product. Barrier would be matched for barrier, concession for concession, trade balance for trade balance — all on a bilateral basis. Certainly that seemed the intent of much of the reciprocity legislation before Congress. In the words of Senate Finance Committee chairman Robert Dole, author of one reciprocity bill,

> [r]eciprocity means a dramatic change from the "most-favored nation" principle. It means that other countries should provide us with trade and investment opportunities equal not simply to what they afford their other "most-favored" trading partners but equal to what we offer them. And reciprocity should be assessed not by what agreements promise but by actual results — by changes in the balance of trade and growth in investment between ourselves and our major economic partners.[45]

How the administration stood on such legislation was not clear. Publicly, spokesmen like Trade Representative Brock repeatedly cautioned Congress not to let the many reciprocity bills become vehicles for protectionism. Yet covertly the administration seemed almost to welcome the threat of congressional action as an additional form of leverage on our trading partners to coerce them into concessions — a traditional tactic of the Executive branch in international trade negotiations. What was clear was that the administration was playing a risky game, skating on very thin ice. Either its approach would have to produce results, in our home market as well as in opportunities to trade elsewhere, or its hand might be forced by a disappointed Congress. Ultimately, reciprocity must either succeed or trigger American retaliation. Yet at the same time we must not provoke our allies into a trade war by seeming to bully them. A few examples illustrate how dangerously thin the ice really was.

Japan

Of all our allies, Japan is regarded in Washington as the most guilty of unfair trading practices. Provoked by Japan's huge and growing surplus in our bilateral trade — over $18 billion in 1981, nearly twice the figure for 1980 — complaints address both sides of our mutual balance. On the export side, the Japanese are criticized for their habitual strategy of massive penetration of export markets in relatively narrow product lines, causing severe injury to local competitors. In addition, Japan's exporters are said to benefit improperly from generous government support, especially at the R & D stage. On the import side, the Japanese are criticized for a whole range of formal and informal nontariff barriers, from special product standards to time-consuming and expensive customs procedures, that limit access to their internal market. If there is any single country that is the implied target of reciprocity, it is Japan.

In many instances, the grievances against Japan appear justified — the Japanese themselves, when pressed, have often implicitly conceded by acting selectively to restrain exports or liberalize imports. However, what was remarkable after the Reagan administration arrived in Washington was the sharp rise in the level of acrimony in American accusations. Neither the administration nor the new Congress had any tolerance for past piecemeal approaches, which, it was thought, had resulted at best in only tactical retreats by the Japanese. The feeling was that only by means of a broad, blunt assault could really significant concessions be obtained. "We needed to get their attention," one administration official said privately. "We had to use the proverbial two-by-four." [46]

The assault began, under pressure from domestic interests, with negotiation in May 1981 of a "voluntary" agreement on the model of earlier negotiated quotas restraining Japanese automobile exports to the United States. Having lost on a petition for escape-clause relief before the International Trade Commission in December 1980, the American automobile industry had turned instead to Congress, where supporters introduced highly restrictive quota legislation. In turn, the administration made use of this threat to persuade Japan to accept an export limit of 1.68 million units in the year beginning April 1st, down from 1.82 million units the previous year, and to continue restraint the following two years. There is no question that the Japanese acceded reluctantly to these limits. Calling them "voluntary," however, allowed the administration to claim no responsibility for a protectionist agreement that it had in fact actively negotiated, thus ostensibly preserving its free-trade credentials.

Subsequently, the focus shifted to Japanese imports. As a result of its many nontariff barriers, the administration noted, Japan imported fewer manufactured goods as a proportion of GNP than any other industrial country (about 1½ percent, as against 3½ percent or more in the United States and Europe); indeed, the share of manufactured imports in GNP had actually declined over the previous two decades, while that of other industrial states had rapidly risen. And Japan also maintained strict controls on imports of agricultural commodities of interest to the United

States, such as rice, citrus, tobacco, and beef. Furthermore, the Japanese were criticized for their strong "Buy Japan" ethic and their complex distribution system, highly dependent on long-standing social relationships, both of which also inhibit imports.

The assault on Japanese import practices was maintained throughout the administration's first eighteen months. In response, Japan announced several liberalization programs. In December, tariffs were cut on some 1,653 items, including such goods as computers and automobile parts. In January, 67 nontariff barriers were eliminated or significantly reduced, out of a list of 99 such barriers culled from previous complaints. And in May, tariffs were cut on an additional 215 items, and import quotas on some farm products were eased. Yet the administration hardly seemed mollified. In fact, the tone of criticisms grew even harsher, despite such concessions. "The atmosphere here is uglier than in the past," noted one knowledgeable Washington observer.[47] In turn the Japanese, gradually abandoning their customary deference, began to lash back, citing their own grievances against this country (discriminatory government procurement programs, restrictions on the sale of Alaskan oil, and alleged dumping of petrochemical products, for example) and challenging Washington's threat of unilateral retaliatory measures. "If the United States does not want to trade with Japan, politics here would change," warned one high trade official in Tokyo. "There would be no benefit for Japan to remain a member of the free world." [48] Though perhaps an extreme example, such a statement is symptomatic of the frictions generated by the administration's attitude.

Europe

In trade relations with Europe, three issues in particular stood out during the administration's first eighteen months: steel, agriculture, and sanctions. Each contributed to what *The Economist* called the "rockiest patch for 30 years" [49] in the Atlantic trading relationship.

The steel issue was inherited from the Carter years. Despite the trigger-price mechanism instituted in 1978, steel imports had continued to increase their penetration of the American market (19 percent in 1981, up from 16 percent in 1980 and only 14 percent as recently as 1976), intensifying industry pressures for relief. The major culprits, the industry charged, were members of the European Community, who were accused of illegal subsidies as well as outright dumping. Reviving a tactic that had been used successfully during the Carter administration, companies such as U.S. Steel again began threatening antidumping and countervailing-duty suits against the Europeans. "The target price is simply out of control," argued the chairman of U.S. Steel in early November. "It is being blatantly ignored by most of the European producers. The time for patience is past. It is time for action." [50] Action finally came in January

1982, when U.S. Steel and six other companies filed more than 190 complaints against seven EC countries, as well as Brazil, Romania, South Africa, and Spain.

The Reagan administration was caught in the middle, between the protectionist demands of the industry and its own free-trade pretensions. Unfortunately, its instincts seemed to place highest priority on the interests of a powerful domestic constituency. Although there seemed much truth in industry charges against the Europeans, American companies had by no means helped their case by repeatedly raising prices in 1980 and 1981, despite weak market conditions. In addition, the European Community could legitimately claim that at least some of its subsidies were legal, being tied to plans for rationalization of its own industry, and in any event were being gradually phased out. Yet the administration never hesitated to keep pressure on the Europeans to restrain their sales here. In late 1981 and again in mid-1982 Commerce Secretary Malcolm Baldridge tried to negotiate a "voluntary" export agreement with the Community similar to the Japanese automobile pact. When these efforts failed, countervailing duties were recommended that would amount to the severest trade restriction by this country in years. In retaliation, the Community began compiling a list of American exports benefiting from tax breaks on which the Europeans could also impose countervailing duties. The bitterness felt on both sides of the Atlantic over the issue was palpable.

Another major irritant was agriculture. For the Reagan administration, one of the most unfair of all trading practices was the Community's common farm policy which, with its high prices and open-ended guarantees, had turned the EC from a net importer of food into a net exporter of such items as dairy products, beef, poultry, sugar, and wheat — thereby threatening traditional overseas markets of the United States. The issue, as the administration saw it, was the Community's aggressive use of export subsidies to gain competitive advantage. For the Europeans, however, this was a case of the pot calling the kettle black. The United States, they pointed out, also provides broad government support for its farmers; and America's share of world agricultural trade has actually grown more rapidly than that of the Community. Objecting to the administration's contentious tone, EC officials warned that any action against European farmers would provoke countermeasures endangering America's traditional surplus in agricultural trade with Europe. Said the United States Deputy Secretary of Agriculture: "I'm not sure we won't have a trade war." [51]

Finally, there were the economic sanctions imposed by the Reagan administration on Poland and the Soviet Union following the Polish government's declaration of martial law in December 1981. As Miles Kahler points out in his contribution to this volume, administration spokesmen criticized the Europeans for their failure to match America's actions, charging that Europe seemed more interested in markets than in the security of the Western alliance. The Europeans, in turn, criticized Washington for overreacting, suggesting pointedly that they might be more willing to cut their trade with the Soviet bloc if the United States were to make an equivalent sacrifice by reinstating the grain embargo that President Reagan had lifted in 1981. Subsequently, the dispute was raised to what *The Economist* described as the "hair-pulling level" [52] by administration efforts to persuade the Europeans to cancel their planned natural gas pipeline from Siberia and to restrict government-subsidized export credits to the Soviet Union. When, in mid-June, the administration decided to extend its ban on sales of American technology and equipment for the pipeline, contrary to understandings reached at the Versailles summit just days before, the Europeans were understandably furious. Said Francois Mitterrand: "We wonder what concept the United States has of summit meetings when it becomes a matter of agreements made and not respected." [53] As summer began, it was clear that the damage done to allied relations by this action would not be easily mended.

Canada

With Canada, the major issues in our mutual relations involved not trade but investment. Since 1974, the Canadian Foreign Investment Review Agency has scrutinized incoming foreign investment on the basis of whether it offers "significant benefit" to Canada, and has both limited the opportunities for foreign investors and imposed trade-related performance requirements on them. For the Reagan administration, such screening was an anathema, not only because it interfered with market forces but because it was inherently discriminatory, contravening international undertakings regarding "national treatment" — the same treatment of foreign and domestic enterprise. In early 1982, after months of complaint, the administration took its case formally to the GATT, where a favorable ruling would authorize Washington to retaliate by curbing Canadian access to the American market. The administration was particularly incensed by Canada's National Energy Program, announced in August 1980 with the goal of "Canadianization" of the country's oil and gas industry. The program seemed aimed directly at American companies, which currently control some two-thirds of all Canadian energy production. In response, Canadians ask how this country would feel if the tables were reversed. Would Americans tolerate such a high degree of foreign penetration of so vital a sector of their economy? More generally, Canadians feel they have a right to develop an independent national identity in the face of the pervasive influence of their giant neighbor — American companies also control some one-third of all manufacturing activity in Canada — and greatly resent the Reagan administration's harsh rhetoric and threats of retaliation. Washington's attacks have served mainly to deepen Canada's own sense of grievance. As a result, according to two astute observers (one Canadian and one American), "Relations between Canada and the United States have become more strained than at any time in recent memory.... The two governments seem to be on a collision course." [54]

Conclusion

It can hardly be said that the Reagan administration's approach to international economic relations fared well during its first eighteen months. Quite the contrary, the combination of Reaganomics at home and reciprocity abroad proved no solution at all to the central dilemma of foreign economic policy — the growing constraints on policy makers. In effect, the administration tried to ignore the new limits of American power, disregarding the lesson learned by the Carter administration. Our accustomed autonomy and influence over economic events would simply be reasserted. The results, predictably, were disappointing. Not only was economic prosperity not promoted, but relations with the other industrial states were brought to a new post-World War II low, endangering the very foundations of the Western alliance. The administration's tradeoffs among policy objectives threatened to be highly costly for the nation as a whole.

Domestically, the costs were evident in the prolonged recession and long unemployment lines. Abroad, the costs were less evident but, potentially, even more severe. By reasserting as forcefully as it did the primacy of American interests, defined in the narrowest possible terms, the administration effectively served notice that it no longer felt any special responsibility for preservation of the economic system as a whole. We too would act as a "free rider," extracting gains where we could. In the short run, such a policy might indeed succeed in wringing concessions from our allies. But the risk is that the more often we do this, the more likely it is that these same allies will feel driven to insulate themselves from us in their trade and monetary relations, just as they felt driven by the chaos of the dollar in 1978 to form the European Monetary System. And this in turn would most certainly deprive us of much of the benefit of global economic interdependence. In the long run, the United States too would be a loser. Like it or not, we still have a vested interest in avoiding undue discord or disruption in the system, and this the Reagan administration has clearly failed to do. Conflict has not been kept manageable. There could yet be an explosion in the kitchen.

Notes

1. Robert O. Keohane, "U.S. Foreign Economic Policy Toward Other Advanced Capitalist States," in *Eagle Entangled: U.S. Foreign Policy in a Complex World,* Kenneth A. Oye, Donald Rothchild, and Robert J. Lieber, eds. (New York and London: Longman, 1979), pp. 118-119.
2. Walter W. Heller, *New Dimensions of Political Economy* (New York: Norton, 1967), p. 5.
3. See, e.g., Richard N. Cooper, "Prolegomena to the Choice of an International Monetary System"; and Lawrence B. Krause and Joseph S. Nye, "Reflections on the Economics and Politics of International Economic Organizations"; both in *World Politics and International Economics,* C. Fred Bergsten and Lawrence B. Krause, eds. (Washington: Brookings Institution, 1975); and Benjamin J. Cohen, *Organizing the World's Money* (New York: Basic Books, 1977), ch. 2.
4. But see, e.g., Benjamin J. Cohen, "U.S. Foreign Economic Policy," ORBIS 15, no. 1 (Spring 1971), pp. 232-246; and Benjamin J. Cohen, "The Revolution in Atlantic Economic Relations: A Bargain Comes Unstuck," in *The United States and Western Europe,* Wolfram Hanrieder, ed. (Cambridge, Mass.: Winthrop, 1974).
5. Robert E. Osgood, "The Revitalization of Containment," *Foreign Affairs* 60, no. 3 (1982), p. 465.
6. For an authoritative statement of the administration's thinking at the time, see Richard N. Cooper, "Global Economic Policy in a World of Energy Shortage," in *Economics in the Public Service,* J. Pechman and J. Simler, eds. (New York: Norton, 1981). Cooper was President Carter's Under Secretary of State for Economic Affairs.
7. See, e.g., Keohane, "U.S. Foreign Economic Policy," pp. 102-109.
8. Council of Economic Advisers, *Annual Report, 1978* (Washington: January 1978), p. 124.
9. Benjamin J. Cohen, "Europe's Money, America's Problem," *Foreign Policy* 35 (Summer 1979), pp. 31-47.
10. Andrew Shonfield, "The World Economy in 1979," *Foreign Affairs* 58, no. 3 (1980), p. 607.
11. Council of Economic Advisers, *Annual Report, 1981* (Washington: January 1981), p. 199.
12. See, e.g., Marina Whitman, "A Year of Travail: The United States and the International Economy," *Foreign Affairs* 57, no. 3 (1979), pp. 543-544.
13. Whitman, "Year of Travail," p. 545.
14. See, e.g., Shonfield, "World Economy," pp. 616-617; and Thomas R. Graham, "Revolution in Trade Politics," *Foreign Policy* 36 (Fall 1979): 55.
15. For evaluations of these two policy measures, see Robert Carswell, "Economic Sanctions and the Iran Experience," *Foreign Affairs* 60, no. 2 (Winter 1981/82), pp. 247-265; and Robert L. Paarlberg, "Lessons of the Grain Embargo," *Foreign Affairs* 59, no. 1 (Fall 1980), pp. 144-162.
16. Council of Economic Advisers, *Annual Report, 1982* (Washington: February 1982), p. 167.
17. Presidential Message to the Congress accompanying his Program for Economic Recovery, February 18, 1981.
18. *Economic Report of the President* (Washington: February 1982), p. 4.
19. *America's New Beginning: A Program for Economic Recovery* (Washington: February 18, 1981), p. 25.
20. As quoted in William Greider, "The Education of David Stockman," *The Atlantic Monthly,* December 1981, p. 29.

21. *America's New Beginning,* p. 12.
22. As quoted in Greider, "Education," p. 38.
23. *Ibid.,* p. 29.
24. Tom Wicker, "Mr. Reagan's Mirrors," *The New York Times,* 11 December 1981, p. A35.
25. According to the Congressional Budget Office, even if all of the President's FY 1983 budget proposals were enacted, the deficits would more likely be $120.6 billion in FY 1983 and $128.9 billion in FY 1984. See *The New York Times,* 25 February 1982, p. A1.
26. September 29, 1981, as quoted in *IMF Survey,* 12 October, 1981, p. 317.
27. Steven Rattner, "U.S. Interest Rates: Currency Mover," *The New York Times,* 10 February 1982, p. D1.
28. Robert Solomon, " 'The Elephant in the Boat?': The United States and the World Economy," *Foreign Affairs* 60, no. 3 (1982), pp. 577-581.
29. Flora Lewis, "Alarm Bells in the West," *Foreign Affairs* 60, no. 3 (1982), p. 556.
30. *The Economist,* 14 February 1981, p. 67.
31. C. Fred Bergsten, "The Costs of Reaganomics," *Foreign Policy* 44 (Fall 1981), p. 25.
32. As quoted in *The New York Times,* 26 April 1982, p. D10.
33. *Financial Times,* 21 July 1981, p. 1.
34. "Living With Mr. Reagan," *Financial Times,* 23 July 1981, p. 16.
35. Leonard Silk, "The Sanctions and the Allies," *The New York Times,* 6 January 1982, p. D2.
36. *The New York Times,* 19 January 1982, p. D1.
37. *The New York Times,* 12 February 1982, p. 1.
38. John Wyles, "Europe: At the Mercy of Outside Forces," *Financial Times,* 7 December 1981, supplement, p. 1.
39. Leonard Silk, "Looking for a Way to Subdue Currency and Interest Discord," *The New York Times,* 5 June 1982, p. 30.
40. *The New York Times,* 7 June 1982, p. D6.
41. Office of the United States Trade Representative, "Statement of U.S. Trade Policy," July 8, 1981.
42. *The Economist,* 4 July 1981, p. 21.
43. Address before the European Management Forum, Davos, Switzerland, 1 February 1982.
44. *Ibid.*
45. Robert Dole, "Reciprocity in Trade," *The New York Times,* 22 January 1982, p. A31.
46. Interview with the author.
47. Philip H. Trezise, of the Brookings Institution, as quoted in *The New York Times,* 27 March 1982, Business Section, p. 1.
48. Kazuo Wakasugi, director of the trade policy bureau of the Ministry of International Trade and Industry, as quoted in *The New York Times,* 27 March 1982, Business Section, p. 32.
49. *The Economist,* 27 February 1982, p. 20.
50. As quoted in *Financial Times,* 4 November 1981.
51. As quoted in *The Economist,* 13 March 1982, p. 23.
52. *The Economist,* 27 February 1982, p. 22.
53. As quoted in *The New York Times,* June 29, 1982, p. A10.
54. Marie-Josée Drouin and Harald B. Malmgren, "Canada, the United States, and the World Economy," *Foreign Affairs* 60, no. 2 (Winter 1981/82), p. 393.

5

Reaganomics
and the Third World

Richard E. Feinberg

The "north-south dialogue" had already fallen from the top of the foreign policy agenda when the Reagan administration entered Washington. Moreover, the new administration was palpably hostile to the very concept of negotiating new international economic structures and even proclaimed disbelief in the existence of the south. Administration officials repeatedly referred to the "so-called" Third World. More generally, the Reagan administration relegated international economics to a lower priority than had any administration in the postwar period. To the extent that international economics was taken into account, it was frequently subordinated to East-West conflict and perceived as a potential weapon for striking at the Soviet Union and its allies. The international affairs budget was tilted heavily toward military spending and security-oriented assistance.

International economic policy was also subordinated to domestic economic interests. This must always be true to a degree. However, in light of the growing openness of the American economy and the sharply increasing interdependence with Third World markets, international economic concerns were unusually and surprisingly subsidiary. The almost exclusive focus on domestic economic policy reflected the background of

Richard E. Feinberg is a fellow at the Overseas Development Council and an Adjunct Professor to the Landegger Program of International Business Diplomacy at Georgetown University. He has worked as an international economist at the Treasury Department and the House Banking Committee and was a member of the Policy Planning Staff of the State Department from 1977-1980. He has published articles in such journals as Foreign Affairs, Foreign Policy *and* The Washington Quarterly. *His books include* The Intemperate Zone: The Third World Challenge to U.S. Foreign Policy *(Norton, 1983);* Subsidizing Success: The Export-Import Bank in the U.S. Economy *(Cambridge University Press, 1982); and (editor)* Central America: International Dimensions of the Crisis *(Holmes and Meier, 1982).*

the Reagan team. Especially before the arrival of George Shultz as Secretary of State, the international experience of many of the administration's top economic decision makers had been only sporadic, and even fewer had in-depth knowledge of developing countries.

The Reagan administration justified its concentration on domestic economic policy on the grounds that an upright American economy would be its best contribution to global welfare. The administration perceived a United States that was still strong, perhaps dominant, not only in military but also in global economic terms. Many Reagan officials felt that the Third World was still weak, and that pandering to its demands unnecessarily inflated its power. Moreover, many administration officials believed that the Third World had only itself to blame for its poverty. The solution to underdevelopment was not to provide more welfare, but for the developing countries themselves to adopt the proven model of the United States.

Beyond seeking to contain Soviet influence, administration policy toward the Third World consisted substantially of a principled defense of select American virtues. Economic rather than political freedom was seen as more readily transmittable to the developing countries. The stimulation of indigenous capitalism became a primary United States interest in many developing nations. Especially at the level of rhetoric, the transfer of American institutions abroad was given greater attention than the advancement of tangible American economic interests. The administration did, however, seek to promote an open international environment where economic decisions responded to market signals and where American firms could prosper.

The administration scored an early diplomatic victory at Cancun, Mexico, where heads of state gathered to discuss the future of the north-south dialogue. There, Reagan emphasized the importance of his domestic economic programs. As Reaganomics faltered, however, its impact on the Third World was far different from the one envisioned at Cancun.

The administration sought to implement its free-market principles in various bilateral and multilateral institutions and supported some programs that were intended to stimulate private capital flows beyond what the market would dictate. It sought to stimulate private investment — American and indigenous — in the developing world through the Overseas Private Investment Corporation (OPIC), the Agency for International Development (AID), and the multilateral development banks. With some exceptions, the administration sought to keep American markets open to foreign commerce. The administration also resisted what it perceived as efforts by international organizations to fetter markets, or to reduce American power. The administration demonstrated its determination to combat efforts to control markets by institutions heavily influenced by the Third World when it refused to sign the Law of the Sea Treaty.

As we shall see, however, the administration's free-market rhetoric ignored important theoretical justifications for government intervention and occasionally led the administration to advance positions contrary to the interests of American business. Moreover, drawing a sharp dichotomy between the free market and government intervention is a poor guide for understanding the actual economies of Third World states and the choices open to them.

Cancun

By the end of the Carter administration, the so-called north-south dialogue had stalled. Progress had been made in some areas,[1] but the spokespersons for the south — the Group of 77 — were dissatisfied. The much-heralded "New International Economic Order" (NIEO) with its long list of recommendations for reform, had for the most part been rejected by the north. The south argued that the essential roadblock to international reform was the lack of "political will" in the north. The statesmen in the industrial West were either too preoccupied with other issues; too subservient to immediate, status-quo interests; or too intellectually narrow to enter into serious negotiations. This analysis was reflected in the report of the Brandt Commission, released at the end of 1979. The international panel composed of leaders from the north and south proposed a summit of world leaders to "forge commitments." [2] The Brandt Commission understood that a meeting of heads of state could not itself negotiate complex agreements, but it felt that a summit could "give guidelines for detailed negotiations in the appropriate international fora, settle the parameters and the format for such negotiations, and decide upon timetables for results to be reached." [3]

While the Brandt Commission was concluding its report, the Group of 77 launched a call for "global negotiations." Global negotiations were to once again take up the array of issues raised in the NIEO documents — but this time in the United Nations framework, where the Third World dominated. The initiation of a fresh round of comprehensive negotiations in a new, more favorable venue might succeed in injecting "political will" into the soured dialogue. The Carter administration balked, not wanting to enhance the power of the United Nations in international economic matters. Specifically, the administration did not want to transfer power from the specialized agencies — the International Monetary Fund, the World Bank, and the GATT, which are dominated by the industrial countries — to the more egalitarian U.N. General Assembly.

Following the suggestion of the Brandt Commission, Canada, Mexico, and Austria decided to convene a summit in Mexico City, with Mexican President José Lopez Portillo and Austrian Chancellor Bruno Kreisky as the cochairmen. The Carter administration was cool to the idea but left the final decision to the incoming administration. To the surprise of many, President Reagan decided to attend the meeting, held in the Mexican resort city of Cancun in October 1981.

Reagan's decision to attend the Cancun Summit ultimately gave the administration its greatest triumph in north-south diplomacy. The administration seemed to shift away from its initially hostile approach toward anything related to the north-south dialogue and the NIEO. Suddenly, it was willing to engage in wide-ranging discussions with southern leaders. The United States appeared amenable to expanding the field of decision makers on international economic matters from the industrial states represented at the annual economic summits to include representatives of the developing world. At Cancun, the United States even seemed willing to enter into "global negotiations," thereby acceding to what had become the south's leading proposal.

Reagan was personally pressed to attend by two of the conference's sponsors, Lopez Portillo and Canadian Prime Minister Pierre Trudeau. Since Reagan was enthusiastically talking about "North American" accords, he was sensitive to their appeal. British Prime Minister Margaret Thatcher, Reagan's ideological soul mate, also reportedly urged Reagan to participate. With the Europeans willing and in some cases even anxious to attend, the United States would have been isolated had it not gone to Cancun. Nevertheless, the United States agreed to attend only after other participants[4] had accepted several crucial preconditions. President Reagan would be happy to discuss an array of issues, but there could be no detailed negotiations, no concrete agreements on substantive issues, no final communiqué, and no Cuban presence. Moreover, the United States made clear that it would consider participating in global negotiations only if the substantive negotiations were done within the specialized agencies and the principle of weighted voting within these agencies would not be challenged. The UN might technically oversee the talks, but it could not overrule any agreements made through these agencies. The global negotiations would also have to address issues of global economic growth and efficiency, not just means whereby existing wealth could be transferred from the north to the south. Finally, the United States warned that it would not participate in negotiations that degenerated into the "sterile rhetoric and unrealistic demands" of the past.[5] The United States thereby assured that the Cancun summit would be safely ceremonial, and that any future global negotiations would be tightly circumscribed.

The United States gave away nothing at Cancun. The discussions among the heads of state were predictably general and superficial, wandering over a wide range of issues including food security, energy, commodity stabilization, and finance.[6] In the absence of precooked agreements or the expertise even to establish frameworks for future discussions, substantive progress was impossible. Thus, much of the time was consumed debating the procedural matter of where and how to begin global negotiations.

Nevertheless, the cochairmen's summary failed to pin down a firm commitment to start the global negotiations. The document noted only that a consensus had been reached "to launch Global Negotiations on a basis to be mutually agreed and in circumstances offering the prospects of meaningful progress." [7] Negotiations had still not begun by the summer of 1982.

Despite the lack of substantive or even firm procedural progress, the summit's participants generally declared the meeting a success. Why were the representatives of the south willing to accept such a paltry outcome with relative magnanimity? The explanation lies partly in adroit administration tactics and partly in the structural weakness of the southern position.

The Reagan administration's early hostility toward the north-south dialogue had sharply lowered expectations among the developing countries. With its free-market rhetoric and denunciation of the NIEO, the Reagan administration seemed to oppose almost any form of official international cooperation. Starting from this low base, merely agreeing to attend the Cancun summit was perceived as an important concession. When Reagan admitted to Tanzanian President Julius Nyerere that concessional assistance, not private investment, was appropriate for constructing basic physical infrastructure, witnesses hailed Reagan's flexibility. The Carter administration had experienced the opposite: When it failed to meet raised expectations, the south was disappointed and less willing to grant credit for the progress that was made. The Reagan administration's success was thus a product of its ability to project a generally positive if ambiguous attitude toward the summit and global negotiations while maintaining a firm position on the less visible substantive issues. Ronald Reagan was the perfect showman to implement a policy of public smiles coupled with private evasion and toughness.

Individual countries had their own reasons for not wanting to confront the United States, at least publicly. Mexico and Canada were the hosts. Venezuela was seeking a preferred relationship with Washington. India and Guyana were hoping to convince the United States to take a less hostile attitude toward loans pending in the international financial institutions. The president of Brazil was recuperating from a heart attack and unable to attend.

The time was also ripe for a thinly disguised jettisoning of the NIEO. The "threat from the Third World," which had intimidated some Western statesmen after the 1973 OPEC oil embargo and price hikes, had dissipated. Other OPEC-like organizations did not follow. For other commodities, producing states were either too weak; too divided by geography, culture, or ideology; or too divergent in interests to form an effective cartel.[8] More generally, it had become increasingly obvious that the economic interests of the 120 members of the Group of 77 were widely disparate and even contradictory. The NIEO itself was a long list of proposals that represented a least common denominator of LDC wishes. Some proposals sounded fine but were too vague to ever be implemented. Other proposals, if implemented, would actually be harmful to the interests of some of the developing states. If serious negotiations were ever to begin, the Group of 77 would find itself in sharp internal disagreement on key issues.

Moreover, as growth began to slow in many developing countries in 1979-1981, their governments became more concerned with pressing domestic adjustments and less interested in windy clarion calls for restructuring the world economy. Each government was scurrying to meet its own needs and had less time to focus on global meetings, especially if they were unlikely to provide tangible resources quickly. Many finance and economy ministers in the Third World had never expected to see most of the NIEO implemented, and were more interested in gaining access to markets and to available resources in the international financial institutions, or from bilateral agencies. As economic times worsened, their views became weightier. Finally, many economists and bureaucrats in the north and south felt that the north-south dialogue had simply run out of steam and that the new emphasis on the procedural issue of global negotiations was a dying gasp.

The Ford and Carter administrations had accepted those aspects of the NIEO that promised mutual benefits for the north and the south.[9] They were willing to increase resource transfers and even to sanction internationally controlled official intervention in markets on behalf of increased efficiency or growth. Both administrations, however, successfully resisted measures that would fundamentally shift power relations. Both, for example, maintained American voting shares in the international financial institutions and preserved the jurisdiction of these institutions over vital international financial matters. The south recognized that the United States had the institutional strength, and the will, to veto reforms. Moreover, it was the north that was expected to finance many of the NIEO proposals. Therefore, a meeting not attended by the United States was like holding a jostling match that the opponent failed to attend. You might score a few points by default, but you could not draw blood.

Whether Cancun represents the end of an era or merely an interlude between periods of north-south dialogue and debate remains to be seen. In the short run, however, it was a tactical success for the Reagan administration. At Cancun, the United States deflected pressures for international economic reform, without having to grant any substantive concessions. Moreover, the Reagan administration used Cancun to broadcast its own alternative economic message.

The Reagan Promise

Prior to traveling to Cancun, President Reagan delivered two major speeches on international economic policy. The first was addressed to the joint World Bank-International Monetary Fund annual meetings in Washington, the second to the World Affairs Council of Philadelphia. In these speeches, Reagan insisted that the best service his administration could perform for the international economy in general, and the developing nations more particularly, was to reawaken the United States economy. "No American contribution can do more for development than a growing, prosperous U.S. economy," Reagan said.[10] "And as the world's largest single market, a prosperous, growing U.S. economy will mean increased trading opportunities for other nations. Lower U.S. inflation and interest rates will translate into increased availability of financial resources at affordable rates." In short, a healthy United States economy would revitalize the world's commodity and capital markets and pull the rest of the world into what Reagan promised would be "a new era of sustained, noninflationary growth and prosperity, the likes of which we have not seen for many years."

This "America first" theme was, of course, correct in the literal sense. Steady growth in the United States would stimulate the economies of other nations. But this had been true throughout the postwar period, when administrations had demonstrated more direct concern for international economic stability and growth. Moreover, the United States economy was no longer so dominant as to be able to function alone as the engine of growth for the entire world.

The "America first" theme nevertheless served several administration purposes. First, it correctly reflected the administration's true priorities and perceptions. Domestic economic policies *were* the principal preoccupation of the White House. An improved domestic economy was seen as both the key to the administration's political fortunes and the necessary underpinning for the resurgence of American military and diplomatic strength abroad.

Top Reagan officials also tended to assume that international economics, like domestic business, was essentially a matter of each country's, or firm's, making the correct decision. If each government adhered to sound monetary policies, international coordination of macroeconomic policies was unnecessary. At the micro level, if markets were functioning without interference, there was little need for a guiding hand. Just as national governments should be minimized, so should international cooperation.

Embedded as it was in a rhetoric that played down the institutions and process of international cooperation and that emphasized traditional American virtues, the "America first" theme took on a go-it-alone tone.

The unwillingness of the administration to genuinely consult even with major European allies[11] or to take into account the likely international implications of its domestic economic policies enhanced the unilateralist flavor of Reagan's economic prescription.

Second, the "America first" theme seemed to justify the administration's desire to restrain spending for foreign assistance and other international economic matters not directly related to perceived security interests. The welfare of the Third World could better be served by balancing the United States budget than by increasing aid flows. While the actual numbers involved in foreign assistance and other international economic projects were small in comparison to the United States budget, the administration concentrated on the theoretical point. In addition, the administration repeatedly argued that foreign aid was useless in countries that failed to adopt efficient economic policies.

Finally, the "America first" theme fitted ideologically. The administration argued that the best contribution it could make to improve economic management overseas was to set an example of good management at home. In his pre-Cancun speech in Philadelphia, Reagan repeated his campaign theme that "In 1630, John Winthrop predicted that we would be a city upon a hill with the eyes of all people upon us." The Third World should follow our example, and grasp the essential truth that "free people build free markets that ignite dynamic development for everyone." Some nations have already learned the lesson. "The developing countries now growing the fastest in Asia, Africa and Latin America," Reagan noted, "are the very ones providing more economic freedom for their people — freedom to choose, to own property, to work at a job of their choice, and to invest in a dream for the future." The Reagan administration's domestic policies were aimed at rekindling John Winthrop's bright beacon to the world.

The Foreign Implications of Reaganomics

The administration's domestic economic policy had two macroeconomic targets: price stability and economic growth. The "supply-side" school promised to attain both objectives with little pain. Taxes were slashed on personal income and the corporate income tax was substantially reduced through accelerated cost recovery, sale-leaseback and other special provisions. The tax cuts were to stimulate personal savings and corporate investment. Surging economic growth would produce sufficient tax revenues to more than offset the tax cuts and to balance the federal budget (the Laffer curve effect). On top of supply-side economics, the administration pursued a reordering of national priorities that had a major impact on the federal budget. In both fiscal years 1982 and 1983, the administration cut deeply into social programs oriented toward the poor, while granting a series of tax breaks that benefited disproportionately the middle and upper classes. At the same time, the administration successfully pushed through Congress a rapid increase in authorizations for defense. Only those who believed in the extremely optimistic assumptions of the supply-side school failed to predict that the mix of tax cuts and heightened military spending would result in a widening fiscal deficit. The three-year Economic Recovery Tax Act of 1981 amounted to some $750 billion in lost revenue for the Treasury. In July 1981, the Office of Management and Budget (OMB) was insisting that federal deficits in the FY1982-1984 period would remain within the range of $50 billion, but in December 1981, OMB leaked a more realistic set of projections that foresaw the deficit rising from $109 billion in FY1982 to $162 billion in FY1984.[12]

The Federal Reserve feared that if it accommodated the fiscal deficit with an expansionary monetary policy, inflation would accelerate. Thus, the Federal Reserve sought to counter the loose fiscal policy with a tight monetary noose. The predictable result was high interest rates. The high cost of money drove the housing and auto industries into a depression and generally discouraged investment. The promised supply-side boom was choked off before it could begin.

Despite its unease, the administration hesitated to criticize Federal Reserve stringency. A priority administration objective was to reduce inflation. The administration also tended to believe that interest rates would fall rather quickly in the wake of decelerating inflation. Nevertheless, to the surprise not only of the administration but to many professional economists, interest rates remained unusually high. Real interest rates (the nominal rate adjusted for inflation) reached historic levels of 4 to 10 percent. West German Chancellor Helmut Schmidt may have been correct at the Ottawa Summit in July 1981, when he said that interest rates were at the highest levels of the Christian era. The administration blamed continuing high interest rates on the slowness of inflationary expectations to adjust. Critics argued that capital markets were responding to the fear that the anticipated large fiscal deficits foreshadowed a continuation of tight monetary policy. Tight money policy in the United States and in many Western European countries was producing a liquidity squeeze that was pushing up the cost of money (the interest rate).

Whatever the cause, the administration refused to alter its priorities. It might have eased the fiscal deficit by postponing tax cuts and slowing defense spending, thereby freeing the Federal Reserve to ease up on its monetary brake. Instead, the administration chose to ride out what had clearly become a recession, always remaining hopeful that the upturn was just around the corner.

The administration apparently paid little attention to the international implications of its policy mix. Had its earlier optimism proved correct, the adverse impact abroad might have been short-lived. But as the American economy failed to respond to supply-side medicine, the adverse international consequences of tight money deepened.

In a world of closely integrated capital markets and a huge volume of outstanding debt, high American interest rates had a profound effect. By 1982, the interest-sensitive long-term external debt of developing countries owed to private sources amounted to roughly $306 billion.[13] This excludes the large volume of loans with maturities under one year. In his Philadelphia speech, Reagan noted, "Every one percent reduction in our interest rates due to lower inflation improves the balance of payments of developing countries by $1 billion." A more likely figure would be $4 billion (1 percent of $400 billion). In its May 1981 *World Financial Markets*, Morgan Guaranty Trust Company noted: "A one percentage point change in [interest rates] now causes more of a variance in LDC financing requirements than does a one dollar change in oil prices." For non-oil developing countries, interest payments on their mounting outstanding debt rose from 5½ percent of exports of goods and services in 1978 to 8½ percent in 1981.[14]

In addition to sharply increasing the service charge on debt, high interest rates in the United States drained developing countries of their own financial resources. The net increase in foreign assets in the United States rose from $38 billion in 1979 to $78 billion in 1981.[15] Over half of the latter came in the form of short-term bank deposits (hot money), with $30 billion originating in Latin America. Moreover, American investors preferred the high-return, low-risk financial investments available at home, and America's foreign direct investment fell precipitously. Whereas global investment by United States-based multinationals had reached $25 billion in 1979, it fell to $18.5 billion in 1980 and to under $9 billion in 1981.[16] The growth of commercial bank lending also slowed.

To stem this hemorrhaging of liquid capital, many developing countries were forced to raise their own interest rates. The setting of positive, real interest rates was a desirable development in some countries where the repression of interest rates had discouraged savings and hindered the efficient allocation of investment. But the sudden and sharp rise in interest rates added another contractionary element on top of a depressing debt overhang and a recessionary global economy.

As growth in the industrial countries slowed to 1 percent during 1980-1982, the volume of their imports stagnated, and they even declined by 2.3 percent in 1981.[17] The prices of primary commodities slumped dramatically, and the terms of trade turned against the developing world. Non-oil developing countries faced a deterioration in the earnings of their exports relative to their imports of approximately 9 percent during 1980-1982.

The impact of high world interest rates and stagnation in trade drained capital from developing countries while making it harder for them to earn foreign exchange. The current accounts of the non-oil LDCs, already reeling under the 1979 oil price rise, deteriorated further. Aggregate deficits rose from $59 billion in 1979 to $99 billion in 1981, with little hope for rapid recovery. Commercial lenders became increasingly alarmed at the deteriorating situation of many LDCs, a concern compounded by the general uncertainty of the international environment. Bankers responded by increasing the spread (the premium over a reference market interest rate) charged to many LDC borrowers, while limiting the growth of new exposure. LDCs were thus deprived of the mechanism they had used to avoid the full impact of the 1974-1975 recession in the industrial nations. This time around, the LDCs could not borrow enough funds to cover current account deficits that were consistent with healthy GNP growth rates. LDCs were forced to adjust to a contracting global economy by cutting their demand for imports and finance — that is, by reducing the levels of domestic economic activity. Output growth in the non-oil developing countries fell to a postwar low of 2.5 percent in 1981, a level insufficient to maintain per capita income in many countries. Thus, the world was gripped by the downward spiral.

The bright dream painted by Reagan at Cancun had turned into a nightmare as the worldwide recession spread and deepened. It would be unfair to blame the Reagan administration for all the ills besetting the global economy in the early 1980s. The administration did, however, turn a deaf ear to those arguing for a new policy mix to alleviate at least some of the adverse international repercussions of Reaganomics.

The Magic of the Market

The administration's domestic stabilization policy was only one element in a broader economic strategy. The administration also held to a structural view of how secular growth occurred. As Reagan stated: "The societies which have achieved the most spectacular, broad-based economic progress ... [are those that] believe in the magic of the market place." [18] The administration tended to equate market mechanisms with private ownership. Individual entrepreneurs, responding to unfettered market signals, would make the most efficient decisions.

In advocating the virtues of market mechanisms, the Reagan administration was, to a degree, knocking against an open door. Many developing country governments had come to acknowledge that some forms of government intervention were ultimately too costly or even counterproductive. Aspects of the import substitution industrialization model, widely adopted in the Third World, were being discarded. To propel industrialization, countries had erected high tariff barriers, overvalued their exchange rates, and repressed agricultural prices. National industry developed, but agriculture often lagged behind domestic demand, exports languished, and balance of payments crises became chronic. Many countries were now seeking to adjust their exchange rates, to rationalize or lower import barriers, to allow interest rates to rise, and to release prices paid to farmers. The intention was to make industry more efficient and able to compete in international markets while stimulating agriculture.

The Reagan administration's rhetoric did not seem, however, to value such marginal reforms. Little to no room was left for government action. In projecting this categorically antistatist view, the administration exposed itself to two types of criticisms. Even in a static, neoclassical model, government has an important role. Moreover, in the dynamic, structuralist view of development, government must perform crucial functions.

Static Welfare

According to neoclassical theory, welfare is maximized in a free market environment where factors of production move freely in response to prices to maximize their marginal products. In the cases of "public goods" and "externalities," however, government intervention may be necessary to correct "market failures" if welfare is to be maximized. Public goods are those goods and services that cannot be provided to an individual or group without being available to a larger population. Nonpayers cannot be excluded from consumption, and the extension of benefits to additional users involves no additional costs. Thus, even where private firms might be willing to produce some of the public goods, production will fall short of socially optimal amounts. Defense, health care, and public parks are examples of public goods.

An "external economy" or "diseconomy" occurs when the actions of a producer or consumer confer as a by-product a benefit (or harm) on others without imposing an appropriate cost (or compensating payment). Divergencies thus arise between private profitability and the net benefit to society. Physical infrastructure projects, such as roads, electric power, and water supply tend to yield positive externalities. Educational systems typically bring societal returns greater than the benefits that accrue to the individual. Pollution is an example of a diseconomy.

Many activities undertaken by governments can be justified by either the public good or externality rationales. The administration did, at times, recognize that the public sector has a legitimate purpose. In his Philadelphia speech, Reagan admitted that "[g]overnment and private enterprise complement each other. They have, can and must continue to co-exist and cooperate." [19] But such lines seemed misplaced in speeches that labeled government action as seeking "to compel, command and coerce people into submission and dependence."

Dynamic Intervention [20]

In many countries, public and private sectors recognize the advantages in a marriage that is positively interdependent and mutually supportive.[21] The exact nature of the relationship is dynamic, changing as a country passes through the various stages of development. Initially, the state builds ports and roads, educates an urban work force, and protects fledgling industries from foreign competition. Only the state can gather the resources to undertake major projects. As development progresses, the state is pressed to increase its technical and financial support to firms. Once, the state protected them against foreign competition. As the firms mature, governmental aid is required still again when the country is capable of constructing the expensive and technologically advanced capital goods industries.[22] Moreover, as the developing nations become more tightly integrated into the increasingly competitive global economy, government involvement in industrial policy intensifies. Proponents of official activism argue coherently that only an aggressive state can hope to overcome the advantages of developed-country firms with their historic head start and their access to subsidies from their own governments.

The state and the private sector in industrial and developing countries can work harmoniously and pragmatically to fullfill each other's priorities. Most American businessmen, at least in large firms, understand this. In a survey whose primary respondents were American business leaders, the overwhelming majority favored an active federal role in promoting the reindustrialization of the United States.[23] The same survey asked, "Should the U.S. encourage LDCs to rely primarily on private development capital?" Forty-two percent disagreed, and only fourteen percent expressed full agreement with such a doctrinaire strategy.[24]

Margaret Thatcher and Ronald Reagan notwithstanding, the clear trend in industrial states is toward governments trying to steer the course of their economies' industrial development. The costs and risks associated with rapid technological change cannot be absorbed by private firms. The complexity and the size of investments now required in some industries argue for an increasing government role. Private enterprise, by itself, may hesitate to risk massive amounts of capital when profits will not be returned for many years. This may be especially true in industries in which other governments subsidize competing firms.[25] Moreover, the quickening pace of international competition compels governments to assist their "sunrise" firms and to soften the impact of foreign competition on "sunset" industries.

"Industrial policy" is a euphemism for the use of government instruments to alter economic structures. Sometimes the policies are planned and consistent, sometimes ad hoc and conflicting. Nonetheless, industrial policies are commonplace in advanced and developing countries. One in-depth study of eight world industries — tobacco, food processing, pharmaceuticals, autos, tractors, tires, electrical machinery, and steel — confirms this trend. It found that "[i]n almost every industry, governments in both home countries and host countries played an important role in shaping industries' development." [26] A separate study calculated that the governments of the United Kingdom, West Germany, France, and Sweden by the mid-1970s were all involved in approximately a quarter or more of total manufacturing investment and research and development. Governmental participation took the form of grants, special loans, loan guarantees and tax reductions. It included small business assistance, sectoral and regional policies, and export promotion. For example, in West Germany, supposedly a bastion of laissez-faire economics, the Ministry of Economics has assisted sectors in structural decline (coal mining, steel, shipbuilding, and textiles) to rationalize their holdings by preserving only their competitive segments.[27] The Ministry for Research and Technology has the task of actively promoting high-technology, knowledge-intensive industries. This conscious national industrial policy is orchestrated to restructure the economy away from firms that cannot be defended against superior foreign competition and toward world-class industries.

Just as capitalist economies do not meet the free-market ideal, socialist states no longer blindly reproduce Stalinist centralization, heavy industrialization, and agricultural collectivization. Indeed, in theory and increasingly in practice, socialists are experimenting with different mixes of centralization/decentralization and of public/private ownership. From China to Nicaragua, socialists are discovering the virtues of market mechanisms. While convergence between capitalist and socialist forms is incomplete, the dichotomy is certainly less stark than ideologues in both camps care to admit.

Most Third World countries that call themselves socialist still contain large private sectors. India, Zambia, Somalia, Egypt under Nasser, and Jamaica under Manley have all proclaimed socialism while permitting a substantial, perhaps still dominant private sector to go on conducting business. The clenched fists and the rhetoric may be Marxist, but the working hands and the politics are often mildly reformist.

Yet even in countries where the leadership is more seriously socialist in the Marxist tradition, the trend is toward pragmatic experimentation. Outside of Eastern Europe, few governments (even when led by self-defined Marxist parties) now seek to nationalize fully their means of production. In Angola, Algeria, and Nicaragua, for example, important sectors of the economy are in private hands. Moreover, even in states with strong public ownership, there is a definite trend toward locating power in the nationalized firms themselves. The hope is that decentralized decision making will be more efficient. Interestingly, the definition of "efficiency" that socialist managers normally accept approximates the capitalist definition. Efficiency is equated with minimizing costs and maximizing net revenue — in other words, with making a profit.

These tendencies toward decentralization and toward efficiency criteria are the result of several converging trends that are gripping Eastern Europe and many developing countries. First, the dynamics of international competition are establishing a demanding yardstick to measure performance. Second, the stagflation afflicting the global economy since 1974 adds further pressure on governments to give efficiency priority over ideology. Third, those who would benefit from decentralization and efficiency add their personal interests to the pressures for reform emanating from the global economy. Decentralization transfers power from government and party bureaucrats toward the managers, technocrats, and skilled workers in firms. Efficiency criteria argue that the latter group ought to be given greater economic incentives; for example, higher salaries, bonuses, and perhaps even access to Westernized consumption styles. Finally, movement toward decentralization of economic decision making dilutes the power of the central bureaucracy and opens space for political relaxation.

Therefore, under these various pressures, many socialist states have been moving not toward communism but toward the capitalist criteria of efficiency, decentralized decision making, less equal income distribution, and an openness to international trade. While these phenomena seem to be accelerating, they are not brand new. In the late 1940s and early 1950s, Yugoslavia was already experimenting in these directions. In the late 1960s, Hungary began to increase the power of firm managers and opened its economy to foreign trade. By 1980, Hungary was earning half its export income in the West and was bringing domestic prices into line with world prices. Small-scale private business also has been encouraged to provide services that would be inefficiently performed by larger, more bureaucratic organizations. Today China,[28] Poland, and to a lesser extent Cuba are in the throes of the same impulse toward reform.

In industrialized and developing countries, whether they are market-oriented or statist, nationalized firms are under mounting pressure to be self-financing. Tight government budgets no longer provide these firms with fat subsidies. With financial soundness as the operating guideline, nationalized firms begin behaving like privately owned firms. For example, Alain Chalandon, the chief executive of the French state-controlled, oil-based conglomerate, Société-Nationale Elf Aquitaine, candidly admitted: "Elf does business in exactly the same way as a private enterprise and with the same motivations: to make money, to expand, to succeed."[29] Neither Marxist nor capitalist ideologues have wanted to recognize this convergence. If public sector firms are governed by efficiency criteria, they no longer seem to be a panacea for capitalism's ills; nor are they the cancers choking off healthy economic growth that capitalism's eulogists regularly diagnose.

American Financial Interests

The Reagan administration's motivation for urging the rest of the world to adopt free-market mechanisms generally seemed more moral than material. If nations would accept this disinterested advice, the benefits would be theirs to enjoy. Nevertheless, the implication was strong, and sometimes made explicit, that American firms were being severely handicapped by the nationalist policies of foreign governments. Certainly, many United States-based multinationals could have done better with less statist intervention. Nevertheless, in the global environment of hybrid mixes of public and private sector activity, American lenders and investors have found ample outlet for their capital and technology.

Nationalizations and public sector interventions have not prevented American firms from expanding their Third World operations. In fact, the trade and international investment activities of American firms have been growing more rapidly than their purely domestic operations. The ability of multinational corporations (MNCs) to adapt to changing circumstances in the Third World has contributed to their success. When many LDCs erected tariff walls against MNC products, the MNCs leapfrogged the barriers by successfully establishing local subsidiaries. Multinational pharmaceutical firms, for example, set up shop in dozens of LDCs, including Costa Rica, India, Pakistan and Sri Lanka. As governments began to demand an equal voice through participation, MNCs learned to live profitably with joint ventures. Where LDCs created state monopolies (as Brazil, Mexico, India, and Turkey did in steel), MNCs entered into licensing, managing, and trading arrangements. Where countries have pressured firms to increase the use of local components, or to export, the multinationals' purchasing and marketing networks have expanded and often become more aggressive.

Indeed, the multinationals have been able to turn each successive set of demands, even those that at first appeared onerous or prohibitive, into advantages. Forced by tariffs to substitute local production for trade, MNCs proceeded to establish a solid presence in the host countries' economy and society. Under the old regime, LDCs could curtail imports of consumer goods when foreign exchange was scarce; but once local production was in place, thousands of local jobs were dependent upon the firms' good health. Governments became obligated to supply the subsidiaries with the required intermediate imports so that local production could continue. The network of workers and consumers that surrounded the subsidiaries acted as a local pressure group on the firms' behalf. Thus, in Allende's Chile, while the old-fashioned copper companies were confiscated outright, manufacturing subsidiaries were treated with care, and the MNCs were often encouraged to maintain their operations.

A rising percentage of foreign investment is being concentrated in such manufacturing firms. They are less visible than large natural resource complexes and so are less likely to become the target of nationalist ire. Even where pressures mount on manufacturing subsidiaries to export a portion of their production to earn foreign exchange, it ultimately benefits the firm, since the subsidiary — and the host country — only become more tightly integrated into the MNCs global operations.

Naturally, multinationals complain loudly about host country policies on taxation, performance criteria, price fixing, credit restrictions, limitations on the amount of profits that can leave the country, and a whole variety of other regulations. Nevertheless, as long as the investment is sufficiently profitable and the business climate is stable, the firms will generally accommodate. As a study of MNC's conducted for the business-oriented Committee for Economic Development concluded, "Multinational corporations now tend to be less ideological and more pragmatic and flexible in their approach to operations in the developing world. . . . By and large, the multinationals understand and accept this [interventionist] role for the governments of developing countries." [30]

The multinationals have also learned to do business in countries with a wide variety of political institutions and ideologies. The Committee for Economic Development study, which surveyed 400 subsidiaries, found that "the transnationals said that if the terms of operation are clear and stable, they can operate in almost any situation, no matter how stringent the regulations, as long as some margin for profit exists. As an example, they pointed to their subsidiaries in Eastern Europe." [31]

The expansion of American bank lending abroad has been even more dramatic. The exposure of American banks and their overseas subsidiaries had reached $287 billion by the end of 1980, $97 billion of which was in developing countries.[32] Banks are even more flexible than direct investors in their willingness to do business in diverse political environments. Indeed, banks have tended to view strong governments as being better sovereign risks. Witness the $60 billion in commercial credits outstanding to Eastern Europe at the end of 1980. Moreover, in making their portfolio choices in more capitalist-oriented countries, banks often lend heavily to government institutions. With their preferred access to government favors and foreign exchange, public sector agencies are a better risk. For example, of the $13.6 billion lent by American banks to Brazil at the end of 1979, $4.1 billion were to government entities.[33]

As a result of the boom in bank lending and the rise in interest rates, bank income in the Third World has soared. In 1980, interest income reached $10.4 billion, outstripping the $7.6 billion in profits earned by nonpetroleum investments.[34] One could, of course, debate whether it is in the American national interest for American capital to have profitable foreign outlets. In any event, the emergence of commercial banks provides American investors with a highly flexible avenue for capital outflow, one capable of adapting to almost any political environment. From the point of view of American financial interests overseas, the Reagan administration's emphasis on the conflict between the public and private sectors was, if not irrelevant, certainly exaggerated and misplaced.

Implementation

Given the administration's misconceptions about the realities of the development process, the complex, dynamic interaction between public and private sectors, and the actual status of private sector activities, it is not surprising that the administration began with few, if any, concrete ideas as to how to put into practice its rhetoric in favor of the private sector. Was the administration talking about correcting market failures, and/or obtaining treatment for American subsidiaries that was equivalent to that extended to national firms? If so, its approach would differ more in spirit than in theory from that of the Carter administration. Or was the Reagan administration in favor of actively subsidizing the export of American investment capital? Alternatively, was the administration really talking about fostering indigenous capitalists? If so, should that be done by concentrating on altering nations' treatment of private investment or by directly assisting local firms? Finally, what instruments might the United States have to implement any of these policies?

The administration did not clearly answer these policy questions. At the level of strategy, it tended to emit contradictory signals. Some officials argued that American policy was still neutral toward international capital flows, while others seemed intent upon directly encouraging foreign investment. State Department officials maintained that nations are free to choose their own development models, whereas the Treasury Department clearly preferred to pressure countries toward a private sector orientation.[35] Lacking clear guidelines, it was not surprising that, at the level of operations, the bureaucracy would opt for a scatter-shot approach, trying to do a little of each. Actual initiatives had to be modest, since the administration was not prepared to place substantial resources behind its rhetoric in favor of the private sector.

Two institutions already existed for the purpose of stimulating foreign investment in the Third World. The bilateral Overseas Private Investment Corporation (OPIC) offers political risk insurance, and small amounts of financing and guarantees to American subsidiaries. The International Finance Corporation (IFC), a member of the World Bank Group, provides equity and technical assistance to ventures in the Third World that involve private capital, foreign and domestic.

In the past, neither institution had been very dynamic. During the years from FY1978-1980, OPIC assisted projects with a total American investment of only $1.7 billion,[36] while the IFC made investments of $1.4 billion.[37]

The Reagan administration sought to expand these two programs. The administration successfully supported an amendment to OPIC's legislative mandate relaxing restrictions on doing business in the wealthier developing countries. The volume of insurance written by OPIC jumped by one-third in FY1981 and again expanded substantially in FY1982. The

IFC expanded its activities 19 percent in FY1981. Despite American prodding, however, IFC investments in FY1982 actually fell below FY1980 levels.

Both programs remain modest in terms of global investment flows. The ability of these programs to effectively stimulate foreign investment is limited by institutional and operational constraints. Both strive to maintain their own profitability and to seek a diversified portfolio. They hesitate, therefore, to undertake risky or very large projects. Moreover, it is not easy to find projects that are considered good investments but which foreign investors would not find attractive without an OPIC or IFC presence. If a project is clearly attractive, the foreign investor may feel that it is not worth paying OPIC's insurance premiums; but if the project is truly risky, the official presence may be an insufficient inducement. Analytically, it is difficult to determine the degree to which the official guarantee or financing has generated additional private investment that would not have been forthcoming otherwise. If the United States exerts pressure for a rapid expansion of OPIC or the IFC, the danger is greater that projects will be supported that would have gone forward in any event.

The administration also seized upon one other existing program that fosters not direct equity investment but commercial banking lending. The World Bank, and to a much lesser degree the regional development banks, had been stimulating international lending through various cofinancing techniques since the mid-1970s. Rather than financing the entire project itself, the multilateral development bank (MDB) finances only a portion, leaving another portion to be financed by private lending. Cofinancing is intended to permit the MDBs to gain greater mileage from their own limited resources and to stimulate private international capital flows into the Third World. Cofinancing is a response both to the constraints on concessional assistance budgets and the greater availability of private finance.

The Reagan administration voiced its support for an expansion of MDB cofinancing. The new president of the World Bank, A. W. Clausen, had been president of the Bank of America and was already disposed to move in the same direction. Clausen urged the World Bank staff to generate more "bankable" projects and initiated an information campaign to make bankers in the United States, Western Europe, and Japan more aware of cofinancing opportunities.

Nevertheless, only sixteen World Bank projects were coupled with private cofinancing in FY1982, five less than in FY1980, when a record twenty-one projects were authorized. The volume of private cofinance in FY1982 reached an estimated $2.8 billion, or $1 billion more than in either of the two previous years, but most of the increase was accounted for by a single project, an Ivory Coast petroleum refinery. Even with this increase, World Bank-associated private cofinance remained a small fraction of total private bank credit extended to LDCs: under 2 percent of the $123 billion in new short-, medium-, and long-term credits disbursed in 1981.[38] Moreover, development bank cofinancing remained small compared to the volume of private loans cofinanced or guaranteed by national export promotion agencies. The U.S. Eximbank alone supported projects with private cofinancing of an estimated $2.8 billion in FY1981 and insured $7.4 billion in private trade credits.[39]

The growth of MDB cofinancing was retarded by certain attitudes of each of the parties involved — the development banks, the commercial banks and the borrowing countries. The MDBs sometimes insisted on a reduction in spread on cofinanced loans, to the disgust of the commercial banks. The MDBs argued that since the risk involved in a project that had been carefully assessed and backed by an MDB was less, the interest charge should be shaved. The commercial banks responded that interest margins were already narrow enough, and the MDBs were neither directly guaranteeing the private loan nor willing to sign a mandatory cross-default clause. The voluntary cross-default clauses left the MDBs with the discretion to not call in their own loan if the borrower defaulted against the private creditor. The World Bank feared that mandatory cross-default clauses would compromise its independence, too closely associate it with creditors, and potentially drag it into reschedulings. The World Bank felt that its record of never having rescheduled a loan was important to maintaining its triple-A bond rating. Neither the World Bank nor the LDCs favored direct guarantees, since the Bank's charter required that such guarantees be charged on a one-to-one ratio against loan authority; that is, guarantees would substitute for concessional loans. The commercial banks complained that the MDBs took much too long to design and approve projects. Furthermore, the commercial banks tended not to be interested in projects in the poorer "uncreditworthy" developing countries. The borrowing countries naturally preferred to maximize the share of concessional finance and feared that the private participation, rather than being additional, was replacing low-interest aid. Both the MDBs and the LDCs worried that the private cofinance would have been forthcoming in any event, if not for the particular project in question than for another one in the same country. Knowledgeable commercial and investment bankers warned that cofinancing would not dramatically increase unless some of these obstacles could be overcome.[40] Gradual but not spectacular increases in cofinancing seem the most likely projection.

Beyond expanding existing programs, the administration launched several new programs to stimulate foreign investment. As part of the Caribbean Basin Initiative, the United States Business Commission on Jamaica, known as the Rockefeller Commission after its chairman, David

Rockefeller, sought to interest American firms in Jamaica. Recently elected Jamaican Prime Minister Edward Seaga was a darling of the Reagan White House, and Reagan repeatedly referred to Jamaica as an economic miracle in the making. The administration sought to lend support to the Rockefeller Commission's efforts by closely identifying with the Seaga government and by increasing bilateral and multilateral assistance. Many businessmen visited Jamaica, but the commission admitted that, at least initially, the number of projects actually begun was disappointing. Businessmen complained about lack of physical infrastructure and skilled personnel, bureaucratic red tape, and continued political uncertainty. They noted that six years of recession in Jamacia had left the island with excess capacity, and export markets were depressed because of the global recession.

The administration decided to go beyond the jawboning approach of the Rockefeller Commission and proposed that American firms investing in the Caribbean and Central America could claim a credit against their total tax liabilities for an amount equal to 10 percent of new investment in plant and equipment. But the proposed investment tax credit ran into opposition in Congress from the AFL-CIO as a stimulus to "runaway shops." The administration also seemed to cool to the idea, according to one official because new calculations indicated that the tax credit would not generate much additional investment.[41] The proposal seemed likely to wither in Congress.

The Reagan administration's natural impulse was to turn the Agency for International Development (AID) into an instrument to promote the private sector. Some of the Reagan appointees, taking a cue from their domestic agency counterparts, declared that many of the poverty-oriented programs of the 1970s "frankly, haven't worked." [42] They tended to paint basic needs projects as short-lived consumption subsidies, although many had actually been designed to create employment and increase productivity.

AID officials announced that they would concentrate not on income redistribution but on wealth generation, not on inefficient and coercive public sector projects but on private sector development. Initially, AID officials had few ideas of how to put this rhetoric into practice, and it appeared as though old-style basic needs projects would simply be relabeled. Thus, projects previously described as targeted at the "rural poor" became projects designed "to assist small agricultural entrepreneurs." Since the end users of most AID projects had, in fact, always been private producers or consumers, the bureaucracy had little difficulty in placing old wine in new bottles.

By Reagan's second year, however, AID began to announce new programs that could fundamentally change the nature of the institution. AID would assist not only small farmers but also agroindustry, finance privately owned development finance companies that on-lend to private firms, encourage the growth of capital markets, and itself make investments in private firms.[43] A special Bureau for Private Enterprise was established, with a modest annual budget of $26 million, to advise governments on how to create a favorable investment climate and to support appropriate projects itself. A Trade and Development Program was initiated to locate projects of interest to American exporters and investors. Moreover, governments judged unwilling to work harmoniously with private capital would receive less aid. AID spokespersons claimed that their main focus was the indigenous private sector, but at least some programs were interested in promoting joint ventures with American capital. While some of these directions were not entirely new, the swerve away from projects oriented directly toward the poor majority was striking. It was unclear to what extent these programs and bureaus would reorient the entire agency.

The policy shift faces several obstacles. First, AID has had difficulty interesting American business. AID has a reputation for being bureaucratic and not particularly astute or businesslike. Large firms find the available resources almost ridiculously tiny and not worth the potential political hazards of being associated with a United States government agency. Attracting smaller American firms will require more time, effort, and ingenuity. Second, AID may be trying to do too much with limited resources. The budget for development loans, at $1.8 billion in FY1983, is not growing in real terms. It is spread thin in many countries and, now, among a widening variety of contrasting projects. Third, AID runs the risk of becoming redundant. OPIC (which was originally a spinoff of AID) and the IFC already foster foreign and indigenous private investment, the Eximbank and the Commerce Department promote American exports, and the multilateral development banks and the International Monetary Fund offer advice on capital market development and private sector stimulation. Fourth, if AID is seen as a subsidy to business, it could lose its most important domestic constituency among liberals. Ultimately, a crisis of identity and legitimacy could destroy the agency. From the perspective of some Reaganites, so long as the security-oriented programs were retained, this might not be an unwelcome outcome.

In summary, the effort to implement the private sector rhetoric had mixed results. A weak grasp of the theory and practice of private enterprise, lack of clear priorities, budgetary constraints, and institutional rigidities were among the obstacles that hindered progress. Most important, the global recession outweighed any official stimuli the Reagan administration could offer to investors. At ehe same time, the administration discovered that it had inherited several programs that were already dedicated to stimulating private capital and strove, with varying degrees of success, to sharpen and expand their operations. These programs may have some impact on select firms and countries. It seemed unlikely, however, that the administration would be able to remake the world in its own image.

Trade

In advocating the free movement of goods and services across international borders, the Reagan administration reaffirmed American faith in an open world trading system. The administration did not move unilaterally to reduce American barriers to trade, as a pure free-market as opposed to bargaining approach to international trade might dictate, but with some exceptions, it did avoid imposing new restrictions on the access of LDC products to the American market.[44]

Consistent with free trade views, the administration took a cool view toward the Common Fund. Adopted in principle in June, 1980, the Fund was to pool the financial resources of various commodity agreements in order to stabilize commodity prices and to assure a steadier flow of financial resources to commodity-exporting developing nations. The administration decided to honor American commitments to the individual commodity agreements, although it refused to sign the Sixth International Tin Agreement.[45] Viewing the Eximbank as a trade-distorting subsidy, the Office of Management and Budget tightened its lending limits, and the Treasury pressed the Europeans to negotiate a meaningful international agreement to restrain export credit subsidies. Despite heavy lobbying by the shoe industry, the orderly marketing quotas on shoes that were negotiated in 1978 were allowed to expire in the Spring of 1981, opening the American market to Taiwanese and Korean producers.

The administration initially took a liberal position during the negotiations on the renewal of the important Multifiber Agreement (MFA). The United States defended those clauses that allowed imports to grow faster than domestic consumption, while the Europeans pressed for greater restrictions. To gain votes for its FY1982 federal budget, however, the administration bowed to pressures from the domestic textile industry and agreed to restrict the rate of textile import growth to the rate of domestic market growth. This was still more liberal than the European position, which interprets the new protocol as allowing for reductions in imports. Actual levels must be hammered out in bilateral agreements.

A bargain struck with domestic sugar producers, also to gain their support for the administration's FY1982 budget, ultimately came into conflict with free trade principles. When the world price of sugar suddenly plummeted, it would have become unexpectedly expensive to maintain the support price that the administration had promised domestic producers. The administration opted for a reinstitution of a quota system as the less expensive way to limit sugar imports.

The textile and sugar policies compromised the administration's highly publicized proposal for a Free Trade Area (FTA) for the Caribbean and Central America. The FTA offered a unilateral reduction in United States tariffs to "non-Communist" Caribbean Basin nations. The potential impact of the FTA on the targeted region was debatable, since 87 percent of the region's exports already entered the United States duty free, and Congress threatened to exclude other items beyond textiles and sugar.[46] Conscious that this unilateral offer represented a major departure from traditional American trade strategy of bargaining global agreements in a multilateral framework, the administration certified that it would not be repeated elsewhere.

The administration did have an agenda for further trade liberalization in the General Agreement on Tariffs and Trade (GATT). United States Trade Representative William Brock wanted the GATT to take up areas where other nations were inhibiting American exports: non-tariff barriers, trade in services (including insurance, shipping, consultancy, and data processing), and agriculture. The administration also wanted to curb the use of "performance criteria" under which host countries require foreign investors to use local components and meet prescribed export targets. The climate for further trade liberalization, however, seemed poor. Moreover, the United States did not seem prepared to make concessions of its own.

While the administration adhered reasonably well to free trade principles, several of its policies threatened to increase domestic pressures for protectionism. The administration endorsed the vague principle of bilateral reciprocity. If taken seriously, "reciprocity" could be interpreted as conflicting with the "special and differential" treatment accorded developing nations. For example, some argued that Mexican truckers should not be allowed on American highways unless American truckers receive equivalent rights. The administration privately justified its rhetorical acceptance of reciprocity as a means of applying pressure to American trading partners, especially Japan, and of deflecting mounting domestic demands for protectionism; but the maneuver could backfire if American trading partners are not seen to be making sufficient concessions.

High unemployment and the global recession, to which administration policies contributed, were basic sources of protectionist pressures. The administration nevertheless slashed Trade Adjustment Assistance from levels near $1 billion in 1981 down to some $200 million in FY1982. While the program was clearly in need of reforms that would concentrate on helping displaced workers find new jobs, the administration chose instead to demolish it. The administration's general distaste for policies that could assist firms and workers to adjust to foreign competition was consistent with belief in market mechanisms; but in the real world, rigid reliance on markets at home could allow protectionist pressures to build that would eventually swamp free-trade advocates and lead to the dismantling of the liberal international order.

International Regulation

In many areas, the Reagan administration's foreign economic policy was a projection into the international sphere of impulses derived from domestic experiences. Reaganites had reacted strongly against the wave of federal regulations governing business conduct promulgated since the New Deal, and especially since the consumer protection movement of the late 1960s and 1970s. These objections were borne of ideological preferences for market mechanisms based on a concern that regulations reduced business production and profits. Not wanting to see international versions of the Federal Trade Commission or Consumer Protection Agency harassing American firms abroad, the administration refused to join either the Law of the Sea or the United Nations code governing the marketing of infant formula. The administration also relaxed controls on the export of hazardous substances and supported initiatives in Congress to limit the Foreign Corrupt Practices Act.

Eight years in the drafting, the Law of the Sea Treaty was completed in April 1980. A complex and comprehensive document, the Treaty established the metallic nodules lying under the oceans as "the common heritage of mankind." The nickel, copper, cobalt, and zinc nuggets would be mined by consortia of private companies and by an official global mining enterprise. The treaty also fixed a universal territorial limit 12 miles out to sea and an "exclusive economic zone" 200 miles out. The intention was to end fishing wars and to establish rights of safe passage for merchant and military ships and planes.

Proponents of the treaty argued that establishing the rules of the game would provide safety and predictability to private mining firms. Moreover, the treaty gave each nation exclusive right to oil and gas 350 miles beyond its coast. Since these resources were more immediately accessible and were plentiful off the United States coasts, these provisions should outweigh the restrictions on deep seabed mining. Moreover, without a treaty, mining consortia would have no clear title to ocean mines, and commercial banks might not extend the necessary credit. Finally, the Pentagon welcomed the guarantees for unimpeded passage through strategic straits.

Despite having gained some last-minute alterations in the draft treaty, the administration voted against it on April 30, 1982. The only other countries voting no — Israel, Turkey, and Venezuela — did so out of parochial reasons that did not concern seabed mining. The administration objected to restrictions on access to mining sites by private firms, production quotas for deep seabed mining ventures, and a provision calling for the mandatory transfer of mining technology from private firms to the official enterprise. The administration also felt that the United States was not given adequate influence in the seabed's new governing authority.[47]

The International Code of Breastmilk Substitutes was endorsed by the World Health Organization (WHO) in May 1981, with the United States alone dissenting. The code's proponents argued that poor Third World parents misuse the formula by overly diluting it; moreover, they do not have access to clean drinking water needed to mix with the formula. The code does not prohibit selling infant formula, but it does instruct governments to restrict its marketing.

American formula makers and producers and merchandisers of other baby foods opposed the code. The State Department Assistant Secretary for International Organizations, Elliot Abrams, explained the principles behind the American dissent:

> The United States is very much opposed to such regulation...by U.N. bodies. The Code in addition interferes with the role of health professionals in dealing with their parents by assigning to governments — not doctors — the central role in informing families about infant feeding. Once again, assigning more and more tasks to the state is a practice favored by many nations, but not one that the United States wishes to encourage by a yes vote.[48]

The negative votes on the Law of the Sea and the infant formula code demonstrated the administration's willingness to stand on principle against world opinion. The votes illustrated the depth of the administration's antipathy to "world order" regulations and institutions and to the sharing of power with Third World states. The votes also suggested the permeability of the administration to narrow business interests. The American posture, however, was not necessarily in the long-run interests of American business. Without a seabed mining treaty, American firms may lack the security and the financing to proceed. And, to the extent that the image of American capitalism is important in the struggle of ideas — a struggle the administration itself deems vital — the rejection of the infant formula code is counterproductive.

The Multilateral Financial Institutions

High-level Reagan appointees to the Treasury Department and the Office of Management and Budget came to Washington with a strong suspicion of the multilateral development banks. An early draft OMB memo accused the World Bank of promoting income redistribution. Indeed, the extreme Right, in Congress, the Heritage Foundation, and elsewhere, had been accusing former World Bank president Robert McNamara of fostering socialism in the Third World.[49] They also tended to view the World Bank and the smaller regional development banks as welfare handouts akin to the domestic programs the administration was determined to slash. Moreover, since the United States had, allegedly, been losing influence in the multilateral banks, they no longer adequately served American security interests.

As senior administration officials came into contact with the multilateral agencies, their own subordinates in the permanent civil service, and their foreign counterparts, their views were softened. The Treasury Department spent a full year in preparing a major study of the multilateral banks, dubbed "the education of Beryl Sprinkel" for the turnabout it appeared to represent in the thinking of the Chicago School Under Secretary for Monetary Affairs. The Treasury assessment, entitled *United States Participation in the Multilateral Development Banks in the 1980s*,[50] directly refuted charges that the MDBs had been providing mere handouts, fostering socialism, or failing to support American political interests. Indeed, the official report was unusually candid in its discussion of American clout in the banks. "A total of fourteen significant issues were identified for a detailed review of how effectively the United States was able to influence the MDBS over the last ten years.... [T]he results were judged fully successful ... in nine instances. We were partially successful in three instances and failed in two of the cases studied.[51] The report concluded that the MDBs contribute to American global economic objectives by encouraging developing countries to participate more fully in an international system based on liberalized trade and capital flows. American commercial objectives were served by the expanded opportunities for American exports, investment, and finance. American political and strategic objectives were advanced by the MDBs' contribution to steady economic growth, which reduces the likelihood of political instability. Moreover, the country allocation of MDB loans had generally been compatible with American foreign policy preferences.

Thus spoke the permanent bureaucracies at Treasury and State, in words apparently convincing to their political superiors. Where Reaganite opinions proved more obdurate, however, was in the budgetary recommendations. The administration called for a major reduction, of roughly 30 to 45 percent in real terms, in American contributions to the "soft-loan" windows of the MDBs. Their highly concessional loans are concentrated in the poorer LDCs. The hard-loan windows, which require less donor government financing, could continue to grow, but at reduced rates. The Treasury report simply argued that, however worthwhile the MDBs might be, American budgetary constraints required cutbacks.

The administration also recommended specific reforms that, while being fully consistent with administration thinking, would enable the MDBs to be more effective with less money. The proposals, for the most part, were not departures from current practices but gave greater emphasis and urgency to select, existing MDB directions. The wealthier developing countries should "graduate" out of the MDBs, since their creditworthiness gave them access to private capital markets. The MDBs themselves should assist countries to develop private capital markets and to gain access to private international finance through cofinancing and an expansion of the World Bank's International Finance Corporation (IFC). The MDBs should also make greater efforts to leverage their own loans on behalf of policy reforms. The regional banks should concentrate on policy improvements at the project and sector levels. The World Banks should, in addition, seek sound — that is, private sector, market-oriented — policies at the macroeconomic level.

In pressing for reforms, the MDBs should coordinate closely with the International Monetary Fund (IMF), the Treasury report argued. At the same time, the administration was urging the IMF to require countries to adjust more rapidly to the adverse global environment. In practice, rapid adjustment often meant sharp devaluations, tight credit, lowered government spending, falling wages, and other austerity measures to correct balance of payments disequilibria and slow domestic inflation. Certainly many developing countries needed to adjust their economies. In 1979-1980, the IMF had briefly experimented with more gradual adjustment programs that tried to lessen the costs of adjustment by maintaining investment and attacking development bottlenecks, especially in energy and agriculture.[52] The Treasury claimed that these programs had been too lenient and had failed to force sufficient adjustment.[53] A substantial portion of the conservative IMF staff agreed, and the IMF seemed to revert to more traditional, rapid adjustment programs.[54]

Administration attitudes toward the MDBs reflected a broader intellectual outlook. On the one hand, the administration believed that the developing world would have to accept slower growth rates: Expanded official lending either won't help, or would be too costly. On the other hand, the administration, at least initially, was sufficiently confident in private capital flows to scoff at those who warned that the global economy might be on the edge of a downward spiral and was susceptible to a major financial crisis triggered, perhaps, by LDC defaults on external debts. When asked in June 1982, whether it was wise to constrain official lending agencies in the midst of a global recession, Treasury Under Secretary Sprinkel confidently responded: "I think it would be shortsighted to assume that the worldwide recession is going to be deeper... recognizing [the problems of] the past doesn't commit us to the same degree of problems in the immediate future. I think the prospect is much brighter." [55] This official optimism rejected the warnings that commercial banks were becoming extremely nervous about the debt servicing capabilities of many LDCs. Many in the financial community were arguing that enhanced official lending would help reduce their perception of international risk; that is, more official finance might be a prerequisite for sustained private capital flows into the developing world.[56]

The administration also argued that a reduction in American contributions would not appreciably harm American influence in the MDBs. The United States would still remain the single largest donor. In the initial round, the Europeans and the developing countries, sorely divided among themselves and often preoccupied with internal crises, did fail to orchestrate a defense against the determined administration offensive. Some, like Great Britain and, to a degree, West Germany, sympathized with the administration. However, in the spring of 1982 France proposed a Special Fund be created in the World Bank to sustain the flow of highly concessional resources to the poorest countries. If the United States refused to contribute, it could lose its voting power and influence in the Special Fund, and the Fund's credits could not be spent on American products. The principles of multilateral development finance, which the Treasury report had praised, were in jeopardy. Yet the administration either thought it could deflect the French challenge or didn't care.

In the fall of 1982, however, administration attitudes toward the IMF shifted abruptly. The administration had brushed aside the accumulating repayment problems of smaller debtors — such as Costa Rica, Bolivia, and Zaire — as not constituting serious threats to the international financial system. But, in late summer, Mexico's announcement that it was suspending payments on principal sent shock waves through the heavily exposed banking community. Mexico was not unique. Other major debtors, including Brazil and Argentina, were also having difficulty meeting their debt service obligations. The banks' natural response was to contract lending. Smaller banks tried to pull up stakes altogether. Larger banks, being more locked into major creditor-client relationships, were generally willing to maintain existing exposure, but balked at extending new loans.

This freezing up of financial markets made it difficult for countries to meet interest payments, no less to amortize principal (which was being rescheduled with increasing frequency). The administration's assumption that private capital markets would continue to function smoothly proved overly sanguine. When finally confronted by a full-blown crisis it could no longer deny, the administration bowed to pressures from commercial banks and western European governments to permit a significant and rapid increase in the lending capacity of the IMF. The IMF management and some Europeans wanted to double the IMF's approximately $65 billion in resources. The administration had originally planned for a 25–40 percent increase, which was to become effective in 1984; it agreed instead to a compromise 40–50 percent increase, effective as early as late 1983. In addition, the administration floated a proposal to make some $20 billion in emergency funds available should the IMF prove unable to meet the balance-of-payments needs of select developing countries. In the interim, the Federal Reserve, working closely with administration officials, demonstrated its ability and willingness to respond to impending or actual debt crises; in conjunction with the Geneva-based Bank for International Settlements (which acts as a coordinating club for central banks), the Federal Reserve quickly extended short-term lines of credit to debt-ridden Mexico and Brazil in excess of $1 billion each.

This partial readjustment in American policy steadied the international financial system, at least temporarily. The additional assistance, however, was still less than most other governments thought necessary, and might be insufficient to prevent further disruptions in international capital markets if the United States and other industrial economies fail to recover in 1983-84. The additional assistance certainly seemed insufficient to permit the hard-hit developing countries to resume healthy growth paths. Nevertheless, the administration gave no indications that it would alter its restrictive budgetary policies toward the investment-oriented multilateral development banks.

Conclusions

The Reagan administration had its greatest success in north-south relations at the Cancun Summit, a meeting it almost refused to attend. This diplomatic triumph, however, was founded more on atmospherics, personalities, and expectations than on substantive progress. Its shine grew dim as the harsh realities of Reaganomics began to have their impact in the Third World. At Cancun, Reagan paid less attention to the immediate problems of LDCs, concentrating instead on the virtues of the free market and the problems of the American economy. He promised that a reformed American economy would reinvigorate the world. Instead, the failure of Reaganomics at home has cost the developing countries dearly.

Presented in its pristine form, the ideology of the free market ignores basic tenets of neoclassical welfare theory and negates the role that governments can and typically have played in promoting dynamic growth. In practice, the administration's free-market ideology frequently ran against the interests of important sectors of American business: Multinational investors generally favored active multilateral development banks, who build infrastructure; the large commercial banks argued that an expanded IMF was needed to balance the global financial system; and mining firms may regret the nonparticipation of the United States in the new regime that will govern exploitation of the oceans.

Some interventions by foreign governments in the marketplace have undoubtedly harmed the interests of American banks and firms as well as reduced the welfare of the populations they were supposed to serve. The low priority that the Reagan administration gave to international economic cooperation, however, may ultimately have a more negative effect on trade and capital flows, and on LDC growth, than many forms of intervention frequently found in developing countries. Certainly, the declining growth of international trade, investment and bank lending in 1981-1982 was the result not of a surge in state intervention but of the inability of the industrial states to manage the global economy. The Reagan administration was unable to put its own house in order and hesitated to initiate compensating actions in the international arena. Its ideology of anti-intervention seemed to have left the administration paralyzed as the international economic situation grew darker and darker. It took an acute debt crisis that threatened the stability of the global banking system to galvanize the Treasury to seek ways to funnel more funds to hard-pressed LDCs.

The administration did have some modest success in implementing its ideas in specific arenas. It reinforced existing institutions (such as the IFC and OPIC), which promote private capital flows. It sought to bend others (the IMF, the World Bank, AID) to adhere more closely to its precepts. Bureaucratic interests within these institutions, however, and the attitudes of other parties, sometimes including business, placed limits on administration enthusiasts. Moreover, these advances paled in relation to the global slump.

Ultimate judgment of the Reagan administration's economic policies toward the Third World will hinge on the validity of key administration assumptions and strategies regarding the nature of systemic stability and the depth of American power. The administration assumed that markets, domestic and international, naturally tend toward stable equilibria. Active government intervention is therefore generally unnecessary, and even counterproductive. This optimism regarding the functioning of markets spilled over into projections of the future growth paths of the United States and the world economy. If these projections continue to prove to be wishful thinking, and the administration adheres to its nonintervention philosophy, the liberal international order could be in jeopardy. At the least, contracting trade, increasing incidents of de facto defaults and debt reschedulings, and declining growth rates could typify the next several years. The American economy itself could suffer significantly from lost export markets.

While economic prosperity does not guarantee political stability, economic suffering makes instability more likely. For an administration extremely unnerved by political upheavals in the Third World, such developments could be traumatic. There is thus a potential contradiction between the inherent logic of the administration's economic policies, which seem to suggest that many of the poorer LDCs are of marginal importance, and a security outlook that is quick to see vital American interests at stake.

The administration also tended to perceive the United States as possessing sufficient potential economic and military power such that it could at least veto undesirable policies of other nations. Other nations would rally to our side, buckle to our pressures, or at least be neutralized. In some areas the administration did gain ground, in part because of the lack of an effective opposition by either the other industrial states or the developing countries. Yet the Law of the Sea may go into effect without a United States signature.[57] The Europeans may establish a separate fund in the World Bank without American participation. Power is to a considerable degree a matter of perceptions, and if other countries perceive that progress can be attained without American leadership or even involvement, American power will be much diminished.

The validity of the administration's assumptions and strategies will depend upon the decisions of millions of lenders, investors, borrowers, and consumers, as well as upon the responses of other industrial states and the Third World. Ironically, during the administration's first phase, the response of individual economic decision makers was the more disappointing. If the global economy continues to worsen, and the administration does not switch the course of its domestic and international economic policies, the risk is great that the diplomatic environment will also deteriorate.

Notes

1. For a summary of reforms made during the Carter period, see C. Fred Bergsten, "North-South Relations: A Candid Appraisal," in *The World Economy in the 1980s: Selected Papers of C. Fred Bergsten, 1980* (Lexington, D.C. Heath & Co., 1981).
2. Willy Brandt, *North-South: A Program for Survival* (Cambridge, Mass.: MIT Press, 1980), p. 265.
3. *Ibid.*
4. The twenty-two participating nations were Algeria, Austria, Bangladesh, Brazil, China, France, Guyana, India, Ivory Coast, Japan, Nigeria, Philippines, Saudi Arabia, Sweden, Tanzania, United Kingdom, United States, West Germany, Yugoslavia, Mexico, and Venezuela.
5. Secretary Haig used this phrase in his address before the UN General Assembly on September 21, 1981, as excerpted in *The New York Times*, September 22, 1981, p. A8. For articles on the Cancun Summit, see Art Pine, "Cancun's Conferees Say Speedy Action Is Needed to Preserve Fragile Consensus," *The Wall Street Journal*, October 26, 1981, p. 4; "Interview with Robert Hormats," *The Inter-Dependent*, vol. 7, No. 6, September/October, 1981, p. 1; and Christopher Madison, "Reagan's Attendance at Cancun Summit Could Be High-Risk Gamble for U.S.," *National Journal*, September 12, 1981, pp. 1625-1630.

6. Interviews with U.S. Government officials, Washington, D.C. October and November 1981.

7. Summary by the cochairman of the International Meeting on Cooperation and Development, release, October 23, 1981, Cancun, Mexico.

8. For a discussion of the flaws of commodity cartels, see Richard E. Feinberg, *The Intemperate Zone: The Third World Challenge to U.S. Foreign Policy* (New York: W.W. Norton, 1983), Chapter 2.

9. See C. Fred Bergsten, *op. cit.*

10. Remarks at the 1981 annual meetings of the World Bank and the IMF, press release No. 3, September 29, 1981.

11. See the essay in this volume by Benjamin Cohen, Chapter 4.

12. Official estimates remained somewhat more optimistic, placing the estimated total FY1984 federal deficit at $97 billion, falling to $83 billion in FY1985. Council of Economic Advisers, *Economic Report of the President, 1982* (Washington, D.C.: Government Printing Office, 1982), p. 98.

13. IMF, *World Financial Outlook* (Washington, D.C., IMF, 1982), p. 170.

14. *Ibid.*, p. 173.

15. Commerce Dept., *Survey of Current Business* (Washington, D.C.: Government Printing Office), June, 1982, Table 1, line 56, and Table 10, lines 72 and 73.

16. *Ibid.*, Table 1, line 48.

17. Figures in this section are from IMF, *op. cit.*

18. Address before the annual meetings of the World Bank/IMF, *op. cit.*

19. The Reagan administration explicitly accepted the public goods and externalities rationales for public sector activity in a Treasury Department Study, *United States Participation in the Multilateral Development Banks in the 1980s* (Washington, D.C.: Government Printing Office, 1982), pp. 8–13. For a similar official exposition, see Council of Economic Advisers, *op. cit.*, pp. 29–36.

20. A fuller exposition of this section can be found in Richard E. Feinberg, *op. cit.*, Chapter 2.

21. For a clear-headed discussion of the interdependence of the public and private sectors by a World Bank economist, see Barend A. deVries, "Public Policy and the Private Sector," *Finance and Development*, Vol. 18, No. 3, September 1981.

22. See World Bank, *The Capital Goods Sector in LDCs: A Case for State Intervention?* Staff Working Paper No. 343 (Washington, D.C.: World Bank, July, 1979).

23. Council on Foreign Relations and the International Management and Development Institute, "New Directions in U.S. Foreign Policy" (1980), appendix p. 3.

24. *Ibid.*, appendix p. 4.

25. A government subsidized firm can accept minimal profits for many years while cutting prices, increasing its market share and adding capacity, thereby achieving a long-term competitive cost advantage. See Telesis, *A Framework for Swedish Industrial Policy* (Somerville, Mass.: Telesis, 1978), Vol. 1, p. 69.

26. Richard S. Newfarmer, *International Oligopoly and Uneven Development*, forthcoming, Chapter 11.

27. On German industrial policy, see Telesis, *op cit.*, Vol. 2, appendix 12. Also, see Ira Magaziner and Robert Reich, *Minding America's Business* (New York: Harcourt, Brace Jovanovich, 1982).

28. For a thorough discussion of the Chinese modernization campaign and its opening to the West, see Doak Barnett, *China in the Global Economy* (Washington, D.C.: Brookings Institution, 1981).

29. *Fortune*, September 7, 1981, p. 93.

30. Isaiah Frank, *Foreign Enterprise in Developing Countries* (Baltimore: Johns Hopkins University Press, 1980), pp. 4, 157.

31. *Ibid.*, p. 112.
32. Board of Governors of the Federal Reserve System, "Country Exposure Lending Survey," press release, May 28, 1981. The $98 billion outstanding to LDCs does not include on-lending from offshore banking centers (Bahamas, Hong Kong, etc.).
33. *Ibid.* Of United States bank loans to developing countries outstanding at the end of 1980, 32 percent were to public borrowers.
34. Calculated in Richard E. Feinberg, *op. cit.*
35. For a State Department treatment of the foreign investment issue, see testimony of Robert Hormats, Testimony before the Subcommittee on International Economic Policy, Senate Foreign Relations Committee, October 28, 1981. For the Treasury Department's attitudes, see Treasury Department, *U.S. Participation . . .*, *op. cit.*
36. Overseas Private Investment Corporation (OPIC), *Development Report FY1980* (Washington, D.C.: OPIC), p. 19.
37. International Finance Corporation (IFC), Annual Report (Washington, D.C.: IFC, various).
38. Calculated by Gary Hufbauer, "Does Private Cofinancing Make a Difference?" *The Future of the Multilateral Development Banks* Hearings, U.S. House of Representatives, Subcommittee on International Development Institutions and Finance of the Committee on Banking, Finance and Urban Affairs, June 17, 1982 (Washington, D.C.: Government Printing Office, 1982).
39. United States Export-Import Bank, *Export-Import Bank Annual Report FY1981* (Washington, D.C.: 1982). Private cofinancing was estimated as equal to 90 percent of the export value of projects supported by Eximbank loans, minus Eximbank loan authorizations. For a comparison of Eximbank and MDB activities, see Richard E. Feinberg, *Subsidizing Success: The Export-Import Bank in the U.S. Economy* (New York: Cambridge University Press, 1982), Chapter 3.
40. See *The Future of the Multilateral Development Banks* Hearings, U.S. House of Representatives, *op. cit.*, especially the testimony by Nicholas Rey and John Niehuss.
41. For a critique of the proposed tax credit, see Richard E. Feinberg and Richard S. Newfarmer, "The Economic Impact of the Caribbean Basin Initiative," testimony before the U.S. Senate, Committee on Foreign Relations, March 31, 1982.
42. As quoted in Christopher Madison, "Exporting Reaganomics — The President Wants to Do Things Differently at AID," *National Journal*, May 29, 1982, p. 962.
43. For example, see M. Peter McPherson, "A.I.D./I.D.C.A. Policies and Programs for Private Sector Involvement in Development Abroad," testimony before the U.S. House of Representatives, Foreign Affairs Committee, February 24, 1982.
44. For a good review of Reagan administration trade policy, see Gary C. Hufbauer, ed., *U.S. International Economic Policy 1981: A Draft Report* (Washington, D.C.: The International Law Institute, Georgetown University Law Center, 1982).
45. Victor Lusinchi, "20 Nations Adopt Tin Price Pact," *The New York Times*, June 24, 1982, p. D15.
46. For a skeptical analysis of the FTA, see Richard E. Feinberg and Richard S. Newfarmer, *op. cit.*
47. Michael J. Berlin, "U.N. Approves Sea Pact Despite U.S. Objection," *The New York Times*, May 1, 1982, p. A1.
48. "Infant Formula Code: Why the U.S. May Stand Alone," *The Washington Post*, May 21, 1981, p. A27.
49. For an early retort to the rightist critique of the World Bank, see Robert Ayres, "Breaking the Bank," *Foreign Policy*, No. 43, Summer, 1981.
50. *Op. cit.*, footnote 19.

51. *Ibid.,* p. 5.
52. For a discussion of loans made under the Extended Fund Facility, see John Williamson, *The Lending Policies of the International Monetary Fund* (Washington, D.C.: Institute for International Economics, 1982).
53. Private discussions with administration officials.
54. See the testimony by John Williamson, Hearings, Subcommittee on International Development Institutions and Finance, *op. cit.*
55. Hearings, Subcommittee on International Development Institutions and Finance, *op. cit.*
56. See the testimony of John Petty, the president of Marine Midland Bank, *ibid.*; also, the forthcoming report on international financial institutions by the Economic Policy Council of the United Nations Association of the USA.
57. For a warning that the Law of the Sea can proceed without U.S. participation, see Leigh S. Ratiner, "The Law of the Sea: Crossroads for U.S. Policy," *Foreign Affairs,* Vol. 60, No. 5, Summer, 1982.

6

Energy Policy
and National Security:
Invisible Hand or Guiding Hand?

Robert J. Lieber

Foreign policy dilemmas facing the Reagan administration have been especially acute in the realm of energy. Here, as in other areas, the administration has tended to hold a Sovietcentric view of the world and to emphasize the market mechanism and a reduced role for government. Yet this approach has imposed costs, both immediate and potential, for the international security of America and its allies. Energy security here means a stable and reliable pattern of energy supply and demand, not excessively vulnerable to interruption or at disruptive prices.

The administration has had tangible achievements in energy. These include cooperation with Congress in accelerated filling of the Strategic Petroleum Reserve (SPR) and continuation of policies to decontrol oil and, in part, natural gas prices. Such measures help to lessen American vulnerability to international oil blackmail or embargo. They also contribute to a reduction in American oil consumption and imports.

Yet the administration's priorities impose a tradeoff against the reduction of allied dependence on Middle East oil. In the case of East-West

Robert J. Lieber is Professor of Government at Georgetown University, specializing in U.S.-European relations, energy security, and American foreign policy. He has held fellowships from the SSRC, Council on Foreign Relations, and Guggenheim, Rockefeller, and Ford Foundations. In addition he has been Research Associate at the Harvard Center for International Affairs; Visiting Fellow at St. Antony's College, Oxford; Research Associate of the Atlantic Institute, Paris; Guest Scholar at the Brookings Institution; Fellow of the Woodrow Wilson International Center for Scholars; and professor at the University of California, Davis. Among his books are British Politics and European Unity; Theory and World Politics; *and* Oil and the Middle East War: Europe in the Energy Crisis. *He is also coeditor of* Eagle Entangled: U.S. Foreign Policy in a Complex World.

policy, they have brought it into sharp conflict with European allies over their imports of Soviet natural gas. In addition, the Reagan administration's emphasis on the market mechanism at times runs counter to other energy security needs. These include the ability to cope with a future oil shock or to meet International Energy Agency (IEA) obligations in the event of an emergency. Free-market principles also motivate opposition to the World Bank program designed to stimulate energy production and conservation among non-OPEC states of the developing world.

In the military sphere, the United States is committed to the buildup of a Rapid Deployment Force (RDF) for military contingencies in the Persian Gulf. The objective of this force is to counter threats to vital allied energy supplies. Yet to the extent that American policies result in slower diversification away from dependence on Middle East oil, the United States and its allies retain a greater degree of vulnerability to the effect of upheavals in one of the most unstable regions on earth.

In the sections that follow, this chapter considers the context in which United States international energy policy takes place. This context includes the legacy of energy crises during the past decade as well as the constraints imposed by an integrated world oil system. This chapter then analyzes the transition in policy from the Carter to the Reagan administrations. Next it explores the premises that underlie administration policy and the tradeoffs that result. It concludes that there must be more concern with the international consequences of administration policies. An effective policy must take far greater account of the enduring risks to energy security and of the imperatives for cooperation among oil consuming countries.

America and the International Oil System

The setting for international energy policy is one in which the role of oil remains overwhelmingly important. In the space of some twenty-five years, from the late 1940s to the early 1970s, North America, Western Europe, and Japan experienced a period of remarkable economic growth and sharply increased living standards. The energy source for this development was oil, available in seemingly limitless quantities and at low prices. In a mere two decades, imported oil replaced domestic coal as the dominant source of energy in most of the developed world.

The United States had long been the leading force and most important producer in the world oil market. Although America became a net oil importer as early as 1948, a substantial domestic and international reserve capacity helped to keep prices low and supplies ample. As a result, neither the Suez Crisis of 1956 nor the Arab-Israeli Six Day War of 1967 caused any sustained disturbance to oil supply or price. Indeed, as late as January 1970, Saudi Arabian light marker crude oil sold for a mere $1.39

per barrel.[1] In constant dollars, the price had actually declined by half over a period of two decades.

The year 1970, however, brought a peaking of American oil production. Thereafter, the balance between world production capacity and demand became substantially tighter. During the early 1970s, a number of additional factors combined to produce profound changes in the balance of international petroleum power. The hitherto unchallenged dominance of the international oil companies, the seven "majors," was eroded by the increased activity of the smaller independent companies and by the growing strength of OPEC. In 1970, the radical government of Libya, under the leadership of Colonel Qaddafi, succeeded in imposing a price increase on the Occidental Petroleum Company. Within a year, at Teheran in February 1971, the OPEC countries managed to negotiate a substantial price increase with the oil majors. In large measure, this was made possible by the erosion of excess world oil production capacity in relation to demand. Some accounts, however, suggest that it may also have resulted from indecisive United States policy, or even that the Shah may have achieved the 1971 price increase with the encouragement of officials in the United States State Department. The balance of bargaining power had now shifted to favor the producing countries, giving them — rather than the companies — the dominant voice in setting prices and production levels.

The onset of the Arab-Israeli war on October 6, 1973, suddenly illuminated the shift in power that had taken place. An Arab oil embargo against the United States and — more importantly — Arab production cuts precipitated an almost fourfold increase in price over a period of several months: Saudi oil rose from $2.70 per barrel on October 4, 1973, to $10.46 by March 1, 1974.[2]

This 1973-1974 oil shock caused serious economic harm to the industrial democracies as well as the non-oil producing less developed countries (LDCs). The Western allies and Japan, members of the Organization for Economic Cooperation and Development (OECD), lost the equivalent of 2 percent of their gross national product (GNP).[3] They also experienced a sharp inflationary jolt, rising unemployment, and substantial balance of payments problems.

Equally important, the United States and its allies found themselves in serious political disarray. They faced sharp differences over Middle East policy, with individual European countries and Japan seeking to make individual bilateral deals with oil producing states at the cost of cooperation on either a European or Atlantic basis.[4] The sole positive outcome of this period was the creation of the International Energy Agency. This new body, established under American impetus and over the opposition of France, was to provide a basis for emergency consumer cooperation and oil sharing in the event of a future crisis. The trigger for such sharing would be an oil shortfall of 7 percent or more.

As the crisis receded, the international oil problem began to ease. A major Western recession in 1974-1975 brought reduction in world oil demand. To a lesser extent, oil price increases also caused a degree of conservation and fuel switching. During the period from late 1974 to late 1978, the economic impact of the crisis was gradually absorbed. The looser supply and demand balance even produced a growing sense of oil "glut." OPEC prices stagnated, and in real terms actually declined by 13 percent between 1976 and 1978.[5]

During the five years from the end of 1973 to the end of 1978, European consumption of petroleum declined by 3.6 percent and imports by 2.2 percent.[6] However, American consumption continued to rise, climbing 11.8 percent in this same period. More dangerously, American oil imports increased even faster. As a result not only of growing consumption but of decreased domestic production, these imports rose by 28.5 percent.[7] At the same time there were reductions in oil available from Canada and Venezuela. American dependence on both OPEC and on Arab oil producers thus soared. For example, between 1973 and 1977, OPEC's share of American oil imports rose from 50 percent to 73 percent, and that of Arab OPEC states from 15 percent to 38 percent (see Table 6-1).

American energy policy remained at a near impasse. Its chief accomplishments were legislation imposing mandatory improvement in automobile fuel economy, consolidation of the IEA, and initiation of the SPR

TABLE 6-1. U.S. Petroleum Imports

Year	Total Net Imports mbd*	Total OPEC mbd	%	Total Arab OPEC mbd	%
1973	6.0	3.0	50	0.9	15.0
1974	5.9	3.3	56	0.8	13.6
1975	5.8	3.6	62	1.4	24.0
1976	7.1	5.1	72	2.4	34.0
1977	8.6	6.2	73	3.2	38.0
1978	8.0	5.8	73	3.0	38.0
1979	8.0	5.6	70	3.1	39.0
1980	6.4	4.3	67	2.6	41.0
1981	5.4	3.3	61	1.8	33.0

* Millions of barrels per day.

Arab OPEC (OAPEC) includes Algeria, Libya, Saudi Arabia, United Arab Emirates, Iraq, Kuwait, and Qatar.

Non-Arab OPEC includes Indonesia, Iran, Nigeria, Venezuela, Ecuador, and Gabon.

Figures include SPR imports.

SOURCE: Based on data in U.S. Department of Energy, Energy Information Administration, *Monthly Energy Review*, December 1982, pp. 31 and 36-37.

(though without substantial purchases of oil for it). Otherwise, the United States experienced a stalemate. Controls on oil kept prices far below world levels and thus worked against efforts to reduce import dependence. Measures to encourage conservation, energy efficiency, fuel switching, and the development of non-oil energy sources were not given the scale of support required to stimulate meaningful changes. And battles over natural gas pricing pitted regions and interest groups in a bitter and inconclusive struggle.

Although a number of serious analysts warned of a future tightening of world oil supply patterns and thus the risk of another oil shock, many observers and policy makers tended to minimize the problem. For example, as late as the autumn of 1978, the then Congressman from Michigan, David Stockman, could write:

> Indeed, the global economic conditions necessary for another major unilateral price action by OPEC are not likely to reemerge for more than a decade — if ever.[8]

Suddenly, in late 1978, upheaval in Iran began to disrupt oil production. That country had been OPEC's second largest oil producer after Saudi Arabia, accounting for 5.5 million barrels per day (mbd) as late as October 1978. With massive political unrest, however, production dropped by 2 mbd in November and an additional 1 mbd in December. With the Shah's ouster in January, Iran's oil production came to a virtual halt. It then slowly began to recover, rising to 2.2 mbd in March and then fluctuating between 3 and 4 mbd for the remainder of the year.[9]

Much of the reduction was offset by increased oil production elsewhere. However, Saudi Arabia exacerbated the situation by reducing its own production from 10.4 to 9.8 mbd in January, and by a further 1.0 mbd in April. This left a net shortfall of approximately 4 percent of world oil demand for the second calendar quarter of 1979. At a time of unusually low world oil stock levels and disruption of established oil market patterns, fierce competitive bidding for oil erupted on international spot markets. Prices surged upward, with consuming countries unable to cooperate effectively. Ultimately, prices rose 170 percent over a fifteen-month period.

This rapid succession of oil crisis, glut, and crisis occurred in a highly intergrated world oil system, or "regime." The functioning of this system shapes the relations among producers and consumers of petroleum outside the Soviet Union and China. It is based on the fact that the production or consumption of a barrel of oil, wherever it occurs, ultimately weighs as part of a world balance of supply and demand.

World prices of petroleum are affected both by political factors and by economic and market mechanisms. Prior to 1970, the role of oil majors was decisive in setting or influencing prices. Subsequently, the emergence of OPEC and especially of Saudi Arabia as the source for meeting marginal changes in oil demand gave those producers an impact even greater than that of their share of world oil production. Nonetheless, the overall pattern of world oil supply and demand does set the framework within which various forces contend. More important, the greater the margin of spare petroleum production capacity and the more diversified among oil producing countries, the less vulnerable the system is to sudden oil shocks.

Wherever they occur, shifts in supply or demand have some overall effect on the system as a whole. On the supply side, increase in Saudi capacity, the development of Alaskan, North Sea, and Mexican oil, and even small-scale increases in oil production among the less developed countries all add to the potential pool of world oil supply. Conversely, conflict in Iran and Iraq and decline in American and Venezuelan production represent real or potential reductions in world supply.

On the demand side, fuel switching from oil to any other energy source (for example, coal, natural gas, nuclear energy, or solar power), reductions in oil consumption, energy conservation and efficiency, the drawing down of stockpiles, or the effects of recession, all result in decreased world oil demand. In turn, factors such as economic growth, development among the LDCs, and the wider spread of automobile ownership, create increased demand pressure.

These forces shape a volatile international oil pattern. When there is little surplus production capacity, the system is especially vulnerable to oil shocks. These can result from any significant disturbance to routine conditions of supply. Thus, after the October 1973 war, a shortfall of roughly 7 percent created the conditions for a 300 percent increase in prices. Again, after the fall of the Shah, a reduction of 4 percent during the spring of 1979 provided the impetus for a 170 percent price increase.

Conversely, when there is substantial spare capacity and an excess of oil production in relation to demand, the system is far more resistant to disruption. The outbreak of the Iran-Iraq war occurred at a time of substantial surplus capacity and record high levels of world oil inventories. As a result, no oil shock occurred. During 1981 and the spring and summer of 1982, continued easing of the supply-demand balance produced a softening of world oil prices and a temporary "glut," though the actions of OPEC in cutting production prevented the occurrence of a major downward price break.

The implications of this integrated oil system are profound. They impose an ineluctable interdependence upon its participants, regardless of whether or not this is consciously a part of their international energy policies.

Illustratively, the 1973-1974 Arab oil embargo against the United States had little direct impact on its target. Oil available internationally was simply allocated on a pro rata basis by the oil majors. In future crises, the emergency oil sharing system of the International Energy Agency would have much the same effect.

On the other hand, the existence of this integrated world oil system sometimes creates unwelcome tradeoffs. Continued American opposition to Western European purchases of Soviet natural gas and embargoes of equipment and technology used in the construction of the pipeline would have imposed an energy security cost, regardless of other foreign policy priorities (including the desire not to strengthen the Soviet economy). To the extent these policies were maintained and resulted in delayed European consumption of this fuel, and to the degree they caused the Soviet Union to lag in the exploitation of domestic oil and gas resources, they would have had the effect of placing greater demand pressure on the world oil market.

Energy Policy: From Carter to Reagan

The administration of Jimmy Carter sought, in a more comprehensive way than any of its predecessors, to make a priority of energy policy. Yet energy-related issues, in the form of the fall of the Shah, the second oil shock, and the Iran hostage seizure, did much to cause the defeat of the Carter administration.

Initially, President Carter had sought to arouse the nation over the energy problem. However, his April 1977 speech, describing the energy challenge as the "moral equivalent of war," failed to make a decisive impact. The call to a massive conservation effort was more hortatory than substantive. Other major portions of his energy program, including a gasoline tax, became entangled in a congressional stalemate over natural gas decontrol.[10] The issues of costs and benefits to industries and entire regions proved particularly unmanageable, and a substantial easing of the international oil balance in 1975-1978 deprived energy policy of much of its urgency.

With the overthrow of the Shah, however, energy policy once again became crucial. In April 1979, Carter used his executive authority to initiate decontrol of domestic petroleum prices over a two-and-a-half year period. The new crisis also led to breaking of the deadlock over natural gas. Congress agreed on a program of phased decontrol extending to 1985, as well as a windfall profits tax on oil.

Overall, the second crisis found the United States and the other major consuming countries still ill prepared to cope with an oil shock. In the United States, there were once again fears of shortage, problems of oil allocation, gas lines, steep price increases, and ample political recriminations. At the international level, political disarray and an inability to cooperate effectively again marked the relationships among the Americans, Europeans, and Japanese.[11]

The difficulty was less acute than during the 1973 crisis, and consultation among IEA members did occur. This produced commitments to reduce oil consumption by 5 percent, but these and other steps were more symbolic than substantive. In any case, they were inadequate to prevent the intensification of the second shock or substantially to ameliorate its effects.

In July 1979, with the administration's overall leadership under serious criticism, President Carter announced a vast $88 billion federal program to accelerate the development of synthetic fuels over the course of a decade. The long-term objective was to produce the equivalent of 0.5 mbd of oil from coal and shale rock by 1987, and 2 mbd by 1992. However, these and other efforts had little direct bearing on the crisis. One tangible program that might have made a difference was use of the SPR. Yet filling this reserve had been slow to develop, due both to technical reasons (the need to prepare oil storage caverns and install pumps) and to budgetary priorities (the cost of oil purchases). As a result, there were only 67 million barrels of oil in the SPR at the end of 1978 — the equivalent of a mere eight days of total U.S. petroleum imports.[12] Indeed, SPR additions were halted in September 1979, in part due to a desire not to antagonize Saudi Arabia (which had increased production by 1.0 mbd in July). Filling of the SPR finally resumed a year later.

Reagan Administration Energy Policy: Premises and Dilemmas

The Reagan administration took office with a set of doctrinal impulses toward energy policy more than with a coherent strategy. Three sets of principles shaped the administration's approach. The first of these lay outside the immediate realm of energy and economic policy. It was an emphasis upon the Soviet threat and East-West confrontation. To the extent that other priorities came into conflict with this, the Sovietcentric priority was likely to take precedence.

A second principle involved "a much heavier emphasis" on allowing energy decisions to be made by the free market.[13] Third, and closely related, was a stress on reducing the role of government and of regulatory mechanisms. Indeed, government was seen as a major cause of the energy problem. This was symbolized in a campaign pledge to abolish the Department of Energy.

These principles were accompanied by a set of beliefs about energy, typified by presidential candidate Reagan's assertion that deregulation could make the United States self-sufficient in energy within five years.[14] Emphasis on the supply side of the energy equation, rather than on demand (except insofar as the price mechanism was involved), was another characteristic. Among specific energy sources, oil, natural gas, coal, and nuclear power, were looked upon favorably, while solar energy, other renewable sources, and energy efficiency, were viewed, at best, with indifference.

In addressing energy, the Reagan administration inherited an international environment that, at least temporarily, had greatly eased. Steep declines in oil demand were occurring as a result of earlier price increases and the most severe economic recession since the 1930s. In addition, non-OPEC production capacity (Mexico, Alaska, the North Sea, and elsewhere) had increased by several million barrels in the years from 1978 to 1982.

These factors, together with approximately 2 mbd of destocking, caused the demand for OPEC oil to plummet. Production of OPEC oil fell from 31 mbd in 1979 to an average of 22.7 mbd in 1981 and as low as 16.7 mbd in the spring of 1982.[15]

As a result of this drop in the demand for OPEC oil, prices softened. Anxieties over security of oil supply eased greatly, and the balance of bargaining power between producers and consumers of oil once again seemed to shift. The shift deprived the producing countries of some of the unilateral advantages they had enjoyed during and immediately after each of the oil shocks.

The Reagan administration came into office under less pressure and with greater room for maneuvering than its predecessors. The president's initial step, within a week of taking office, was to end price controls on domestic crude oil. These controls were begun in 1971, but decontrol had already been initiated by Carter. At the time of Reagan's action, less than one-fourth of domestic oil remained to be affected. In any case, controls had been due to expire on September 30th. The administration also abolished complex emergency allocation procedures for gasoline as well as regulations affecting the entitlements program. (This had required transfer payments among companies to equalize the competitive conditions for those without access to cheap domestic oil.) Because of the soft international oil market situation, oil decontrol was completed without causing disruptive price increases.[16]

Another significant component of Reagan energy policy concerned the Strategic Petroleum Reserve. Under congressional pressure, additions to this had been resumed in the waning months of the Carter administration. Support for the SPR had also figured in the 1980 Republican platform.

Despite differences between the Reagan administration and Congress over funding for the SPR and the rate at which purchases would be made, additions to the reserve were accelerated. During 1981, these averaged over 300,000 barrels per day. By the summer of 1982, the SPR had reached 275 million barrels. Although the administration preferred to place the funding for the program off-budget, and appeared to favor purchases of 200,000 barrels per day rather than 300,000 sought by the Senate for the 1983 fiscal year, a substantial fill rate continued.

The growing size of the SPR made the United States somewhat less vulnerable to the effects of a future oil emergency. Reductions in American oil consumption and imports — which were occurring independently of government policies — also meant decreased dependence on foreign oil. Net petroleum imports, which had been 8.0 mbd in 1979, fell to 6.4 mbd in 1980 and 5.4 in 1981. Both phenomena, the growth of the SPR and reduction in import dependence, contributed to American energy security.

East-West Priorities and Energy Tradeoffs: The Soviet Gas Pipeline

Other central attributes of administration policy had opposite effects when judged by the criteria of energy dependence and vulnerability. The most visible of these policies concerned Soviet exports of natural gas to Western Europe. These were to be delivered beginning in 1984 via a 3,700-mile pipeline from Western Siberia. In this case, decisions of the Reagan administration to oppose the project were taken with the intent of punishing the Soviet Union for repression in Poland. The action was also based on two additional reasons. One was concern over the possibilities of Soviet leverage against Western Europe, for example, in a future opportunity for the Soviet Union to threaten to curtail natural gas supplies. (The Soviet Union had previously manipulated its exports of oil as a political tool in 1948 against Yugoslavia, in 1956 against Israel, in 1964 against China, and in 1968 to influence Cuba.)

The administration also sought to deny the Soviets hard currency earnings of $8 to $10 billion per year by its own estimates (though less than $4 billion by a different forecast)[17] that West European gas exports would bring. It thereby aimed to squeeze the Soviet economy and hence made it more costly for the Soviet Union to devote scarce resources to military spending. The immediate American expectation was that restrictions would delay completion of the gas pipeline by roughly two years.

The specific American measures began with a December 1981 decision preventing the General Electric Corporation from exporting turbine rotors to the Soviet Union. This restriction also applied to GE agreements with three European manufacturing associates: AEG-Telefunken in West Germany, John Brown in the United Kingdom, and Nuovo Pignone in Italy. In addition, the American firm of Caterpillar Tractor was prevented from selling $90 million worth of pipe-laying vehicles to the Soviet Union.

In June 1982, the administration extended the restrictions to overseas subsidiaries of American firms and to foreign companies that held GE licenses; in this case, the French firm of Alsthom-Atlantique, which had a contract to supply complete turbines on its own.[18] Firms in Britain, Italy, and West Germany were also affected. In addition, the American decision resulted in collapse of Japanese negotiations for joint oil exploration with Russia on Sakhalin Island.

The American decision left unanswered questions, particularly as to its effectiveness. It was not clear whether the pipeline project would be delayed for a matter of years, if at all. For example, the Japanese Komatsu firm was believed to have stepped in to provide the pipe-laying equipment, and the Soviets appeared to have other possibilities (albeit at additional cost) for turbine rotors. In any case, energy tradeoffs were readily apparent.

From the perspective of the Western European countries most concerned (France, West Germany, and Italy), the gas deal was a pragmatic way of diversifying energy import sources. In this case, relying upon the Soviets for approximately 25 to 30 percent of their natural gas supplies (but just 5 to 6 percent of total primary energy) offered a means of lessening oil and gas dependence on the Middle East and North Africa — and hence reducing European vulnerability to the effects of a crisis in that region.

Indeed, the Germans, French, and Italians already relied on Soviet gas, apparently without putting themselves at undue risk. In 1980, the Soviet Union provided 17.5 percent of gas supply in Germany, 13.3 percent in France, and 23.7 percent in Italy.[19] Moreover, the increases in 1990 gas dependence (to 29 percent in Germany, 23-28 percent in France, and 29 percent in Italy) would roughly offset the decline in Soviet oil exports to Western Europe. These amounted to 1.1 mbd in 1979 and accounted for more than half of the Soviet Union's earnings of essential hard currency.[20] Thus, controversy over the gas pipeline tended to obscure the fact that Western Europe was already importing Soviet oil and gas. The issue, therefore, was less one of dependence on the Soviet Union per se than of whether, or at what level, these imports might pose unacceptable risks.[21]

To the extent that American sanctions had proven effective, they would have imposed a second energy tradeoff — in this case, requiring Western Europeans to rely on the world oil market for fuel that would otherwise have been offset by Soviet gas. Indeed, if the Soviets are less able to exploit indigenous oil and gas resources for their own and Eastern European use, an additional net increment to demand will be placed on an integrated world oil supply system.

Finally, the June 1982 measures caused bitter recriminations with America's European allies. There was ample reason to prefer that the repression in Poland not be cost-free to the Soviets. Yet European skepticism about the efficacy of sanctions (based in part on their own previous experience — for example, that of the Federal Republic in the 1950s and 1960s) was combined with a cynical view toward the continuing American grain exports to the Soviet Union. The Europeans were particularly irked that the Americans had not taken the occasion of the Versailles Summit or of the NATO meeting in Bonn, which immediately followed, to consult over the impending expansion of restrictions. Even as staunch an anti-Soviet as Conservative British Prime Minister Margaret Thatcher attacked the American actions, in this case, on the grounds that it was wrong for a powerful nation to seek to prevent existing contracts from being fulfilled.[22]

Within weeks of the American action, the governments of France, Italy, Britain, and (indirectly) Germany ordered their firms to proceed with contractual commitments for work on the Soviet pipeline project. American restrictions were rejected on the grounds that they constituted an unacceptable extension of United States law into the internal affairs of Western Europe.[23]

While discussions about increased exports of American coal or more rapid development of Norwegian oil and gas suggested longer term alternatives to dependence on Soviet gas, these sources were not available in time to meet projected European energy needs during the last half of the 1980s. However, an alternative American approach could have allowed the Europeans to draw upon Soviet gas while minimizing the risks of Soviet leverage. Once it became apparent that it was too late for the Europeans to obtain North American or North Sea energy in the time required, and that the deal could no longer be prevented (because contracts had been signed by the early months of 1982, and because of the European jobs involved in pipeline contracts), continued American opposition was likely to be counterproductive. At this point, there would have been more purpose in promoting a comprehensive and fully funded series of gas security measures. These would include a coordinated program of gas storage, improved integration of pipeline networks, dual capacity (gas-oil) boilers, and interruptible contracts (requiring large-scale users of fuel to switch to oil or coal in a crisis, thereby avoiding possible cutoffs for millions of individual households).

In addition, development and planning for reserve or surge capacity, based on Dutch and Norwegian gas, could have been sought systematically. Instead, many of these measures were pursued on a partial or haphazard basis, and with uncoordinated national programs.

Faced with blanket opposition from allied governments and a deep split within its own bureaucracy (essentially pitting the State and Commerce Departments against the National Security Council and elements of the Defense Department), the administration sought a face-saving means of retreating from its policy. On November 13, 1982, after consultations with the Europeans, President Reagan announced the lifting of sanctions against companies taking part in the Soviet-West European gas pipeline project. The action was based on "substantial agreement" among the allies on economic relations with the Soviet Union. The United States and the Europeans were to avoid trade agreements that aided the Soviets militarily, especially in high technology projects, including oil and gas. Pending an allied study, no new Soviet gas contracts were to be signed, allied controls on transfer of strategic items to the Soviet Union were to be strengthened, and procedures to monitor and harmonize allied financial relations with the Soviet Union were to be sought.

The American actions at least temporarily ended an acrimonious dispute within the alliance, but not without further political cost. The French government announced it was not a party to any new agreement, the British Foreign Minister termed it a "unilateral decision" by the Americans, and German officials described the language of the agreement as merely parallel to the June 1982 Versailles summit communiqué.[24] A European verdict on the American policy was offered by *The Economist*, which termed it "a catalogue of muddle of near-Carteresque proportions." [25]

The Free Market
and Energy Security Externalities

The Reagan administration's National Energy Policy Plan emphasized use of the market mechanism for making energy decisions. It held that market forces would cause beneficial increases in petroleum investment and production. Not only was this approach to determine choices in resource allocation, but it was also to prevail in times of emergency: "In the event of an emergency, preparedness plans call for relying *primarily* on market forces to allocate energy supplies." [26]

At the domestic level, this free-market emphasis caused a drastic reduction in the level of governmental incentives and support for conservation, fuel switching, solar energy, and renewable sources of energy. Whereas the Carter administration had encouraged solar and renewable energy, with a view to encouraging these to provide 20 percent of America's primary energy supply in the year 2000, the Reagan administration preferred that development of these sources be left to the private sector. In this, as in other areas, the administration disregarded barriers to market penetration as well as the historical role the public sector had played in providing massive subsidies and incentives for the development of coal, oil, hydroelectric, and nuclear power. Yet the desire to reduce government support was highly selective. The Department of Energy planned to allocate a mere 2 percent of its research, development, and commercialization funds for 1983 to conservation, while devoting no less than 84 percent to nuclear energy.[27] Administration policy also seemed to suggest a reduction in American efforts to prevent nuclear proliferation.

Emphasis on the market meant an unwillingness to promote development of synfuels. The 1981-1982 glut had softened oil prices and left questions about long-term energy price trends. In April and May of 1982, in response to these uncertainties, as well as rising development costs, the major Colony Shale and Alsands heavy oil projects were abandoned by the private firms involved. Meanwhile, the administration discouraged activities of the quasi-public U.S. Synthetic Fuels Corporation.[28] Only two years after inception of the Carter plan, American synfuels efforts were now moribund.

The administration's petroleum policies were consistent with its overall philosophy. Initially, it rejected an increased gasoline tax. This had been proposed as a measure to reduce federal budget deficits and to reinforce long-term trends toward fuel economy (at a time when gasoline prices had eased by as much as 20 cents per gallon). The administration also refused to support subsidies for fuel switching, which might have saved an additional 1 mbd. It took no action to discourage private company destocking, although in the first six months of 1982 the depletion of these reserves took place at three times the SPR fill rate.[29]

At the international level, administration opposition was largely responsible for blocking expansion of a World Bank energy program. The initiative had been proposed by the bank's outgoing president, Robert McNamara. It would have increased lending by an additional $16 billion between 1982 and 1986 in order to stimulate oil and gas exploration and development as well as encourage other sources of energy, such as hydroelectric and fuel wood. The plan was a response to expectations that the non-oil producing LDCs will be a major source of increased world oil demands during the remainder of this decade. By 1990, the expanded World Bank program was expected to have been responsible for the equivalent of 1.3 mbd of oil. It would also have reduced LDC oil import bills by $25 to 30 billion.[30]

In opposing the program, the administration rejected arguments that it was necessary to offset political uncertainties and to provide financing for small- or medium-scale efforts that would otherwise prove less attractive to private firms, even though of considerable value to individual LDCs. It preferred to rely on the private sector for LDC energy development.

A pattern thus became clearly evident. Apart from its efforts to encourage the nuclear industry and subsidize breeder reactor development, the administration would not normally employ governmental efforts and resources in order to promote decreased reliance upon oil. Indeed, the National Energy Plan had been remarkably explicit in rejecting reductions in oil imports as a key objective. The position bears quoting, for it reflects the predominance of doctrinal consistency over both strategic considerations and a decade's experience of international energy instability:

> [*A*]*chieving a low-level of oil imports at any cost is not a major criterion for the nation's energy security and economic health.* Even at its current high price, imported oil is substantially less expensive than available alternatives.[31]

The administration's policies evoked questions about its ability to meet a future oil emergency. This was not only a domestic matter. It also concerned obligations to the International Energy Agency — a body created largely through the efforts of two previous Republican administrations — and relationships with Europe and Japan. In the words of a former high official with responsibility for international energy security: "How can there be cooperation [with allies] if the United States dismantles almost completely its preparations to deal with emergencies." [32]

The measures that gave rise to these concerns were often highly detailed or technical in nature. The more important of them included the following:

— Virtual dismantling of the DOE (Department of Energy) apparatus for handling emergencies.[33]
— President Reagan's March 1982 veto of legislation that renewed his specific authority to allocate oil supplies and set prices in an emergency.[34] (The Senate narrowly failed to override the veto.)
— Opposition to a bill, passed by a bipartisan Senate majority seeking to fill the SPR at a rate of 300,000 barrels per day in 1983 and requiring that the president submit a plan for SPR use in an emergency. (The administration preferred a 200,000-barrel rate and opposed the provision for an emergency plan.)[35]
— Possible inability to comply with IEA emergency procedures. In the event of a general oil supply shortfall exceeding 7 percent of IEA's normal consumption, members are required to reduce consumption by 7 percent. (A shortfall above 12 percent requires a 10 percent restraint.) Yet, as of the summer of 1982, there appeared to be no effective emergency plan for such a reduction, apart from an expressed intent to rely on the market. Indeed one proposal, to draw upon oil stocks or the SPR for this purpose, could violate IEA obligations.[36]
— Refusal to take part in IEA discussions for coping with subtrigger emergencies. (Note that the 1973-1974 and 1979 oil shocks were both caused by shortfalls below the formal 7 percent trigger.)

In short, overwhelming reliance on the market mechanism tended to exclude consideration of energy security externalities. Whatever the virtues of the market and simplifying or reducing an elaborate regulatory system, it was as though the Department of Defense determined to have all American combat aircraft manufactured in Japan because a firm there could provide the lowest bid. Indeed skeptics, including leading Republicans in Congress and even the GOP Governor of Texas, were concerned that the administration appeared to attach no national security premium to oil imports at all.[37]

Ironically, an inconsistency exists between the administration's energy policy and the objectives of its military policy toward the Persian Gulf. In looking toward that region, conventional force planning had sought to deter military threats that would reduce the flow of Middle East oil to the United States and its allies. The Rapid Deployment Force (begun under the previous administration), as well as other forces capable of projecting American power, have thus been bolstered for possible Gulf contingencies. They have accounted for substantial increases in the defense budget.

Yet the security interests of the United States and its allies would be enhanced by a coherent program that steadily decreased their long-term reliance on Middle East oil and thus reduced the strategic importance of an unstable Gulf region. While useful increases in world oil production outside the Middle East have been achieved, and some reductions in relative dependence on this region have occurred, these have not eliminated the strategic dependence of the industrial democracies on Middle East supplies.[38] The point is not that preparation of the RDF is undesirable, nor that it may not have a significant utility. Deterrence of Soviet threats and support for the governments of oil producing states threatened by outside forces may prove effective. However, these are not necessarily the most likely sources of instability and of possible oil disruption.

Internal upheavals (as in the case of Iran), as well as endemic regional conflicts (such as the Iran-Iraq war), are more likely causes of instability. Yet these provide difficult circumstances in which American or allied military forces can effectively be brought to bear. As Barry Rubin demonstrates in Chapter 12, it is hard for the United States to control events in the region. In view of the likely sources of instability, there are thus limits to the utility of the RDF. In short, the Persian Gulf and the Middle East region as a whole present a series of nearly intractable problems. Recognition of this underscores the need for coherent energy policies aimed at further reducing Western and Japanese oil import dependence on the region.

America's Energy Security: Autonomy or Interdependence?

The Reagan administration established its energy policies at a time of sizable oil glut. Were this eased oil pattern to continue over the long term, there would be little reason for concern. However, three sets of uncertainties profoundly affect this picture in the remaining years of the 1980s, and in each case they suggest the need for greater attention to energy security.

The first of these uncertainties concerns the reasons for decreased oil demand in the 1980-1982 period. The twenty-one countries of the IEA consumed 5.4 mbd less petroleum in 1981 than in 1979.[39] In the United States alone, average consumption fell by 2.5 mbd, and net imports by 2.6 mbd.[40] However, the reasons for this decline are not entirely certain. IEA analysts estimate that roughly half the reduction results not from long-term adaptation to higher prices (fuel switching, energy efficiency, etc.), but from the effects of economic recession. In addition, despite decontrol, American oil production is likely to decline at least slightly by the end of the decade, and possibly by as much as 2.5 to 3 mbd. (It is sobering to realize that, even in the face of sharply higher oil prices and the coming on stream of Alaskan oil, domestic oil production actually fell from 9.2 mbd in 1973 to 8.6 mbd in 1981.[41]) Together with the reduction in private oil stocks, these factors work against long-term continuation of an oil glut.

Second, world oil demand is likely to increase among three groups of countries during the remainder of the 1980s: the non-oil producing LDCs, the Communist countries, and the OPEC states themselves. Assuming Western economic recovery and that oil prices remain constant, OPEC production of 25 mbd could be required in 1985, and as much as 30 mbd in 1990.[42] This is approximately the amount produced by OPEC in 1978-1979.

Third, and even more imponderable, is the risk of unexpected future events (war, domestic upheavals, accident, even sabotage) acting as catalysts to touch off new oil shocks. Prediction of any one specific occurrence is foolhardy; expectation that some kind of disruptive turmoil will occur is far more plausible.

To be sure, there are other factors to take into account, particularly the behavior of the OPEC countries individually and OPEC as a group. Although the possibilities of ample world supply and stable or declining oil prices through the next decade cannot be ruled out, this would be based on a good deal of luck. While uncertainties abound, many forecasts suggest a tightening oil pattern in the last half of the 1980s.[43] It is precisely this, however, that makes for a volatile world oil pattern, and one vulnerable to sudden new oil shocks. Hence the fact of continued American and allied dependence on imported oil from the middle East poses a major, enduring energy security risk.

Administration policies have left the United States well positioned neither to cope with a future oil crisis nor to cooperate effectively with its allies. A new oil shock could prove as damaging as either of the first two crises, or even more so. Serious economic disruption, weakened alliance relations, and further harm to the internal fabric of Western societies would all be likely to occur.

An underlying theme of this volume has been that the world of the 1980s imposes a multiplication of issues and tradeoffs. It constrains U.S. ability to go it alone, whether in terms of minimizing the impact of external events or overlooking the consequences of its actions on others. Benjamin J. Cohen has observed in Chapter 4 that for the new administration it was simply inconceivable the United States could not reclaim its accustomed autonomy and influence over events. What Cohen has identified in the economic realm holds equally for energy security. In this case, the existence of both an integrated world oil regime and the global consequences of energy shocks imposes a tenacious interdependence. Yet just as domestic economic policy was made with limited regard for the outside world, so it has been with energy choices.

All of this suggests that the administration's concept of free world leadership is too narrow, with insufficient attention to issues outside the realm of East-West security. The approach of the United States also represents a break with a decade of policy, followed by both Republican and Democratic administrations, in seeking to manage interdependence rather than ignore or transcend it. Yet in energy security, as in economic policy, defense problems, and important regional areas, the contemporary realities are those of interdependence. A policy framed with insufficient regard for these may at times succeed through luck, but this is no cause for complacency.

Any policy choice must be made in conditions of partial uncertainty. This is no less true in the realm of energy. However, the international context of this problem calls for policies that better incorporate the imperatives of cooperation with allies and the security externalities of dependence on imported oil. At a minimum, the criteria for energy policy should include a recognition of tradeoffs, with the aim of giving greater priority to reduced oil consumption and imports. Far more effective planning for emergencies is also needed, both in long-term measures such as expansion of governmental and private oil stocks as well as in specific preparations for dealing with a crisis.

Finally, there must be greater attention to cooperation with allies. Even if the United States imported no oil from the Persian Gulf, it would still be greatly affected by a major crisis there. The impact would be felt soon enough, whether through soaring prices of our now decontrolled oil and of other forms of energy, or through the economic and political harm inflicted on the industrial democracies of Europe and Japan. The fate of these regions is inextricably linked: An energy policy based on this recognition is a matter of enlightened self-interest.

Notes

1. Source: Exxon Corporation, *Middle East Oil* (2nd edition, September 1980), p. 26. For an analysis of the evolving importance of oil and subsequent shift in bargaining power, see Robert Stobaugh and Daniel Yergin (eds.), *Energy Future: Report of the Energy Project at the Harvard Business School* (New York: Ballantine, 1980), Chapters 1 and 2.
2. Exxon, *Middle East Oil*, p. 26.
3. Organization for Economic Cooperation and Development, *Economic Outlook* (Paris), No. 27 (July 1980), p. 114.
4. For a detailed analysis of this period, see Robert J. Lieber, *Oil and the Middle East War: Europe in the Energy Crisis* (Cambridge, Mass.: Harvard Center for International Affairs, 1976). An invaluable inside account can be found in Henry Kissinger, *Years of Upheaval* (Boston, Little Brown, 1982), especially Chapters 16, 19, and 20.
5. OECD figures, based on oil import prices deflated by the prices of OECD manufactured exports, showed a decline from an index figure of 271 in 1976 to 236 in 1978 (1972 = 100). OECD, *Economic Outlook*, July 1980, p. 116.
6. "European" figures for consumption are for OECD less United States and Japan. Import figures are adjusted to exclude the United Kingdom and Norway (the North Sea oil producers). Consumption is based on total oil requirements but excludes marine bunkers. Percentages calculated from data in OECD *Economic Outlook*, No. 25 (June 1979), p. 62.
7. Calculated from data in OECD, *Economic Outlook* July 1979, p. 140.
8. David A. Stockman, "The Wrong War? The Case Against a National Energy Policy," *Public Interest*, Autumn 1978, pp. 3-44, at p. 21.
9. Figures from *Monthly Energy Review*, March 1980, p. 92; and April 1981, p. 92.
10. For a thoughtful treatment of Carter programs and problems, see Daniel Yergin, "America in the Strait of Stringency," Chapter 4, in Yergin and Martin Hillenbrand (eds.), *Global Insecurity: A Strategy for Energy and Economic Renewal* (Boston: Houghton Mifflin, 1982).
11. See Robert J. Lieber, "Cohesion and Disruption in the Western Alliance," In Yergin and Hillenbrand, *Global Insecurity*, Chapter 11.
12. *Monthly Energy Review*, October 1982, pp. 31 and 33. U.S. oil imports in 1978 averaged 8.0 mbd.
13. The National Energy Policy Plan, U.S. Department of Energy, July 1981. Summarized in *Energy Insider*, August 3, 1981, pp. 3-6.
14. *Wall Street Journal*, September 5, 1980.
15. Figures from *Monthly Energy Review*, December 1982, p. 95.
16. Gasoline prices rose approximately 14 cents per gallon and then drifted lower in response to conditions of oil glut.
17. Jonathan P. Stern, "Specters and Pipe Dreams," *Foreign Policy*, No. 48 (Fall 1982), p. 23.
18. A detailed account appears in *The New York Times*, July 1, 1982, p. D2.
19. *Financial Times* (London), February 25, 1982.
20. Figures for 1990 are CIA estimates. See *International Defense Review*, 1/1982, pp. 15-18. EEC estimates are somewhat higher: Germany, 34 percent; France, 26 percent; and Italy, 35 percent. *Ibid*. Oil import figures are from CIA, *International Energy Statistical Review*, February 22, 1982, p. 24. The total volume of Soviet gas exports to Western Europe in 1990 has been estimated as the equivalent of 1.0 to 1.1 mbd.
21. For an illuminating account of allied disagreements over Soviet *oil* exports to Western Europe in the early 1960s, see Bruce W. Jentleson, "Krushchev's Oil

and Brezhnev's Natural Gas Pipelines," in Robert J. Lieber (ed.), *Will Europe Fight for Oil?* (New York: Praeger, 1983).

22. *The New York Times*, July 2, 1982.

23. On June 22nd, for example, the EEC Council attacked the United States decision to prohibit the export of components and ban the use of licenses already granted and the use of components already supplied:
    > This action taken without any consultation with the Community implies an extra-territorial extension of the U.S. jurisdiction which, in the circumstances, is contrary to the principles of international law, unacceptable to the Community, and unlikely to be recognized in courts in the EEC.

    Source: quoted in "Policy Statement by Chancellor Helmut Schmidt, "Federal Republic of Germany, *Statements and Speeches*, Vol. V, No. 15 (June 24, 1982), (New York: German Information Center), p. 4.

24. For French and British reactions, see the *Washington Post*, 15 November, 1982. The text of the Reagan statement can be found in *The New York Times*, 14 November, 1982.

25. *The Economist* (London), 20 November, 1982.

26. Summary of National Energy Policy Plan, U.S. Department of Energy, *Energy Insider*, August 3, 1981, p. 3. Emphasis added.

27. *Washington Post*, October 28, 1981.

28. This had been established under the 1980 Energy Security Act. See the account in *Congressional Quarterly*, May 29, 1982, pp. 1249-1252.

29. A 35-million-barrel increase in the SPR was offset by a 100-million barrel reduction in private stocks. See *Business Week*, June 14, 1982. Other figures suggested an even sharper contrast: daily additions of 200,000 barrels per day to the SPR versus destocking of 1.4 mbd. *Congressional Quarterly*, May 29, 1982, pp. 1249-1252. A five cent per gallon gasoline tax was enacted in late 1982.

30. *Bulletin of the Atomic Scientists*, April 1982. Also see Edward R. Fried, "The World Bank and Energy Investments," in the Brookings Institution, *The Future of the World Bank* (Washington D.C.: Brookings Dialogues on Public Policy, 1982), pp. 27-31.

31. Quoted in *Energy Insider*, August 3, 1981, p. 3. Emphasis added.

32. Private communication, May 12, 1982.

33. Even emergency planning was downgraded. In the words of an administration official sympathetic to the president, "We have options but not a policy." Interview by the author, Washington, D.C., May 17, 1982.

34. The vetoed legislation was the Standby Petroleum Allocation Act. Previous legislation (the Emergency Petroleum Allocation Act) had expired on September 30, 1981. *Congressional Quarterly*, May 29, 1982. The administration argued that it already possessed sufficient legislative authority.

35. *Ibid.*

36. Technically, this hinges on whether the stocks to be drawn upon are sufficiently in excess of the 90-day import level required by IEA. See U.S. Department of Energy, "Domestic and International Energy Emergency Preparedness," Assistant Secretary for Environmental Protection, Safety and Emergency Preparedness, DOE/EP-0027 (July 1981), pp. 4-5, 17, and 19.

37. *Dallas Morning News*, April 20, 1982, p. 1A.

38. In 1981, the volume of U.S. oil imports from OPEC and OAPEC remained higher than in 1973. American imports from OPEC were 3.3 mbd in 1981, compared with 3.0 mbd in 1973. Oil from the OAPEC states amounted to 1.8 mbd in 1981, as against 0.9 mbd in 1973. (See Table 6-1.)

39. *Monthly Energy Review*, December 1982, p. 96. Consumption was 35.9 mbd in 1979, 33.0 in 1980, and 31.3 in 1981.

40. *Ibid.*, p. 31. 1979 equaled 8.0 mbd; 1981 equaled 5.4 mbd.

41. Data from *Monthly Energy Review*, October 1982, p. 32.

42. Edward R. Fried, "After the Oil Glut," *The Brookings Bulletin*, Winter/Spring 1982, pp. 6-11.

43. See e.g., Robert Stobaugh, "World Energy to the Year 2000," in Yergin and Hillenbrand, *Global Insecurity*, Chapter 2. This is also foreseen in the projections of Exxon, the CIA, DOE, and the IEA.

III

Regional Problems

7

Reagan and the Russians: United States Policy Toward the Soviet Union and Eastern Europe

Alexander Dallin and Gail W. Lapidus

Introduction: The Promise and the Reality

The Reagan administration came into office on the strength of a pledge to bring about a fundamental change in the direction of American foreign as well as domestic policy. Central to this promise was the determination to initiate a new departure in both the substance and the conduct of American policy toward the Soviet Union. The repudiation of detente and the reassertion of American primacy were the key elements of this new orientation. Alleging that previous administrations had permitted the erosion of American economic and military strength and had acquiesced in a dangerous expansion of Soviet power, the new administration assigned

Alexander Dallin is Professor of History and Political Science and chairman of the International Relations Program at Stanford University. Formerly director of the Russian Institute and Adlai E. Stevenson Professor of International Relations at Columbia University, he has served as chairman of the National Council for Soviet and East European Research. He is the author and editor of a number of books and articles, of which the most recent include "Domestic Sources of Soviet Foreign Policy," "Soviet-American Relations in the 1980's," and "Soviet and East European Studies in the United States."

Gail W. Lapidus is Associate Professor of Political Science and Director of the Center for Slavic and East European Studies at the University of California at Berkeley. She is the author of Women in Soviet Society, *of "Soviet Society in the 1980's" (in Robert F. Byrnes, ed.,* After Brezhnev: Sources of Soviet Conduct in the 1980's, *Indiana University Press, 1983), and other articles and monographs. She is currently a Kennan Institute fellow at the Woodrow Wilson Center in Washington, D.C., studying Soviet national policy.*

The authors wish to thank Mark D. Wilson for his assistance with research for this chapter.

highest priority to reversing these trends and to challenging "Soviet imperialism" politically, economically, and militarily.

The new administration promised major changes in the conduct of American policy as well: greater consistency of purpose; greater coherence in linking assumptions to policy instruments to goals; greater competence in the management of national affairs; and above all, strong executive leadership to eliminate the multiplicity of competing views and policies that had, it claimed, undermined the credibility of American policy under the Carter administration among friends and foes alike.

Finally, the new administration held out the hope that this new approach would have a desired impact on the Soviet Union itself, at the least modifying Soviet behavior so as to produce greater restraint and reciprocity, and at best transforming the very nature of the Soviet system.

Although the full record remains to be written, there is still no broad political strategy for dealing with the Soviet Union. American policy toward the Soviet Union during the initial years of the Reagan administration has been characterized by (1) an unprecedented shift in the center of gravity of American policy to the political right, with alarmist rhetoric at times reducing international relations to a world-wide struggle against the Soviet Union; (2) a lack of conception, coherence, consistency and competence in the formulation and conduct of American policy toward the Soviet Union and Eastern Europe, and at best uncertain executive leadership; and (3) an impact on the Soviet Union that is not yet fully defined but that risks, in the long run, giving support to the views of those within the Soviet policy making community who see the "American threat" in the most extreme and alarmist terms, who are most skeptical of the prospects for cooperative relationships between the two superpowers, and who prefer greater reliance on Soviet military and economic power to increased interdependence with the United States.

Soviet-American Relations: The Historical Context

The Perennial Problem

The Soviet Union has been the single most important problem for American foreign policy makers since the defeat of Germany and Japan in World War II. It has been the primary cause of huge military expenditures, of a network of alliances, of a far-flung and complex intelligence effort, and of a public state of mind that has fluctuated between an exaggerated optimism about the prospects of Soviet-American collaboration and, more frequently, an obsessive anxiety about the "Soviet threat."

From the very start, the Reagan administration thus confronted the fundamental challenge that has preoccupied American foreign policy for over three decades: to define an appropriate balance between the pursuit of containment and the pursuit of accommodation. Its answer, as we shall see, differs sharply from the mix adopted by previous administrations. But to locate the Reagan policy — its underlying assumptions, choice of instruments, and objectives — along the broad spectrum of competing approaches to the Soviet Union, it is necessary first to review the evolution of American attitudes and policies toward the Soviet Union, and the elements of continuity and change that have characterized them.

Containment

The United States and the Soviet Union emerged from the Second World War as the two new superpowers: an unprecedented and challenging role for each. But the attitudes the leaders of the two nations brought to this new role were far from symmetrical. Stalin's determination to use the unique opportunity — the Axis powers defeated; the European powers prostrate; and the United States distant, uncertain, and eager to return to normalcy — led to the Soviet effort to expand and consolidate the area of Soviet control in Eastern Europe and the Far East. This sequence of events confirmed the worst fears and biases of some American observers, confused others, and launched the two powers on the intense and dangerous adversary relationship we call the Cold War.[1]

The original American policy of "containment" was the response to what was perceived to be the Soviet threat in Europe. One of its elements was to contain the Soviet Union "horizontally," that is, to forestall a march of the Red Army into Western Europe. The effort at alliance-building and a restoration of West European military capabilities was to produce the North Atlantic Treaty Organization (NATO). The second element stemmed from the fear that the Communist parties in Western Europe would subvert their political allies, destroy all political opposition and (in close cooperation with the Soviet Union) undermine the Western democracies and substitute systems modeled on the Soviet Union internally and allied with it internationally. The Marshall Plan was meant to be the response to this seeming danger, an effort to strengthen the economic and social fabric of European democracies and to reduce their internal vulnerability to "vertical" subversion. Most brilliantly analyzed in George F. Kennan's famous "X" article, this perspective also assumed that by blocking the further expansion of Soviet power such a policy would ultimately accomplish the larger task of transforming the Soviet system from within.

For some twenty years — until well into the 1960s — there was a far-reaching American foreign policy censensus that it was essential for the United States to contain, compete with, and under crisis conditions confront the Soviet Union. What this meant, and what this required, remained open to some dispute; continuing controversy over the meaning of "containment" only highlighted the areas of ambiguity.[2] Some thought of it as primarily geopolitical, seeing a threat of Soviet expansion primarily into neighboring territories, not only in Europe but also in the Far East (and later on, the prospect of Soviet power projection elsewhere as well). Others, by contrast, saw Soviet aggrandizement as primarily ideological, with "world Communism" the ultimate goal.

In either case, the common denominator of American policy throughout these Cold War years amounted to (1) being prepared to fight and win a war if it came to that; (2) trying to stop what was commonly assumed to be the spread of Communism; (3) insofar as a diminution of the Soviet-American conflict was perceived to be possible, achieving it by bringing about an alteration of Soviet behavior.

The most extreme version that the policy of containment took in the upper reaches of the American government was the outlook reflected in a document known as NSC 68, and drafted in the first months of 1950. The product of a study directed by the State Department's Policy Planning Staff headed by Paul H. Nitze, it accepted the notion that the Soviet Union was committed to the defeat of the United States and was preparing to launch an attack on it. It called for a tougher policy in dealing with Moscow and for a massive program of American rearmament. While the circumstances have of course changed enormously in the intervening years, the document illustrates the continuity of an influential American mind-set.

> The Soviet Union [the document stated], unlike previous aspirants to hegemony, is animated by a new fanatic faith, antithetical to our own, and seeks to impose its absolute authority over the rest of the world....

Significant here is the perception (as of 1950!) of the Soviet challenge:

> [Recent technological developments] have greatly intensified the Soviet threat to the security of the United States.... In particular, the United States now faces the contingency that within the next four or five years the Soviet Union will possess the military capability of delivering a surprise attack of such weight that the United States must have substantially increased general air, ground, and sea strength, atomic capabilities, and air and civilian defenses to deter war and to provide reasonable assurance, in the event of war, that it could survive the initial blow and go on to the eventual attainment of its objectives.

In fact, "without superior aggregate military strength, in being and readily mobilizable, a policy of 'containment' — which is in effect a policy of calculated and gradual coercion — is no more than a policy of bluff."

More broadly, NSC 68 characterized the policy of containment as one

> which seeks by all means short of war to (1) block further expansion of Soviet power, (2) expose the falsities of Soviet pretensions, (3) in-

duce a retraction of the Kremlin's control and influence, and (4) in general, so foster the seeds of destruction within the Soviet system that the Kremlin is brought at least to the point of modifying its behavior to conform to generally accepted international standards.[3]

Accommodation

The dominant adversary perspective, just sketched, was in practice modified, in the minds of many American policy makers and diplomats, by their recognition of the existence of mutual or parallel interests shared by the two superpowers. Without dismissing or ignoring the antagonistic strain, these actors were prepared to undertake or promote a variety of forms of accommodation, cooperation, and/or negotiation with the Soviet Union.

During the Second World War and in the first months thereafter, there had been widespread illusions about the nature of the postwar international order: They all hinged on Soviet-American concord. Whatever the historians' retrospective assessment of responsibility, it did not take long for these illusions to vanish. A better-founded and sustained re-emergence of the accommodationist outlook had to await the mid-1950s, following Joseph Stalin's death in 1953, when changes in the Soviet system and in Soviet policy created real possibilities for mutual efforts — such as the end of the Korean war, the Austrian peace treaty, renewed "Big Four" summits, and improved Soviet relations with West Germany, Finland, Japan, and Yugoslavia — while the acquisition of nuclear capabilities by the Soviet Union made such efforts more imperative than ever.

The mutual interest in survival prompted efforts at conflict avoidance and crisis management, such as the exploration of agreements to reduce the dangers of accidental nuclear war. The hot line between Moscow and Washington, established in 1963, symbolized this effort. More complex was the attempt to negotiate constraints on the arms race itself, with results ranging from narrow and specific agreements, such as the limited Test Ban Treaty of 1963, to protracted and wide-ranging negotiations, such as those that resulted in 1972 in SALT I and, after another seven years, in the SALT II treaty (which was never ratified by the United States).

Other areas of attempted cooperation or accommodation included relatively nonpolitical and functional areas of shared interests; joint space exploration (such as the Soyuz-Apollo mission in 1975), a sharing of information on environmental pollution, joint scientific and medical work such as cancer research, and exchanges of scholars and graduate students. They also included cultural exchanges aimed at providing not only mutual enjoyment but also better knowledge of "the other side."

On some occasions the United States and the Soviet Union found themselves on the same side of the diplomatic barricades, for example, in the negotiations for a non-proliferation treaty, in which the nuclear powers both sought to convince the others to sign and also resisted their entreaties to commit themselves to a more ambitious and specific arms control agenda; or in some of the discussions of North-South economic relations, in which the less developed countries tended to charge both the United States and the Soviet Union with neglect of their obligations to assist the poorer economies.

Finally, there were some activities that involved a calculus that whatever concessions were required, they were outweighed by the resulting benefits. Such a view presumably underlay the agreements calculated to increase Soviet-American trade (frustrated though they were by congressional action, such as the Jackson-Vanik and Stevenson Amendments). It also underlay the Helsinki accord of 1975, which, in effect, recognized Eastern Europe as a Soviet sphere. Insofar as this constituted at least a symbolic concession by the United States, it was argued, the commitments the Soviet Union undertook in regard to human rights amounted to more than a quid pro quo — either in presaging an improvement of conditions or by providing the West with a legal foundation for future concern with compliance with the Helsinki provisions.

We lack a document comparable to NSC 68 arguing the "accommodationist" side with equal vigor at similarly high levels of the United States government.[4] In part this is because suspicion or fear of the Soviet Union has invariably exceeded a sense of affinity for the leadership in Moscow; in part because bureaucrats intuitively find it less risky for themselves to argue a hard rather than a soft position; and in part because Soviet behavior or intentions, as perceived in Washington, were bound to brand a strongly accommodationist approach naïve or unrealistic. To the extent that such views became articulated and respectable, they were most likely to be voiced in the early 1970s, at the height of detente.

While the protagonists of this approach built on varying underlying assumptions, they tended to see the Soviet Union as undergoing significant internal changes in institutions and attitudes that could be promoted by an appropriate American policy. Implicit too was the view that the Soviet Union was becoming a status quo power, which might find it in its own interest to accept and cooperate in the stabilization of the international order. It was also widely believed that the transfer of goods and services to the Soviet Union inevitably and unwittingly led to the transfer of Western ideas and values as well. Trade, technology transfer, perhaps credits, arms control agreements, grain sales, and cultural exchanges were all elements of a pervasive web of interdependence that, first, would demonstrate to the Soviet elite that getting along with the West was a matter of Soviet self-interest and, second, would make any departure from this system of interdependence in the future exceedingly costly for the Soviet Union and would thus serve as a reliable brake on adventurism.

If such was the typical long-range vision, in the shorter term more specific agreements would provide for tangible benefits as well as rules of the game for both sides. In the less naïve (and less grandiose) versions, this strategy called for the use of American (or, more broadly, Western) resources as both carrots and sticks in dealing with the Soviet Union.

United States Policy as a Mix

American policy toward the Soviet Union may be described as an ever-changing mix between containment (confrontation, challenge, or hostility short of war) and accommodation (coexistence, adaptation, or cooperation). What has affected the particular mix at any given time? Both secular trends and unique occurrences, personalities, and accidents must be invoked here. Most broadly, the major shifts may be summed up as the results of three interacting and interdependent complexes: (1) the nature of American power, values, and morale; (2) Soviet capabilities, perceptions, and priorities; and (3) changes in the international system, above all the emergence of third actors, the change in the strategic balance and in weapons technology, and the loss of American hegemony. These have often been ably described.[5] In the present context, the evolution of the Soviet system deserves to be singled out. In the aftermath of the Second World War, which had cost huge losses in human lives and enormous devastation, the Soviet Union did not even remotely constitute a threat to the United States proper (at a time when, moreover, Moscow had no — or later, very few — atomic weapons). By the 1970s this had begun to change fundamentally. The Soviet Union had attained essential parity in strategic weapons; it was acquiring influence worldwide and for the first time could claim truly to have global interests and global reach; and it demanded recognition as the equal of the United States politically as well — a status of political parity that mattered to Moscow and that Washington alternately conceded and denied. While the Soviet economy suffered from numerous difficulties and Soviet science and technology lagged behind those of the West, and while specialists pointed to a troublesome cumulation of unresolved sociopolitical problems in the Soviet Union (let alone Eastern Europe), there was little doubt of the formidable Soviet ability to wage both conventional and nuclear war. Moscow stood to benefit from the political fallout of this military potential.

If, then, the West's initial fears in the 1940s had centered on Soviet *intentions*, by the 1970s Soviet *capabilities* gave substance to the notion of a Soviet "menace," whereas the nature of Soviet intentions remained for many observers obscure, contested, and perhaps in flux.

Yet another set of foreign policy determinants was locked within the American political system itself. The characteristics of particular administrations and the key actors within them — say, a John Foster

Dulles or a Henry Kissinger — have played an important part; so have institutional arrangements, such as the role of the National Security Council. More broadly, the policy mix has been affected by the whole range of domestic constraints on foreign policy, which have often powerfully affected, distorted, or frustrated the conduct of foreign affairs.

Perhaps the most important yet amorphous cluster is the world of interest groups, formal and informal. Lobbies for ethnic groups (Poles, Jews), defense industries, and many other special causes groups (business groups, farmers, and organized labor) have a particular stake in policy toward the Soviet Union and Eastern Europe. The four-year cycle of presidential elections and administrations adds to the difficulty of sustaining a coherent foreign policy over time. By their very nature, Soviet-American relations require patience and steadfastness. These are hard to come by in Washington, where the temptation to resort to a quick fix is high. Moreover, bureaucratic politics shapes and misshapes foreign policy, as will be amply apparent from the record of any recent administration. Contests over "turf," jurisdiction, and resources, interagency fights, interservice rivalries, executive-legislative splits, and personal feuds often overwhelm the particular issues and policies at stake.

And, in regard to the Soviet problem in particular, note should be made of the pervasive responsiveness of the American public, of the media, and of politicians to anti-Communist and anti-Russian themes. From cartoon strips to spy novels, the Soviets are readily portrayed as villains. And American politicians will be only too cognizant of the danger of being portrayed as soft on the communists, let alone appeasing the Russians. If these have been fairly constant sources of domestic constraints, others have over time made for a changing balance. Notable among these has been the breakdown of the foreign policy consensus accelerated by what has been called the Vietnam syndrome, including a reluctance to use or even contemplate the use of force in support of American interests or clients abroad.

However we wish to delimit the Cold War years, clearly a new phase opened in 1969 and in effect spanned the 1970s. This new period is identified with detente, and it illustrates many of the factors just cited as making for change. The motivations and calculations on both sides included some well-known and some less obvious factors. In the short run, Henry Kissinger hoped to use the Russians to apply pressure on North Vietnam to settle the conflict in Southeast Asia on terms acceptable to the United States. In Europe, the Federal Republic of Germany had blazed the trail of agreements with Moscow and Warsaw that at last normalized relations and seemed to settle the explosive Berlin issue. American observers thought, correctly, that they saw signs of earnest Soviet interest in an arms limitation treaty. And if, as it appeared, Moscow was seriously interested in American goods and know-how, this provided an opportunity, Kissinger and others argued at the time, to involve the Soviet Union precisely in the sort of web of interdependence that would, in the long haul, help make it a more responsible member of the international community.

As seen from Moscow, by the late 1960s the Soviet Union was for the first time approaching the United States in strategic power. The prospect of gross strategic parity created finally a realistic basis for meaningful arms control accords with the United States: Now the consequences of reductions or limitations would be substantially symmetrical in impact on both sides. It also gave substance to the Soviet claim for recognition of its status as a coequal superpower. Another important Soviet purpose in moving toward detente was the desire to benefit from imports of Western technology that might accelerate Soviet economic modernization; this may be understood as a preference for imports from abroad over, and substituting for, potentially destabilizing and uncertain attempts at economic reform at home. Such a perspective marked a fundamental departure from the traditional Soviet pursuit of *autarky*, or self-sufficiency.

Finally, the Soviet-American rapprochement was given additional impetus by the Sino-Soviet split. The Kremlin hoped to improve relations with the United States in order to increase the isolation of the People's Republic of China internationally and from the United States in particular. Some Soviet representatives even explored the possibility of a Soviet-American condominium, including the prospect of joint action against an "aggressive" China.

In retrospect, it is clear that both sides oversold detente, though the characteristic American swing from hostility to euphoria went well beyond Moscow's more restrained tones. The following years were to show that unsettled issues and ambiguities in agreements rapidly overtook the accords that had been reached. What particularly upset the American calculations and expectations were (1) the relentless Soviet buildup of military might, which seemed to proceed at a steady rate, in defiance of American expectations, all through the 1960s and 1970s; and (2) the Soviet effort to take advantage of instabilities, power vacuums, and political opportunities in areas from which logistic limitations and Western predominance had previously all but excluded the Soviet Union: Angola and Ethiopia were the prime examples, particularly galling to the United States because they involved the use of Cuban troops and instructors as proxies for the Soviet Union. Moscow in turn had its own list of grievances concerning American behavior, and while some items on the list were no more than propaganda gambits, the remaining ones — from impediments to expanded trade and credit to exclusion from Middle Eastern negotiations to delays in concluding SALT II — made Moscow increasingly skeptical about the benefits of detente with the United States. After a long hiatus, Soviet media in the late 1970s began once again to speak of a hostile encirclement, conjuring up a coalition of the United States, NATO, China, and Japan against the Soviet camp. The Soviet invasion of Afghanistan, at the end of 1979, killed whatever was left of detente and accelerated a shift in American attitudes and policies in the final year of the Carter Administration, including the withdrawal of SALT II from the United States Senate and a buildup of American defenses.[6] The 1980s thus began with a seriously damaged Soviet-American relationship, which the new administration inherited from the Carter years.

The Legacy of Ambiguities

The seventies had produced an unprecedented accumulation of un-certainties and ambiguities in the American view of the Soviet Union. Was it a potentially responsible treaty partner, sharing a serious interest in arms limitation, or would it continue to "violate all the treaties it ever signed"? Was it bent on expansion, as the attack on Afghanistan seemed to argue, with all talk of peace and friendship little more than deceit or tactics, or had it assumed that the United States had written off Afghanistan — a special case rather than a first step on the road to the Persian Gulf and the Indian Ocean? Was the Soviet Union increasingly powerful militarily, or was it a house of cards, a system so weakened by a failed ideology and a failed economy that its decay was already under way? Had the Soviet system begun to change significantly in the years after Stalin, or were these in the last analysis but cosmetic alterations that did not touch on the evil or dangerous essence of the system itself?

As American disenchantment became more pronounced, it also became more difficult to tell whether detente had failed or had never been given a fair try. It is scarcely surprising that there were profound questions and differences concerning the Soviet Union, and few informed and conclusive answers to them, as the United States went into the presidential elections of 1980.

The Reagan Years

On the Eve

It was clear from the political career and rhetoric of Ronald Reagan, and from his choice of foreign policy advisers during the campaign of 1980, that his election was meant to stand, among other things, for getting tough with the Russians. Candidate Reagan's speeches and press conferences had for some years been peppered with remarks more blunt in their hostility toward the Soviet Union and more sweeping in their condemnation of "Marxism" than those of any other major candidate of recent vintage.

Scarcely less damning was his critique of the Carter administration (and implicitly, its Republican predecessors) for its acquiescence in the decline of American power and a corresponding expansion of Soviet power in the intervening years. A post-Vietnam excess of guilt and breast-beating had undermined both confidence in American purposes and the will to lead, while the wearisome sequences of negotiations and under-standings epitomized by detente had conferred a one-sided advantage on the Soviet Union.[7]

The pronouncements from the Reagan camp focused particular atten-tion on the contrast between the continued Soviet military buildup and the alleged failure of the United States to keep pace. The doomsday scenarios to which a tilt in the strategic balance gave rise were reinforced and elaborated, moreover, by the Committee on the Present Danger, a group of concerned political figures and academics who warned that the United States was becoming number two, that the Soviet Union remained committed to the goal of a world controlled from Moscow, and that the liberals were in effect practicing appeasement of the Soviet Union by seeking to prolong detente. The deteriorating international situation, in their view, required immediate and drastic action. In the words of Norman Podhoretz, one of the most articulate if intemperate spokesmen for this approach, "I think if present trends continue, there may be a Cuban missile crisis in reverse in the Persian Gulf.... Then [the Soviet Union] will be in a position to dictate terms to almost everyone in the world, including us...." [8]

It was indeed easy for critics to point to a seeming American retreat in the aftermath of Vietnam, illustrated by the congressional ban on assistance to "anti-Communist" forces in Angola, the embarrassment caused by the Iranian seizure of American hostages and the failure of the American raid to free them, and American inaction in the face of the extension of Soviet influence to Somalia, and then Ethiopia and South Yemen. Never mind that this was at best an incomplete picture, which ignored both Soviet setbacks — most notably, the Sino-Soviet split — and Soviet restraint on other occasions. The Soviet invasion of Afghan-istan, in December 1979, was thus bound to trigger a more extreme re-sponse from the Carter administration, lest it lend further credence to the charges of indecision and softness raised against it from the Repub-lican right.

There was less clarity on the causes of this decline in American power. While it was easy for critics to point to a self-imposed retreat from American involvements and commitments abroad, there was a tendency to minimize changes in the structure of the international system itself that reduced the relative share of American power in the world. There was also a tendency to ignore the gap between public expectations, based on assumptions of omnipotence fed by the unique but temporary circumstances of the postwar era, and limited American capabilities to affect political developments in different regions of the world.

The ineptness of the Carter administration provided another element of obvious consensus in the Reagan camp prior to the election: the determination to avoid the images of naïveté, divisiveness, incoherence, and backbiting that plagued the Carter team, especially in the field of foreign affairs. The transition teams in the foreign affairs and defense fields, appointed by President-elect Reagan in November 1980, seemed to confirm by their composition that the new administration would pursue a clear and more militant anti-Soviet course. Yet a close student of Reagan's backers might well have recognized even before the inauguration of the new president that there were muted ambiguities and contradictions in the victorious team's view of Soviet power, objectives, and capabilities — due in large part to the composition of the political coalition that the Reagan strategists had put together. Including as it did old-line Republicans favorably oriented toward business interests; neoconservatives hyperbolically dramatizing the options America faced between gloom and doom or newfound glory; professional politicians blithely ignorant of more than shopworn stereotypes when it came to explaining Soviet affairs; right-wing Democrats captured by — or indeed in the lead of — the Committee on the Present Danger; and retired military officers welcoming the prospect of unprecedented defense budgets and "sticking it to the Reds," it was a coalition unlikely to find a common ground once the new administration was obliged to turn from a critique of past policies to the formulation and implementation of its own.

Key Actors and Institutions

Many of the actors and agencies central to this chapter are described elsewhere in this volume. Several deserve to be singled out because of the central role they were to play in the making and conduct of American policy toward the Soviet Union.

The White House has of course the last say in critical and contentious matters, a fact reconfirmed in the resignation of Alexander Haig as Secretary of State. The president himself appears to have less of a personal interest in foreign policy than his predecessor had and relies heavily on his subordinates to provide information and structure policy options. His choices seem to be based on instinct and deeply rooted prejudices, and his advisers often tend to tailor their recommendations to fit his presumed views and biases.

In its first year this gave considerable power to the trio of presidential assistants. In the second year, the forced retirement of Richard V. Allen brought William P. Clark to the critical position of head of the National Security Council. Judge Clark, whose previous experience had been in California politics and law, thereafter played a key role in funneling and filtering foreign policy proposals and recommendations from various agencies to the White House.

Though he failed to receive presidential sanction for the sweeping direction of all foreign affairs activities in the government, which he had solicited without false modesty when first appointed, Secretary Haig during his tenure in office had formally (though not always in practice) the preeminent role in the articulation of foreign policy, such as it was. This was constitutionally proper and remains so under Secretary Shultz. It was also inevitable with an individual such as General Haig. Ambitious though disciplined, outspoken though inarticulate, often concealing common sense amidst clouds of bluster, Haig was in spite of himself more experienced than his cabinet colleagues in European (or for that matter, military) affairs.[9] His two immediate subordinates (after Clark moved to the NSC) brought an element of experience and professional competence to the management of Soviet-American relations: Walter J. Stoessel, a former ambassador to Moscow and Bonn (who retired in 1982) and Lawrence E. Eagleburger, who had served with Haig under Kissinger.

The arrival of George P. Schultz enhanced the role and effectiveness of the Secretary of State within the United States government. In style, it made for more discretion and quiet diplomacy. Shultz was both willing and able to listen and learn. In substance, his own views on the Soviet Union remained to be spelled out; but, along with a greater preoccupation with economic issues, he made clear his continued concern with managing relations between the United States and its allies (as was apparent over the question of pipeline sanctions, discussed below) as well as its adversaries, and in contrast to some of the administration ideologues, he espoused a more pragmatic approach to foreign affairs.

The major institutional and political counterweight to the State Department was the Department of Defense under Caspar Weinberger, Jr. An experienced administrator who had run a number of agencies, he had no systematic knowledge of foreign affairs. Among his major assets were the president's confidence in him and his ability to reduce complicated problems to very simple terms. Insofar as the Soviet Union was concerned, Weinberger came to his job with little knowledge; no ideological fanaticism but strong convictions concerning the need for a no-nonsense, massive buildup of American strength; a total lack of trust in Soviet promises or pronouncements; and a predisposition to believe alarmist, worst-case allegations. Among those whose views and information influenced Weinberger, Richard N. Perle, Assistant Secretary for International Security Affairs, occupied a prominent place. A long-time adviser to Senator Henry Jackson, Perle was an effective political operator on the militant right insofar as Soviet relations are concerned, with close contacts to the neoconservatives and easy access to many Washington influentials.

It is ironic that, among other executive agencies, the Central Intelligence Agency should have been viewed as less than reliable by the militant right, which had long suspected it of underestimating Soviet military capabilities and expenditures, while the United States Arms Control and Disarmament Agency should have become the stronghold of a number of veteran hawks, whose appointment properly raised questions about the administration's commitment to arms control. Even more remarkable was the political twist by which the initial Reagan appointee to head that agency, Eugene V. Rostow, an uncompromising veteran anti-Communist, should have been dismissed in January 1983, in part for what he described as an excess of zeal. The choice of Kenneth L. Adelman as his replacement did not betoken an ungrading of the enterprise by the White House. It was no less ironic that the chief arms control negotiator, Paul H. Nitze, who had earlier resigned from the American negotiating team when he found SALT II overly favorable to the Soviet Union, was reprimanded by the Reagan White House for exceeding his instructions in exploring an agreement with his Soviet counterpart.

While appointments elsewhere have varied in quality, virtually none has brought into the administration individuals with either personal or professional knowledge of Soviet affairs. Loyalty to the president and managerial experience account for most senior appointments dealing with the Soviet Union. Whether out of disillusionment with "expertise" or out of the conviction that decision makers have little to learn about the Soviet Union, the Reagan administration finds itself singularly lacking in individuals at critical policy making or advisory positions who are knowledgeable about Soviet affairs.[10] While no doubt a diversity of points of view on the Soviet Union exists at lower levels of the governmental bureaucracy, these are scarcely represented where it counts.

More surprising perhaps was the near absence from the administration of representatives of an assortment of views on the political far right. From the outset no room was found for Maj. Gen. George Keegan, formerly chief of Air Force Intelligence, or Lt. Gen. Daniel O. Graham, former head of the Defense Intelligence Agency, both outspoken alarmists about Soviet capabilities and intentions. And by mid-1982 a new "rightist opposition" was beginning to form among publicists and others who shared a "neo-conservative anguish over Reagan's foreign policy," which one of their number published prominently as a contribution to the backstage debate only weeks prior to Haig's resignation.[11]

Initial Policy Orientations

From January 1981 on, the initial orientation of the Reagan administration was to deal with the Soviet Union in three ways: first, to distance itself from previous policies, making clear its rejection of detente, the SALT II treaty, and other such arrangements; second, to propose major increases in American defense appropriations and unprecedented procurement to restore American military superiority; and third, to engage in rhetorical political warfare with the Soviet Union. The president demonstrated the new line at his first news conference after his inauguration, in replying to a question about Soviet intentions:

> I know of no leader of the Soviet Union ... that has not more than once repeated ... their determination that their goal must be the promotion of world communism and a one-world socialist or communist state. ...
> Now as long as they do that and as long as they, at the same time, have openly and publicly declared that the only morality they recognize is what will further their cause: meaning they reserve unto themselves the right to commit any crime, to lie, to cheat, and to obtain that and that is moral, not immoral, and we operate on a different set of standards, I think when you do business with them — even at a detente — you keep that in mind.[12]

As for the proposed defense buildup, Secretary Weinberger justified it in a statement before the Senate Armed Services Committee by asserting:

> It it is neither reasonable nor prudent to view the Soviet military buildup as defensive in nature. It would be dangerously naïve to expect the Soviet Union, if it once achieves military superiority, not to exploit their military capability even more fully than they are now doing. We must assume some rationale behind the Soviets' enormous allocation of resources to the military at the expense of basic human needs. In fact, we have clear evidence of aggressive Soviet behavior around the globe. ...
> This Soviet activity, unchallenged in recent years by the United States, has led to Soviet gains and the growing perception that the Soviets and their proxies can act with impunity. This trend must be halted and then reversed.[13]

The new defense program was meant to serve a variety of purposes. It could be seen as an end in itself, intended to reverse the widening gap between Soviet and American expenditures and narrowing the gap between military capabilities; it meant to stop Soviet initiatives and, ideally, isolate or roll back the Soviet Union; it was part of an effort intended to postpone serious negotiations until the United States reached a stronger bargaining position. Domestically the attempt to dramatize the urgency and magnitude of the need for a stronger posture was meant, in the first place, to secure prompt congressional approval — where it implied a growing budget deficit and a sacrifice of social programs — with a minimum of difficulty or delay. But when all is said and done, talking tough and carrying a big (and expensive) stick do not constitute a political strategy for dealing with the other superpower. As Zbigniew Brzezinski remarked, "A stance is not a policy."

Assumptions and Mind Sets: In Search of a Typology

To understand why no systematic political strategy toward the Soviet Union was formulated for a long time, it is necessary to step back from the bureaucratic feuds, from the preoccupation with the domestic economy, and from the elements of intellectual helplessness occasionally manifest in the administration — all of which impeded the formulation of foreign policy — and sketch more broadly the often conflicting assumptions that different political actors held and the conflicting policy preferences that these assumptions prompted.

Analysts of United States foreign policy have devoted considerable effort to the task of distinguishing in some systematic way the different orientations toward the Soviet Union that have characterized the policy making and specialist communities and of grouping them into various schools or camps on the basis of their underlying assumptions about the nature of the Soviet system or Soviet behavior and their recommendations for American policy. While the terminology varies greatly, as do the criteria used to classify these different orientations, there are some common and consistent threads that weave across a number of such attempts.

The majority of such groupings are dichotomous ones: They treat approaches to the Soviet Union in terms of a dialogue between two opposing orientations. In simplest form, this is the cleavage between left and right, soft and hard, or dove and hawk. In the more sophisticated recent versions, this is Daniel Yergin's contrast between what he calls the "Yalta school" and the "Riga school"[14] or Robert Osgood's contrast between what he calls "Analysis A" and "Analysis B."[15]

These labels, and similar ones used by others, do capture a real and profound split in American perceptions. Yet this dichotomous framework fails, in our view, to differentiate adequately among what are three distinct and significant perspectives: an "essentialist," a "mechanistic," and an "interactionist" approach.

The essentialist approach focuses its attention not on what the Soviet Union does but what it is. Highly determinist in approach, it defines the Soviet system as inherently evil, sees little prospect for change, and denies the benefits of piecemeal accommodation.

The mechanistic approach is concerned with Soviet behavior, not essences. It views the Soviet threat as primarily geopolitical and takes the traditional view that power can and must be checked with equal or superior power: The answer to Soviet ambitions is containment.

The interactionist approach (which has at times been labeled cybernetic or organismic) involves greater recognition of differences, even uncertainties, within the Soviet elite, rather than seeing Moscow as a unitary purposive actor. It assumes a learning process that includes significant feedback from Soviet experience abroad to decision makers' assumptions. It implies the need for greater fine-tuning of analysis and policy responses and generally assumes a more pervasive interdependence between the two adversary systems than the other two approaches would grant.[16]

Schematically we may now distinguish the three approaches in terms of a number of linked assumptions about the nature of the Soviet Union and its implications for American policy. (1) In regard to the *sources of Soviet behavior*, the essentialists see the Soviet system as inherently evil and inherently expansionist (although they may differ on whether the reason for this is its Russian, Communist, or totalitarian essence); they see it as substantially unchanging; and they minimize the importance of Soviet elite politics and the differences among individual actors in Moscow. The mechanists see the Soviet threat as primarily geopolitical, but are likely to differ among themselves on the sources and likelihood of change in the future and on the role of politics in Moscow. The interactionists see the sources of Soviet-American conflict in both structural — superpower — elements and in mutual perceptions and misperceptions. They are more likely to see elements of diversity, if not pluralism, in Soviet elite politics and to anticipate the possibility of significant evolution in the Soviet system.

(2) In respect to the *nature of the Soviet threat*, the essentialists will divide between those who see world revolution and those who see Russian hegemony as the ultimate object of Soviet intentions. They will agree on the formidable military challenge the Soviet Union represents and are likely to see Communism and Soviet society increasingly in a state of crisis. They are inclined to believe that domestic crises in the Soviet Union and Eastern Europe are apt to propel the Soviet leadership into compensatory adventures abroad. They tend to see the Soviet Union as a unitary actor with a coherent long-range blueprint or master plan and both the intent and the capability to carry it out; this perspective moves from imputed intent to outcome without particular concern about intervening constraints. Finally, they incline to a two-camp view of the world — a bipolar approach that tends to see conflicts anywhere in terms of the superpower relationship, minimizing local and regional factors.

The mechanistic approach is likely to see Soviet superpower preponderance as the ultimate objective, with the quest for greater security (as defined by Moscow) and superpower status as more immediate goals. It may be more agnostic in regard to the effect of internal Soviet crises on foreign policy and on the Soviet responsibility for violence and instability the world over.

The interactionist approach, finally, may lead to various assessments of Soviet intentions and capabilities. Rejecting the notion of a blueprint, it tends to see in Soviet foreign policy a greater reactive element to events abroad. It also sees the Soviet Union as beneficiary, and not necessarily as instigator, of instability in Third World areas, which may create opportunities for the Soviet Union. And it inclines to conclude that domestic difficulties, rather than push it outward, are more likely to constrain Soviet foreign policy.

(3) As for the *prospects of Soviet-American accommodation*, the essentialists judge the likelihood of war, and quite possibly nuclear war, between the two powers to be high. Some have argued that Moscow seriously contemplates launching an all-out nuclear strike against the United States. They believe that the Soviet Union has no interest in a stabilized world order acceptable to the United States. They see little point or consequence in limited negotiations or partial agreements. To them, the only viable policy is one that seeks to weaken the capabilities or to affect the survival of the system itself.

The mechanistic approach, by contrast, takes a more open-minded approach to the possibility of useful negotiations — not as a substitute for force but as a supplement to it — and accepts the possibility of effective deterrence of Soviet military initiatives. While the more militant approach may still place a high likelihood on the prospect of a Soviet-American conflict, the more moderate variant is likely to focus on the need, and the possibility, to "manage" the adversary relationship by means short of war.[17] Believing in "leverage," it is likely to use a combination of both carrots and sticks to shape Soviet behavior abroad.

The interactionists would agree with such a "managerial" perspective, emphasize the possibility of identifying areas of parallel Soviet and American interests, and favor a step-by-step approach to the negotiation of agreements. They would hope that over time a common code of rules of the game and restraint could gain acceptance. Because they see the climate of relations as important in affecting the Soviet elite's attitudes and perhaps the balance of power within the Soviet elite, they ascribe importance to American and other foreign behavior as a determinant of Soviet foreign policy and reject the notion that it is entirely internally driven. More inclined to see the loss of American hegemony as an inevitable product of secular trends, they would settle for world order rather than attempts at American primacy.

In terms of this typology, one might summarize the policy controversy within the Carter administration as centering on the tension between the mechanistic and interactionist arguments, while in the Reagan administration the debate has shifted: the interactionists are missing, and the essentialists have landed in unprecedented force. Insofar as they are derived from different conceptions of the Soviet Union, the current policy feuds may be said to range between essentialists and mechanists.

Political actors obviously do not always adhere to what logically should be their consistent operating assumptions or policy preferences. Some will change their minds; others will prefer not to commit themselves. In the top echelons of the Reagan administration, one "insider" was quoted as saying,

> There are no groups. There is a continuum from purists to pragmatic conservatives, with one and the same person falling in different places on different issues. The purists are Manichaean in the medieval sense. They believe the Soviets are the devil, and that you can't bargain with the devil without losing your soul. The pragmatists take into account the world as it is.[18]

Moreover, the mechanistic approach covers a broad spectrum. Henry Kissinger and Zbigniew Brzezinski would both have fitted here. In the Reagan administration, Haig, Shultz, and Weinberger might all be included in this bracket. Distinguishing further between moderate and militant views within this group, Reagan belongs closer to the essentialist end of the spectrum but with distinct overtones of militant mechanistic assumptions, while a number of officials, such as William P. Clark, Richard Perle, and Richard Pipes, would be assigned to his right. Secretaries Weinberger and Shultz occupy opposite ends of the mechanistic sector. The continuing ambiguities of the administration's approach are thus due in part to unresolved conflicts over assumptions and policy preferences among key officials.

A Strategic Consensus?

If there existed a paper outlining in broad strokes United States policy toward the Soviet Union — and there is no indication that such an official paper exists — its outlook would, in all likelihood, be more consistent, more uncompromising, and more extreme than its implementation might require. Its assumptions include dichotomist, globalist, and unilateralist elements.

The point of departure is a dichotomous view of the world: "we" and "they." It classifies people as friends or enemies, with little room for anything else. It tends to see neutrality as suspect and its advocates as potential dupes of communism. It tends to dismiss shadings, be they among different Soviet officials or between Soviet and other Communist actors, as curiosities at best, essentially trivial and insignificant. While ideological in origin, its political corollary is simple: "He who is not with us is against us." If the advocates of a nuclear freeze or the West European allies dissent from the official American position, they must be either infected by or vulnerable to Communist propaganda.

At the same time, a globalist "two-camp view" greatly simplifies the perception of world affairs, especially in the Third World, where events can be seen in terms of the overriding world-wide struggle between East

and West, to the exclusion of local wants or needs. As the president remarked in an interview prior to his election, "Let's not delude ourselves,
the Soviet Union underlies all the unrest that is going on. If they weren't
engaged in this game of dominoes, there wouldn't be any hot spots in the
world." [19] To be sure, this perspective makes it hard to explain differences
among friends and allies, be they between Taiwan and the People's Republic of China, or between the United States itself and Japan or Western
Europe. The globalist perspective underlay the predictably futile idea of
forging an anti-Soviet regional security pact in the Middle East compris-
ing states from Israel to Saudi Arabia. It ignores the fact that global and
regional tensions need not be antithetical, and it ignores the rule that a
globalism that is insensitive to regional needs and concerns cannot be
effective in drawing regional actors into a broader, global alignment. In
fact, such an outlook produces a dangerous temptation to identify one of
the adversaries in regional conflicts with the Soviet camp — mildly, as in
the case of Argentina in the Falkland Islands dispute, or more blatantly
(but equally misleadingly), as in the case of the Ayatollah Khomeini.

Such an attitude also reflects a unilateralist American approach, rather
than a commitment to a "multilateralist" alliance system and shared values.
It mirrors skepticism about the steadfastness and commitment of friends
and allies, and it often reflects a sense of moral righteousness. As a member of Congress declared after the proclamation of martial law in Poland,
this time the United States should proceed to do "what is right" without
worrying too much about its allies.

If in this overall perspective Soviet-American enmity is a given and
a constant, policy making becomes a technical question of how best (and
at a reasonable cost or risk) to pressure or injure the adversary. What follows from such an approach amounts to a massive military buildup and a
confrontational strategic doctrine and an effort to maximize the strains
sustained by the Soviet Union, by engaging in campaigns of both economic and political warfare against it.

In practice, however, the implementation of American policy toward
the Soviet Union was more pragmatic than this stance would have required. It reflected both a need to modify some of these broad policy
prescriptions and a continued tug-of-war between advocates of different
orientations within the administration.

Issues and Policies

Defense Policy. A key area of consensus between essentialists and
mechanists, as well as a personal commitment by the president, was the
priority given to a major buildup of both conventional and strategic
capabilities. This buildup was defended on several grounds. First, they
argued that the Soviet Union was outspending the United States by a
large margin, that official estimates understated the seriousness of the

problem, and that domestic equanimity (as well as excessive spending on social programs) had seriously compromised American power. The spending gap had in turn produced a gap in capabilities: Sustained Soviet efforts had finally brought American military superiority to an end; some, including the president, spoke of a clear-cut American inferiority to the Soviet armed forces. This analysis rested on both a pessimistic assessment of American capabilities and vulnerabilities and an exaggeration of Soviet strength. To sell the largest program in defense spending in the nation's history to Congress and to the public required an ambitious and sustained effort at threat inflation in portraying Soviet intentions and capabilities in the most alarming possible terms.

This unprecedented budget did not reflect a coherent military strategy or careful planning that assigned tasks to specific weapon systems and units under different scenarios of conflict. (See Chapter 3.) It was in effect a "wish list" of the Secretary of Defense based on the assumption that "more is better" and on a simplistic comparison of Soviet and American expenditures without weighing the relative efficiency of the defense dollar or the implications of asymmetrical force structure.[20]

Some elements of the new approach to strategic planning became apparent in 1981-1982. In substance, they reflected a more explicit commitment to "warfighting," both conventional and nuclear, than had previously been true. While the Pentagon insisted that its primary purpose continued to be to deter a Soviet attack, the doctrine that the United States must be in a position to prevail in an all-out nuclear exchange was at best highly ambiguous, and at worst a substantial alteration of strategic doctrine. Renewed discussion of antiballistic missile defense and civil defense programs reflected the view that Soviet warfighting preparedness must be matched by an equivalent American commitment.

While the formulation of a new, "confrontational" strategy followed the budget request, the problems of the defense program were illustrated by the fate of the MX missile. Intended as an alternative to the ostensibly vulnerable land-based ICBM, the mobile basing mode for the MX was dropped when domestic opposition developed. The fall-back proposal to base the MX in existing silos amounted to placing domestic politics ahead of what were alleged to be security needs, failed to address the threat that had justified the MX program in the first place, and left open the supposed "window of vulnerability." When late in 1982, on Weinberger's advice, Reagan came out for a so-called "dense pack" basing of the MX (in Wyoming), Congress refused to go along with what was palpably a half-baked technical argument, and the administration was obliged to settle for an uncertain and embarrassing compromise that left the basing mode open.

Like the new campaigns of economic and political warfare, discussed below, the Weinberger approach to strategic planning sought to take advantage of potential Soviet vulnerabilities. It too sought to take the initiative, for instance, in power projection by means of a huge new navy. It would retaliate for Soviet forward moves at places of American choosing. And insofar as this was accompanied by reduced reliance on European allies, it represented a unilateralist spirit in defense strategy.

Few voices in American public life dissented from the necessity of maintaining rough strategic parity with the Soviet Union and of continuing to improve the quality and readiness of American forces. Differences, discussed elsewhere in greater detail, have arisen, however, over a number of questions relating centrally to the United States defense posture. These include, for instance, (1) whether the new strategy is based on a correct reading of Soviet military doctrine and capabilities: (2) whether the drive for American military superiority is either necessary or realistic; (3) whether the magnitude of the defense budget is disproportionally damaging to the American economy; (4) whether the proposed defense program can be politically sustained given the cost in social programs at home, support from allies abroad, and credibility in American intentions and commitments.

Economic Relations with the Soviet Union. In shaping economic policies toward the Soviet Union that would serve its broader political objectives, the new administration faced the task of reconciling its commitment to economic deregulation and expanded free trade with its desire to constrain the Soviet military buildup by economic as well as by political and military means. The urgency of the latter task foreclosed a laissez-faire approach to Soviet-American economic relations and imposed instead a choice between a strategy of leverage and a strategy of denial. Both entailed enhanced government control over the flow of trade, the transfer of technology, and the availability of credits to the Soviet Union.

The first approach, advocated in particular by the Departments of State, Commerce, and the Treasury, would have had as its objective the close coordination of all economic relations with the Soviet Union on the part of the United States and its allies in order to elicit more "responsible" Soviet behavior. It would have relied on a combination of economic incentives — the further development of mutually beneficial economic relations — and implicit threats — to reduce or cut off such opportunities — to influence Soviet policies in a more benign direction.[21]

A strategy of denial, promoted by the Department of Defense as well as by neoconservative supporters of the administration, based on greater skepticism about the possibilities and effects of leverage, sought to affect Soviet capabilities rather than Soviet behavior. Its intent was to impose maximal costs and burdens on the Soviet system by reducing Soviet gains from trade, constricting the availability of technology and credits, and more generally subjecting the Soviet economy to increased strain. This strategy rested on an assessment that Soviet gains from East-West trade and technology transfer were both substantial and asymmetrically advantageous to the Soviet Union, that the Soviet economy, as it faced the prospects of long-term retardation, was highly vulnerable to external pressure, and that Western policies that deprived it of the economic resources with which to pursue a military buildup at home and expansion abroad would compel the Soviet leadership either to divert resources from military to civilian uses or face growing social unrest as a result of declining mass consumption.[22]

Three specific issue areas formed the focus of policy debates: trade in strategic goods and technologies, general trade, and the problem of credits. In the case of the first, the administration chose to pursue a more complete strategy of denial. Arguing that past policies had permitted the transfer of technologies that had contributed to Soviet military power, and that previous controls had been largely ineffective, the Reagan administration sought to tighten controls over the export of all goods and technologies, including ideas themselves, that might contribute even indirectly to the Soviet military potential. This involved an effort to further tighten interallied Coordinating Committee (CoCom) guidelines, to enforce export controls more stringently, to step up measures to prevent Soviet industrial espionage, and, most controversially, to reduce the scope of, and introduce closer controls over, scientific and cultural exchanges that might offer the Soviet Union access to key technologies in areas such as computers or artificial intelligence.[23]

While the need to bar Soviet access to technologies of direct military significance was unquestioned, the effort to define whole classes of advanced technology that have indirect military applications was fraught with difficulties, and the task of controlling their export still more so. The Defense Department's "Initial List of Militarily Critical Technologies," issued in 1980, contained, in the words of one analyst, "a virtual roll-call of leading contemporary techniques, including videodisk recording, polymeric materials, and many dozens of others equally broad. If this collection had automatically become the basis for the official Commodities Control List (as some had urged during the debate over the 1979 Export Administration Act), the entire Department of Commerce would not have been large enough to administer the export-control program." [24]

When it came to general trade, in which United States grain sales figured most prominently, domestic political considerations triumphed over foreign policy consistency. Over the objections of Haig and others, who argued that his actions would undercut both leverage and denial, in April 1981, President Reagan honored his campaign pledge to the farm vote by lifting the embargo on agricultural commodities that Carter had imposed after the invasion of Afghanistan.[25] The president defended his decision on the grounds that the embargo had been ineffective (thus undercutting the key assumptions of a strategy of denial) and that it had imposed excessive burdens on one segment of the American economy (thus illustrating the political difficulties entailed in the pursuit of leverage), but the major impact of his decision was to undermine the credibility of American demands for greater economic sacrifices by its European allies in dealings with the Soviet Union. West German Chancellor Helmut Schmidt pointedly observed that grain is also a strategic commodity.

In approaching the problem of credits, the administration's task was eased by the fact that government credits were not at issue; they had not been available to the Soviet Union since 1975. It was the restriction of private credits that the militant wing of the administration sought, on the grounds that such indirect subsidization of the Soviet economy was "selling the Russians the rope" by which they would hang us. The pervasive unwillingness to interfere with the operation of market forces, and the desire to promote free trade and expanded exports, here clashed most directly with the conviction that American business shortsightedly pursued narrow economic interests at the expense of national security goals, permitting the Soviet Union to engage in its customary practice of playing off one against the other. This concern reached its height over the economic relations of the West Europeans with the Soviet Union. In the administration's view, the use of export credits and government-backed loans to finance commercial transactions with the Soviet Union violated free-trade principles, alliance commitments, and the canons of good sense to boot.

The protracted and bitter controversy over the projected Soviet-West European natural gas pipeline project (discussed at greater length in Chapters 6 and 9) dramatized the degree to which the administration's economic policies had departed from those of its predecessors as well as its allies and had moved in the direction of outright economic warfare. Fusing as it did the issues of technology transfer, trade, and credits in one single project, the pipeline issue offered a litmus test of the different assumptions held by different actors about East-West economic relations and their political and military implications. To the advocates of denial, which here included Weinberger and the president himself, the pipeline project involved the export of critical technologies that would contribute to Soviet economic, and thereby military, power; it relied heavily on Western credits, which constituted an additional indirect subsidy to the Soviet economy; it enmeshed the West Europeans even more deeply in asymmetrical trade relationships, which magnified their alleged dependence on the Soviet Union; and by alleviating its chronic shortage of hard currency, it would enable the Soviet Union to circumvent efforts to constrain its future economic growth.[26] Rejecting the advice of Haig and others, who urged acceptance of the West European commitment as a *fait accompli,* and shifting the focus to improving credit terms and reducing the possible risks of the undertaking, the president in June 1982 made a last-ditch effort to thwart the project by attempting to block the transfer of components manufactured by foreign subsidiaries of American companies or by European firms under license from American corporations. This decision, of dubious legality and high political cost, not only helped trigger the resignation of Haig but provoked a crisis within the alliance, which Foreign Minister Cheysson characterized outspokenly as a progressive "divorce."

The crisis was itself an indication of the distance the Reagan administration had traveled in moving from the pursuit of leverage to a strategy of denial, if not outright economic warfare. Where Kissinger and Vance, as well as Schmidt and Mitterrand, had sought to enmesh the Soviet Union in a network of economic links viewed as mutually beneficial and as promoting a desirable interdependence, the new administration viewed such relationships as intrinsically one-sided and costly to the West, and sought rather to isolate the Soviet Union from Western technology and trade. Where earlier policies sought the discriminating use of both carrots and sticks to shape Soviet perceptions and behavior, the Reagan administration had little confidence in either the prospects of achieving such fine-tuning or its effectiveness in moderating Soviet actions. The effort to bring about greater relaxation in Soviet outlook and policy was rejected in favor of policies meant to maximize pressure on the Soviet system and to limit its capabilities. Where others had been prepared to recognize Soviet superpower status and had sought to reduce Soviet insecurities, the White House sought instead to exploit all possible Soviet vulnerabilities.

While the merits of this approach remained untested, it soon became clear that a strategy of denial that was pursued unilaterally, and that demanded major economic sacrifices from allies while exempting American grain exports, had no prospect of success. Indeed, as Secretary Shultz soon realized, its pursuit placed far greater strain on the alliance than on the Soviet Union, at a time when alliance unity was critical to the success of any effort to apply economic pressure on the Soviet Union. By November 1982 his efforts culminated in a face-saving arrangement by which the United States lifted its sanctions against West European companies in return for a vague understanding with the Allies to study trade and credit issues further.

Eastern Europe and the Polish Crisis. The heightened preoccupation with the "Soviet threat" and the black-and-white view of world affairs made it especially difficult for the Reagan administration to develop a coherent policy regarding Eastern Europe. Should the states of the region be treated as an integral part of the Soviet empire — in effect, as allies of the adversary? Or should they rather be viewed as reluctant subjects seeking to maximize their autonomy? The first approach dictated a policy of greater economic and political pressure, whereas the second suggested a differentiated strategy aimed at encouraging greater foreign policy independence from the Soviet Union or domestic political and economic liberalization in Eastern Europe.

The evolution of American policy toward Eastern Europe in the postwar period has covered a whole gamut of alternative policies. At the height of the Cold War, American policy denied the legitimacy of these Soviet-sponsored regimes, treated them as mere appendages of the Stalinist system, and sought to keep alive the symbolism of Eastern Europe as captive nations. As evidence gradually mounted, in the post-Stalin era, of both pluralism and nationalism among East European political elites, American policy shifted toward an effort to encourage diversity and autonomy within the Communist bloc. Yugoslavia provided the precedent of American support for a Communist country that had become independent of the Soviet bloc; events in Hungary, Poland, Czechoslovakia, and Rumania in subsequent years raised the possibility of substantial changes within the existing political framework which the United States might welcome and support.

The effort at West European and American cultural and political bridge-building to Eastern Europe in the late 1960s was followed in the 1970s by an expansion of economic relations.[27] By the mid-1970s a three-tiered policy had developed, in which Yugoslavia was the object of especially favorable political and economic treatment, while Poland, Hungary, and Rumania were eligible for preferential trade arrangements and access to official export credits on terms that were denied to the Soviet Union and its more orthodox allies.[28] Despite the sweeping human rights rhetoric of the Carter administration, charges of violations were largely confined to the Soviet Union.

To supporters of detente, expanding contacts between East and West in a more benign international environment and growing liberalization and diversity within Eastern Europe were among the most salient achievements, and mounting Eastern bloc indebtedness a relatively small price to pay.[29] To its critics, however, the costs of detente far outweighed its benefits: By helping ameliorate economic conditions in Eastern Europe, the West helped legitimize what were at bottom oppressive, Soviet-dominated regimes; by subsidizing East European economies through snowballing credits it had contributed, however indirectly, to the Soviet military buildup; it had failed to bring about any visible Soviet restraint abroad; and far from increasing Western political leverage over Eastern Europe, it had had the opposite effect, creating "reverse leverage" over Western creditors who were too fearful of losing their investments to refuse requests for additional aid.

To the incoming Reagan administration, mounting economic difficulties in Eastern Europe were further evidence for what it saw as the failure of both Communism and detente. At the same time, the success of Solidarity as an independent trade union movement in Poland and its association with Polish nationalism and Christian values attracted sympathy across an exceptionally broad spectrum of American opinion, from the left to the Reagan conservatives. The overhanging threat of Soviet military intervention in Poland prompted repeated warnings by the United States to the Soviet leadership that such action would have the most serious consequences. Meanwhile, the United States sought to strengthen the hand of the Polish authorities by granting them debt relief and emergency credits for the purchase of agricultural commodities. In its first year the new administration therefore had the luxury of being able simultaneously to support Polish resistance to Communist rule, a liberalization of the existing system, and a weakening of the Soviet bloc.

The imposition of martial law in Poland in December 1981 — a development that in its preoccupation with the possibility of a Soviet military intervention the administration had failed to anticipate — transformed the situation overnight, and a major controversy over policy toward Poland erupted within both the United States and the Western alliance. Some interpreted the imposition of martial law as a desperate effort by the Polish leadership to forestall Soviet military intervention on the one hand, and a breakdown of domestic controls on the other, and urged policies that would simultaneously maximize political pressure on Warsaw while maintaining its limited autonomy from Moscow. Others saw the events as confirmation that political developments in Poland were entirely orchestrated in Moscow and urged the harshest possible American response directed against both the Polish and Soviet leadership. Among the measures advocated were calling off all Soviet-American negotiations, the imposition of sharp economic sanctions, and the declaration of default on the Polish debt.[30]

The controversy over default crystallized a larger debate over American policy toward Eastern Europe. For the advocates of a formal declaration of default, such a pronouncement would simultaneously serve as a token of Western outrage at the suppression of Solidarity, a symbol of the bankruptcy of Communism, a gesture that would end the "reverse leverage" ostensibly operating against Western creditors of Communist regimes, and a measure that would further strain the Soviet system by compelling it to assume the full economic burden of a crippled Polish economy. To opponents of default, such a declaration would be an empty gesture of potentially greater cost to the West than to its intended victims, a measure that would deprive the West of whatever leverage it still had to influence the course of events in Poland, and a step that would force Poland back into the Soviet camp.[31]

The administration's response straddled the two positions. On the one hand, the president accepted the view that the Soviet Union had been centrally responsible and should be the object of serious sanctions along with Poland itself. On the other hand, the administration stopped short of imposing either a total embargo on both countries or a declaration of Polish default, holding out the possibility that economic relations and even assistance might be restored if and when three preconditions were met: an end to martial law, the release of political detainees, and a resumption of the government's dialogue with the Church and Solidarity.[32]

If in this instance, unlike many others, the administration chose a course less extreme than that advocated by a wide array of public figures, from Caspar Weinberger to Henry Kissinger to Felix Rohatyn, several possible explanations can be advanced. First and foremost, since the effect of a declaration of default on the West European banking system was bound to be both enormous and incalculable, to have triggered default over the opposition of the West Europeans would have entailed disproportionate costs. The White House preferred to retain its freedom to opt for default later, but in effect it accepted the argument that to invoke it would be counterproductive in that it would (1) relieve Poland and the Soviet Union of their financial obligations, (2) destroy such leverage as the West possessed, and (3) disrupt the Western banking system. The stakes were so high and the consequences so uncertain that the balance within the Reagan cabinet tipped in favor of the business-oriented technicians, beginning with the Treasury, over the ideologically oriented crusaders.

If the controversy over default was too arcane for much of the public, it also beclouded the basic fact that there was little the United States could or would do. There were no obvious weapons in the political or economic arsenal that the administration could wield to affect significantly the course of events in Poland — and not even the most extreme activists advocated American military action. This again became evident when in December 1982 the Polish authorities, having banned Solidarity, "suspended" martial law and released most of the detainees held since the crackdown a year earlier. Washington declared that the changes were insufficient to warrant lifting United States sanctions.

In view of the limited options available to the United States, the high prospects for continuing political turbulence and economic crises in Poland and elsewhere in Eastern Europe, as well as the inherent complexity and ambiguity of developments there, this area will necessarily continue to present difficult choices and produce divided counsel within the Reagan administration.

Political Warfare. According to the more militant planners of the new administration, political warfare was to be the counterpart to economic warfare with the Soviet Union. It was intended (1) to exploit and enhance political and social vulnerabilities within the Soviet Union, (2) to combat Soviet ideological influence and challenge Soviet political prestige abroad, and (3) in effect to isolate the Soviet Union from the outside world.

Most novel but also unclear was the desire to promote "destabilization" in the Soviet camp. Whereas previous administrations had sought to influence Soviet officialdom through proper channels — "from above" — the new policy would seek to appeal to a target audience "from below," as was entirely congruent with the essentialists' commitment to delegitimizing the Soviet regime. If this meant intervening at least verbally inside the Soviet bloc, to the pragmatists this looked like a welcome way of getting even with the extensive Soviet propaganda effort abroad. Officially the effort was described as giving "vigorous support to democratic forces wherever they are located — including countries which are now communist.... A free press, free trade unions, free political parties, freedom to travel, and freedom to create are the ingredients of the democratic revolution of the future." [33]

President Reagan chose the occasion of his address to the British Parliament on June 8, 1982, to make public his plan:

> What I am describing now is a plan and a hope for the long term — the march of freedom and democracy which will leave Marxism-Leninism on the ash heap of history as it has left other tyrannies which stifle the freedom and muzzle the self-expression of the people....
>
> The objective I propose is quite simple to state: to foster the infrastructure of democracy — the system of a free press, unions, political parties, universities — which allows a people to choose their own way. ... This is not cultural imperialism: it is providing the means for genuine self-determination and protection for diversity.... It would be cultural condescension, or worse, to say that any people prefer dictatorship to democracy.[34]

Other than in the proposed expansion of broadcasting to Communist countries, the implementation of such a program remains to be spelled out. What it has done is to stimulate a keen new interest in Washington in the nature and scope of Soviet vulnerabilities, from social cleavages to ethnic tensions to unmet consumer needs. The only follow-up event was a State Department conference on "democratization of Communist countries," held in October 1982. While it was apparently the first of its kind, the meeting did not seem to lead to any new initiative or organization.

The Voice of America (VoA) has been an obvious element in the attempted mobilization for political warfare, with increased funding for transmissions across Soviet jamming and the addition of broadcasts in minority languages of the Soviet Union. VoA has also, understandably, been the object of bitter controversy, in large part between those who would have it report candidly and "objectively" and those who would seek to transform it into a propaganda agency. According to the outspoken views of Phil Nicolaides, who was appointed deputy program director of VoA but was soon forced out after a bitter feud, this was to be the Voice's purposes:

> We must portray the Soviet Union as the last great predatory empire on earth, remorselessly enslaving its own diverse ethnic populations, crushing the legitimate aspirations of its captive nations.... We must strive to "destabilize" the Soviet Union and its satellites by promoting disaffection between peoples and rulers.[35]

More than previous administrations this one has been prepared — at times, eager — to challenge Soviet influence abroad. This has included the president's repeated references to the failure of communism as well as specific releases and allegations, for example, on a systematic Soviet campaign of "disinformation" in the West. As a pet project of Secretary Haig, the Soviet Union was blamed for training and supporting international terrorism. Whatever the Soviet role in particular instances, especially in supporting "national liberation movements," the charges were so sweeping and indiscriminate that other United States government agencies were unable to support or substantiate them.[36]

Negotiating with the Soviets. The whole strategy of political warfare implied an effort to isolate the Soviet Union; to deny it symbolic recognition, parity, or legitimacy; to cut back on scientific, educational, and cultural interactions as well as trade; and, in effect, to ostracize it in the international community. The logical corollary was to refuse all negotiations with Moscow: Negotiating was at the opposite pole from political warfare on the spectrum of political relations. To refrain from negotiations also fitted the pragmatic argument that at some future point the United States would be in a stronger bargaining position, thanks to the military buildup the administration had launched and because of looming crises in the Soviet system. Moreover, in such critical areas as arms control, the Reagan team arrived without any negotiating strategy, given the rejection of the SALT II treaty as "fatally flawed" and the antagonistic attitudes that the new officials brought to the Arms Control and Disarmament Agency and to the Department of Defense.

But such an approach was bound to go against the grain of professional diplomats and of at least some businessmen serving the new administration. Whether or not to negotiate with the Soviet Union became and remained a matter of intense dispute. Only rarely did it come to the surface, as it did once in perhaps the most "moderate" policy statement which Secretary Haig made during his seventeen months in office. Describing Soviet-American relations as a "challenge to develop and to sustain a relationship with the Soviet Union which recognizes that the competition will proceed but constrains the use or threat of force," Haig went on to declare, "We can develop a lasting framework for this relationship if we avoid the extremes that have distorted American foreign policy over the postwar period." Goodwill and negotiations were no substitute for strength, he remarked but continued significantly: "We cannot claim that we are too weak to negotiate and at the same time insist that we are strong enough for a policy of all-out confrontation."

Rather unusually in the Reagan era, Haig went on to propose the use of carrots as well as sticks: When the coming new leadership in the Soviet Union faces economic and other difficulties at home, "the United States must make clear to the Soviet Union that there are penalties for aggression and incentives for restraint. . . . We are prepared to show the Soviet leaders that international moderation can help them face painful domestic dilemmas through broader relations with the United States and other Western countries." To make his point even clearer, he added: "We can signal the benefits of greater restraint" to the Soviet Union.[37] There was no echo to this theme. Two months later Haig was out.

A second occasion that illustrated the differences at the apex of the American government arose with the death of Leonid Brezhnev on November 10, 1982. When the president turned down Shultz's recommendation that he go to Moscow for the funeral to meet the new Soviet leaders, Vice President George Bush and Secretary of State Shultz attended instead and met the new Soviet First Secretary, Yuri V. Andropov. While their public comments did not go as far as the extravagant opinion in American media regarding the new opportunities that the change in Soviet leadership presented for Soviet-American relations, Bush and Shultz were upbeat and cautiously encouraging concerning the future. At the very same time President Reagan, at a meeting with the new West German Chancellor Helmut Kohl, reverted to the customary confrontational rhetoric concerning the Soviet Union.

As in other areas, it proved to be impossible to stick to what the militant pursuit of the new strategy would have demanded. The pressure to negotiate with the Soviet Union — over the whole complex of arms control issues, ranging from strategic weapons to the deployment of theater forces in Europe — mounted steadily, especially in Western Europe since the commitment to negotiate had been part of the bargain that had led the European allies to accept the American program for the modernization of Theater Nuclear Forces, an essential part in their minds of the agreement to install Pershings and cruise missiles on the European continent.

Public opinion, first in Europe and then in the United States as well, began to pressure the administration, especially in regard to nuclear weapons, and in November 1981 the White House decided to reverse course on two key issues — first, tacitly to abide by the terms of the

SALT II agreement, later inflated into a public statement by the president that the United States would not undercut the terms of SALT II so long as the Soviet Union observed them; and second, to take the initiative on arms control negotiations, hoping to take the wind out of the sails of the arms control advocates and the vociferous proponents of a nuclear freeze. The United States in the process moved from the search for arms limitations to a pledge to seek meaningful arms reductions — hence the change in acronym from SALT (Strategic Arms Limitations Talks) to START (Strategic Arms Reduction Talks). By mid-1982 the United States and the Soviet Union were engaged in arms control discussions in several different forums (although the administration refused to resume talks on a comprehensive nuclear test ban treaty).

The negotiations on intermediate-range missiles in Europe offered the best prospects for agreement on arms control. The American proposal — the so-called zero-zero option — would have required, as a condition to forestall the deployment of new Pershing II and cruise missiles in Western Europe, the removal of all equivalent Soviet missiles. Particularly in the face of various Soviet counterproposals, the zero-zero option was widely perceived as unrealistic, and the American commitment to it threatened to produce a stalemate in the talks and a public-relations setback for the United States. In early 1983, rising European protests and Soviet ability to exploit the issue persuaded at least some officials to move to a more flexible negotiating strategy in these — though not in any other — arms control talks and to perhaps accept a low number of equivalent "Euromissiles" for each side. The effort to regain some propaganda advantage prompted Reagan's offer, on January 31, 1983, to meet with Andropov to sign a treaty banning intermediate-range missiles, substantially on terms Moscow had already rejected.

The administration has been divided over the utility of the arms talks. To some senior officials they are largely a nuisance, at best a device to gain time. For others, they are important; and by midterm the negotiations had acquired a life and logic of their own. They may prove too costly to turn off, both for domestic reasons and for the sake of relations with America's allies. Their role surely had not been anticipated when the Reagan administration took office.

Conclusions

Washington: Blinders, Beliefs, and Bureaucracies

As the Reagan presidency unfolds, observers see both shifts and continuities in its policies toward the Soviet Union. There is no indication of any change in the underlying assumptions of either the president or his close associates. The commitment to the major buildup of American defense capabilities remains as firm as ever. The Kremlin remains *the* adversary with whom (as Ronald Reagan remarked privately to his colleagues at the Versailles summit in June 1982) "we are at war."

Yet eighteen months after he assailed the SALT II treaty as a dangerous giveaway, the president agreed to observe its provisions so long as Moscow does the same. The shrill campaign against Soviet responsibility for international terrorism petered out without much ado or explanation. After first shying away from arms control negotiations, two years later the administration was deeply involved in a series of talks about arms reduction and force deployment abroad. The idea of an anti-Soviet "strategic consensus" in the Middle East, including both Israelis and Arabs, was quietly dropped as palpably naïve. On Poland the hyperbolic American announcements yielded, after the proclamation of martial law, to a policy of restraint. The change in the position of secretary of state eliminated some idle, and counterproductive, bravado. Yet on all sides evidence of zigzags and seeming incoherence of policy has remained. Why?

(1) The mind sets of the new policy makers have encountered the reality of the world abroad, and it has turned out that some of their prior beliefs don't fit. Some were plainly wrong; more often they were too simple-minded: Reality proved to be far more complex. As we have seen, the White House strategy was based on a "two-camp" view of the world, which was at best obsolete and at worst primitive. Albert Einstein once remarked that it was essential to simplify all problems as much as possible — but not one iota more. It is as misleading to exaggerate Soviet power and to underestimate its limits as it is to portray the Soviet system as hovering on the brink of collapse. It is as erroneous to deny Soviet expansionism as it is to posit it as inevitable and irreversible. George F. Kennan writes:

> In a relationship of such immense importance as the Soviet-American one there should be no room for such extremisms and oversimplifications. Not only do they produce their counterparts on the other side, but they confuse us. They cause us to see as totally unsolvable a problem that is only partly so.
>
> Soviet society is made up of human beings like ourselves. Because it is human, it is complex. It is not, as many of the oversimplifications would suggest, a static, unchanging phenomenon. It too evolves, and the direction in which it evolves is influenced to some degree by our vision of it and our treatment of it.[38]

Especially the far right is attracted to a style of unilateralist crusading that enables it to dispense with the finer points and brings little knowledge of the outside world to the policy arena — and sees little need for it.

The lack of fit between prior beliefs and present reality generates several types of outcome. One is the disjunction between the articulated world view and foreign policy behavior. Indeed, it would not be the first time in American foreign policy that the bark is worse than the bite. The ideological rhetoric has its political and psychological uses at home but need not inform all policy. A news weekly, mindful of the president's past, has aptly if unkindly suggested that at times the foreign policy posture turns out to be more stagecraft than statecraft. Surprisingly, perhaps, the vigor in rhetoric appears to be coupled to an instinct for *in*action as well. For instance, the administration's actual support for the Afghan rebels — perhaps the only ones physically fighting the Soviet system — seems to have been quite modest. If it wished its own dire prognoses, from Central American and Caribbean revolutions to Libyan terror squads, to be taken seriously, it might have been expected to have acted more forcefully. It failed to put together, prior to the imposition of martial law in Poland, a package of proposals of economic assistance in return for political guarantees. Its eloquent rhetoric concerning democratization from below" in Communist countries appears to have been little more than words.

The dissonance between beliefs and experience can also produce tactical adaptation. The reversal in the arms control field must be seen primarily as a response to pressures — from the allies, from the European and then the American public, and from the media. There is no evidence, as yet, that the changes in policy reflect (or cause) a change in the underlying attitudes and assumptions.

Finally, as a policy maker comes to grips with reality, there is apt to occur a (sometimes unwitting or unwanted) learning process. No doubt this has in fact been taking place, especially among officials with little previous experience with foreign affairs. Moreover, the ideological biases contained in the essentialist mind set tend to focus on a limited number of salient issues; policy problems of lower attention may typically be handled in more pragmatic fashion and may be open to less constrained learning. The willingness not to undercut the terms of the SALT II treaty is an example of new information and judgment (perhaps presented by senior military men) altering prior beliefs.

(2) The mind sets of the new ideologues have also encountered the reality of domestic politics, and here too there has ensued an awareness of the costs attached to the pursuit of some prior beliefs. It is in the nature of American politics that special interests and lobbies often distort, constrain, or propel foreign policy in fundamentally unsound directions. At times they may encourage grandstanding; at others, as in the lifting of the grain embargo and the decision not to institute the draft, they may work against a tougher foreign policy. But in either case domestic politics tends to undercut the coherence of policy. This is particularly true where, as in the Reagan administration, the choice of particular policies (for instance, economic warfare) to be successful requires a high

degree of mobilization and coordination of domestic interest groups as well as of foreign allies.

The lack of fit between commitments and constituency becomes especially troublesome politically when, as in this case, the political constituency is heterogeneous. If the farm vote applauded the lifting of the grain embargo, to the neoconservatives it was only one of many tokens of the administration's suspected downhill slide from the peak of anti-Sovietism. Policy incoherence was well demonstrated when the White House reversed itself twice on the Siberian pipeline — imposing sanctions soon after a series of representations against "creeping Haigism" on the part of the New Right, and lifting them four months later when both their futility and the cost in conflict with the NATO allies became manifest.

The flip side of the administration's sensitivity to domestic constituencies is the fact that, especially until the appointment of George Shultz, people who lacked experience in foreign affairs had a heavy influence on the making of foreign policy. It is characteristic of the Reagan wing of the Republican party — largely outsiders until 1980 — that it has a paucity of competent foreign policy specialists. This is particularly true of experts on the Soviet Union.

(3) Beyond these traits, the administration suffered from the unresolved and often fundamental differences in outlook among the many actors and bureaucracies dealing with Soviet affairs. What became clear over time, as it had not been at the outset, was the unresolved ambiguity between essentialist and mechanistic orientations; whether ideological preconceptions guided American policy or pragmatic considerations prevailed; whether to use American assets to apply leverage on Moscow or to strive to isolate, pressure, and transform the Soviet system. Ultimately it was the ambiguity between the goals of "transformation by victory" and tension management. In substance, this meant that there was no single coherent policy toward the Soviet Union.

(4) To be sure, some of the causes of seeming incoherence are not specific to this administration. The cycle in turnovers of administrations and key officials has meant that there is no continuity of institutional memory, a need every four years to reinvent the wheel. A good case can also be made that the functional differences — say, between State and Defense — are bound to make for differences in policy preferences, and that the mechanism of the National Security Council, instead of resolving them, adds another source of conflict.[39]

(5) Finally, there are elements in the structure of the international system itself that place limits on the exercise of American power. The tendency of the Reagan administration has been to ignore the secular trend reducing the ability of the United States to play a hegemonic role.

Yet the American preponderance after the Second World War was an aberration, bound to be altered as other economies (including those of the loser states, Germany and Japan) worked their economic miracles and as the Third World began its faltering march to development. If in 1945 the United States had a monopoly of atomic weapons, this situation was bound to change and will continue to change, reducing the American role. If in the early years the United States had its way in the UN virtually all the time, in a UN of over 150 members such a prospect would be illusory. Only to a small degree has this process been the result of Soviet actions. The postwar experience has made clear the limits of American power.

Yet in the Reagan camp there remains a deep nostalgia for hegemony, and a belief that it can be restored by an act of will. The president's rhetoric reflects an intuitive assumption of the universality of American values; Paul Nitze's statements mirror the nostalgia for the simpler days of NSC 68, the Marshall Plan, and an evil Stalin; in the writings of neo-conservatives the loss of hegemony becomes virtually an indictment of past policy makers for criminal negligence, or worse.

The fact remains that one major source of problems in American foreign policy, including policy toward the Soviet Union, is the gap between aspirations and capabilities, or at least our ability to act at a reasonable cost or risk. Afghanistan and Poland both exemplify cases of frustration due in large measure to our inability to affect the outcome without assuming undue costs. Bringing objectives and capabilities into better balance must be a major strategic objective for the United States: it requires adjustments on both sides of the equation. The Reagan administration is committed to an increase in military capabilities (the economic universe proves to be far more recalcitrant) but has also raised its foreign policy objectives, so that the gap between the desired and the possible fails to shrink.

Moscow: The Impact of the Reagan Administration on the Soviet Union

In the last analysis, the crucial test of the Reagan foreign policy is its effect on Moscow. In trying to gauge this effect, we labor under several handicaps. For one thing, it is too early to be sure. In the long run, the impact on Soviet elite images and perceptions may be far more important than the immediate responses in diplomatic notes or statements to the press. For another, we face the usual problems of assessing Soviet attitudes and behavior from very inadequate information, and virtually no access to insiders. It may be necessary to argue by analogy with precedents, but obviously precedents provide an imperfect source of forecasts. Even if a desired change in Soviet behavior should occur, it is methodologically next to impossible to show just what will have brought it about or whether American policy was the crucial or even a necessary precondition for it. Finally, foreign policy is often based on assumptions whose soundness is bound to be a matter of judgment — until it is too late to change it. The following therefore amounts to a set of tentative hypotheses.

(1) The buildup of the American armed forces, the apparently greater willingness of the Reagan administration to risk military confrontation with the Soviet Union, and increased discussion of scenarios that involve the risk of nuclear war — from limited to protracted — have probably strengthened a belief in responsible Soviet quarters that in a future international crisis the United States may be prepared to resort to, or stumble into, the use of force, including nuclear weapons. It is at least possible that this perception reinforced the inclination on the part of the senescent Brezhnev leadership toward restraint in the projection of Soviet power abroad. It is impossible to tell what risks Moscow might have been prepared to take under different circumstances (and Soviet policy makers have typically avoided high risks), but it may be that (a) if there is a Soviet risk assessment, American policy has raised the Soviet calculus of risk, and (b) the internal arguments in favor of caution in dealing with Iran, desisting from new African adventures, and the singular Soviet passivity in the Middle East crisis of mid-1982 have been reinforced by a wish to avoid tangling with an increasingly unpredictable but dangerous United States.

(2) How the American defense effort will affect the military balance between the superpowers is not yet clear. The Soviet military budget is subject to two contradictory pressures: on the one hand, to respond to American increases in defense appropriations and military capabilities by offsetting increases on the Soviet side; on the other hand, to respond to the pressures of economic stringency within the Soviet Union. How these conflicting demands will be balanced out remains to be seen. It should also be added here that there is always considerable uncertainty as to what the military balance is. Nor is it necessarily the case that increases in military spending produce commensurate increments in military capability, let alone in security.

While it is not yet apparent how the new Soviet leader will choose to respond, the best indications are that, having at last achieved something like strategic parity with the United States and having begun to overcome the prolonged handicap of a political inferiority complex, Moscow is not prepared to yield that status at the first signs of an American decision to launch a new arms race.

Given the many demands on scarce resources, the share of the defense burden in the total Soviet economy may well become the object of political controversy. The best estimates are that with some slowing in the growth of consumption the Soviet economy can continue to sustain current levels of defense.[40] Politically, it may indeed be easier for the Soviet system to sustain a military buildup than it would be for the United States, since it need face no vocal opposition or public policy debate. Much will no doubt depend on Moscow's perception of the seriousness of the American threat. While the long-run effect must be left somewhat open, previous experience suggests that in the short run the impact of the American defense effort is almost certainly to strengthen an attitude of belt tightening at home and a return to the familiar Soviet images of a threatening international environment, in which American interventionism abroad, threatening aggression and subversion, obliges the Soviet Union to defend its own and its allies' gains. Such a defensive theme has invariably been more successful in Soviet domestic mobilization than a missionary theme.

(3) American words and deeds have confirmed the Soviet judgment that detente, as we knew it in the 1970s, is over. They must also have enlivened the Soviet debate over its relative costs and benefits. Such a reassessment involves a judgment in Soviet policy making circles that the prospects of settling any significant issues on acceptable terms are dim indeed as long as the Reagan administration pursues its present course.

To be sure, Soviet "Americanists" were initially divided over the likely policy of the new administration; some invoked the Nixon precedent of an ardent anti-Communist converted by pragmatic need into a partner of sorts; others welcomed an end to the unpredictability of the Carter years; and some banked on American business to promote expanded trade and credits. By late 1981 the leading Soviet analysts appeared to have reached a consensus that "the present Washington leadership . . . is trying to attain a one-sided military superiority over the Soviet Union. . . . All positive gains have been reversed." [41] Nonetheless, the Soviet leadership has been eager to avoid a complete rupture with the United States. Especially since the accession of Andropov, a number of Soviet statements and proposals have sought to engage the United States in an effort to renew detente, including arms limitation proposals and a possible summit meeting.

(4) A Soviet appeal to the allies of the United States as well as China was a logical corollary of this conclusion. Given (in the view of the dominant orientation in Moscow) the continued desirability of greater economic, technological, and perhaps political interaction with the outside world (albeit now with greater vigilance about unwanted political effects at home) and given the American withdrawal from this interaction, Moscow chose to step up its efforts to propitiate and get along with the European allies of the United States, notably West Germany and France.

Supported by a respectable tradition in Soviet diplomacy, going back to the Rapallo agreement with the Weimar Republic in 1922, this policy now aims to secure from others some of the technology, services, and know-how that the Soviet leaders had initially hoped to procure from the United States; to circumvent the political, economic, and cultural isolation that the Reagan policy has sought to impose on it; to encourage a perception among European elites and public opinion that American policy has been irresponsibly heedless of the overriding importance of preventing nuclear war and a new arms race; and for the first time to envisage as a realistic maximum objective to deepen the split between the United States and its overseas allies. That indeed was a prospect to which, Soviet observers cheerfully noted, Washington contributed at least as effectively as did Moscow. Here was in fact a dramatic example of the counterproductive consequences of the Reagan policy, which for too long had ignored the link between modernization of Theater Nuclear Forces and arms control talks, and which so weakened the Western alliance that NATO was able to bring less, not more, pressure to bear on the Soviet Union.

Similarly, Moscow now made a more vigorous and public appeal to the Chinese leadership to mend relations with the Soviet Union, which had been virtually ruptured throughout the 1970s. While it dealt with a variety of issues, the effort — begun under Brezhnev and stepped up under his successors — sought to capitalize on Chinese disillusionment with the Reagan administration.

(5) Turning to the administration's impact on Soviet allies and clients, we find that it has failed to pursue a consistent line on whether it makes a meaningful differentiation among them or tends to lump all "satellites" and "client regimes" together with the Soviet Union. Whether in regard to Hungary and Rumania, or to Cuba and Vietnam, a frequent fallacy has been to assume that whatever they do must be at the behest of Moscow; at times the behavior of Libya or the P.L.O. has similarly been assumed to be the product of Soviet orders. The "two-camp" approach denies or minimizes diversity within the adversary coalition and tends to overlook opportunities for increasing the room for maneuver of particular actors or states. Reinforced by a sweeping condemnation of all "Marxism," this orientation often tends to push back into official orthodoxy individuals or regimes interested in alternative opportunities.

(6) Most difficult but most important to establish are the intangible effects of the Reagan policy — including its behavior at home and elsewhere in the world — on the domestic political dialogue and political climate in the Soviet Union. Its impact came against the background of a Soviet leadership divided over the calculus that led to the improved relations of the 1970s. Whatever the balance of considerations that led to the removal of a number of leading Party and state officials from office in the 1970s, including Politburo members Peter Shelest and Alexander Shelepin, there are solid indications that a high number of them were more skeptical of the prospects of detente than the survivors. The skeptics

remained (tacit or vocal) participants in the discussions on Reagan policy. On the other hand, the termination of detente was something of a setback for those who had advocated it and acquired a stake in its success.

The dominant impact of the Reagan policy thus far appears to be that it has provided the Soviet authorities a very welcome external enemy whose existence permits them to mobilize public opinion and resources. The result of the pressure applied by the Reagan administration must almost certainly be to get the backs of the Soviet elite up; it strengthens belligerence and hostility to the outside world, and it helps support a hardening of the line at home. It means greater vigilance and suspicion of anyone with deviant, pro-American interests and attitudes. It means greater risks for closet liberals who speak out for improving living conditions or relaxed censorship policies. It means fewer opportunities for travel and contacts abroad (including more jamming of radio broadcasts from the West, a sharp restriction in direct-dialing telephone service out of the country, and greater constraints on cultural and academic contacts and exchanges). It means mounting, if still subtle, pressures for more conformity and discipline, thus easing the task of the regime and especially of its most unimaginative law and order spokesmen.[42]

The effort to isolate the Soviet Union from contacts with Western goods and services, and the ideas that come with them, is bound to play into the hands of the surviving Stalinists and their younger disciples inside the Soviet Union. That used to be precisely their policy. It is the more independent and curious souls who demanded access to foreign books and magazines, films and art. Along with tourists and technology, Soviet citizens encounter new ideas about the quality of life, human rights, and openness in interpersonal relations.[43] Emigration from the Soviet Union reached its peak during the years of greatest interaction. So did diversity, both in the Soviet Union and in the East European bloc, where contact with the West was the necessary condition for the ferment and pressure for change that have been so manifest in Poland and, less dramatically, in Hungary. Isolation fosters a siege mentality that brings back a sense of crisis, with overtones of sacrifice and repression, and with a premium on military virtues and ardent patriotism, at the expense of civilian, humanitarian, and consumerist values.

For at least fifteen years there has been a quiet debate in Soviet elite circles about the possibilities of improving Soviet-American relations. One question in dispute has been the prospects of reaching agreements in areas of mutual interest, such as arms control and trade. Another has been the willingness of the United States to recognize the Soviet Union as coequal not only militarily but also politically. Now the events appear to validate the arguments of the Soviet essentialists, who can insist, looking at current American policy, that it was a delusion to think that the United States was prepared to make equivalent concessions and to stick to, and ratify, treaties and agreements reached between the two superpowers. "The USA is again acting as an unreliable partner with whom one cannot have any dealings on a long-term basis." [44]

Of course, insofar as the essentialist view prevails in Washington, it is not the purpose of the administration to encourage more cooperative relations with the Soviet government: It is to transform it. Such a construction of the purposes of the Reagan administration is not calculated to endear it to the Soviet elite. If, as is at times proposed, it should be our purpose to convince the next generation of Soviet leaders that they have more to gain by getting along with the United States than by confronting it, it must be said that the Reagan program has done more to kindle fears than to awaken hopes; on the basis of the present policy, "future Soviet leaders cannot avoid feeling that the option of a more constructive relationship has been foreclosed." [45]

The final cost of the Reagan administration's foreign policy approach is to the American political process itself. To the extent that it rests on unrealistic assumptions about the vulnerability of the Soviet system and about the costs and limits of American power, it encourages a mistaken belief that the United States is in a position to force a major reorientation of Soviet domestic priorities. To the extent that it perpetuates a deeply rooted American propensity to search for easy panaceas, whether through accommodation or through confrontation, it perpetuates the costly oscillation of American foreign policy from one extreme to another. To the extent that it widens the gap between ambitions and capabilities, it increases the risk of disillusionment and policy instability and prevents the formation of a stable domestic foreign policy consensus. And to the extent that it substitutes rhetoric for policy, it risks letting slip a real opportunity to shape a coherent and long-term strategy for managing a Soviet-American competition that will continue to be with us for decades to come.

Notes

1. Among the voluminous and controversial literature on the origins of the Cold War, see John L. Gaddis, *The United States and the Origins of the Cold War* (Columbia University Press, 1972); Charles Gati (ed.), *Caging the Bear* (Bobbs-Merrill, 1974); Gary R. Hess (ed.), *America and Russia: From Cold War Confrontation to Coexistence* (Thomas Y. Crowell, 1973); Vojtech Mastny, *Russia's Road to the Cold War* (Columbia University Press, 1979); Daniel Yergin, *The Shattered Peace* (Houghton Mifflin, 1980).

2. See Gati, *op. cit.;* John L. Gaddis, "Containment: A Reassessment," *Foreign Affairs,* July 1977, and Gaddis, *Strategies of Containment* (Oxford University Press, 1982).

3. On NSC 68 (which appears in *Foreign Relations of the United States, 1950,* I, 237-292), see Samuel F. Wells, Jr., "Sounding the Tocsin: NSC 68 and the Soviet Threat," *International Security,* IV:2 (1979), 116-158; also Yergin, *op. cit.,* pp. 401ff.

4. Some approximation of it may be found in the arguments made by Secretary Kissinger at the time of the debate over the Jackson-Vanik Amendment (rather than in his later comments); and in Marshall D. Shulman, "Toward a Philosophy of Coexistence," *Foreign Affairs,* October 1973. See also Lawrence T. Caldwell and William Diebold, *Soviet-American Relations in the 1980's* (McGraw-Hill, 1981); and Dan Caldwell, *American-Soviet Relations From 1947 to the Nixon-Kissinger Grand Design* (Greenwood Press, 1981).

5. See, in particular, Stanley Hoffmann, *Primacy or World Order* (McGraw-Hill, 1978).

6. See, e.g., Robert Legvold, "Containment Without Confrontation," *Foreign Policy,* no. 40 (Fall 1980).

7. According to one of the most imaginative publicists of the neoconservative camp, Norman Podhoretz, if the assumptions on which detente was based were not abandoned, ". . . it would signify the final collapse of an American resolve to resist the forward surge of Soviet imperialism. In that case, we would know by what name to call the new era . . . : the Finlandization of America, the political and economic subordination of the United States to superior Soviet power." (Norman Podhoretz, *The Present Danger* [Simon & Schuster, 1980], p. 12.)

8. Podhoretz, in *Book Digest,* December 1980, p. 30. Prominent members of the Committee on the Present Danger included Paul H. Nitze, Eugene Rostow, and Richard Pipes. Others members included William J. Casey, Director of the CIA; Jeane Kirkpatrick, Ambassador to the United Nations; and Richard N. Perle, Assistant Secretary of Defense. For a fuller list, see Robert Scheer, *With Enough Shovels* (Random House, 1982), pp. 144-146.

9. Cited in Leslie H. Gelb, "How Haig Is Recasting His Image," *New York Times Magazine,* June 6, 1981.

10. An exception was Richard E. Pipes, who was appointed to the National Security Council staff but chose after two years to return to his position as professor of history at Harvard. A specialist in Russian history, Pipes has stressed the continuity of historical factors to explain contemporary Soviet perceptions and values.

11. Podhoretz, "The Neo-Conservative Anguish Over Reagan's Foreign Policy," *The New York Times Magazine,* May 2, 1982. See also George Will's columns, e.g., *Newsweek,* January 18 and June 21, 1982.

12. *The New York Times,* January 30, 1981. In a subsequent explanation, Reagan attributed Soviet immorality to the fact that Marxist-Leninists do not believe in an afterlife.

13. *The New York Times,* March 5, 1981.

14. According to Yergin, the advocates of the "Riga axioms" saw the Soviet Union as a revolutionary state committed to a drive for worldwide mastery and to ideological warfare; the logic of their views, at the end of World War II, led to the dominant idiom of the Cold War. The "Yalta axioms," by contrast, tended to depict the Soviet Union as a great power, different only in degree from other great powers, and correspondingly played down the role of Communist ideology as a source of Soviet behavior abroad as well as the foreign policy consequences of domestic Stalinism. See Yergin, *The Shattered Peace.*

15. According to Osgood's "Analysis B," the Soviet Union is relentlessly expansionist,

out of an inner compulsion rooted in one or more of the following: Communist ideology, which moves the Soviet elite; the totalitarian nature of the system, which requires expansion; a search for legitimacy at home, for which the regime strives by adventures abroad. According to this view, the Soviet leadership does have a grand strategic design, which it seeks to implement; it is increasingly prepared to use armed force to advance its objectives. "Analysis A," by contrast, sees the Soviet regime as pragmatic, opportunist, increasingly conservative but expansionist, seeking status and security abroad. Though Soviet and American objectives are likely to come into conflict, they can probably be compromised. In Osgood's astute analysis, "A" permits disaggregating the conflict so as to deal with issues one by one; "B" sees the relationship as a zero sum game, a seamless web. See Robert E. Osgood *et al., Containment, Soviet Behavior, and Grand Strategy* (Berkeley: Institute of International Studies, 1981).

16. For earlier variants and more detailed discussions of the characteristics of these three models, see William Welch, *American Images of Soviet Foreign Press* (Yale University Press, 1970); William Zimmerman, "Containment and the Soviet Union," in Gati (ed.), *Caging the Bear,* pp. 85-108; and Lawrence T. Caldwell and Alexander Dallin, "U.S. Policy Toward the Soviet Union," in Oye, Lieber, and Rothchild (eds.), *Eagle Entangled* (Longman, 1979), especially pp. 215-219.

17. For an able discussion contrasting the commitment to conflict termination (either by accommodation on the left, or by victory on the right) with conflict management (again, with soft and hard variants), see John Van Oudenaren, *U.S. Leadership Perceptions of the Soviet Problem Since 1945* (Rand Corp., 1982, Doc. R-2843-NA).

18. Gelb, *op. cit.*

19. *The Wall Street Journal,* June 3, 1980. Conscious of the fact that this statement constituted a gaffe, the presidential speech writers inserted in his address to the United Nations a different statement: "We look around the world and see rampant conflict and aggression. There are many sources of this conflict — expansionist ambitions, local rivalries, the striving to obtain justice and security." (*The New York Times,* June 18, 1982.)

20. See, e.g. David Holloway, "Military Power and Political Purpose in Soviet Policy," *Daedalus,* Fall 1980; and Abraham S. Becker, *The Burden of Soviet Defense* (Rand Corp., 1981, Doc. R-2752-AF) and sources cited therein.

21. See, for example, the statement of Myer Rashish, Under Secretary of State for Economic Affairs, before the Senate Foreign Relations Committee's Subcommittee on International Economic Policy, September 16, 1981. Differences among Cabinet officers and their departments are reflected in U.S. Congress, Joint Economic Committee, *East-West Commercial Policy: A Congressional Dialogue with the Reagan Administration* (Government Printing Office, February 16, 1982).

22. The rationale for such an approach is spelled out in Carl Gershman, "Selling Them the Rope: Business and the Soviets," *Commentary,* 67:4 (April 1979), pp. 35-45. Gershman's critique of leverage deserves to be cited:

" 'Economic diplomacy' is no substitute for a policy of military deterrence and common sense should dictate that anything the Russians want badly enough to forgo opportunities for expansion is probably something they should not have in the first place. A policy of controls... would not be tied to politics, but ... could in the long run limit the Soviet Union's ability to threaten the security of the West."

A more sophisticated treatment is offered in Thomas A. Wolf, "Choosing a U.S. Trade Strategy Towards the Soviet Union," U.S. Congress, Joint Economic

Committee, *Soviet Economy in the 1980's: Problems and Prospects* (Government Printing Office: forthcoming).

Critics have argued that East-West trade occupies too limited a place in total Soviet imports to make the Soviet Union seriously vulnerable to efforts at economic warfare; that except for grain its supplies are too diversified to make a total embargo possible; and that even if economic pressure could have an effect on Soviet performance, it is more likely to be detrimental than helpful to Western interests. See, for example, Edward Hewett in *The Washington Post*, July 16, 1982.

23. The effort to limit scientific contact embroiled the administration in a controversy with the scholarly community, which led to the appointment of a National Academy of Sciences panel on communication and national security. For its report, see *Scientific Communication and National Security* (National Academy Press, 1982).

24. Thane Gustafson, *Selling the Russians the Rope? Soviet Technology Policy and U.S. Export Controls* (Rand Corp., 1981, Doc. R-2649-ARPA), p. 4.

Critics have argued that the administration has overstated the degree of Soviet dependence on Western technology, and that its case rests on faulty assumptions about the impact of Western technology on the Soviet economy. The diversion of dual-use technologies from civilian to military purposes is more complex than is suggested; technological imports do not necessarily free domestic resources but may require additional investments to exploit them. The Soviet system is not, on the whole, able to assimilate new technologies effectively and rapidly. And, it has been argued, the costs of proposed controls far outweigh their possible benefits. Among many studies, see in particular Philip Hanson, *Trade and Technology in Soviet-Western Relations* (Columbia University Press, 1981); and U.S. Congress, Joint Economic Committee, *Issues in East-West Commercial Relations*, Part I (Government Printing Office, 1979).

25. In August 1981 the president announced a one-year extension of the Soviet-American grain agreement and increased the quantity the Soviet Union would be allowed to purchase. In August 1982 he extended the agreement for another year but resisted farm state pressures to negotiate a new long-term pact. In October 1982, two weeks before the mid-term elections, Reagan appealed to the farm vote by offering the Soviet Union an opportunity to purchase up to 23 million tons of grain on terms that for some six months would be exempted from any new future sanctions against the Soviet Union.

26. As Senator Jake Garn graphically put it,

"The pipeline project ... will provide the Soviet Union with a much-needed boost in foreign-exchange earnings, help the Soviets maintain their control over Eastern Europe, bail the Soviets out of serious energy and economic difficulties, expose West European banks to a heightened risk of financial ruin, and grant Moscow large-scale economic and political influence over Western European affairs that could sap the vitality from the NATO alliance. In return, the Western Europeans get the privilege of turning over to the Soviets billions of dollars in technology, goods, and equipment, paid for almost entirely by Western loans that are secured by as yet unrealized energy supplies sold at some unknowable market price in the future. All this so that our major allies can become dependent for up to 25 per cent of their natural gas supplies on the country that didn't hesitate to cut off energy shipments to Yugoslavia in 1948, to Hungary and Israel in 1956, to Czechoslovakia in 1968, and that used its energy leverage over Poland in 1981."

(*The Wall Street Journal*, May 20, 1982.) For a more balanced treatment of the pipeline issue, see Angela Stent, *Soviet Energy and Western Europe* (Washington Papers, no. 90) (Praeger, 1982), and her *From Embargo to Ostpolitik ... 1955-*

1980 (Cambridge University Press, 1981); John P. Hardt and Kate S. Tomlinson, "Economic Interchange with the USSR in the 1980's" (California Seminar on International Security and Foreign Policy, April 1982); Jonathan Stern, *Soviet Natural Gas Development to 1990* (Lexington Books, 1980); and Jonathan Stern, "Specters and Pipe Dreams," *Foreign Policy*, no. 48 (Fall 1982), pp. 21-36.

27. The actual volume of East-West trade remained comparatively small. NATO imports from the countries of CMEA (Council for Mutual Economic Assistance) in 1980 represented 3.2 percent of their total world trade, and exports 3.4 percent of their total. As in previous years, the Federal Republic of Germany had the largest share, followed by France, Italy, the United Kingdom, and then the United States. U.S. imports from CMEA countries in 1980 amounted to $1.4 billion, while exports totaled nearly $3.9 billion — 0.6 and 1.8 percent of the U.S. imports and exports respectively. (U.S. Department of State, Special Report no. 92, November 30, 1981, pp. 1-2.)

28. U.S. Congress, Joint Economic Committee, *East-West Commercial Policy*, pp. 4, 13.

29. By 1981 the six East European countries of the Soviet bloc had accumulated a net debt of roughly sixty billion U.S. dollars to the West, of which just over five billion was owed to the United States. Poland accounted for some 22 billion of this total. (Wharton EFA, "Centrally Planned Economies Current Analysis," April 27, 1982.)

30. Henry Kissinger, "Poland's Lessons for Mr. Reagan," *The New York Times*, January 17, 1982.

31. Arguments in favor of default were presented in testimony before the Senate Appropriations Committee Subcommittee on Foreign Operations, among others by Felix Rohatyn. The administration position was defended by Assistant Secretary of State Robert Hormats. A more technical analysis of the consequences of declaring the Polish debt in default is found in Wharton EFA, "Centrally Planned Economies Current Analysis," February 12 and May 17, 1982.

32. U.S. sanctions in response to the proclamation of martial law included the suspension or cancellation of a number of exchange agreements with the Soviet Union, and the cancellation of airline landing rights and of fishing rights previously granted to Poland and the termination of Export-Import Bank insurance for credits granted to Poland. The U.S. did not cancel Soviet-American foreign minister talks, arms control negotiations, or participation in multilateral conferences attended by both the U.S. and the Soviet Union.

33. Secretary Haig's speech of April 27, 1982. See also *The New York Times*, May 30, 1982.

34. *The New York Times*, June 9, 1982.

35. See the rather partisan account by Tom Bethell, "Propaganda Warts," *Harper's*, May 1982, pp. 19-25.

36. See, e.g., *The New York Times*, February 9, 1981; San Francisco *Chronicle*, March 30 and April 27, 1981.

37. Address to the U.S. Chamber of Commerce, Washington, D.C., April 27, 1982.

38. George F. Kennan, "A Risky U.S. Equation," *The New York Times*, February 18, 1981.

39. For a thorough discussion, see Alexander L. George, *Presidential Decisionmaking in Foreign Policy: The Effective Use of Information and Advice* (Westview Press, 1980).

40. Daniel Bond and Herbert S. Levine, "The Soviet Economy to the Year 2000: An Overview" in Abram Bergson and Herbert S. Levine (eds.), *The Soviet Economy: Toward the Year 2000* (Allen and Unwin, 1983).

41. *Izvestia*, August 30, 1981.
42. See also Thompson R. Buchanan, "The Real Russia," *Foreign Policy*, no. 47 (Summer 1982); and Andrew J. Glass, "Moscow's Reagan Jitters," *The New Leader*, July 12-26, 1982.
43. See Alexander Dallin, "A Balance Sheet of Soviet-American Exchanges," in *A Balance Sheet For East-West Exchanges* (IREX Occasional Papers, vol. I, no. 1, 1980); and Gail W. Lapidus, "Studying the Soviet Social System: *The Soviet Citizen* Revisited," IREX Occasional Papers, vol. I, no. 4 (1980).
44. S. A. Losev, "Vashington: Uzhestochenie kursa antirazriadki," *SShA*, 1982, no. 2, p. 59.
45. Marshall D. Shulman, "Sensible Policy Toward Moscow," *The New York Times*, June 27, 1982.

8

China Policy and
the Constraints of Triangular Logic

Banning Garrett

In China policy making under the Reagan administration, the logic of geopolitics and national interest confronted the pressures of ideology and domestic politics. President Ronald Reagan found himself torn between his anti-Communist pro-Taiwan sentiments and his ambitious anti-Soviet goals.

Like Presidents Nixon, Ford, and Carter before him, President Reagan viewed China policy through the lens of the triangular relationship among the United States, China, and the Soviet Union. Despite his fervent anti-Communism, Reagan supported developing strategic relations with the "Chinese Communists" as a counter to the growing power of the Soviet Union. The president also felt a strong loyalty to the Nationalists on Taiwan and had committed himself during the presidential campaign to restoring "official" ties with Taipei.

President Reagan hoped to avoid a policy tradeoff in achieving these aims by trying to gain Chinese acquiescence to upgraded American ties with Taiwan while offering expanded American military ties to China. Beijing's rejection of Reagan's two-edged approach to China and Taiwan led to the worst crisis in Sino-American relations since the opening of ties in the early 1970s. President Reagan's room for maneuver domestically and internationally was narrow. He was forced to choose between the imperatives of the strategic triangle and the demands of traditional loyalties. To understand the triangular dilemma faced by President Reagan in policy making toward China requires analysis of the dynamics of American-

Banning Garrett is a Washington-based defense consultant specializing in U.S.-Soviet-Chinese strategic relations. He is also the author of a forthcoming book entitled The "China Card" and Its Origins: U.S. Bureaucratic Politics in the Strategic Triangle.

The author wishes to thank Bonnie S. Glaser for her extensive research, editorial, and analytical assistance in preparing this chapter.

Soviet-Chinese relations and of United States bureaucratic politics that led to the quasi-alliance between the United States and China that existed when he entered office.

Global Realignment

For China, the 1971-1972 rapprochement with the United States followed a strategic assessment that the Soviet Union was a greater threat to China than the United States and that Washington was a potential military partner in a global strategy aimed at countering expanding Soviet military power and political influence. The Sino-Soviet split, which emerged into the open in 1960, and the Cultural Revolution that began in 1966 had left China isolated internationally and weak and divided internally as hostilities between Moscow and Beijing escalated at the end of the decade. China's decision to break out of isolation and seek a strategic counter to the Soviet Union in an American connection followed the Soviet invasion of Czechoslovakia in August 1968, the Sino-Soviet border clashes, beginning in March 1969, and veiled Soviet threats to launch surgical strikes against Chinese nuclear forces. Chinese leaders, especially Chairman Mao Zedong and Premier Zhou Enlai, judged the Soviet Union to be a greater danger to China than the United States, which they considered a declining power that would begin withdrawing from Asia.

Chinese leaders also saw their strategic realignment with the West as the underpinning of a modernization strategy that aimed at gaining access to Japanese and Western civilian and defense technology. The full extent of Chinese ambitions was not evident in the West until the Four Modernizations program was announced in February 1978, more than a year after Mao's death and the purge of the Gang of Four radical leaders. But it was foreshadowed in the large purchases of whole plants and high technology from the West in the 1972-1975 period [1] and the goals set forth by Premier Zhou at the Fourth National People's Congress in January 1975.

The rapprochement with the United States allowed China to shift from planning for war on two fronts — against the Soviet Union in the north and the United States and Taiwan in the southeast — to concentrate their forces primarily on the Soviet threat. The American connection also raised the spectre for the Soviets of possible American assistance to China in the event of a Sino-Soviet war. China was no longer isolated in the face of superior Soviet military power, however uncertain any American aid might be. The rapprochement also reduced the likelihood of American-Soviet collusion against China, although that concern continued to ebb and flow, especially at times of stagnation in relations between Washington and Beijing and improvements in relations between Washington and Moscow.

While Mao and Zhou sought to end China's economic and political isolation and to establish a reliable American counterbalance to Soviet power, President Richard Nixon and his national security adviser, Henry Kissinger, sought to:

— gain Chinese support for stability in Asia as the United States scaled down its defense posture in the region;
— capitalize on the Sino-Soviet split to gain diplomatic leverage over both the Soviet Union and China and create a new structure of global power relations that compensated for perceived American weaknesses;
— head off a possible Soviet attack on China and a Sino-Soviet war, which could become global or could lead to Soviet domination of China;
— head off a Sino-Soviet rapprochement, which, like imposed Soviet domination, could lead once again to a coordinated Soviet-Chinese strategy against the United States.

Before the Nixon administration shifted American strategy in 1969-1970, American military posture since the early 1950s had presumed a monolithic Sino-Soviet threat and was ostensibly based on a "two-and-a-half war" strategy that envisioned fighting major wars simultaneously in Asia against China and in Europe against the Soviet Union — and at the same time meeting a "minor" contingency elsewhere, such as in Vietnam. In his memoirs, Henry Kissinger notes that the United States never had sufficient forces to implement such a strategy, and he argues that if war had broken out simultaneously against the Soviet Union and China, it would likely have escalated to use of nuclear weapons to compensate for weakness in conventional forces.[2] The United States also secretly had planned to "swing" much of its conventional force capability — naval and air forces primarily — to the European theater in the event of a NATO/Warsaw pact conflict.[3]

The change to a "one-and-a-half war" strategy was announced in February 1970, which Kissinger says was a signal to China that the United States publicly acknowledged the unlikelihood of Sino-Soviet cooperation and "would no longer treat a conflict with the USSR as automatically involving the People's Republic."[4] In 1972, Kissinger says, the Chinese gave the United States the assurances he and Nixon had sought that China would support stability in Asia while the United States reduced its force levels in the region.[5]

For Moscow, the Sino-American rapprochement appeared to give viability and permanency to China's split with the Soviet Union and created the possibility of a simultaneous two-front war against NATO and China. Moscow had been building up its forces in the Far East since 1965 — from fifteen to thirty-three divisions by 1969 — as its conflict with China had become more volatile. In the 1960s, however, China was isolated and the Soviets had a potential free hand to use military force against the Chinese, who were seen as adventurist and expansionist by Washington. Indeed, in the early 1960s, President Kennedy had seen China as a more dangerous enemy than the Soviet Union and had considered military action to take out China's nuclear facilities before Beijing could produce its first atomic bomb.[6] Washington's open discussions of this may have given Moscow the impression that the United States might even cooperate or at least acquiesce in a Soviet strike against China. But, when Soviet officials probed the United States for such cooperation in 1969 and 1970,[7] the Nixon administration rejected the overtures and indicated Washington's disapproval of such action. This signaled Moscow that a triangular strategic arrangement was now operative and that the Soviets faced the prospect of Sino-American collusion against them in both peacetime and wartime.

Although wartime cooperation between Washington and Beijing seemed quite unlikely in the early 1970s, Kissinger recounts that he and Nixon were committed to preventing Soviet domination of China. According to Kissinger:

> From the beginning Nixon and I were convinced — alone among senior policymakers — that the United States could not accept a Soviet military assault on China. We had held this view before there was contact of any sort; we imposed contingency planning on a reluctant bureaucracy as early as the summer of 1969. Obviously, this reflected no agreement between Peking and Washington.... It was based on a sober geopolitical assessment. If Moscow succeeded in humiliating Peking and reducing it to impotence, the whole weight of the Soviet military effort could be thrown against the West. Such a demonstration of Soviet ruthlessness and American impotence ... would encourage accommodation to other Soviet demands from Japan to Western Europe, not to speak of the many smaller countries on the Soviet periphery.[8]

During the India-Pakistan War of December 1971 — six months after Kissinger's secret trip to Peking — Nixon and Kissinger apparently were prepared to risk war with the Soviet Union if Moscow attacked China.[9] In the decade that followed, the likelihood of American assistance to a besieged China increased as the United States and China established a "new relationship" in 1972 and moved in 1978 toward building a military and strategic dimension to Sino-American ties. Although the Chinese still could not be assured of American support, the Soviets could not rule out an American response if they attacked China. And China's strategic concern that the Soviets not succeed in achieving domination of Western Europe, through appeasement or military defeat, created the possibility of Chinese intervention to help prevent a Soviet victory in the west that could allow for a redeployment or "swinging" of Soviet forces to overwhelm China in the east. Thus, by the early 1970s, the Soviets had found themselves facing the prospect of a two-front war, a concern heightened by the development of American-Chinese military ties at the end of the decade. Ironically, Soviet fears of Sino-American military collusion against them had predated the idea of such collaboration within the United States Government and may have contributed to its formulation.[10]

Although Nixon and Kissinger perceived strategic military benefits from the global realignment of 1969-1971, their more immediate goal was to capitalize on the Sino-Soviet split and Chinese overtures to the United States to gain diplomatic leverage over the Soviet Union on SALT, Vietnam, and other bilateral and multilateral issues. The Soviets, fearful of Sino-American collusion against them, sought to improve relations with the United States in competition with Beijing. Nixon's dramatic summitry of 1972 consolidated this new situation: Within four months, the American president formally established the "new relationship" with China and detente with the Soviet Union. The Shanghai Communiqué, signed by the president at the end of his February visit to China, set forth the principles of the new Sino-American relationship, including a declaration suggesting Washington's opposition to any effort by the Soviet Union to dominate China.[11] Nixon then went to Moscow in May, where he signed the first Soviet-American strategic arms limitation agreement (SALT I) and the principles for conduct of Soviet-American relations, thus formalizing "detente" between Moscow and Washington.[12]

Nixon and Kissinger sought to use the new relationship with China to gain leverage over the Soviet Union. But the policy had an inherent contradiction in that the Chinese were seeking to pull the United States into an anti-Soviet alignment and to undermine detente, while the Nixon administration was seeking to further negotiations and cooperation with the Soviet Union by using Soviet fears of Sino-American collusion to pressure the Soviets to compromise. Thus, if American policy toward China were successful in furthering detente, China's security would be diminished, the usefulness of the Washington connection put in doubt, and Sino-American relations would likely deteriorate.

Military Ties with China?

In the 1971-1972 period, Soviet fears of Sino-American collusion, and Chinese fears of United States-Soviet collusion produced a desire in both Moscow and Beijing to move forward in relations with Washington. But the contradiction between Chinese security interests and Soviet-American detente soon began to pose a dilemma for the United States, at the same time a debate heated up in Washington over the viability of United States detente strategy.

By 1974-1975, the idea of developing a Sino-American military relationship began to percolate inside the United States government.[13] The notion of Sino-American defense ties, although stimulated in part by quiet Chinese probes to the United States as early as 1973, nevertheless contradicted the conventional wisdom of China experts in the United States, who believed the Chinese would never abandon self-reliance and seek military ties with the United States. Some defense planners, however, could see the strategic logic and benefits for both the United States and China of a military relationship, and the idea received attention within the Defense Department beginning in the fall of 1973. By December 1974, Secretary of Defense James Schlesinger was briefed on the pros and cons of military ties with China, and by the fall of 1975, the outlines of a sharp debate over China's role in American strategy toward the Soviet Union had emerged with "military ties" the key issue. This debate was part of a larger struggle over detente, in which Schlesinger was pitted against Secretary of State Kissinger.

The purported benefits of a defense relationship with the "Communist Chinese" — ranging from exchange of defense attaches to sales of advanced weapons — included:[14]

— gaining leverage over Moscow to restrain its behavior internationally and to pressure the Soviets in the SALT talks and other bilateral negotiations;

— preventing a Sino-Soviet rapprochement by maintaining suspicion and tension between Beijing and Moscow on the one hand, and by tying Chinese leaders, including military leaders, to the policy of tilting toward the United States on the other;

— giving Moscow reason to plan for possible U.S. wartime aid to China in the event of a new Sino-Soviet military conflict;

— strengthening China's military capability through the transfer of certain advanced weapons and military technology, thus helping China deter the Soviets and possibly leading Moscow to redeploy some of its conventional forces to the Far East, thereby reducing pressure on NATO in the west.

Strategic Debate

By 1975, both Kissinger and Schlesinger were attracted to the idea of military ties with China, but for different and conflicting reasons.[15] Both officials viewed China in a triangular context, but they saw China's role in the strategic triangle differently, based primarily on their conflicting views of United States-Soviet relations and on their conflicting institutional concerns.

For Kissinger, detente was aimed at "strategic enmeshment" of the Soviet Union in a web of relations with the United States and the West, which could be used to constrain the extension of Soviet influence at a time when Moscow's global power, especially its military power, was growing, and American power seemed to be peaking in relative terms. Detente was intended to employ carrots as well as sticks to induce acceptable Soviet behavior by linking issues in bilateral relations with global politics. SALT was to be the political underpinning as well as the arms control foundation of detente.

Although strong American military power, including maintenance of "essential equivalence" of strategic forces in the face of a major Soviet nuclear arms buildup, was said to be a prerequisite for carrying out this strategy, it was fundamentally a diplomatic approach to the problem of coping with Soviet power. For Kissinger, the problem was strengthening the American position in the peacetime balance of power through political and economic means at a time of Vietnam War-induced defense spending cuts in the United States.

Kissinger — and Nixon in the 1969-1974 period — approached China largely in the context of Soviet strategy and policy. Since they sought to gain leverage over Moscow by manipulating Soviet anxiety about possible Sino-American collusion against them, any gestures toward military ties with China would have to be aimed at maintaining and increasing Washington's leverage over Moscow. At the same time, such attempts to gain leverage could be counterproductive if moves toward China provoked the Soviet Union to adopt a harder line toward the United States and engage in more aggressive international behavior, thus undermining the entire detente relationship.

For Schlesinger, coping with Soviet power was more a military than a diplomatic problem. In his view, detente had not slowed the buildup of Soviet strategic and conventional military power, nor had it altered the long-term "hegemonistic" goals of Soviet leaders. The benefits accruing to the United States in the global military balance resulting from the Sino-Soviet split and then China's tilt toward the United States had become increasingly important factors in efforts to maintain or improve the American military position vis-à-vis the Soviet Union, especially in the Far East. As a strategic ally, China offered great potential to tie down a substantial portion of Soviet military capabilities and resources, and to greatly complicate Soviet defense planning for both conventional and nuclear war with the West. From Schlesinger's more military point of view — and his concern about the wartime balance of forces — the preservation of detente had less significance than did the maintenance of a favorable balance of military power.

Kissinger's Moves Toward Military Ties

Moves toward American military ties with China were first considered in the fall of 1975 as Washington's relations with both Moscow and Beijing deteriorated, and the president was under increasing domestic pressure to take strong action against the Soviet Union. At the same time, a power and policy struggle was intensifying within the Ford administration. Kissinger was facing strong opposition to his detente policies, especially from Schlesinger and from vocal members of Congress. The secretary of state's efforts to finalize the SALT II agreement based on the Ford-Brezhnev Vladivostok formula were stalled. Kissinger's strategy of "strategic enmeshment" had been seriously undermined by the December 1974 Jackson-Vanik amendment, which tied improved Soviet-American trade relations to Soviet emigration policies and led Moscow to abrogate the 1972 Soviet-American trade agreement. Soviet actions in the Middle East and Angola had eroded the credibility of Kissinger's detente strategy and further strained United States-Soviet relations. Kissinger also was under attack for the Helsinki agreement, signed in July 1975 by President Ford, and for his failure to criticize the Soviets directly on human rights violations. Although Kissinger was trying to defend and repair his faltering detente policy, he also was becoming increasingly disenchanted with the Soviet view of detente.[16]

Kissinger was under attack from the Chinese as well. They had begun accusing him of "appeasement" of the Soviet Union and indicating that American weakness vis-à-vis Moscow raised serious doubts about the reliability and usefulness of the United States as a strategic counter to the Soviets. Kissinger had failed to follow through on the Shanghai Communiqué and normalize relations with Beijing, and he was under pressure to do something to move Sino-American relations forward.[17] It was in this context that "administration officials" — almost certainly Kissinger or his deputy Winston Lord — expressed concern in an interview with *The New York Times* that the slippage in Sino-American relations had weakened Washington's leverage over the Soviet Union.[18] The "officials" said that in their view, Soviet fear of United States-Chinese collusion against them had greatly diminished and that the Soviet concern over Sino-American ties that had moderated Moscow's behavior in the early 1970s no longer was a factor restraining Moscow's "adventurism" in Portugal and Angola.

A move toward military ties with China offered Kissinger a means of improving Sino-American relations and thereby of regaining leverage over Moscow in the SALT II talks, which were to be resumed in early 1976, as well as over Soviet actions in Angola. At the same time, a gesture toward military ties with China would allow President Ford to give the Chinese something significant at a time when he was unwilling because of a conservative challenge in the 1976 elections to compromise on Taiwan. Kissinger and Ford made that gesture in December 1975 during a trip to Beijing. They approved the British sales to China of Rolls Royce Spey jet engines — used in the British version of the F-4 Phantom fighter bomber — and a Spey factory to build engines in Xian,[19] a deal that had been under discussion since 1972. The United States had the ability to block the deal through CoCom, the Western allies' "coordinating committee" for controlling the transfer of strategic technology to the Soviet Union and other Communist countries.[20]

The next move on the military-ties track followed the death of Chairman Mao Zedong on September 9, 1976, and the arrest of the Gang of Four on October 6. Kissinger was sufficiently concerned that a post-Mao power struggle could yet turn against American interests that he urged the National Security Council on October 12 to approve the sale to China of two advanced Control Data Cyber 72 computers with military applications. Subsequently, at a news conference on October 15, he warned Moscow and reassured Beijing that "the territorial integrity and sovereignty of China is very important to the world equilibrium and we would consider it a grave matter if this were threatened by an outside power." Although Kissinger's moves may have been effective in reassuring the Chinese of American support and in signaling the Soviets that Sino-American collusion was a live option in United States policy, the secretary of state was a lame duck, and his actions did not constitute an overall policy that was necessarily to be continued by the new administration.

Carter and the China Card: To Play or Not To Play?

When Jimmy Carter assumed the presidency in January 1977, he and Secretary of State Cyrus Vance had already indicated that improving Soviet-American relations would be of paramount concern for the new administration, while Sino-American relations were far down the list of foreign policy priorities. Vance indicated that he would not let Washington's relations with Beijing interfere with SALT and other outstanding issues between Washington and Moscow,[21] and throughout his tenure as secretary, Vance opposed moves toward military ties with China on the grounds that they would damage Soviet-American relations.

But Vance was not the only foreign policy maker in the administration, and his desire to concentrate on improving Soviet-American relations while playing down relations with China was soon challenged by other officials — and by events. The "China card" — as it was coming to be called — was pushed to the top of the presidential options deck ten weeks after Carter was inaugurated. The president's explicit statements criticizing human rights violations in the Soviet Union quickly soured the atmosphere in Soviet-American relations, contributing to Soviet suspicions of the new administration's intentions when Vance presented a SALT "reductions proposal" during his visit to Moscow at the end of March. Soviet leaders angrily rejected the proposal and denounced Carter's human rights policy. In response, the administration considered playing the China card for the first time. The idea — which was strongly backed by National Security Advisor Zbigniew Brzezinski — was rejected at the presidential level in June, after months of internal debate. Officials from the Pentagon, the National Security Council, and the CIA favoring military ties with the Chinese were pitted against State Department officials, who argued that such moves might be too provocative toward the Soviets.[22] The option of some sort of defense ties with China, such as transfer of military-related technology or allowing Western European arms sales to Beijing — was put on the back burner for the rest of 1977. But the issue continued to be the subject of intense debate and political struggle within the administration.

The internal debate was unresolved with the June 1977 rejection of the China card option, which represented a temporary victory for the Vance "pro-detente" faction of the administration. Besides seeking to reassure the Soviets that the United States was not moving toward a military alliance with China,[23] at Vance's urging President Carter toned down his criticisms of Soviet human rights policy and backed off from his tough SALT proposals. The administration seemed to be moving quickly toward a SALT II agreement with Moscow, and in October President Carter erroneously predicted that an accord might be reached "within the next few weeks." [24]

In this period, the National Security Council concluded a major interagency study of the global balance of power — Presidential Review Memorandum (PRM) 10 — which concluded that growth in Soviet military and economic power was slowing down and that long-term trends favored the United States.[25] The massive study concluded that the Soviet-American military balance was roughly equal at present but contrasted the strength and scope of the American economy and capacity for technological innovation with forecasts of impending Soviet capital and labor shortages. In addition, PRM 10 noted Moscow's problems with political succession, agricultural failures, and the continuing Sino-Soviet split as factors exacerbating Soviet long-term weakness and tilting the balance of power toward the United States. Vance and other pro-detente officials argued on the basis of the PRM 10 assessment that Soviet weaknesses and American strengths provided a basis for Soviet interest in accommodation with Washington. Brzezinski and others, however, viewed the conclusions of PRM 10 as arguing for exploitation of Moscow's vulnerabilities to diminish Soviet power, a view that did not prevail within the administration until the spring of 1978.

Chinese leaders reacted negatively to Vance's strategic assessment based on PRM 10 and to his desire to avoid provoking Moscow through developing military ties with China and to instead deal with Sino-American relations as primarily a bilateral matter.

The Chinese conveyed their disapproval of the American strategic view and the administration's policy toward the Soviet Union during a visit to Beijing by the secretary of state in August. Privately, American officials worried that the failure to move forward in relations with China resulting from Vance's trip was more a function of fundamental differences in strategic views than of a highly publicized impasse over conditions for normalization of relations. The conclusions of PRM 10 were a direct challenge to China's view of the United States as a declining superpower, with the Soviet Union as the superpower on the ascendancy. They also raised questions about the usefulness of America as an ally if Washington failed to see the need to take a strong global stand against Soviet expansion. In major press commentaries in the fall of 1977, the Chinese charged that "advocates of appeasement" in the West — apparently including Vance and some other members of the Carter administration, if not the president himself — "hope they can divert the Soviet Union to the east so as to free themselves from this Soviet peril at the expense of the security of other nations." [26] The commentaries also questioned the reliability of the United States commitment to Western Europe and, by implication, to China.[27]

Chinese leaders nevertheless hoped Washington would assume a tougher anti-Soviet posture. Their hopes for a change in American policy heightened in early 1978 as United States-Soviet relations again deteriorated. President Carter was under mounting domestic pressure to take a tougher position in the SALT talks and to respond forcefully to Soviet and Cuban military intervention in Ethiopia. Carter departed sharply from his previously conciliatory approach to the Soviets in a speech at Wake Forest University on March 17. The address, which was prepared by Brzezinski and his NSC staff, took a generally harder line toward Moscow.

Although Brzezinski had won the battle to toughen up the administration's rhetoric toward Moscow, Carter rejected his proposals for a show of American military force in the Horn of Africa and for linkage of progress in the SALT talks to Moscow's international behavior. But Carter's decision to side with Vance on these issues made the "China card" a more attractive option to punish and pressure Moscow. Over Vance's objectives, the president decided to send his anti-Soviet national security adviser to China in May — a signal to both Moscow and Beijing that the United States had made an important shift in its triangular policies.

Carter's new tougher line toward Moscow was well received during Brzezinski's visit to Beijing May 21-23. The White House officially denied that Brzezinski's trip was intended to send any signals to the Soviets. But administration officials said privately that the visit's primary purposes were to reassure the Chinese about American defense policies vis-à-vis the Soviet Union, to reaffirm Washington's desire to pursue parallel interests with China globally, and to keep the Soviet Union off balance by holding out the possibility of increasingly close Sino-American cooperation if American relations with Moscow deteriorated further. Brzezinski told his Chinese hosts in his opening speech: "We approach our relations with three fundamental beliefs: that friendship between the United States and the People's Republic of China is vital and beneficial to world peace; that a secure and strong China is in America's interest; that a powerful, confident and globally engaged United States is in China's interest." He emphasized that "the United States does not view its relationship with China as a tactical expedient," but rather as "derived from a long-term strategic view" as "reflected in the Shanghai Communiqué." He added that the United States recognizes and shares "China's resolve to resist the efforts of any nation which seeks to establish global or regional hegemony." Brzezinski mentioned Africa, Europe, the Middle East and Asia as areas where "we can enhance the cause of peace through consultations and, where appropriate, through parallel pursuit of our similar objectives."

Brzezinski and his staff added to Soviet concern about his visit by leaking to the press that the sale to China of American dual-purpose, military-related technology and Western arms had been discussed in Beijing, and that Chinese leaders had been given detailed briefings on the SALT II negotiations and on the administration's global strategic assessment, PRM 10. They stressed that Soviet weaknesses and long-term American advantages should be exploited to extract greater concessions from Moscow and to contain its influence, even at the expense of possible deterioration in Soviet-American relations. This view was far more acceptable to the Chinese than Vance's strategic assessment, and it indicated a greater American willingness to pursue a potentially provocative informal alliance with Beijing against Moscow. Chinese officials, who were dissatisfied with Vance's Beijing visit, indicated they were pleased with the Brzezinski trip. Both Deng Xiaoping and Brzezinski later said that agreement on strategic views had made possible rapid movement toward normalization of relations, which had been deadlocked since the 1972 Shanghai Communiqué.

Brzezinski's visit was intended to "play the China card," and it was perceived that way in Moscow as well as in Beijing. On June 25, Soviet President Brezhnev charged that "recently attempts have been made in the U.S. at a high level, and in quite cynical form, to play the China card against the USSR." Brezhnev called Carter's China policy "shortsighted and dangerous." A week earlier, *Pravda* had stated more explicitly that American "alignment with China on an anti-Soviet basis would rule out the possibility of cooperation with the Soviet Union in the matter of reducing the danger of a nuclear war and, of course, of limiting armaments."

Some senior American officials, including the secretary of state, sought to maintain at least a public image of "evenhandedness" in Washington's dealings with Moscow and Beijing. Hoping to limit damage to Soviet-American relations, they also sought to slow if not reverse the momentum of the "new phase" in Sino-American relations. But the direction of the Washington-Beijing relationship had been set, resulting first in the normalization of relations and finally in the administration's decision in the wake of the Soviet Afghanistan invasion to permit sales to China of nonlethal military equipment.

While Vance was unable to alter the direction of China policy, he managed to obtain a SALT II agreement with Moscow in the spring of 1979, even though the "China factor" continued to have a major impact on United States-Soviet relations, which had continued to deteriorate after the winter of 1978. The announcement December 15, 1978 that the United States and China would normalize relations January 1, and that Deng would visit Washington, was made less than a week before Vance and Gromyko were scheduled to meet in Geneva for what was billed by the United States side as the final round of SALT talks before a Carter-Brezhnev summit to be held in Washington in mid-January. But those talks failed. Administration officials attributed the failure in part to a Soviet desire to put off finalization of the accord and a Carter-Brezhnev summit until after Deng's visit to Washington in order to assess how the United States dealt with the Chinese leader. Soviet officials publicly denied that Sino-American ties were the cause of the delay, apparently because they did not want to acknowledge a linkage between SALT and China.

The normalization agreement and Deng's visit to the United States January 29–February 5 were victories for those officials in the administration seeking to develop strategic ties with China. But the Chinese invaded Vietnam less than two weeks after Deng left the United States.[28] President Carter refrained from all-out support for China, and at Vance's urging secretly resumed SALT discussions during the invasion. The arms limitation agreement was finalized in the spring and signed at a Carter-Brezhnev summit meeting in Vienna. The June summit was limited to signing the SALT II accord, however, and United States-Soviet relations failed to improve significantly. The Chinese, meanwhile, made new overtures in April for talks with Moscow on normalizing relations, thus keeping the Soviets off balance and showing their dissatisfaction with Washington's failure to give all-out support for their attack on Vietnam.

Cold War with Moscow, Quasi-Alliance with Beijing

Although Sino-American relations cooled in the aftermath of the Vietnam invasion and the conclusion of the SALT II agreement in May, President Carter approved further steps toward military ties with China in the summer and fall of 1979. These began with a visit to Beijing in August by Vice-President Walter Mondale, who broadened the implied security guarantee given to China by Kissinger in 1976. Mondale stated on nationwide Chinese television that "any nation which seeks to weaken or isolate you in world affairs assumes a stance counter to American interests." [29]

By the time the vice-president returned to Washington, the United States and the Soviet Union were on a collision course over American intelligence leaks of an alleged Soviet "combat brigade" in Cuba. While Carter's public response to the "crisis" on October 1 focused on stepped up surveillance activity and naval operations aimed at Cuba, and on a strong appeal for Senate ratification of the SALT II treaty, the president quietly approved several measures to intensify pressure on Moscow. These included moves indicating that the United States would begin to further restrict the flow of high technology to the Soviet Union and that the administration would move toward overt military ties with China. On the same day Carter announced the measures against Cuba, the White House leaked to the press that Secretary of Defense Harold Brown would visit China.

A few days later, administration sources leaked a secret Pentagon study, "Consolidated Guidance Number 8: Asia During a Worldwide Conventional War," which concluded that in view of China's "pivotal role" in the global balance of power, it would be in the American interest "to encourage Chinese actions that would heighten Soviet security concerns." [30] "CG 8" recommended possible American military assistance to China to increase the likelihood of Chinese participation in a global war, including provision of advanced technology and intelligence data, sale of advanced arms, Chinese production of American weapons, and joint military exercises. Although Vance denied that any change had taken place in administration policy, State Department officials interviewed by the author in early December 1979 said that the "China tilters" had won the battle for military ties with China and predicted that the United States would move closer toward an alliance with China, including sales of military-related technology and possibly even arms.

The Soviet invasion of Afghanistan in late December created a new crisis in Soviet-American relations and sharply weakened the position of those in the State Department who had hoped to limit the substance of Defense Secretary Brown's upcoming trip to China to prevent further damage to the remaining shreds of Soviet-American detente. A "senior official" — probably Brzezinski — told *The New York Times* on the eve of Brown's departure for China in early January that the Soviet invasion had given Brown's mission a "new dimension" and asserted that "the Soviets have forced us and the Chinese into a posture in which we both see the world in the same way." [31] Brown apparently received new instructions in response to the Afghanistan invasion that included informing Chinese leaders that the United States was now willing to consider the sale of nonlethal military equipment to China on a case-by-case basis.

Vance continued fighting a losing battle against Sino-American strategic ties, apparently with hopes of reversing the continuing deterioration of United States-Soviet relations. But his influence within the administration had been dealt a mortal blow by the crisis over the Soviet brigade in Cuba. He finally resigned from office in April after opposing the ill-fated Iranian hostage rescue mission. With Vance's departure, the position of officials opposed to military ties with China was further weakened. Although President Carter did not lift the arms sales ban, there were indications that he would have done so had he been reelected, and that American officials had already led the Chinese to believe the arms sales ban was only temporary.[32]

By the end of 1980, outgoing Carter administration officials described the pace of improvement of relations with China as remarkable. Talks with the Chinese on military matters were described as "almost like talking to an ally." Although no military equipment sales had been consummated by the end of the Carter administration, cooperation was developing in other areas — including, according to officials, a "joint intelligence" project.[33]

Shifting Debates Under the Reagan Administration

President Reagan inherited a nascent quasi-alliance with China and near Cold War tensions with the Soviet Union. Reagan's harsh anti-Soviet rhetoric and his determination to take a tough global stand against Moscow made the "China card" naturally attractive to him. And indeed, during his unsuccessful bid for the Republican presidential nomination in 1976, Reagan had said that selling arms to China to counter the Soviet Union would be a "natural development." But Reagan's fervent anti-Communism also made him highly suspicious of "Chinese Communists" as well as "Russian Communists." On the eve of his inauguration, Reagan revealed such ideological views when he described China as a "country whose government subscribes to an ideology based on a belief in destroying governments like ours."

Added to this tension between viewing China as a potential ally against the Soviet Union and as a perennial Communist foe was Reagan's long-time commitment to his anti-Communist friends on Taiwan. Reagan had charged during the campaign that President Carter had made unnecessary concessions to Beijing in normalizing relations, and the new president apparently hoped to roll back some of those concessions. But he also sought to avoid a policy tradeoff: He wanted to continue the

Carter administration's policy of building a strategic anti-Soviet relationship with China while resurrecting official ties with Taiwan.

Reagan's approach to China produced the worst crisis in Sino-American relations since the rapprochement of 1971-1972. The Chinese reacted sharply to what they perceived as Reagan's attempt to "roll back the clock" in Sino-American relations. Not only was movement forward in strategic relations stalled despite a Reagan administration decision to lift the ban on arms sales to China, but Beijing repeatedly threatened to downgrade Sino-American diplomatic ties. At the same time, domestic politics and triangular interactions created pressures on President Reagan to preserve Sino-American relations at the expense of fulfilling his promises to upgrade Washington's relations with Taipei.

While President Reagan was buffeted by these conflicting pressures, his top aides were as deeply divided on China policy and global strategy toward the Soviet Union as senior officials of the Carter administration had been. The nature of the debate over triangular policies shifted with the change in administrations, however. The primary focus of differences on China policy in the Carter administration had been on the issue of the impact on Moscow of military ties with Beijing. Neither Vance nor Brzezinski was ideologically committed to Taiwan, however, although they felt strong political pressure from Taiwan's supporters in Congress in negotiating the terms of normalization with Beijing. But Taiwan was considered a secondary matter compared with the American global strategic interests at stake with Beijing.

In the Reagan administration's debate over strategy toward Moscow, there was far less concern over a potentially negative impact of United States-Chinese ties on the Soviet Union. The new secretary of state, Alexander Haig, favored a coalition strategy, similar to Brzezinski's, that relied on forging closer security ties with allies and friends, including China. While Haig supported Reagan's call for an American military buildup, he also called for arms control talks and other measures to manage the Soviets through negotiations, and he opposed strong economic sanctions against Moscow if they endangered relations with American allies. Caspar Weinberger, the new secretary of defense, stressed the unilateral buildup of American military power and a more "go it alone" strategy, however, that would reduce reliance on other states, thus mitigating the need to bend to pressure from allies on such issues as arms control talks with the Soviets and trade sanctions against Moscow.

Chinese leaders might have been expected to be reassured by Reagan's strong anti-Soviet, anti-detente statements. But the "go it alone" policy current — with its implied reduction in China's strategic importance to the United States — along with changes in American policy toward the

Third World and Western Europe, provoked concern in Beijing about the viability of the Sino-American strategic partnership. Even before he was elected president, Reagan's statements on Taiwan led the Chinese to suspect that the new president might seek to use China to pursue his anti-Soviet objectives while at the same time trying to reverse the progress achieved between the United States and China with respect to Taiwan and implement a "two Chinas" policy. Reagan's Taiwan statements raised hopes in Moscow, however, that his China policy would damage Sino-American relations and reduce the threat of United States-Chinese collusion.

President Carter had left unresolved the issue of future American arms sales to Taiwan. At the time the normalization agreement with Beijing was announced, December 15, 1978, American officials had said the United States would continue to sell "arms of a defensive character" to Taiwan on a restrained basis, although the administration suspended the arms sales for calendar year 1979. During a visit to China in August 1981, former President Carter said he had committed the United States to sell only "strictly defensive" and "not advanced" weapons that would "pose no threat to the mainland." He said the agreement was based on the premise that a prudent supply of weapons would be provided to Taiwan without time limit, but with the hope of a peaceful resolution of disputes between Taiwan and the mainland. The question of future arms sales to Taiwan was also addressed by Congress in the Taiwan Relations Act (TRA) of April 1979, which said the United States would "provide Taiwan with arms of a defensive character" in order to help the island "maintain a sufficient self-defense capability." [34]

At the time normalization was announced, Chinese Premier Hua Guofeng noted that China and the United States had "differing views" on the issue of arms sales to Taiwan, adding that "we absolutely could not agree to this," and that "it would not conform to the principles of normalization." "Nevertheless," Hua said, "we reached an agreement on the joint communiqué" announcing full normalization of relations. The arms sales issue was thus put on the back burner in 1978, to be finnessed and quietly resolved — or to become a source of conflict in the future.

Chinese willingness to tolerate further arms sales to Taiwan under some circumstances was demonstrated when the Carter administration announced the resumption of sales on January 3, 1980 — on the eve of Secretary of Defense Brown's visit to China and less than two weeks after the Soviet invasion of Afghanistan. The State Department announced $280 million in sales of "selected defensive equipment," while rejecting for the time being Taiwan's request for an advanced fighter plane on the grounds these planes could be used to attack the mainland. China did not publicly protest the announced sales and voiced only muted criticism of the American move in private sessions with Brown, indicating the strategic importance the Chinese attached to cooperation with the United States.

Washington and Beijing at Odds over Taiwan

The Chinese did not remain silent, however, in May 1980 when presidential candidate Ronald Reagan said he would consider restoring an "official" relationship between Taipei and Washington.[35] A commentary in Beijing's *People's Daily* warned that "if the United States reestablished 'official relations' with Taiwan according to the policy announced by Reagan, it would imply that the very principle which constitutes the foundation of the Sino-American relationship would retrogress against the will of the two peoples." In an effort to reassure the Chinese after his nomination in August, Reagan sent to China George Bush, his vice-presidential running mate and former chief of the United States liaison office in Beijing. But a statement by Reagan August 25 upon Bush's return heightened Chinese fears that a Reagan administration would attempt to "turn back the clock" in Sino-American relations. In the August 25 statement, Reagan said that the TRA of April 1979 provided an "official basis for our relations with our longtime friend and ally," and that he would "not pretend" that our relations with Taipei are not official. Reagan said he would develop relations with Taiwan in accordance with the TRA, and asserted that "by accepting China's three conditions for normalization, Jimmy Carter made concessions that Presidents Nixon and Ford steadfastly refused to make" — a comment that led one former Carter administration official to note that Reagan had spoken "without knowledge of the negotiating record." [36]

Following Reagan's victory in the November election, the Chinese refrained from sharp criticism on the Taiwan issue, apparently in the hope that Reagan's comments were campaign rhetoric that would not necessarily become Reagan administration policy. Although statements by the president-elect and his advisers were often conflicting, two parallel tracks were perceptible to the Chinese: an interest in anti-Soviet strategic cooperation with China, and a desire to improve American ties with Taiwan.

Chinese concern that the new president might upgrade ties with Taiwan was expressed in a strong statement in December warning the Netherlands against selling two submarines to Taiwan and admonishing "certain people" who wanted more than unofficial ties with Taiwan. China later downgraded diplomatic ties with the Dutch government to chargé d'affaires level when the submarine sale was consummated in May 1981. In a warning, then directed at other nations, the Chinese Foreign Ministry said that the "creation of 'two Chinas,' sale of" weapons and armaments to the Taiwan authority "or the establishment of" official relations "with Taiwan will be firmly rejected."

At the outset of the Reagan administration, China policy was low on the president's list of foreign policy priorities as it had been when Jimmy Carter had taken office four years earlier. During this period, the administration continued to send conflicting signals to Beijing. In late January, President Reagan sent a personal, unpublicized note to Chinese Premier Zhao Ziyang reassuring Chinese leaders that the new president would abide by the normalization communiqué.[37] Administration support for the normalization communiqué was publicly confirmed by the State Department on February 6. The following month, Secretary of State Haig stressed in an interview that normal relations with China were "a strategic imperative ... of overriding importance to international stability and world peace." [38] But Haig also asserted that Reagan's August 25, 1980, statement, which called for "official" relations with Taiwan, represented administration China policy.

Despite Haig's public endorsement of Reagan's statement, he privately advised the president against taking any actions to enhance Taiwan's standing in Washington during a China policy review then under way for fear that China would lose interest in strategic cooperation with the United States. No moves toward Taiwan were made during the review period leading up to a visit to Beijing by Haig in June. But administration officials continued to make conflicting statements, while Reagan remained silent on the China-Taiwan issue, reportedly causing confusion and irritation among Chinese officials.

On the eve of Haig's trip to China, Beijing responded to reports that the administration would try to gain Chinese acceptance of American arms sales to Taiwan by offering arms to Beijing as well. An authoritative Xinhua commentary rejected Reagan administration attempts to "sell arms to China in exchange for China's consent to U.S. arms sales to Taiwan," charging that this was "nothing but superpower logic to split China." The commentary for the first time linked "further strategic relations" between the United States and China to a halt in administration efforts to develop contacts with Taiwan that went "beyond nongovernmental relations."

Chinese fears about Reagan administration policy were not unfounded. The administration did decide that Haig should tell Chinese leaders that the United States would consider specific Chinese requests for purchase of lethal weapons on a "case-by-case" basis, a decision that the secretary of state made public in Beijing. At the same time, Haig informed Chinese leaders that the United States would manage its relations with Taiwan on a strictly unofficial basis, but that it would continue to supply defensive military equipment to Taipei.

The upcoming visit by the secretary of state had forced the administration to make a series of decisions on China policy. As in previous administrations, the "event-driven" decision-making process did not result in an overall coherent China policy that was also integrated with Soviet policy and strategy. The administration had not yet reached any consensus on basic issues of Soviet-American relations,[39] and the National Security Council meetings in early June in preparation for Haig's visit resulted in tradeoffs on specific decisions and not agreement on general policy toward Beijing. The decision to allow China to purchase American arms on a case-by-case basis — which two months earlier had been threatened as a possible American response to a Soviet invasion of Poland that had not materialized — apparently was viewed by Chinese leaders as simply a ploy to gain their acceptance of continued arms sales to Taiwan, as Xinhua had warned.

Secretary Haig had tried to prevent actions toward Taiwan that could jeopardize what he viewed as the larger American strategic interests at stake in relations with China. But some White House officials ascribed greater value to Taiwan's security interests and feared the political repercussions of "abandoning an old friend" which was strongly supported by key members of Congress and the Republican right wing. The lack of consensus in the administration resulted in decisions to continue arms sales to Taiwan and to offer arms to China. But the administration did not decide which was the primary U.S. interest: strategic ties with Beijing or traditional ties with Taipei.

At the time of his departure from Beijing, however, Haig appeared to have been successful in his aims. He said: "It is apparent that the strategic realities which prompted reconciliation between the U.S. and China more than a decade ago are more pressing than ever. U.S. and Chinese perceptions of the international situation have never been closer. Our common resolve to coordinate our independent policies in order to limit the Soviet Union's opportunities for exploiting its military power has likewise grown stronger." Haig had earlier said his talks with Chinese leaders would "open a new era of strategic and economic cooperation with the PRC," and that President Reagan had made a "firm commitment" to advance the strategic relationship.

Evidence of Beijing's willingness to move toward a closer military relationship with the United States was demonstrated in the announcement that Liu Huaqing, vice chief of the PLA general staff, would visit Washington in August with a shopping list for arms purchases. At the time, the Chinese press echoed Haig's words, saying that the meetings showed that both sides hold "similar, if not identical, views in estimating the world strategic situation and on a series of important international problems." [40]

Despite the progress made during the trip, the Taiwan issue had been neither resolved nor shelved. A Chinese commentary on the day of Haig's departure called American arms sales to Taiwan the "key stumbling block" in development of United States-Chinese relations.[41] Significantly, the commentary refrained from identifying Haig as a supporter of continued arms sales to Taiwan, and rather blamed "Americans in the U.S. Government and of the opposition" who still advocated such a policy. Chinese displeasure with the administration's attempt to pursue an "arms for China and arms for Taiwan" policy soon was demonstrated by the indefinite postponement of Liu Huaqing's visit to Washington. The Chinese did not want to give the impression that they had agreed to continued American arms sales to Taiwan in exchange for the right to buy American arms themselves.

The administration's first approach to the China-Taiwan problem had failed despite the rhetoric of common strategic interests and the American offer during Haig's visit to sell arms to China. Progress in Sino-American strategic cooperation stalled, and Washington and Beijing moved toward their worst crisis in relations since the 1971-1972 rapprochement. United States-Chinese relations had reached points of stalemate in the past, from the signing of the Shanghai Communiqué in February 1972, to the actual normalization of relations January 1, 1979. In that period there were cooler and warmer periods of Sino-American relations. But there was never a period of threatened retrogression of relations. Now, in 1981, Beijing was warning that it might downgrade diplomatic ties with the United States if Washington were to go ahead with further arms sales to Taiwan. Although Beijing had accepted — by agreeing to disagree — further sales of defensive arms to Taiwan after a one-year hiatus in 1979, Chinese leaders apparently had perceived President Carter as intending to reduce and possibly eliminate arms sales to Taiwan in the long run while strictly adhering to the normalization agreement pledge of nongovernmental ties. The Chinese had indicated they would be patient on the Taiwan issue if they felt the trend was toward American disengagement from Taipei. But when it appeared that President Reagan, who was even more anti-Soviet than Carter had been in the second half of his administration, was seeking to reverse that trend, then Beijing apparently decided to press for resolution of the issue of future arms sales to Taiwan as a litmus test of American intentions toward China.

While refusing to renounce its right to use force to reunify Taiwan with the mainland, Beijing also sought to signal Washington and Taipei that its intentions toward Taiwan were peaceful. In a nine-point proposal for reunification on September 30, 1981, by Ye Jianying, chairman of the Standing Committee of the National People's Congress, Beijing called for Kuomintang (KMT) leaders to participate in the government of the People's Republic while allowing for the retention of the island's armed forces as well as its economic, political and cultural system.

Chinese leaders probably expected the KMT's prompt rejection of the proposal, but they were less certain about Washington's reaction. Beijing may have hoped for a positive response from the United States that acknowledged, if not endorsed, Beijing's overtures to Taiwan as a step toward peaceful reunification. But the Reagan administration was silent for a month and a half, until Haig cautiously noted that the Chinese proposals were "rather remarkable" and "not meaningless."

Haig's comment on Ye's offer to Taiwan was made a few weeks after his meeting in Washington with Chinese Foreign Minister Huang Hua, at which Huang reportedly said China was willing to accept continued American arms sales to Taiwan if the weapons did not exceed current levels of sophistication, and if the United States agreed that such sales would gradually diminish in quantity and would not continue indefinitely.[42] But at that point, the White House was not considering reducing arms sales to Taiwan but rather whether to sell the FX, which would increase the level of sophistication of weapons sold to Taipei.

Triangular Logic and Reagan's China Policy

Secretary of State Haig had consistently fought against selling the FX to Taiwan. In late November, he had sent a comprehensive memo to President Reagan outlining what he saw as the causes and the solution to the problems that had developed in relations with China. In the November 26 memo, which was leaked to the press in January,[43] Haig warned the president that Sino-American ties stood at a "critical juncture" and cautioned that in relations with Beijing, "careful management is essential, if we are to avoid a setback which could gravely damage our global strategic policy." Assessing the origins of the crisis in relations, Haig said that one factor was "our campaign rhetoric and subsequent behavior which gave Peking the impression we wanted to reverse normalization and pursue a 'two-China' policy." Haig went on to say that this impression of reverting to a "two-China" policy had "transformed the aircraft replacement question, which might otherwise have been manageable, into a symbolic challenge to China's sovereignty and territorial integrity."

Haig, addressing the president's ideological predilections and his concern for Taiwan's security, argued that the Taiwanese did not need an advanced fighter; he added that "we must recognize that mainland capabilities and intentions do not require a level of U.S. arms sales above the final year of the Carter administration, which provided an unusually high ceiling." Haig said that the United States could "agree to stay within this level, so long as Peking pursues a peaceful Taiwan policy," and that the FX decision could be made "in this context." Haig thus proposed to Reagan a formula for resolving the issue: "[W]hile we cannot specify a time certain for ending arms sales, we can develop formulation linking our future actions to genuine progress on peaceful reunification."

Besides rejecting the sale of the FX to Taiwan and seeking a formula for reducing other arms sales as progress is made on peaceful reunification, Haig proposed two other steps the president could take to improve relations with Beijing. First, Reagan could make a positive statement on China's September 30 proposal to Taiwan. Haig suggested to the president that he "state publicly, without pressuring Taipei, that you view Peking's effort as a constructive and hopeful sign that the Taiwan issue, ultimately, can be peacefully resolved."

Second, Haig noted Chinese "disillusionment" with "the lack of tangible benefits to China in the technology transfer and economic modernization areas since normalization, and a perception that this administration, like the last, says it wants to further the process but in practice still treats China as an enemy." Haig asked Reagan to reaffirm "your determination to treat China as a friendly nation," to "help in dealing with entrenched bureaucrats who continue to treat China as a quasi-enemy." [44]

Haig's arguments were unpersuasive to White House officials, however, who reportedly were determined to go ahead with the FX sale for ideological and political reasons and were maintaining that potential Chinese response was overstated. Ultimately, Haig won the policy battle. But the basis of his victory was not his arguments about the bilateral implications for Sino-American relations of the sale of sophisticated aircraft to Taiwan. Rather, it was the strategic situation that persuaded the president to reject the FX sale. The administration was seeking to organize a global united front in response to the Soviet-backed imposition of martial law in Poland December 13. On January 10 President Reagan decided to reject the FX sale but to allow Taiwan to continue coproducing the less-sophisticated F-5E aircraft.

Although administration officials viewed the FX decision as favorable to Beijing, Chinese leaders protested the continued sale of F-5E fighters to Taiwan, and complained that China had not been consulted prior to the decision.[45] Despite these objections, Beijing did not downgrade Sino-American relations in response to the F-5E decision. In fact, Chinese press statements in the wake of the decision adopted a more conciliatory tone, publicly indicating the flexibility earlier demonstrated privately by Huang Hua in his November meeting with Haig. A Xinhua commentary January 31 expressed China's willingness to negotiate a time limit on arms sales to Taiwan, which would allow China to "safeguard its own sovereignty" while giving "due consideration" to the American side to work out its obligations to Taiwan, adding that this flexibility demonstrated China was "always mindful of the larger interests."

From the beginning of the Reagan administration, the sale of arms to China was considered as an option to respond to a possible Soviet invasion of Poland. Even before Reagan took office, the incoming chairman of the Senate Foreign Relations Committee, Charles Percy, reportedly told a group of his colleagues in early December that he had warned Soviet officials an invasion of Poland would result in a political climate in the United States favorable to expanding military ties with China. In early April, Percy said that he had "reason to believe" that the Carter administration had asked the Defense Department in December to draw up a list of weapons that "possibly would be sold or provided" to China "if force was used by the Soviet Union in Poland."

A few days later, Secretary of Defense Weinberger made the first administration statement linking arms sales to China with Soviet action in Poland. In a reply to questions by reporters, Weinberger said that the Soviet Union was continuing to build up its forces in and around Poland and that the American response to Soviet intervention in Poland could include trade sanctions and the sale of weapons to China. Other administration officials, including Haig, reportedly were unhappy about Weinberger's statement, which led the Secretary of Defense to say later that selling arms to China was not under "active consideration."

Although the anticipated Soviet invasion of Poland never took place, the Reagan administration decided to approve arms sales to China on the eve of Haig's visit to Beijing. Officials in Haig's party during the China visit told the press that the decision was seen as a way to "get Moscow's attention." This triangular context for the decision was explained in comments by administration officials that American willingness to sell arms to China signaled the Soviet Union that a Sino-American alliance, although not yet politically feasible, had moved a step closer to realization. It was also intended to assure China that the United States was serious about its determination to stand up to the Soviets. Officials noted in addition that a more important development than arms sales might be an agreement for closer coordination with China in all fields against the Soviet Union, including opposition to Soviet involvement in Afghanistan and Kampuchea. Haig was reported to believe that the United States could not stand alone against the Soviets and seemed to be seeking to coordinate an anti-Soviet stance with China, Europe, and Japan. Not only was the arms sales decision part of this strategy, but, according to one press account of Haig's trip, there was "reason to believe that the two nations" were already engaged in "substantial intelligence cooperation." On the eve of Haig's discussions with Chinese leaders, *The Washington Post* revealed the existence of an electronic intelligence facility, established under Carter for joint United States-Chinese monitoring of Soviet missile tests from Chinese territory.[46]

Despite the symbolic significance of the American decision to allow arms sales to China, Haig's visit did not lead to more extensive military cooperation. The indefinite postponement of Liu Huaqing's arms buying trip to Washington signaled that there would be no new cooperative efforts until the Taiwan issue was satisfactorily resolved — even though Haig had found a receptive audience in Beijing for his harsh anti-Soviet rhetoric and calls for a united front against Moscow.[47]

China Doubts Effectiveness of American Strategy

China's criticism of American intentions on Taiwan was part of a larger concern about the Reagan administration's strategy toward the Soviet Union. Despite Haig's assurances that the United States did not plan to stand alone against the Soviet Union and needed to cooperate with China and other countries to contain Soviet power, the Chinese perceived an administration divided over strategy, with the president's views and intentions uncertain. The Chinese concern about Secretary of Defense Weinberger's "go it alone" strategy was reinforced by the views expressed in his speeches and in Defense Department documents that emphasized strengthening America's unilateral military capability.[48] China consistently received little mention and its strategic importance to the United States was played down.

Weinberger's statements on strategy paralleled a view from the White House that China needed the United States more than the United States needed China. One White House official commented to the author in the summer of 1981 that the Chinese were worried that their own importance to the United States had diminished. They are right, he said, in that the United States will be less concerned about offending them. The notion in the past that the United States had to do what the Chinese wanted — for example, come through on military ties — is gone. This administration will do with China what it sees as in its interest, the official added, and it is not about to be stampeded into selling arms to the Chinese.

From the beginning of the Reagan administration, the Chinese perceived America's Taiwan policy to be indicative of its global strategy. Yuan Xianlu, foreign editor of Beijing's *People's Daily*, had directly addressed this issue on the eve of Reagan's inauguration. He wrote in *The New York Times*:

> There are those who believe that China will accept every United States action regarding Taiwan as long as Ronald Reagan is tough on the Soviet Union. Such a belief is totally erroneous.... [P]recisely because Sino-American relations must be viewed from a global perspective, China cannot but look upon the United States' China policy as a most important factor in evaluating the strategic measures and foreign policy of the United States government. This means that whoever truly fights hegemony must not retreat in their policy toward China. If anyone deliberately damages Sino-American relations, this

certainly shows that he lacks a correct strategic point of view and also cannot really play an active role in the overall anti-hegemonistic strategy.[49]

Chinese commentaries also rejected the view of some administration officials and Reagan advisers who argued that the United States should hold on to Taiwan as a "key bastion of the Pacific."[50] A pro-Beijing Hong Kong newspaper argued that "Reagan should know that the peaceful reunification of the Chinese mainland and Taiwan will be beneficial to peace in Asia and the world. A reunified China means a great increase in the strength of forces opposing hegemonism."[51]

The Chinese perceived dual threats to China's security from Reagan's strategic view: On the one hand, Reagan was confrontational in his rhetoric toward Moscow and could conceivably drag China into a conflict against its interests; and on the other, the administration might flip-flop and seek collusion with the Soviets at China's expense.

The Chinese had begun developing a strategic "partnership" with the United States under the Carter administration in which consultations on matters of global strategy and American policy toward the Soviet Union were a major factor. But the Reagan administration's reduced reliance on allies and friends implied reduced coordination of policy. As Sino-American relations deteriorated, "consultations" between United States and Chinese officials became restricted to trying to prevent further backsliding. This failure to consult increased China's concern that, despite his harsh anti-Soviet rhetoric, Reagan could collude with the Soviets on some issues without regard to China's security interests. This was especially a concern in arms control negotiations, including the Intermediate-range Nuclear Forces (INF) talks opened in November 1981, and Strategic Arms Reductions Talks (START) begun in June 1982.

Chinese uncertainty about the reliability of the United States as a quasi-ally was compounded by what the Chinese perceived as counterproductive American Third World policies. In the first year of the Reagan administration, the Chinese became increasingly vocal in their criticisms of the administration's policies in the Middle East, Southern Africa and Central America, and on North-South issues. These criticisms represented a disagreement with Washington over the best way to counter Soviet expansion, however, and were not the harbinger of a more ideological approach to international politics.

The Chinese argued that American policy contradicted stated American strategy: "[J]udging from the announced objectives of U.S. foreign strategy and President Reagan's words," a Xinhua commentary in July 1981 argued, "it is obvious that the U.S. Government is aware of the fact that the main danger to the security of world peace comes from the Soviet Union and that the U.S., on its own, cannot restrain the Soviet Union. To counter Soviet expansionism and aggression, it is necessary to unite all possible forces, including those of the Third World.[52] But the Reagan administration's bias toward its "old friends" — Israel, South Africa, South Korea, and the "Taiwan authorities" — poised the United States "against the Arab and African peoples and the peoples of many other Third World countries." The result of this strategy, the commentary argued, was to provide "the Soviet Union with more opportunities for its hegemonic aims." Thus, the commentary concluded, "U.S. policies toward certain areas of the Third World are in sharp conflict with its overall strategy."

Another major Chinese critique of Reagan's foreign policy, published in January 1982, in the new *Journal of International Studies*,[53] criticized the administration's handling of relations with Western Europe. While the United States wanted to restrict East-West trade, it said, especially to halt the Soviet gas pipeline deal, it was "the Reagan administration itself" that "lifted the grain embargo against the Soviet Union." The article charged Reagan with too great a focus on the Soviet Union as the source of all problems in the world to the point of ignoring local and regional sources of conflict. It also said that "most of the Reagan administration's foreign policy practice has in fact shown U.S. inconsistency, has made people suspect that it is unreliable and has given the impression that it lacks balance in dealing with the relationships between individual problems and in distinguishing the priorities of various problems."

Soviets Hopeful of United States-China Rift

Soviet leaders, while still voicing concern over American military ties with China — especially Haig's announcement of American willingness to supply arms to the Chinese — were hopeful that the conflict over Taiwan would continue to divide Washington and Beijing and prevent further Sino-American collusion against the Soviet Union. Brezhnev sought to capitalize on the Taiwan issue in a speech March 24, 1982, at Tashkent. During a period of delicate United States-Chinese negotiations on Taiwan, the Soviet leader pointedly remarked that "we have never supported, and do not now support in any form the so-called concept of two Chinas." Brezhnev also made another offer for talks between Moscow and Beijing to improve relations. As in the past, this overture failed to elicit a positive response from the Chinese, who said the Soviets would be judged by their deeds rather than their words. The Soviets rejected China's demand for "practical deeds," but renewed their offer for negotiations without preconditions. An I. Aleksandrov article — which represents the views of the Central Committee — in *Pravda* May 19, 1982, called for "detente" between the Soviet Union and China, adding that "it is our profound belief that there exists a real possibility for improving Soviet-Chinese relations."

The May 1982 Aleksandrov article was considerably softer in tone than a previous Aleksandrov commentary that had followed Haig's visit to Beijing in June 1981.[54] That article had charged that Reagan had gone much farther than Carter had by deciding to sell lethal arms to China, and warned that "the Soviet Union cannot remain indifferent to the dangerous new turn taken by Sino-American relations." But even at that time, some Soviet analysts perceived contradictions between the United States and China that could limit the threat to the Soviet Union posed by potential Sino-American military ties. N. V. Shishlin, head of the Consultants Group of the Central Committee International Department, said on Soviet television that the "extraordinary scope and scale" of the military and strategic cooperation reportedly discussed by Haig with Chinese leaders "leads to the thought that what is being discussed is precisely the establishment of an alliance, although it is not being called this. All this of course is very, very serious. However, I would not say that everything put down on paper and everything in the minds of those who spoke recently in Beijing will occur or turn out as planned, at least not at the present time."

When the United States and China had decided to forge a strategic relationship in 1978, the Soviets had reacted with alarm and raised the specter of a vast American-aided buildup of Chinese military capability. But by 1981, the Soviets' fears had diminished as China cut defense spending for a second time and the United States transferred to China very little military-related technology. In interviews conducted by the author in Moscow in February and August, Soviet analysts acknowledged that Chinese defense modernization was proceeding slowly and that the United States was not likely to provide large amounts of military equipment to China.[55] They also acknowledged that the Soviet Union's favorable military balance with China was not likely to change, and that the gap between Soviet and Chinese military capabilities might even grow wider over the next ten to twenty years, even if some American military technology were transferred to China. Although Soviet propaganda was continuing to warn against the "dangerous partnership" between Beijing and Washington, Soviet analysts had become increasingly hopeful that the "contradictions" between the United States and China, especially over Taiwan, would worsen, and that the military relationship would move forward slowly if at all. Brezhnev's March 1982 overture to the Chinese, along with other Soviet gestures,[56] was likely aimed at reducing the specter in Beijing of a Soviet threat to China. This would presumably weaken the hands of those Chinese leaders arguing for greater concessions to Washington to resolve the Taiwan problem — and thus keep the United States and China divided over Taiwan.

In the mid-1970s, when the Soviets were also less worried about Sino-American collusion against them, the Chinese had become increasingly concerned about what they charged was Washington's detente strategy of "appeasement" of the Soviet Union. The Chinese saw the United States as unwilling to develop strategic ties with China for fear of provoking the Soviet Union, as well as failing to take a strong enough stand against Moscow on other issues. Chinese fears diminished in May 1978 after Carter decided to pursue a strategic relationship with China as part of a tougher policy toward the Soviet Union.

Three years later, however, the Chinese again feared that Washington was following a strategy toward Moscow that jeopardized China's security. In this case, the United States strategy was strongly anti-Soviet and anti-detente. But it was also "unilateralist" in relations with allies and friends, and "hegemonist" and counterproductive in the Third World. Instead of Washington's being reluctant to play the China card for fear of provoking Moscow, as Carter was before 1978, the Reagan White House seemed to be willing to risk damaging Sino-American ties out of skepticism about China's strategic value and desire to improve ties with the president's "old friends" on Taiwan.

Geopolitics over Ideology

Despite the White House's predilections, however, there were strong internal and external pressures on the administration to avert deterioration of relations with China. The president's conservative constituency, including key members of Congress, was strongly pro-Taiwan and pushing hard for continued arms sales to Taiwan and upgraded ties with Taipei. Nevertheless, most of the key concerned officials in the United States government other than Reagan's conservative political appointees opposed risking ties with China by altering the status of American ties with Taiwan.

Probably more compelling for the president, and more likely to continue to shape Sino-American relations in the long run, was the external factor of triangular relations. Whatever the ideological predilections of the American leader and his advisers, the perceptions of American national interest that drove the United States toward rapprochement with China in the 1969-1972 period during the presidency of the staunchly anti-Communist, pro-Taiwan Richard Nixon still existed in the 1980s. Even if a particular United States president — or Chinese leader — were to damage Sino-American relations for ideological or other reasons, the realities of geopolitics would likely lead to an eventual renewal of the strategic relationship to counter growing Soviet power. These "realities" became apparent to President Reagan when Soviet-American relations reached crisis points or required a strong American reaction in the administration's view, as was the case after the declaration of martial law in Poland in December 1981.

President Reagan acted in the tradition of his three predecessors in trying to prevent a rift in Sino-American relations. Triangular concerns, combined with an appreciation that China would not accept unlimited arms sales to Taiwan as the price of United States-Chinese strategic cooperation, led the president to involve himself directly in new efforts to resolve the Taiwan issue in early 1982. He delayed formal notification of Congress on the already approved sale of the F-5E jet fighters to Taiwan while the administration negotiated with Beijing on the terms of a communiqué on the arms sale issue. After several months of fruitless negotiations, Reagan sent Vice-President Bush to Beijing in May. Bush was followed a few weeks later by Senate Majority Leader Howard Baker, who convinced Chinese leaders that congressional concern about Taiwan placed strict limits on Reagan's ability to compromise.

Ten weeks later, on August 17, 1982, after intense negotiations on final wording, the United States and China issued a joint communiqué on American arms sales to Taiwan. The carefully worded document used ambiguous language that enabled both sides to maintain their differing views on the arms sales issue. The United States stated that "it does not seek to carry out a long-term policy of arms sales to Taiwan, that its arms sales to Taiwan will not exceed, either in qualitative or in quantitative terms, the level of those supplied in recent years since the establishment of diplomatic relations between the United States and China, and that it intends to reduce gradually its sales of arms to Taiwan, leading over a period of time to a final resolution." The United States also reaffirmed its recognition of Chinese sovereignty over Taiwan, and explicitly said it would not pursue "a policy of 'Two Chinas' or 'one China, one Taiwan.'" The Chinese, while not explicitly agreeing to linkage, stated they had a "fundamental policy of striving for peaceful reunification of the motherland."

The compromise communiqué defused and shelved the Taiwan arms sales issue. But the possibility that the dispute could return to haunt Sino-American relations was portended in conflicting interpretations of the communiqué: Washington claimed the agreement committed the United States only to limiting and reducing gradually arms sales to Taiwan, while Beijing insisted that the United States had agreed to "gradually reduce and finally stop" weapons transfers to the island.

But the communiqué also embodied strong statements of mutually acceptable intentions. The Chinese, while refusing to explicitly rule out use of force against Taiwan, stressed their desire for peaceful reunification. The United States rejected any policy of maintaining indefinitely a separate Taiwan entity and, as Haig had suggested in his November 26 memorandum to Reagan, favorably acknowledged China's peaceful reunification policy. A *People's Daily* commentary on the communiqué said China was "satisfied with a U.S. promise to do its best to adopt measures and create conditions for the problem to be resolved thoroughly at an early date."

Ronald Reagan, who had charged President Carter during the 1980 presidential campaign with having made unnecessary concessions to Beijing in the normalization agreement, two years later strongly reaffirmed the terms of that accord and went a step further toward resolving the issue of arms sales to Taiwan. Geopolitics and national interest had compelled the pro-Taiwan, anti-Communist president to put aside his ideological preferences and political loyalties and reach a compromise with Chinese leaders. "Building a strong and lasting relationship with China has been an important foreign policy goal of four consecutive American administrations," President Reagan said in a statement released with the communiqué. "Such a relationship is vital to our long-term national security interests and contributes to stability in East Asia. It is in the national interest of the United States that this important strategic relationship be advanced."

The development of strategic relations between Washington and Beijing had stalled while the United States and China had been at odds over the Taiwan arms sales issue. Despite President Reagan's statement that "this important strategic relationship" should be advanced, his administration continued to be divided over United States global strategy toward the Soviet Union and China's significance and role in that strategy. In reaching agreement with Chinese leaders on the communiqué, Reagan had halted the downward trend in Sino-American relations that had been created in large part by his own statements and actions. But he had also left unresolved within his own administration the basic strategic issues of China policy and triangular relations.

Despite the August 17 communiqué and Reagan's affirmation of the importance of the Sino-American strategic relationship, the Chinese remained suspicious about American intentions toward Taiwan and continued to criticize the administration's global strategy and its "hegemonist" policies in the Third World. At the same time, Beijing responded cautiously but positively to Soviet gestures for improved ties and opened talks in October aimed at normalizing Sino-Soviet relations. The atmospherics in relations between the two countries continued to improve following the death of Leonid Brezhnev and the reaffirmation of Moscow's policy of seeking improved ties with China by his successor, Yuri Andropov. Chinese leaders nevertheless reassured the West that they did not expect any major improvements in relations with the Soviet Union in the short term, and that significant improvements would occur only if Moscow began to meet Beijing's unchanged demands.[57] Chinese leaders also stressed that there would be no shift in China's strategic posture. How long China's more "equidistant" political posture between the superpowers would last, however, was likely dependent on perceptions and decisions in Washington and Moscow as well as in Beijing.

"China Policy and the Constraints of Triangular Logic" was written for this volume. Copyright © 1983 by Banning Garrett.

Notes

1. Stanley B. Lubman, "Trade and Sino-American Relations," in *Dragon and Eagle: United States-China Relations: Past and Future*. Michel Oksenberg and Robert B. Oxnam (eds.) (New York: Basic Books, 1978), p. 195.
2. Henry Kissinger, *White House Years* (Boston: Little, Brown, 1979), p. 222. Kissinger notes that the shift from a 2½-war to a 1½-war strategy was publicly announced in Nixon's first *Foreign Policy Report to the Congress*, 18 February 1970.
3. According to *The New York Times*, 9 October 1979, Nixon endorsed a secret "swing strategy," which had actually been the basis of U.S. planning since the mid-1950s and which reflected the inability of the U.S. to achieve a 2½-war capability.
4. Kissinger, *White House Years*, p. 222.
5. *Ibid.*, p. 1062. Kissinger says that Mao, in his conversations with Nixon during the president's February 1972 visit, gave assurances that China would not intervene militarily in Indochina and that China posed no threat to South Korea and Japan. Kissinger also says that Mao made clear that the Soviet Union was his principal security concern.
6. One strategist at the time, Morton H. Halperin, argued that the United States "might well wish to explore with the Soviet Union the possibility of joint action to halt the Chinese nuclear program or to render it politically and militarily useless.... The most extreme form of joint Soviet-American action (or unilateral action by one or the other) would be a military move designed to destroy Chinese nuclear facilties...." *China and the Bomb* (New York: Prager, 1965), pp. 124-125, 138. Several former government officials told the author that President Kennedy personally considered a military strike against China's nuclear facilities.
7. See John Newhouse, *Cold Dawn: The Story of SALT* (New York: Holt, Rinehart and Winston, 1973), pp. 188-189; and H. R. Haldeman, *The Ends of Power* (New York: New York Times Books, 1978), pp. 89-94. Some officials interviewed by the author said they thought the Soviet overtures were a bluff to pressure the Chinese while others believed they were serious.
8. Kissinger, *White House Years*, p. 764.
9. *Ibid.*, p. 910.
10. For a detailed account of the origins of the idea of military ties with China, see Banning Garrett, "The Origins of the Strategic Relationship between China and the United States," testimony before the Subcommittee on Asian and Pacific Affairs of the Committee on Foreign Affairs, 26 August 1980, in *The United States and the People's Republic of China: Issues for the 1980's* (Washington: GPO,

1980), pp. 102-108. See also Banning Garrett, "The United States and the Great Power Triangle," in *The China Factor: Peking and the Superpowers,* Gerald Segal (ed.) (London: Croom Helm, 1982), pp. 76-104.

11. See Robert Sutter, *China-Watch: Toward Sino-American Reconciliation* (Baltimore: Johns Hopkins University Press, 1978) pp. 3, 109-112.

12. See Newhouse, *Cold Dawn,* pp. 100, 168-169, on the China factor in detente and the SALT negotiations.

13. The idea of military ties with China originated with Michael Pillsbury, then a RAND consultant, who wrote the first study exploring the subject in detail in early 1974. Pillsbury went public with his ideas in September 1975 in an article in *Foreign Policy* magazine, Fall 1975 issue number 20, "U.S.-Chinese Military Ties?", the publication of which was encouraged by high-level administration officials.

14. These ideas, some of which were first proposed by Pillsbury, *ibid.,* are outlined in Banning Garrett, "The United States and the Great Power Triangle," and in "China Policy and the Strategic Triangle," in *Eagle Entangled: U.S. Foreign Policy in a Complex World* (New York: Longman, 1979) pp. 228-263.

15. This assessment is based largely on dozens of interviews with government officials and other informed sources. See Garrett, "The United States and the Great Power Triangle," p. 84.

16. See Robert Legvold, "Containment Without Confrontation," *Foreign Policy* No. 40, Fall 1980.

17. According to several sources, by Fall of 1975, Schlesinger was pushing hard for a positive response to Chinese probes for military ties.

18. Leslie Gelb, "Washington Senses Loss of Leverage Against Soviets," *The New York Times,* 30 November 1975. Peter Osnos, writing from Moscow for the *Washington Post,* 7 December 1975, concluded that the Soviets "apparently believe that relations between China and the United States are essentially stalled," and consequently seem relatively unconcerned about possible Sino-American collusion against them.

19. The role of the U.S. in "acquiescing" to the British deal was not revealed until four months later in a leak to Leslie Gelb of *The New York Times,* 25 April 1976. The leak to Gelb was itself intended to be a gesture toward a presumed pro-U.S. element of the Chinese leadership during the power struggle following the Tian An Men riots of 5 April 1976, and to provide pressure on Moscow in response to Angola and other sources of U.S.-Soviet tension.

20. CoCom includes the NATO countries, minus Iceland, plus Japan, and was founded in 1949 to control strategic exports to Communist countries. Gelb, *ibid.,* reported and other sources have confirmed to the author that Kissinger agreed to allow the British to bypass CoCom to facilitate the sale of the Spey engines.

21. *Newsweek,* 13 December 1976.

22. See Garrett, "The United States and the Great Power Triangle," p. 88, and "China Policy and the Strategic Triangle," pp. 235-243.

23. In a speech to the Asia Society in New York on June 29, 1977, Vance emphasized that U.S.-China relations would be dealt with primarily in a bilateral context, and that they would "threaten no one," i.e., the Soviet Union. The leak to *The New York Times* five days earlier of a major interagency review of U.S. China policy, "PRM 24," also reassured the Soviets that the "China Card" had been rejected, although it also served as a warning that the option of U.S.-China military ties had been considered at the highest levels of the government and could be reconsidered at a later date, as indeed it was in the spring of 1978.

24. Speech to the United Nations, 4 October 1977.

25. See *The New York Times,* 8 July 1977 and 6 January 1978 on PRM 10's contents.

26. "Chairman Mao's Theory of the Differentiation of the Three Worlds Is a Major Contribution to Marxism-Leninism," by the editorial department of *People's Daily*, translated in *Peking Review*, No. 45 (4 November 1977).
27. Jen Ku-ping, "The Munich Tragedy and Contemporary Appeasement," *Peking Review*, No. 50 (9 December 1977).
28. *The Washington Post*, 1 February 1979. For a detailed analysis of the Chinese invasion of Vietnam and U.S. policy, see Banning Garrett, "The Strategic Triangle and the Indochina Crisis," *The Third Indochina Conflict*, David W. P. Elliott (ed.) (Boulder, Colorado: Westview Press, 1981).
29. *The New York Times*, 23 August 1978. See also the comments by Carter NSC China specialist, Michel Oksenberg, "The Dynamics of the Sino-American Relationship," *The China Factor: Sino-American Relations and the Global Scene*, Richard H. Solomon (ed.) (New York: Prentice-Hall, 1981), p. 53.
30. *The New York Times*, 4 October 1979.
31. *The New York Times*, 3 January 1980.
32. During a visit to the U.S. in late May, China's Defense Chief and Vice Premier Geng Biao, when asked if China would seek to buy arms from the U.S., responded: "I don't think there is such a possibility at present. But I believe there might be such a possibility in the future." *The New York Times*, 30 May 1980.
33. Philip Taubman, "U.S. and China Forging Close Ties: Critics Fear that Pace Is Too Swift," *The New York Times*, 8 December 1980.
34. See Oksenberg, "The Dynamics of the Sino-American Relationship," pp. 37-38.
35. See *The Washington Post*, 22 June 1980.
36. See Oksenberg, "The Dynamics of the Sino-American Relationship," p. 53.
37. *The Washington Post*, 14 March 1981; *Newsday*, 29 March 1981.
38. *Time*, 16 March 1981.
39. A rare glimpse at the administration's decision making process was provided by an account of a major struggle a month later over U.S. trade policy toward the Soviet Union in preparation for the Ottawa summit of leaders of seven major industrial democracies. According to Leslie H. Gelb, "Reagan, at Ottawa Talks, to Ask for Caution in Allies' Soviet Trade," *The New York Times*, 19 July 1981, the struggle pitted Haig against Weinberger in NSC meetings July 7 and 9. After fruitless debates over general issues of how hard to push the Soviets through trade sanctions and how the Soviets would respond to such pressure, the officials agreed they were getting nowhere and turned instead to make decisions on three specific issues: strategic export controls policy; the West European-Soviet gas pipeline deal; and a Caterpillar contract to supply pipe laying tractors to the Soviet Union.
40. Ji Lun, "Alexander Haig's Visit to the Asia and Pacific Region," *Guangming Ribao*, 28 June 1981, Foreign Broadcast Information Service (FBIS)-*China*, 8 July 1981.
41. Xinhua, 18 June 1981, "Commentary: A Key Link in Development of Sino-U.S. Relations," FBIS-*China*, 19 June 1981.
42. The Taiwan arms issue was also discussed by President Reagan with Chinese Premier Zhao Ziyang, at Cancun, Mexico, apparently without any resolution.
43. The November 26, 1981, memorandum was leaked to free-lance journalist Tad Szulc, "The Reagan Administration's Push Toward China Came From Warsaw," *The Los Angeles Times*, 17 January 1982.
44. This problem is discussed by Oksenberg, "The Dynamics of the Sino-American Relationship," p. 53.
45. *The Los Angeles Times*, 18 January 1982, reported that Haig had promised further talks with the Chinese before a decision was made on the FX and other other arms sales to Taiwan.

46. The story of the leak is detailed by Murrey Marder, "Monitoring: Not-So-Secret Secret," *The Washington Post*, 19 June 1981. Marder had first alluded to the facilities in the *Post* five days earlier.

47. One White House official told the author in August 1981 that Haig had given the Chinese an anti-Soviet lecture that took them aback and made their own rhetoric pale by comparison.

48. See reports on Weinberger's "Defense Guidance," *The Washington Post*, 17 and 19 June 1981; *New York Times*, 19 April, 17 May, and 28 June 1981; *Wall Street Journal*, 15 June 1981; major policy speeches by Weinberger 14 July 1981 at Fort McNair and 20 April 1982 at the Council on Foreign Relations in New York.

49. "China and Reagan," *The New York Times*, 17 January 1981.

50. *China Daily* (Beijing), 7 April 1982. See also Hua Xiu, "The Limp U.S. Policy Toward China," *Liaowang*, No. 4, July 1981, FBIS-*China*, 6 August 1981.

51. *Hsin Wan Pao*, "New Talk" column, "The Dialogue Between Zhao Ziyang and Reagan," FBIS-*China*, 23 October 1981.

52. Mei Zhemnin, "U.S. Relationship with the Third World," *FBIS-China*, 9 July 1981.

53. Jin Junhui, "The Reagan Administration's Foreign Policy," *Journal of International Studies*, no. 1, January 1982, FBIS-China, 18 March 1982.

54. I. Aleksandrov, "Escalation of Recklessness," *Pravda*, 27 June 1981, FBIS-*Soviet Union*, 29 June 1981.

55. For a detailed report on Soviet views, see Banning Garrett, "Soviet Perceptions of China and Sino-American Military Ties," prepared for the SALT/Arms Control Support Group, Office of Assistant Secretary of Defense (Atomic Energy), June 1981, Harold Rosenbaum Associates, Inc., Arlington VA. The report is based in part on extensive discussions with Soviet-China experts held during a visit to the Soviet Union in February 1981 as a guest of the Institute for the Study of the U.S.A. and Canada.

56. For summaries of those gestures see Nayan Chanda, "Chinese Acrobatics," 19 March 1982, and "Brezhnev Breaks the Ice," 2 April 1982, *Far Eastern Economic Review*.

57. Beijing's demands included a Soviet troop pullback from China's border with the Soviet Union and Mongolia, a Soviet military withdrawal from Afghanistan, and an end to Moscow's support for the Vietnamese occupation of Cambodia.

9

The United States and Western Europe: The Diplomatic Consequences of Mr. Reagan

Miles Kahler

Some day, it appeared to me, this divided Europe, dominated by the military presences of ourselves and the Russians, would have to yield to something more natural — something that did more justice to the true strength and interests of the intermediate European peoples themselves.

> — George F. Kennan, *Memoirs, 1925-1950* (p. 464)

Hail Mr. President, we who are about to die, salute you!"

> — Banner in a demonstration
> during President Reagan's visit
> to West Berlin, 10 June 1982

Another "crisis" has been declared in relations between the United States and Western Europe; but the jaundiced observer might well ask: What is new about the latest disarray? No aspect of American foreign policy is so carefully observed. Entire squadrons of scholars and politicians prod and poke the alliance to see if it is still alive. Its temperature is taken so often that one is tempted to declare it a hypochondriac.

This "crisis," like so many others, may pass. Many observers, pointing to the continuing security dependence of Western Europe on the United States and the underlying bipolar structure of the international system, suggest that the divided European state system will persist, and with it

---

Miles Kahler is Associate Professor of Political Science at Yale University. His book, Domestic Consequences of International Politics, *will be published by Princeton University Press in 1983. His present research compares foreign economic policies of industrial societies toward the developing countries.*

the structures tying together Western Europe and the United States.[1] Others, however, note certain trends that set apart the present crisis from those in the past and indicate disintegration beneath a façade of stability:

— *Structural changes.* Despite underlying structural stability in the security sphere, changes underway since the 1960s point to divergence in the definition of West European and American interests. The achievement of nuclear parity by the Soviet Union has had a significant impact on the perception of relative vulnerabilities and heightened the level of mistrust between Europe and the United States. Growing European weight in the world economy has been accompanied by a different pattern of economic vulnerability that reflects on European security: a more significant level of economic transactions with Eastern Europe and the Soviet Union and a higher level of dependency on imported Middle Eastern oil.
— *Cumulation.* The present rifts appear at the end of a decade of increasing friction: The Nixon "shocks" of the early 1970s were followed by divisions during the October War in the Middle East and the subsequent oil shock. Arguments after the Soviet invasion of Afghanistan took on a particularly sharp tone as a result.
— *Disagreement along a spectrum of issues.* The United States and Western Europe have had conflicts regarding policy outside the Atlantic area (1950s), nuclear strategy (1960s), and economic competition (1970s). With the resurgence of concern over the possibility of nuclear conflict in Europe, the politicization of economic issues in the guise of economic sanctions against the Soviet Union, and divergence over strategies to ensure a stable supply of oil from the Middle East, the issue-specific debates of the past have broadened into different perceptions of "Western" interests in Europe and elsewhere.
— *European insulation.* Although European vulnerabilities may have grown in the last decade, the capabilities of the superpowers to influence events in Western Europe have declined. The United States, like the Soviet Union, can no longer count upon docile proxies who will spring loyally to its bidding. It is difficult to imagine an earlier German Chancellor, for example, expressing the open contempt that Helmut Schmidt expressed for Jimmy Carter. The United States therefore finds it more difficult to reconstruct the elite solidarity that enabled it to overcome earlier crises.
— *Democratization of security policy.* Perhaps most important, the present conflict is no simple crisis of elites. Calling into question the traditional strategy and assumptions of the alliance is a broadly based, popular, and Europe-wide movement that challenges elite judgments and has begun a reevaluation of security policy more radical than any since the war.

This "crisis"— whether a temporary conjuncture of events within an essentially stable set of boundaries or a reflection of deeper changes that cannot be reversed — began in the final years of the Carter administration, as the American attitude toward the Soviet Union hardened dramatically in response to international and domestic politics. The Reagan administration is a symbol of those domestic events, an illustration of widening differences in perceptions on either side of the Atlantic, and a further test of the two contending views of the future: stability versus disintegration. The administration's efforts to restore American military power, and to impose its conception of the Soviet threat on Western Europe, exacerbated conflict between the United States and its allies until pressures building on the European side forced a partial revision of the administration's distaste for detente and arms control. An elite compromise was ratified at the Versailles and Bonn summits, only to come apart with renewed American efforts to overturn European energy links with the Soviet Union. Finally, an elite bargain was reestablished on the question of East-West economic relations, though its resilience remained in doubt. Any final assessment of the rift in American relations with Western Europe— whether it is a conjunctural dispute subject to diplomatic mending or a structural shift that requires more drastic measures — remains open.

The United States and Western Europe: The Historical Givens

The reality that frames and limits United States relations with Western Europe is the security dependency of Western Europe on the United States: the *separateness* and *lack of equality* in that relationship have been at the core of many of the security disputes within the "troubled partnership" since the 1950s. *Separateness:* obviously, if Europe were Illinois or Wyoming (or even Canada), the American guarantee would not be questioned; much American effort has been devoted to making both the Soviet Union and the Europeans believe that Western Europe *is* the practical equivalent of American territory, that the United States would risk nuclear annihilation in defending its NATO allies. *Lack of equality:* since, until the construction of the British and French nuclear forces (and many would argue even after their construction), the final guarantee of Western Europe's security lay in the hands of a political class in a different country, a galling situation for a continent that once dominated the international system.

These underlying features of the security system were expressed in conflict about NATO strategy during the 1950s and 1960s: the failed European Defense Community and German rearmament, followed by Gaullist questioning of the American guarantee and the building of an independent French nuclear deterrent. While political campaigns were mounted against the European Defense Community and German rearmament in the early 1950s and against the stationing of tactical nuclear weapons in Germany in the latter part of the decade, these disputes remained, by and large, elite disputes: The challenge to the alliance was never so widespread nor so politically significant in Europe as it was in Japan. Related to Europe's newfound security dependence was another element of conflict between the superpower and those European states that had not discovered the limited capabilities of a medium-sized power: defining the interests of the alliance outside the European theater. Sharp disagreement, over Suez and Algeria in particular, resulted from the limits to action and the lack of support that America imposed on the allies. Ironically, positions would later be reversed as the United States pleaded for an expansion of alliance responsibility and the Europeans resisted.

Until the late 1960s, economic conflict remained at a relatively low level among a set of states basically capitalist in structure and enjoying a buoyant set of international circumstances: an international monetary regime that ensured stable exchange rates, a trading system that moved toward liberalization despite lingering protectionist exceptions, and cheap energy supplies. The increasing prosperity of the West Europeans was related to security through the issue of burden sharing, but an expanding economic base made budgetary compromises relatively easy to negotiate. Even after the eruption of serious economic conflict in the early 1970s, there was little direct linkage to security questions: the years of economic disruption were also years of a mutually agreed policy of detente with the Soviet Union.

Nineteen seventy-three, the year of the October War in the Middle East and the first oil shock, saw American and European divergence on two key questions — the Middle East and energy — that had not been at the core of postwar relations, but were inextricably entwined with *both* economic well-being and national security. Although an energy program of sorts was patched together under American leadership, the American ability to insure against an oil shortfall, as it had in previous crises, was gone, never to return. The Middle East question brought to the fore fundamentally different readings (influenced by domestic politics) of events in that region, producing a pro-Arab shift in Europe and hardening of support for Israel in the United States. Less noticed, but equally important, the war had given the opponents of detente in the United States a crucial piece of ammunition to use in overturning the fragile domestic support for Kissinger's policies.

The election of a trilateralist, Jimmy Carter, as president might have augured well for American policies toward Western Europe, but the growing self-confidence of the Europeans in economic policy and their continuing dependence on the American security guarantee brought sharp criticism of American leadership: too much of the wrong sort in managing the international economy, too little of an erratic kind in dealing with the Soviet Union. Complaints of the first sort centered on American efforts to use the economic summits to tie together a "locomotive strategy" for lifting the world economy out of lingering recession, resisted strenuously by the West Germans. Other criticisms centered on the unsteadiness of American policy. The shifts of Carter foreign policy on the neutron bomb question demonstrated the difficulties that could arise when an American president, intending to share decision making in defense, encountered the realities of European domestic politics: Burden sharing came to mean the sharing of political costs, which no politician cares for. The bungling of the neutron bomb decision led to renewed American resolve not to waver in the future and a determination to offer assurances to the Europeans of American commitment to their defense. One result was the decision to deploy a new generation of theater nuclear forces, taken by NATO in December 1979, a collective decision whose consequences have shaken the alliance.

The early squalls of the Carter administration derived from increasing European self-confidence, a result of Europe's growing economic weight internationally, and an American administration dedicated, at least rhetorically, to a more pluralistic view of the world and a more collegial model of alliance management. As the balance within the administration and within American domestic politics shifted toward a harder posture in relations with the Soviet Union, European complaints were the reverse of those voiced earlier. By early 1978, Soviet involvement in the Third World had convinced some members of the Carter administration, notably the National Security Advisor, Zbigniew Brzezinski, that a new line toward the Soviet Union was needed. Even without such an internal shift within the administration, the Carter presidency was beleaguered from without by a resurgent Republican right, hostile to arms control and willing to accept the most dire portrait of Soviet intentions. SALT II, which had first concerned Europeans with the possibility of a deal made "over their heads" and at the expense of their security, was now in trouble, bringing European statements of support for the treaty, even from hard-liners such as Britain's Prime Minister Margaret Thatcher. The full degree of European attachment to past assumptions about the international environment (whatever their concern over changes in the military balance), did not become clear until the end of 1979, however.

Since then, the Europeans — and the use of that term globally will be qualified below — have found themselves in a sort of time warp, confronting a United States whose perceptions had altered dramatically, away from the presuppositions of detente and toward those of confrontation with the Soviet Union. At the heart of the divergence were a series of overlapping crises — a resurgence of concern over the Middle East and the Persian Gulf, opposition to aspects of American nuclear strategy —

all of which found their beginnings in late 1979, after the collapse of the Shah's regime in Iran and the taking of American hostages, the invasion of Afghanistan by the Soviet Union, the NATO decision to deploy new theater nuclear forces, and renewed conflict over economic issues.

The invasion of Afghanistan crystallized growing concern within the Carter administration over an "arc of crisis" around the Indian Ocean littoral and awarded victory to the opponents of detente in the administration and the country: SALT II was shelved, economic sanctions were imposed by the United States, and President Carter proposed a boycott of the Moscow Olympics. Many within the administration and the American political leadership undoubtedly thought that this new show of American leadership would meet earlier European criticisms of the Carter administration and bring a rallying of the alliance in support of the new, tougher line toward the Soviets.

But Afghanistan was not to be Korea: Rather than viewing the Soviet invasion as indicative of renewed global hostility on the part of the Soviets toward the West, many Europeans refused to accept in full the American reading of the situation and its proposed strategy. They at first preferred to define Afghanistan as an "East-South" question and chose not to endanger detente in Europe (viewed as a long-term investment and a success) by following the American rhetorical lead too wholeheartedly. While pledging not to undercut American sanctions against the Soviet Union and reluctantly agreeing to support those imposed by the United States on Iran, it was clear that the West European governments, including the Conservative Thatcher government in Britain (which was in accord with much of the new American analysis), were skeptical of the usefulness of economic sanctions as a means of exercising leverage over the Soviet Union and hostile to the extension of American sovereignty implied by the financial sanctions against Iran. European leaders, particularly Helmut Schmidt in West Germany and Valery Giscard d'Estaing in France, also expressed alarm that the two superpowers were permitting their competition to move out of control, and they put themselves forward as mediators.

The invasion of Afghanistan not only brought to the fore a divergence in attitudes toward the Soviet Union and the value of preserving the fabric of detente in Europe, it also led to quarreling over the alliance's role outside the European theater, a question of particular sensitivity for the West Germans. The theater in question, the Middle East and the Persian Gulf, was one in which the perceived interests and preferred policies of Britain and France in particular often conflicted with those of the United States. The Europeans viewed the principal threat to the region and its oil supplies, not as a further military drive by the Soviet Union, but as intraregional disputes (such as the warfare between Iran and Iraq that erupted in September 1980) or internal conflict, symbolized by the attack on the Great Mosque at Mecca. While accepting the need for a larger Western presence in the region, the Europeans argued for a "division of labor," which would permit them to concentrate on diplomatic and economic instruments. The United States, which placed the Soviet military threat to the region much higher, saw such a division as awarding them the military risks, in spite of the far greater dependency of the West Europeans on oil imports from the region.[2] The regionalist perspective of the Europeans (and different domestic political givens) also influenced their judgment and implicit criticism of American policy toward the Arab-Israeli conflict. Instead of endorsing the Camp David peace process, an alternative European strategy for the Middle East was made clear, to American displeasure, in the Venice Declaration of the European Community in June 1980: a comprehensive peace process; a reaffirmation of Israel's right to existence and security "within secure; recognized and guaranteed borders"; support for self-determination of the Palestinians; and association of the PLO in the negotiations.

The Carter Administration had witnessed the beginnings of what some called a "crisis" in relations between the United States and Western Europe, but the swing of the American administration away from detente policies in the wake of Afghanistan remained in large measure a judgment of strategy toward the Soviet Union, not a divergence of fundamental views about the character of the Soviet regime or its foreign policy.[3] Differences between Europe and the United States concerned the appropriate mixture of carrots and sticks in a strategy that both agreed must be, at base, a mixed one. Questions of efficacy, such as the use of economic sanctions to influence Soviet behavior, and the separability of detente (Europe versus the Middle East) seemed to be the core of disagreement: important differences, but not fundamental. The differing givens in domestic politics on either side of the Atlantic had not yet resulted in different world views, despite the American change of line. Even though months of bickering occurred, the NATO allies were able to coordinate their warnings to the Soviet Union after the eruption of the Polish crisis: Overt Soviet intervention to crush Solidarity would mean the end of detente in Europe. The Carter administration had, however, contributed new sources of conflict that would only become apparent under its successor — the mixing of the two tracks of economics and security in the form of the sanctions question, the apparent move toward a nuclear strategy that offered options for nuclear warfighting, the tenacious defense of a Middle East peace program that failed to bring a settlement of the Palestinian question. It was only when domestic politics in the United States took a further sharp turn to the right, in the presidential election of 1980, however, that the disarray in the alliance deepened. This disarray was grounded in very different perceptions of the Soviet Union that were in turn rooted in political givens in Western Europe and the

United States. And, deepening the rift, the new political givens fed into one another in a particularly perverse way.

The Reagan Administration and Western Europe

The Reagan administration from its first days confronted one element in the apparent Atlantic rift that was not typical in past administrations: the consequences of cumulation. While most administrations had made their own discrete crises in relations with Western Europe, the positions of the new team, swinging even more sharply in the direction taken during the last years of the Carter administration, built on an existing sense in Europe of an American ally oblivious to the European point of view. The administration also confronted, though it took some time to become aware of it, a series of overlapping European-American disagreements that concerned not only the older and better-known questions of nuclear strategy, burden sharing, and international economic management, but also the orientation of the alliance outside Europe and a growing gray area of economic issues with security implications (or, in European eyes, political manipulation of economic transactions). Finally, the Reagan administration was, in the political and economic coalition that supported it, the least "Atlanticist" of any recent American administration. Its concern for Latin America and the Middle East suggested a shift in American economic and political power toward the West and the South domestically and away from traditional allies.

As it had in policy toward the Soviet Union, the Reagan administration brought with it a very simple and coherent strategy for mending ties to the West Europeans. Curiously, that strategy echoed the criticisms that *Europeans* had made of the Carter administration, that the source of division was an absence of leadership on the part of the previous American administration and not disagreement over appropriate strategy, much less structural change. With the reassertion of a clear American line toward the Soviet Union and demonstrated American willingness to undertake a military buildup vis-à-vis the Soviets, the West European allies would respond as they had in the (distant) past.

The pursuit of this strategy pointed up the Reagan administration's contribution to further deterioration in relations with Western Europe. While certain elements of the security relationship, and particularly European security dependency, remained unchanged, other features had altered, particularly Europe's greater political self-confidence (based on its greater economic weight internationally) and the greater insulation of Europe from the manipulation of either superpower. Just as the Soviet Union had lost its hold over most of the West European left, so the United States could no longer play the European center and right as it could in the 1950s. Western Europe was more insulated from direct manipulation but remained highly sensitive to changes affecting its security. The Reagan administration, unwittingly, ensured that such sensitivity would grow and produce, through a democratization of the European foreign policy debate, a popular movement intensely critical of American aims and military strategy.

Sources of Conflict:
Two Views of the "Giant with Feet of Clay"

In his interpretation of Soviet behavior, the scales had fallen from the eyes of Jimmy Carter, by his own admission, at the time of the invasion of Afghanistan, a turning point in the domestic politics of foreign policy in the United States. The Reagan administration brought to power a view of American relations with the Soviet Union and a preferred American and Western policy that was even more sharply hostile and skeptical of negotiations and remnants of detente.[4] The new (or very old) views espoused by the Reagan administration in policies toward the Eastern bloc were at the core of division with the Europeans.

The position of the two administrations in relation to the views of European elites and the growing "peace constituency" in Europe are outlined in Figure 9-1. Even in the shift that occurred late in the Carter administration, the common ground between the American political elite and the European elites remained wide. The Soviet Union, which might be aggressive and expansionist, was also ultimately a manageable threat, an opportunistic power that could be stopped with some variation of the traditional policies of containment applied to new areas of perceived threat — the Middle East and the Persian Gulf. The mixed strategy had to include many more sticks than carrots in the present phase, but the future use of positive incentives was not ruled out. The victory of the hardliners in the Carter administration (and the divergence from the European elites) came in the disappearance of any notion that the Soviet Union behaved defensively (particularly in Afghanistan) and in the calculation of Soviet vulnerability to external pressure from the West, particularly the exercise of leverage through economic sanctions.

In the Reagan administration, an "essentialist" view of the Soviet Union seemed to hold the dominant position, at least in the early months: the Soviet Union was implacably hostile to the West for reasons of domestic ideology, militarism, nationalism, or some mix of the three. The rhetorical picture painted of the Soviet Union by the president was reminiscent of the 1950s: an inherently "evil force," a group of leaders whose morality permitted them "to commit any crime, to lie, to cheat." Soviet expansionism was ceaseless, and it was global: American concern (and allied coordination) had to meet the threat wherever it presented itself. Yet the Soviet Union was also a "giant with feet of clay," and the ad-

FIGURE 9-1.   Perceptions of the Soviet Union

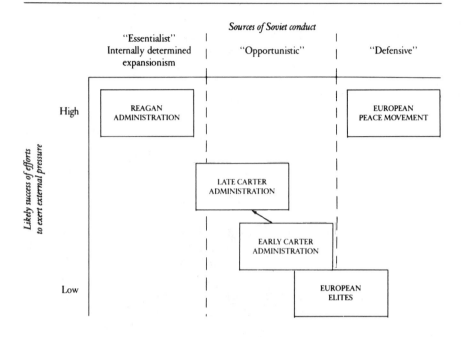

ministration chose to paint different portraits of the adversary at different times. Because of the weakness of its economy in particular, the Soviet Union *was* vulnerable to Western economic pressure. Confronting such a foe, a mixed strategy was hardly possible; rather, "early Reagan" policy suggested that only military buildup, coupled with resolute rhetoric and ideological confrontation, would suffice to contain the Soviet menace.

But not to strengthen the alliance, as it turned out. For elite and public opinion in Europe, however jaundiced a view it took of the Soviet Union, still persisted in seeing the country as a state, however troublesome and even aggressive, that could be bargained with, *must* be bargained with, a state with which the Europeans had lived in very close quarters for many years. And for the building European peace movement, a defensive view of Soviet behavior was often endorsed that had virtually disappeared in American political discourse.

For the European elites, a mixed strategy was not dead at all, and however much they had disagreed with the mix chosen by the Carter administration, they viewed with positive alarm the denigration of negotiation in the rhetoric of the Reagan administration. While they made polite noises of appreciation for the clear direction now visible in Washington (and quietly asked, for how long this time?) they also, in the early months of the administration, made clear that they expected the policies of arms control to continue and that they hoped for an early summit meeting between Reagan and Brezhnev. Like the Reagan administration, the Europeans often accepted a "giant with feet of clay" image of the Soviet Union, but they drew very different conclusions. First, the weaknesses that they perceived (perhaps they saw the feet of clay because they were closer) suggested a more manageable threat. They firmly rejected the ability of Western economic pressures to change the Soviet system or Soviet foreign policy in any predictable way (the source of conflict described below). If anything, much of the European peace movement and segments of the elite saw pressures on a fragile Soviet system as leading not to collapse or conciliation but to closure and greater hostility. Ironically, those who endorsed the defensive view of Soviet motivations agreed with the Reagan line on the susceptibility of the Soviets to external change: Their reading of the internal Soviet dynamics, however, and their prescription — conciliatory, even unilateral policies — was radically different.

As the anti-Soviet rhetoric of the American administration increased, pressure on European elites from the growing peace movement — already perceptible under Carter — brought forth hostile statements of scorn from the Reagan administration. In March, National Security Advisor Richard V. Allen condemned the "outright pacifist sentiments" in Europe. The American line seemed to soften in Haig's speech in New Orleans in August, which called for a "constructive relationship" with the Soviet Union, but concentration on military instruments for dealing with the Soviet Union and comments from Washington about nuclear strategy provoked furor in Western Europe and contributed to a further surge in the strength of the peace movement.

Sources of Conflict:
Nuclear Strategy Enters European Politics

On October 16, 1981, in a speech to American newspaper editors, President Reagan claimed that the United States and the Soviet Union could engage in a tactical nuclear exchange without escalation into all-out nuclear war. A few weeks later, then Secretary of State Haig claimed that NATO had plans for a low-level nuclear explosion to warn the Soviet Union of further escalation if it made a conventional attack on Western Europe. Such public statements reflected an internal debate over nuclear strategy within the administration and the increasing influence within the Department of Defense of those who believed that the United States should develop a nuclear warfighting capability. The movement of what had been an arcane debate into the public arena, through such prominent American leaders, however, could not have happened at a more inopportune time. The comments echoed and reechoed in a Europe already divided by its own debate over the proposed deployment of long-range theater nuclear forces (LRTNF), agreed by NATO in December 1979. That decision, meant to ease the fears of Europeans that American strategic doctrine might delink European defense from the use of American nuclear weapons, ultimately came to be seen, under the Reagan administration, as precisely a means to such delinking. Rather than ensuring a firmer American commitment, when combined with arguments in favor of capabilities for fighting limited nuclear war, many Europeans saw the December 1979 decision as the first step toward a strategy of limited nuclear war in Europe.

Curiously, the 1979 decision had its roots in the equivocations of the Carter administration over the neutron bomb and in the concern of some European leaders and defense analysts that nuclear parity, combined with arms control foreseen in SALT II, would lead to the possibility of dangerous imbalances in nuclear forces at lower levels on the escalation ladder. It was, in fact, Chancellor Helmut Schmidt of West Germany who raised such a danger in a public lecture given in October 1977:

> SALT codifies the nuclear strategic balance between the Soviet Union and the United States. To put it another way: SALT neutralizes their strategic nuclear capabilities. In Europe this magnifies the significance of the disparities between East and West in nuclear tactical and conventional weapons.[5]

While many would later challenge the logic of such concerns and the breadth of European consensus on the need for countermeasures, for the Carter administration such expressions of alarm were serious, particularly after the neutron bomb debacle.

Concern centered on Soviet deployment of a new generation of medium-range ballistic missile, the SS-20, targeted on Western Europe (and China) and possessing larger numbers of warheads and greater mobility than the SS-4 and SS-5 systems that it was replacing. More significant in the eyes of some analysts was the growing vulnerability of NATO theatre nuclear forces to Soviet deployments of all kinds, not simply to the much-discussed SS-20s. Yet, even those who defended the NATO decision to deploy air-launched cruise and Pershing II missiles, often conceded that the military argument in favor of that number of those systems was "not compelling," either in the reading of the consequences of parity at the strategic level or in the appropriate response to the problem of vulnerability, which could be better met by a sea-based deployment.[6]

The deployment of cruise missiles and Pershing IIs was, as had been the case with previous decisions (or nondecisions) on theater nuclear forces, a political decision. The problem addressed by the December 1979 decision was the perennial one of European and Soviet perceptions of possible decoupling of the American nuclear deterrent from the defense of Western Europe. This fear had been the original source of European claims for a counter to the SS-20 deployments. As Bertram would have it, "U.S. nuclear forces *in Europe* will be a more credible and more proportionate demonstration of that link than U.S.-based strategic nuclear systems alone would be."[7] In any case, the political or perceptual argument carried the day, although the political sensitivity of the decision, even in those pre-Afghanistan days, was recognized in Europe. Germany, the most affected nonnuclear power, wanted as many other nonnuclear European countries (and at least one continental country) to accept the deployment as well. European sentiment also saw to it that the decision was tied, for the first time in NATO history, to an effort at arms control with the Soviet Union (the "two-track" aspect of the decision). The Germans also made certain that there would *not* be a "double key," reinforcing the "American" character of the weapons.[8] Also for the first time, the production decision on the new systems was made collectively by NATO, but, as would soon be discovered, the second track of the decision, arms control negotiations with the Soviets, remained in American hands.

As Bertram has noted, the December 1979 decision was an effort to cure a problem of political trust with a military deployment: "What may be desirable today, for political reasons, may become for other political reasons less desirable tomorrow."[9] The political givens on which the NATO decision was based quickly shifted. Instead of a decision taken within a continuing, if fragile, setting of arms control negotiations, the SALT II treaty was shelved a few weeks after the decision, and serious negotiations between the superpowers became moot. With the election of Ronald Reagan on a platform rejecting SALT II and the formation of a foreign policy and defense team more skeptical of arms control than any since World War II, the second track of the NATO decision, the politically essential commitment to arms control, seemed endangered.

Administration skepticism about arms control reinforced perceptions in the burgeoning European peace movement, and in a European public increasingly concerned about superpower conflict, that the new administration took a somewhat casual attitude about the possible danger of nuclear war. Not only were the possibilities of surviving a nuclear war touted by some, but planning for fighting a limited nuclear war, a "tit for tat" exchange, received considerable play as well. To those who were already hostile to the strident anti-Soviet rhetoric of the administration and its shunting aside of arms control, such an apparent shift in doctrine — the development of warfighting capabilities was not portrayed as part of an overall strategy of deterrence — clearly suggested that Europe would probably be the first theater of such a war. The likely result would be the end of European society.

As such fears grew, the Reagan administration, breaking with the style of the Carter presidency and displaying its new ideas of alliance leadership, chose to announce its decision to produce the neutron bomb in August 1981, without consulting its European allies. The decision was only partially tempered by a statement made by Reagan a week later that the weapon would not be deployed without such consultation. Loyally, and at considerable political risk, Helmut Schmidt stated that under the conditions already agreed in 1978, the weapon could still be deployed on West German soil, though the problem was not an "immediate" one. The neutron bomb decision, contributing to the fears of nuclear war in Europe, was followed by the comments of Reagan and Haig noted earlier. This lent credence to a shift away from the very coupling that the LRTNF decision was meant to convey and generated further doubts about American commitment to the doctrine of nuclear deterrence.

With such stimulus from Washington, the European peace movement grew enormously. Particularly in Scandinavia, in the Benelux countries, and in West Germany, the pressures on the political elites were enormous. Even those countries already possessing nuclear weapons (such as Britain), those previously unaffected by European disarmament movements (such as Italy), and those which were not yet members of NATO and did not confront a decision on deployment (such as Spain), witnessed major efforts at organization and demonstration. An antideployment demonstration in Bonn in April 1981 drew 15,000; after ten months of the Reagan administration, demonstrations in October and November 1981 were attracting hundreds of thousands of demonstrators (estimates of 250,000 in Bonn, 150,000 in London, over 200,000 in Florence). Only France seemed exempt from the marshaling of antideployment support on such a scale.

Efforts were made, particularly by Secretary of State Haig, to quiet European elite anxieties by assuring the Europeans that arms control negotiations on LRTNF — the second track — would begin by the end of 1981. But the crowds were not listening to such assurances. As the political pressures against deployment grew in Western Europe, it was now the Americans who began to emphasize the political necessity of the deployment: The Europeans had to share some of the nuclear risk to which the American population was exposed; the deployment became a crucial "expression of Alliance solidarity." [10] Not stated publicly was the view that any willingness of the European governments to bow to the peace movement (viewed by American conservatives as the proxy of Moscow) would simply be another bit of evidence that Europe was on the road to Finlandization.

Reagan's speech on arms control to the National Press Club (November 18, 1981) was in large part a response to growing opposition in Europe to the deployment of new theater nuclear forces. The importance of West European perceptions in planning the address was made clear in its unprecedented live satellite transmission to Western Europe. The tone of the president's speech, meant to convey the image of a man of peace, was decidedly different from Reagan's earlier anti-Soviet rhetoric: he spoke directly to the peace movement, the "young people" who questioned a strategy based on nuclear weapons, emphasized "America's commitment to the Atlantic Alliance and our resolve to sustain the peace," and emphasized the defensive mission of NATO forces. Many of the arms control proposals presented remained vague, save for that on the European theater nuclear weapons: Reagan endorsed the "zero option," committing the NATO allies to cancel their planned deployment if the Soviet Union removed all of their SS-20s (even those east of the Urals).[11] This was a shrewd bit of politics for the European public, it seemed at first glance, since the missile question was batted firmly into the Soviet court. A refusal would make it clear that the obstacle to arms control lay in Moscow. Of course, if the Soviet Union responded with a partial acceptance (a reduction in SS-20 numbers), then the politics of alliance policy would become sticky once again. Collectively, NATO would have to decide how many missiles would be enough.

The response from the European elites was heartening: Schmidt and Thatcher hailed the Reagan speech, Schmidt repeatedly labeling it (for his own public) as the "American peace strategy." It provided the elites in Germany and the Benelux countries with an important card to play in favor of pursuing the 1979 decision, since the second track was now visible. It also gave Schmidt another opportunity to portray himself as the loyal ally who was also a skillful mediator between the superpowers, since the speech came just before Brezhnev's visit to Bonn, the first by the Soviet leader to a Western capital since the invasion of Afghanistan.

The peace movement did not die, however. The opening of negotiations on theater nuclear forces on November 30, 1981, was only a tentative beginning, one that promised a reduction in the visible dangers to Europe from a strategy based on nuclear weapons only in the distant future, if ever. Criticisms of that long-standing strategy surfaced in early 1982 in an unlikely spot — *Foreign Affairs*, usually regarded as the house organ of Atlanticist views on foreign policy in the United States. The authors of the article in question were equally surprising — four of the most senior members of the foreign policy establishment: George Kennan, Robert McNamara, McGeorge Bundy, and Gerard Smith. Their arguments, which were repudiated in advance of publication by Secretary of State Haig, suggested the concerns for the NATO alliance that had grown during the first year of the Reagan administration as the opposition to nuclear weapons in Europe had grown:

> The events of the last year have shown that differing perceptions of the role of nuclear weapons can lead to destructive recriminations, and when these differences are compounded by understandable disagree-

ments on other matters such as Poland and the Middle East, the possibilities for trouble among Allies are evident.[12]

Their case in favor of a declared NATO policy that nuclear weapons would be used to retaliate only against nuclear attack challenged the imprecise, but politically useful, compromise on flexible response reached in 1967. Replies by Haig and German Foreign Minister Genscher suggested that, despite other disagreements within the alliance, that doctrine was still perceived as sound by the elites in both Europe and the United States. The appeal for a policy of no first use of nuclear weapons did, however, find support among those more sympathetic to the peace movement in Europe and found some reflection in the conventional defense emphasis of the communiqué of the Bonn summit in June 1982.

Sources of Conflict:
Politicization of Economic Relations —
Poland and Sanctions

Nuclear strategy was an old battleground in disputes between Europe and the United States, the mirror-image fears of decoupling and becoming a nuclear battlefield were at least two decades old. What was new was the scale of politicization of these issues and the Europe-wide character of such concern. Equally grounded in divergent perceptions of the Soviet Union and in the history of the 1970s was a new source of dispute, less tied to mass politicization, but deeply embedded in the contrasting patterns of economic relations that had developed over the last decade as a result of declining East-West tensions. The use of economic sanctions against Iran and the Soviet Union by the Carter administration had been endorsed by the Europeans only reluctantly, and they had made clear their resentment of the administration's extension of sovereignty to American banks in Europe in the Iranian case. In the Reagan administration, it first seemed that laissez-faire ideology would triumph over anti-Soviet ideology. Reagan, despite resistance from Haig (who saw the lessons that the Europeans and Japanese would draw), decided to lift the partial grain embargo imposed on the Soviet Union after the invasion of Afghanistan: business as usual all around, or very nearly. It soon became clear, however, that the new administration's position on economic transactions with the East would be dominated by assumptions widely different from those of the Europeans, and, unlike questions of military policy, where the British and the French often partially endorsed the more pessimistic American view, on the question of economic sanctions the Europeans stood united against American effort to burden them and their underemployed economies with a dubious foreign policy strategy.

The divergence of views stemmed from the structural place of the two economies, European and North American, in the pattern of East-

West trade; from different conceptions of how to influence Soviet behavior; and from differing readings of the history of the years of detente. The contrasting stakes of the American and European economies in East-West trade were clear, and the proponents of sanctions in the United States saw European reluctance to exert economic pressure on the Soviet Union as further evidence that the years of detente had begun to erode the Western will to resist Soviet expansionism. Even though the Europeans were more deeply involved in East-West trade, however, the dependence of their economies on the East was hardly large enough to support such charges. More important than volume in determining their position on sanctions was the composition of their trade with the Soviet Union and Eastern Europe. Unlike that of the United States, which is concentrated in agricultural exports, European trade is heavily weighted toward manufactures, particularly capital goods. The Europeans argued that trade in such products, unlike trade in grain, could not be turned on and off like a tap without risking disruption to their own economies and the larger pattern of East-West economic transactions.

If the material burden of sanctions seemed heavy for the West European economies, the Europeans also disputed the notion that economic sanctions were an effective means of influencing Soviet behavior. At least three different justifications — symbolism, leverage, and economic warfare — could be found in American arguments for economic sanctions. During the Carter administration, sanctions were usually proposed for reasons of symbolism (to condemn the adversary, even when admitting that his behavior was unlikely to change) and as an attempt to exercise leverage (to change a specific aspect of Soviet behavior through the withholding of specific desired goods). Leverage was the typical argument of those seeking to change relatively minor aspects of Soviet behavior — the linkage of oil drilling equipment to the arrest of Soviet dissidents — while even proponents of sanctions were forced back to arguments of symbolism in the case of Afghanistan, in which the Soviet stakes were clearly too great to be changed by the modest economic weapons at the disposal of the United States. The Reagan Administration, however, took office with at least a part of the administration (and a part that grew in influence) arguing that the Soviet economy was in dire straits and that economic warfare on the part of the West would weaken Soviet ability to pursue expansionist policies abroad and to continue its military buildup at home. Here, the question was not an effort to change specific Soviet policies — the "essentialist" view of Soviet behavior could hardly admit that — but rather to weaken the Soviet capability to pursue policies that were unlikely to change. There was no need for fine-tuning: any denial of Western trade or credits would serve the larger purpose, and, conversely, any trade or transfer of technology was viewed as contributing to the freeing of Soviet resources for military purposes.[13]

The Europeans took a wholly different view, which might be termed automatic destabilization. While agreeing on the restrictions of strategic technologies toward the East (a long-standing alliance policy under the Coordinating Committee on East-West Trade (CoCom), they argued that Western credits, trade, and technology transfers were not easily absorbed without change in the Soviet and East European economies; the growing crisis in Poland seemed to demonstrate that detente policies had worked and that growing interdependence with the West forced hard choices on the Communist regimes. Dependence of the Polish economy on a continued flow of Western credits made it much more unlikely that the Soviets would intervene to quell the rise of Solidarity, since, whatever the risk of Western reaction, the Soviets could not deliver what the Polish economy needed. Opening economies produced rising and difficult-to-satisfy expectations internally and wove the "web of detente" more firmly externally, forcing all parties to move more cautiously than they would have in pre-detente days.

The European view of economic transactions with the East fitted with a third justification for resisting economic sanctions: their reading of detente in Europe. While the Reagan administration saw the years of detente as ones in which the Soviet Union increased its military edge over the West and skillfully exploited Western divisions to win economic concessions and Third World influence, the Europeans did not see detente as a one-way street. Reagan administration statements increasingly portrayed economic transactions of any kind as a "gift" relieving the Soviet bloc's economic difficulties; the Europeans saw not only economic benefits from their trade with the East (as with other trade) but also political benefits in furthering the stabilization of political relations between East and West in Europe.

Poland provided the occasion for demonstrating the fundamental differences between Americans and Europeans on all of these issues. Even those who espoused the automatic destabilization view of East-West trade admitted that an overt Soviet invasion of Poland to crush the insurgent Solidarity movement would necessarily call for a unified and tough NATO response. Since military action had been ruled out, economic sanctions of some kind were necessarily on the agenda. In any event, the declaration of martial law in Poland on December 17, 1981, without Soviet military intervention caught the alliance without a prepared position, and European, particularly German, analyses of the situation and those of the Reagan administration once again swung sharply apart.

The United States announced economic sanctions against the martial law government of General Jaruszelski, quickly followed by a charge of Soviet responsibility, and the declaration of further sanctions directed against the Soviet Union. Even though the American sanctions were not particularly harsh given earlier administration statements, the initial European response was less than enthusiastic: no government endorsed the American sanctions or hastened to impose its own. Divisions appeared within European ranks in response to the ambiguous involvement of the Soviet Union. Germany, in particular, was at first unwilling to state that the Soviet Union had played a role in the martial law declaration. Among those most critical of German equanimity was the Socialist government of France. An interview with Helmut Schmidt at the turn of the year reinforced the impression of German complacence: Schmidt conceded that it was proper to warn the Soviet Union against direct intervention, but he emphasized that the West had agreed at Yalta (red flag to American conservatives!) to divide Europe into spheres of influence, and that any attempt to alter the existing balance of power would mean war.[14] The German reaction and the opposing response of the Reagan administration suggested a very deep difference over the accomplishments and meaning of European detente. On the one hand Germany seemed to uphold the status quo in the face of movements for change in the East; on the other, the Americans condemned detente yet seemed to argue that detente had changed the ground rules in Europe, so that the Soviet Union no longer had an unchallenged right to settle the fate of its sphere of influence.

Despite earlier displays of disunity on what the alliance should do, NATO ministers were able to agree on a common reading of responsibility: The Soviet Union was condemned for its support of "systematic suppression" in Poland and warned of possible European sanctions if the situation in the country did not improve. (Only Greece dissociated itself from the warning.) The Europeans also agreed not to undercut sanctions imposed by the United States, but their interpretation of that assurance was once again different from that of the Americans, particularly when the United States homed in on two questions which had been sources of friction since the Carter administration: the natural gas pipeline deal that was being negotiated between the Soviet Union and West European consumers and subsidized export credits in European trade with the East.

The pipeline would prove the most contentious, and no single issue better symbolized Western Europe's dogged attachment to East-West policies that ran counter to United States views. In scale alone, the proposed pipeline was symbolic of European reliance upon a minimal level of stability in East-West relations: the building of a pipeline 3,500 miles long to transport natural gas from Siberia to the West European market. Western Europe had imported Soviet natural gas for some time, but the new pipeline, when fully on-stream in the mid-1980s, would nearly triple the imports (over 61 billion cubic meters as compared to the present 24) and would ultimately involve ten European countries as consumers. Financially, the deal also represented an unprecedented scale of interdependence between the Soviet Union and Europe: the total construction costs, largely financed by the West, were likely to reach $15 billion. There was no question that the pipeline relied heavily, not only on Western credits but also on Western (and American) technology.

Plans for the Siberian pipeline had been underway for several years, and the Carter administration had expressed concern, which intensified after the Soviet invasion of Afghanistan. The worries of that administration were defined narrowly: fear that increased European dependence on Soviet natural gas would lead to increased leverage by the Soviet Union, enabling the exertion of subtle (or not so subtle) pressure on its European customers. Typically, in the dispute over dependence, the Europeans chose one set of figures, the Americans another. For the United States, the important projection was growth in European natural gas dependency on the Soviet Union: by the 1990s, EEC dependency was projected to grow to 20 percent; for certain countries, particularly West Germany, the level of dependence would be higher. The Europeans retorted that the appropriate figure to examine would be overall energy dependency: In terms of total energy consumption, the share of Soviet natural gas imports would remain less than 5 percent.[15] To the Europeans, Soviet natural gas was a means of necessary diversification of their imports of energy away from the insecure Persian Gulf and Middle East; the United States refused to perceive the Soviet Union as a supplier like any other, and ultimately questioned the wisdom of any increase in dependence on the Soviet Union during a time of increasing East-West tension.

While the Carter administration expressed its disquiet, the dispute broadened under the Reagan administration. Even before the imposition of martial law in Poland, the pipeline had become a virtual idée fixe of the new administration, a potent demonstration that the Europeans did not share its overall view of East-West relations and the place of controlling economic transactions in Western strategy toward the Soviet Union. The pipeline symbolized "web of detente" arguments that the administration totally rejected. For the Reagan administration the pipeline was doubly condemned not only for the asymmetric dependency that it imposed on Western Europe (which the Europeans argued was ultimately symmetric) but also for the contribution that it made to Soviet economic well-being and ultimately to Soviet military gains. The economic warfare theme grew more and more prominent in the administration's case against the pipeline, and particularly the contribution that the sales of natural gas would make in resolving Soviet shortages of hard currencies in the years ahead.

For the Europeans, this new theme was even more unacceptable than the old attack via dependence, for it called into question virtually all East-West economic ties, carefully constructed during the 1970s. According to this view, any gain for the Soviet Union economically was automatically a loss for the West, a zero-sum view that they could hardly accept. The Europeans also rejected American efforts to portray the Soviet economy as a "basket case" that could be seriously damaged by restraint in Western credits and technology transfers. They had heard such predictions of Soviet economic collapse before (since 1917 in fact) and yet the Soviet system staggered on: Surely the state of the economy was no worse than in the years of postwar devastation, when Western quarantine had been nearly total. The European governments also pointed to the closed character of the Soviet economy, which reduced any leverage that the "economic warriors" might hope to use. And finally, it was not at all clear how foreign exchange gains contributed, except in a very indirect fashion, to Soviet military expansion: The Soviet military establishment was certainly not the most dependent on Western assistance. Politically, the Europeans saw important gains for their recession-plagued economies in the pipeline deal, particularly for such hard-pressed industries as steel.

The suppression of Solidarity in Poland seemed to give the Reagan administration a final opportunity to convince the Europeans to call off the deal. As part of its economic sanctions against the Soviet Union, the American government had prevented General Electric Company from selling $175 million worth of components for gas turbine compressors that were to be built under license for the pipeline by three European firms: the troubled West German AEG-Telefunken, Britain's John Brown Engineering, and Italy's Nuovo Pignone. That measure did not seal off the technological loophole, however, since at least one European firm, the recently nationalized French company, Alsthom-Atlantique, was also capable of supplying the components, which it produced under license from General Electric. Despite this evident signal of American intent, the Europeans refused to overturn the deal.

At the same time, the allies were wrestling with the question of the Polish debt. The explosion of the Solidarity movement into Polish politics only worsened the difficult financial situation of Poland, already the most heavily indebted of the East European economies. Throughout 1981, as lines of private credit to Poland and the rest of Eastern Europe tightened, the Reagan administration demonstrated its willingness to assist in the rescheduling of Poland's public debt in order to ease the way for continued liberalization. After the declaration of martial law, however, pressure mounted from the hawks in the administration to declare default on the Polish debt. It was an argument made primarily on the grounds of symbolism — to demonstrate the bankruptcy, literally, of the old regime in Communist Europe — but also on the increasingly popular grounds of economic warfare. Within the administration, the pro-default line was taken by the Defense Department, backed by the CIA and UN Ambassador Kirkpatrick; arrayed against this position were the Treasury and

State Departments, who argued successfully for leverage, and therefore against default, since that would permit the Polish government and the Soviet Union to free themselves of any commitment to repay. This was, in the words of Haig, "the hard position, the more rigid position." But such arguments, made for the domestic audience, were in fact less important than the dangers that were seen to the international monetary and financial system from an abrupt declaration of default, and the resistance that would be mounted by European governments, whose banks and firms were more deeply involved in Eastern Europe.[16]

Faced with European recalcitrance, the administration developed a compromise position on East-West economic relations that it hoped to sell to its allies. Although the argument was more leverage than economic warfare, it satisfied the proponents of both positions. As Robert Hormats, Assistant Secretary of State for Economic and Business Affairs (and hardly a hawk), described before a Congressional committee:

> The question most on our minds is "How do we put the most pressure on the military government in Poland and therefore on the Soviet Union?" and one of our answers is "Less hard currency."

Less hard currency would, according to this "grand leverage" view, force not only the Poles, but also the other Eastern bloc regimes to confront their economic failings. It would also lead — a crucial assumption — to the liberalization of their economic systems and ultimately political conditions in those societies. The unspoken side benefit was, of course, that fewer economic resources would be devoted to military expenditures.

Undersecretary of State William Buckley took this more subtle grand leverage argument on a mission to the European capitals in early 1982. The response he met was distinctly cool. Not only were the European leaders, confronting deep economic recession that they blamed in large measure on American economic choices (particularly large budget deficits and high interest rates), unwilling to bear economic burdens that the Americans themselves refused to take (in the form of a grain embargo), they also detected, under the "grand leverage" arguments of Buckley, the old assumptions of the economic warfare school. Even the leverage arguments that were advanced were not convincing: Why should anyone assume that harder economic pressure from the outside would lead to internal liberalization of the Eastern economies, when historical evidence suggested that a move toward autarchy and the exaction of greater sacrifices from the populations was at least as likely? The shift in Reagan administration strategy from trade sanctions (which raised the embarrassing question of grain) to financial sanctions also called into question the fabric, however tattered, of detente. And once again, the European assessment of that fabric was different.

The Buckley mission had failed to achieve anything more than agreement to continue discussions on the terms of credit offered the Soviet Union within the context of the OECD "gentlemen's agreement" on export credits. Nevertheless, the administration continued to beat the drum for its new course in the months before the Versailles economic and Bonn NATO summits. What was clear after March was an implicit bargain offered to the Europeans: no further American resistance to the gas pipeline (and more generally, a turn away from trade sanctions) in exchange for European concessions in tightening the terms and amounts of credits offered to Eastern bloc countries. It was on the basis of that bargain that the State Department thought it could find consensus at the Versailles economic summit in June.

The Third World: Global Anti-Communism Meets French Socialism and British Nationalism

Even in its anti-Soviet final months, the Carter administration had preserved some elements of the regionalist view on the Third World, crediting Third World politics (and the disputes in which they were embroiled) with a certain life of their own. The Reagan administration rejected this perspective, seeking to build up clients in Asia, Africa, and Latin America whose anti-communist credentials were impeccable. The administration soon discovered that the Europeans would choose their own friends among the developing countries.

In the Middle East, despite their clear disagreement with the Camp David strategy of the Carter administration, the Europeans did not press their peace-making initiatives during the first year of the Reagan administration. As the United States set out to construct a "strategic consensus" encompassing Israel and "moderate" Arab states, the Europeans held back in part because of the administration's own rifts with the Begin government and in part because of the change of government in France. The new Socialist government of President François Mitterrand seemed destined to quarrel with the new administration in Washington, yet, together with the Thatcher government in Britain, it proved the most consistent supporter of the American position toward the Soviet Union and in the Middle East. The personal sympathies of the new president of France definitely tilted French policy away from the clear-cut pro-Arab position that France had followed since 1967.

But if the new French government gave unexpected support to the Reagan administration on Soviet and Middle Eastern questions, the two countries were distinctly at odds on the administration's first "test case" of global anti-communism: Central America. The Europeans in general were skeptical of the American position on the conflict in Central America, and their own political connections — particularly those of the Socialists and the Social Democrats — led them to a close relationship with the opposition to the Duarte government. In the terms of past American debates, the Europeans in general took a distinctly "regionalist" position, critical of imputing all revolutionary change in the Third World to Soviet intervention, and, in the French case particularly, displaying a far more sympathetic attitude toward revolutionary movements. The support lent by the Mitterrand government to the Sandinistas in Nicaragua, dismissed by the Reagan administration as pawns of the Cubans and Soviets, illustrated the importance of ideological differences at least in the Third World arena.

Elsewhere, the administration's policy of polishing its relationship with authoritarian regimes in the Third World met obstacles, not from the ideological sympathies of French Socialists, but from the unexpectedly resolute defense of national interest by Margaret Thatcher's government in Britain. The conflict between Britain and Argentina over the Falkland Islands posed enormous difficulties for the Reagan administration, not the least because it did not fit with the dominant, anti-Communist world-view of the American government. Either the conflict resulted from a dictatorial regime attempting to seize the territory of another country in violation of the norm of self-determination (the British position) or it was at base a North-South issue, a decrepit imperial power attempting to retain the last illegitimate remnants of colonialism (the Argentine position). But in any case the Falklands crisis was only very indirectly an East-West question — in the damage that it could do to relations with an important and ideologically sound ally or to the new policy of forging ties with authoritarian regimes in the cone of South America that could assist American combat against revolutionary forces in Central America (as Argentina had reportedly begun to do). The embarrassment of the administration was evident, but the outcome of the internal debate was never really in doubt, particularly after the European Community so surprisingly and unanimously backed the British position with economic sanctions against Argentina. The United States itself soon applied sanctions and offered its logistical support of Britain during the conflict, while at the same time, like the Europeans, pushing the British government toward a settlement of the Argentine claims that would reduce damage to relations with that country and Latin America as a whole. Although the dissents of neoconservatives and the New Right were of interest in predicting future Reagan policy toward Western Europe, the position of the "Latinos" was quickly overwhelmed.

The elections in El Salvador and the lowering of American rhetoric about Central America, together with the speedy victory of the British in the Falklands, left little in the way of disagreement between European and American leaders on Third World issues by the time of the summits in June 1982. But the Middle East intruded, in a very direct way, on those summits, and left a trail of disagreement suggesting that strains over policy outside the Atlantic area would not disappear.

Versailles and Bonn:
The Limits to Elite Reconciliation

European discontent with the economic policies of the Reagan administration went beyond the question of economic sanctions. Recurrent trade disputes (notably over agriculture and steel) had flared up again in conditions of recession; American macroeconomic policy, which had produced high interest rates and a robust dollar, was seen as thwarting European efforts at economic recovery. As Benjamin Cohen discusses in Chapter 4, the administration's model of leadership, as in other areas of alliance relations, seemed to foreclose any examination of the effects of American policies on other economies. Despite mounting discontent on these issues, however, the months before the Versailles economic summit (June 4-6, 1982) had left little doubt as to which issue would be at the top of the American agenda: economic relations between East and West. It was evidence of the changing climate under the new administration that an *economic* summit in the midst of a serious recession would devote so much time to this question.

The final bargain at the summit involved the same principals as that at the first of these summits, at Rambouillet in 1975 — France and the United States. France won American agreement to the North-South section of the communiqué as well as a pledge of greater monetary cooperation among Europe, the United States, and Japan; and American reiteration of its willingness to intervene in the foreign exchange markets to counter "disorderly market conditions." The French relented — slightly — on the issue of East-West trade by consenting to the inclusion of the word "limits" in the final communiqué on export credits for trade with the Eastern bloc.[17]

Yet, as each side — François Mitterrand for the Europeans and Donald Regan for the United States — hailed their "victories," one could detect that the "agreement" at the summit meant very different things to each. The United States won three commitments: improved control of exports of strategic goods (little European opposition there); an exchange of information on East-West economic transactions within OECD (the Americans hoped that collective scrutiny would lead to greater stringency); and finally, agreement

> to handle cautiously financial relations with the USSR and other Eastern European countries in such a way as to ensure that they are conducted on a sound economic basis, including also the need for commercial prudence in limiting export credits.

In this third clause, the Americans emphasized "limiting"; Regan interpreted it as meaning "cutting back." The Europeans made clear that they would accept no criterion other than "commercial prudence" for those limits, and no hint of economic warfare. As Mitterrand commented to the press, the new commitments would not be permitted to become "an instrument of tension" in relations with the USSR; the objective was "to influence this dialogue with the Soviet Union and not to hinder or prevent it from being carried out."[18] In similar fashion, the Americans explained away their commitment to intervene in the foreign exchange markets, disclaiming any novelty in the final communiqué.

In many respects the NATO meeting of heads of state and government on June 10 was a more impressive demonstration of American-European consensus, since the Reagan administration had come much further toward the European position on arms control in its first year and because the French tended to sympathize with the American position. Indeed, the decision of the French president and prime minister to attend the summit discussions was only the latest evidence of the "Atlanticist" inclinations of the new French government in matters of defense.[19] If the lines of division at Versailles pitted the United States against France and Germany, at Bonn the task was matching German sensibilities and desires for continuing detente policies with American hostility toward those policies. The United States obtained support for its proposals on arms control and condemnation of Soviet actions in Afghanistan and Poland, while the West Germans obtained agreement on "genuine detente" as the aim of East-West relations. In other parts of the NATO communique and in Reagan's public addresses in Western Europe, appeals were made to a European public that had substantially affected American foreign policy, and every effort was made to reinforce the president's image as a man of peace.

Although the president's visit to Europe had not eradicated doubts about his mastery of foreign policy, it seemed to produce a consensus among the elite on some of the points at issue between Europe and the United States: a firmer commitment to arms control while strengthening military forces (how strong those forces needed to be before success in negotiations was left aside), greater caution in East-West economic relations (without making clear whether that caution was simply good business sense or a strategic decision), and at least the appearance of unity (or unified floundering) in the first days of Israel's invasion of Lebanon. But the Israeli invasion and the Falklands imbroglio also demonstrated to the satisfaction of many Europeans that the East-West vision of the Reagan administration was seriously flawed, that the world could no longer be reduced to such a simple Manichaean design, however important an underlying bipolarity remained. More significant, this tenuous reconciliation among the elite appealed to, but could not incorporate, the peace movement in Europe. While Reagan spoke before the German Bundestag, air raid sirens wailed, and across the Rhine, over 300,000 demonstrators gathered to display their resistance to the deployment of nuclear arms in Europe. In Berlin, which John Kennedy had entered like a conquering hero in 1962, Reagan entered as if he were in a hostile camp; despite bans on political demonstrations of any kind, there were still running battles between police and demonstrators. Not only were Reagan's words doubted (one peace movement spokesman declared, "Only when he comes here with a hammer and screwdriver to dismantle nuclear missiles will we believe one word of what he says") the peace movement showed few signs of slowing its momentum, with plans to move from mass demonstations to mass civil disobedience if the deployment of missiles was attempted.[20]

The Pipeline Ban:
The United States Concedes

American representatives at Versailles made clear that no final decision had been made on further American efforts to stop European participation in the Siberian natural gas pipeline. Nevertheless, the State Department had been busily constructing an implicit bargain that seemed to be sealed at Versailles: European willingness to tighten up in some measure on economic transactions with the East in exchange for American willingness to stop its efforts to thwart the pipeline. That implicit bargain, however, was abruptly overturned on June 18, when President Reagan extended the existing American embargo on components for the pipeline to those component manufacturers that were either subsidiaries or licensees of American firms.

The West European response was swift and uniform, since the administration's action had not only reopened the question of economic relations with the Soviet bloc, but added to it the equally sensitive issue of extraterritoriality. The foreign ministers of the European Community, meeting on June 22, displayed a united front in opposition to the ban and to new measures that the United States had taken against European steel exports. They declared that the American measure was probably in violation of international law and would not be upheld by European Community courts. One by one, the European governments set out to compel their firms to disobey the American ban. The United States also raised the stakes, first by threatening and then by imposing its own sanctions on those European firms that continued to participate in the pipeline construction.

Other issues complicated the pipeline dispute as the Versailles consensus disintegrated. Suspension of American action against European steel imports required the concurrence of American steel producers, an agreement that the Reagan administration seemed unable to obtain. Renewed European activity in the Middle East during the Israeli invasion of Lebanon did not at first result in closer convergence of views with the United States. A plan offered by France at the United Nations, calling for Israeli and Palestinian withdrawal from Lebanon, was supported by all of the European members of the Security Council and vetoed by the

United States. The European summit reiterated a formula for peace in the Middle East that had angered the Carter Administration two years earlier: The PLO "should be associated with negotiations" for a Middle East settlement.

Since extension of the pipeline sanctions had figured in the resignation of Secretary of State Alexander Haig, his successor, George Shultz, could not move immediately to reverse the decision. However, the State Department, seconded by the president's economic advisers, finally reconstructed the bargain overturned after Versailles. Domestic pressures in the United States provided support for Shultz's efforts: The House of Representatives passed a resolution opposing the Reagan ban and House Minority Leader Robert Michel discovered that the sanctions did not play in Peoria.

Attempting to disguise its concession as part of a new and tougher joint strategy on East-West economic relations, on November 13 the administration lifted the sanctions applied to American and European firms engaged in building the Siberian gas pipeline. The French government immediately rejected any notion that the American step had been part of a bargain struck with the Europeans. Despite Shultz's claim that, the French had joined in a new consensus on East-West trade in December, the Europeans had accepted no new policy commitments, apart from agreeing to avoid new natural gas contracts with the Soviet Union while studies were being completed.[21] The Shultz-Cheysson announcement only underlined the impression that the economic-warfare view had lost and that the question of trade with the Soviet bloc would be simply studied to death.

The Consequences of Mr. Reagan: Conjunctural Spat or Structural Shift?

Skillful reassertion of the State Department's Atlanticist views under the new Secretary of State seemed to indicate that conflict between the United States and Western Europe was a conjunctural ripple in an essentially stable set of relations. Shultz had managed to defuse the East-West trade issue by papering it over with studies and concentrating on points of likely consensus — tightening the CoCom controls on technology with potential military uses, and applying standards of commercial prudence in granting credits to Eastern bloc economies. In the meantime, recession and the fading credit-worthiness of the Soviet bloc would lend an economic basis to efforts at finessing the opposed points of view.

In the Middle East a new Reagan plan also bore the stamp of the Secretary of State. The sense of movement that it gave following the Israeli invasion of Lebanon and participation of France and Italy in the Lebanese peace-keeping force removed the Arab-Israeli conflict as a point of contention between the United States and Europe. Economic peace had been declared in the steel dispute as well, following European export restraints; and the GATT ministerial meeting, while hardly a tribute to trade liberalization, had not worsened economic disagreements among the industrial countries.

The apparent success of the Shultz strategy seemed to lend strong support to the view that any crisis in relations with Western Europe was conjunctural, resulting from mistaken Reagan administration policies and economic recession. With those two elements changed, conflict would evaporate as it had in the past. Those who espoused the conjunctural view emphasized persistent structural conservatism in the Atlantic alliance — the enduring fact of superpower bipolarity, and the fundamental dependence of Western Europe upon the United States for its security. Following the arguments of Anton DePorte, the Atlantic alliance should continue to provide a framework for American policy toward Europe and a steady assurance of security for the Europeans. In this view economic change — the growing weight of Western Europe in the world economy or the diverging external orientations of the European and American economies — did not have significant spillover effects on the security sphere. For such observers, the current conflict was simply another example of elite division, complemented by popular concern imparted by the loose rhetoric of the Reagan administration. Popular fears of war and particularly nuclear war had appeared in the past in Western Europe: during the "peace campaign" of the Korean War, at the time of the *Kampf dem Atomtod* and the Campaign for Nuclear Disarmament in the late 1950s. European publics behaved rationally: Their mobilization on the issue of peace increased as the perceived risk of conflict between the superpowers increased *and* the probability grew that any war would be nuclear. The Reagan administration had managed to increase both probabilities in the eyes of many Europeans.

Since the rift was a relatively superficial one in this view, the strategies proposed were familiar and minimalist. At the elite level, the favored panacea was increased consultation, perhaps in new organizations.[22] At the popular level, the Reagan administration had to reverse its public relations fiascoes of the first year and to portray itself as the party of peace: a strategy already undertaken in the address of November 18 and the visit to Europe in June. With such policies, a pattern of stability should return to American relations with Europe — until the next patch of turmoil.

Others, however, pointed out that the apparently stable security relationship between the United States and Western Europe in fact masked deeper changes. The achievement of parity by the Soviet Union had produced doubts of American willingness to defend Europe by nuclear means at risk to itself. But that security dependency had also created a parallel fear, fueling the nuclear disarmament movement, that American nuclear weapons could be used to fight a nuclear war *in Europe*. Diverging economic orientations had produced differences in stakes: Western Europe was far more dependent on an assured supply of petroleum from the Middle East; and the European investment in detente — economic and political — was much higher. As a result, Western Europe viewed the Arab-Israeli conflict and relations with the Soviet Union from a different perspective.

Perhaps most significant, and most difficult to assess among structural shifts, are long-term political changes. The democratization of the security debate had already influenced elite divisions; the peace movement encompassed more European societies and had deeper organizational roots than its predecessors. Also, the initial Reagan administration strategy had called forth unusual unity among the Europeans in their dealings with the United States; the new Californian Gaullism called forth collective European Gaullism in response.[23] The European Community served increasingly as a useful forum for developing a joint foreign policy, as its support for Britain in the Falklands crisis had demonstrated. Instead of playing upon European divisions, the Reagan administration, in choosing the issue of East-West trade ensured that the Europeans, including the Thatcher government in Britain, would all stand against its strategy. Such unity was not evident on every issue: Britain — and more surprisingly, socialist France — tended to support the American view of the Soviet threat and necessary defense measures, while the Benelux countries and Germany had proven the most recalcitrant in defending detente policies. To complaints by the German Social Democrats that they were being treated like a colony by the United States, the French Socialists turned a deaf ear. The fact that the French had possessed nuclear weapons for some time and that the new deployment of theater nuclear weapons did not directly concern them were only partial explanations for the position of the new French government and the weakness of the French peace movement. The dynamics of electoral competition explain much more of its anti-Soviet stance: the Socialists were not out of power, competing with an Atlanticist rival (as with the Spanish Socialist Party or the Greek PASOK until its election victory) and, most important, unlike British Labour or the German SPD, the French Socialists were engaged in a continuing battle to reduce the French Communist Party to the status of a fringe political group. Any foreign policy that emphasized the pro-Soviet orientation of the French Communists served that purpose well.[24]

Socialist governments in France and Greece symbolized a final political change, the consequences of which have not yet been fully measured: ideological evolution. The installation of these governments marked an end to the careful balance of center-left and center-right that had characterized European politics in the postwar era. Despite support from France on military questions and its sharp verbal condemnation of the Polish martial-law regime, the French were no more willing than the Germans to join in economic warfare against the East. In many ways the Reagan stance threatened them most directly, since it called into question state intervention in the supply of export credits for Third World and East European markets. Although conflict with the Reagan administration over Central America had subsided, the French were likely to lead the European case against unquestioning American support for Israeli policies in the Middle East should the Reagan plan fail. If a European Gaullism persisted, Socialist France would be at its center.

In the face of such structural changes, three different sets of prescriptions — restoration, devolution, and transformation — have been advanced to bring policy into line with present and future realities.

Restoring American Power: Nostalgia Undefeated

The original strategy of the Reagan administration had offered a simple solution to a perceived drift of Western Europe from the Atlantic alliance: restoring American military power and economic well-being, and reclaiming the role of leadership that had been dropped in the years of retrenchment after Vietnam. Despite the weaknesses in this strategy (described by Kenneth Oye in Chapter 1) and the increased conflict that it had introduced in relations with Western Europe, those who backed restoration had been bowed but undefeated by Reagan administration compromises on arms control and East-West trade. The Defense Department and National Security Council, supported by conservative congressmen, still held to the original strategy in uncompromised form. Despite apparent victory for Shultz's point of view, the ultimate balance within the administration was far from clear.[25] Even Shultz's attitudes were far from an endorsement of the European position. It was George Shultz, after all, who had proclaimed "Santa Claus is dead" after the Nixon shocks of 1971. Although Shultz does not fit the mold of an old Reagan sidekick from Sacramento, his international business connections, like the rest of the administration's "boys from Bechtel," point more toward the Middle East and the Third World than toward Western Europe.

Even if the State Department continues to endorse compromise with the Europeans, an appearance of continuing American concessions might once again win the President to the restorationist point of view. Their winning argument could be the defense budget, which now faces cuts that will impose choices avoided up to this time. As Leslie Gelb has noted, the Reagan budgets have already embodied a strategy of globalization, with the sharpest increases for the Rapid Deployment Force: "This represents a growing shift in priorities toward seapower and a global

maritime strategy and away from land forces and the European theatre." [26] If restorationist views on East-West strategy were not accepted
by the Europeans — and there is little to suggest that they would be —
the Defense Department could provide a strategic rationale and the
budgetary base for a unilateralist position of disengagement from Europe.
The political base for unilateralism would be the Republican right wing,
quiescent as moderation infested the Reagan foreign policy. Certainly
this administration more than any other in recent memory represents a
shift in representation from East Coast Atlanticism toward an orientation
more in tune with the Far West and the South, areas historically less in
touch with Western Europe and its point of view than the Northeast.
Of course, as the pipeline conflict demonstrated, any resurgence of ideological conservatism would make bargaining with the Europeans more
difficult and European unity more likely.

Less Is More:
The Temptations of Devolution

Structural change leads others to recommendations that echo those
of the unilateralists, though the changes would be implemented with
European cooperation and not from pique over rejected leadership. Some
Europeans, witnessing the democratization of the security debate and the
rise of the peace movement, argue that NATO's policy of flexible response is no longer tenable. As an alternative, Lawrence Freedman has
urged "a clear doctrine that both redressed the nuclear bias in NATO
strategy and provided a new approach to the design and deployment of
conventional forces." [27] This group of observers takes the sentiments expressed by the peace movement seriously — the fear of nuclear war in
Europe is real and is not likely to be dissipated by public relations techniques. What is required is a clear strategic shift away from over-depen-
dence on nuclear weapons.

Others see the need for more than a revision in NATO strategy.
Rather than responding to a fear of nuclear war that has resulted from
changes in the nuclear balance and in declared doctrine and military
technology, the European discontent can also be seen as emerging
from the relationship of security dependency itself, the resentment and
sense of helplessness that it induces, and the feeling of being a "colony"
of the United States. To relieve such resentment and to shift defense
burdens in the face of yawning budget deficits in the United States, some
have advocated a division of labor very different from that endorsed by
the Europeans after Afghanistan. The United States would take on the
responsibility for naval and mobile ground forces required to defend
Western interests in the Middle East while the Europeans would assume
a greater share in the defense of Western Europe.[28]

Such arguments are usually coupled with an enlarged role for a

European defense entity, whether based on the Western European Union, a subgroup of NATO, or even on the European Community. Despite the appeal of such a solution, it continues to confront the same obstacles that have been apparent since the 1960s, as recently reviewed by Stanley Hoffmann.[29] The core of such a European defense entity would have to be the French and British nuclear deterrents, but Germany, as the most significant conventional power, would have to be included in decision making without having a hand in controlling or manufacturing nuclear weapons. Some Europeans might also fear that a move to such an independent defense posture would give the United States grounds for a withdrawal from Western Europe. And perhaps most important, a common defense presupposes a common foreign policy of which it is the instrument. Despite the growing displays of unity within the European Community, such a level of common management of defense policy seems well beyond present capabilities.

Arguments for a different division of labor and a common European defense to relieve dependence on the vagaries of American policy can be combined with proposals to narrow the alliance, taking into account diverging European and American interests outside the Atlantic area. These underlying tugs on the alliance could be diminished if it were restricted to a more purely military arrangement in the European theater. The decisions of the Bonn summit suggest, however, a reluctant European acceptance of the need to *widen* the scope of the alliance somewhat since the core problem of energy security lies outside the geographical ambit of traditional NATO concerns. It is also questionable whether a strategy of "less is more" for the alliance would satisfy the domestic political requirements of a coalition that depends on a supply of resources from increasingly hard-pressed national economies. Underlying public support might dry up with a policy of narrowing and distancing, well before any European defense capability had emerged to replace existing structures.

The Peace Movement and Transformation of the European Security System

Even these more radical suggestions do not meet the final set of domestic political criticisms, those advanced by the European peace movement. A nuclear Europe, under European control, would be no more satisfactory than one in which the United States controls Europe's fate. Attitudes within the movement opposing the deployment of new theater nuclear weapons are hardly monolithic; in many respects, the spectrum parallels that just described. Some challenge the Reagan administration's seriousness of intent on arms control; others seek a turn toward a denuclearized Europe through emphasis on conventional defense; still others see the sources of European insecurity in the connection to the

United States itself, and argue for a denuclearized Europe between the superpowers.[30] The peace movement has stimulated the most far-reaching debate on European security and its requirements since World War II; its political presence has already pushed the NATO summit toward an emphasis on the defensive and deterrent function of existing forces and the shifting of defense requirements to conventional weapons. At its core, however, the argument of the peace movement is one of skepticism about deterrence. Instead of a balance of forces that has brought Europe decades of peace and is likely to persist, its spokesmen point to the fragility of other systems of deterrence in the past and the element of chance and miscalculation in the outbreak of international conflict.

The peace movement, which seeks a unified European security sphere absent of nuclear weapons, confronts the old problem of national divisions, East and West: West, in the differing attitudes of the European Left toward military questions that have been evident in the last two years, particularly the contrast between French Socialists and German Social Democrats; East, in the strategy of the peace movement in confronting the irreducible hold of the Soviet Union. A similar grass roots movement of support for new security arrangements cannot exist in the East; the suppression of the Solidarity movement in Poland and the tiny East German and Soviet peace movements suggests an imbalance in political givens that will not be erased. The movement in the West is therefore forced back on one form or another of unilateralism or the acceptance of a purely defensive view of Soviet motivations in defense policy. The movement, particularly in Germany, has also failed to face the paradox that movements such as Solidarity, which might provide the basis for desired grassroots change, also threaten the fabric of detente. The German response to the martial law declaration in Poland evinced a certain relief that the status quo was not endangered.

The choice among predictions and prescriptions ultimately lies in an assessment of the permanence or transience of recent changes in the politics of Western Europe and the United States, just as the present set of disputes can be traced to the turning in American politics since 1979 and the concomitant rise of the European peace movement. It may be that the European popular mobilization will fade as other such movements have in the past, if the Reagan administration offers some progress on arms control and tempers its rhetoric regarding the Soviet Union. The Reagan administration may yet solidify a new political realignment that would provide the base for continuing those conservative policies, particularly on defense and East-West relations, that have produced the existing collision with Western Europe; or the United States may witness yet another turning, a "Europeanization" of the politics of American foreign and defense policy, as described by William Kincaide:

Increasing accuracy, shorter times to target, reduced decision or response time, large numbers of more versatile weapons, and lengthening lists of feasible targets and creating circumstances for Americans similar to those Europeans have experienced for twenty-five years: life at the epicenter of a potential nuclear battlefield where the likelihood of intentional or accidental war is remote, but never quite remote enough.[31]

That sense of increasing risk has already spawned a massive American peace movement parallel to that in Western Europe, which could prod American foreign policy toward convergence with the West Europeans. A heightened sense of risk could also reinforce tendencies toward unilateral or cooperative disengagement from Europe, however. Under a veneer of renewed elite consensus, strategic choices remain in American relations with Western Europe.

Notes

1. The most powerful statement of this point of view is given by Anton DePorte in *Europe Between the Superpowers* (New Haven: Yale University Press, 1979).
2. For the United States, the ratio of oil imports from the AOPEC countries in the late 1970s to domestic production plus imports was about 25%; for the West Europeans, excluding the United Kingdom, the ratio is between 70% and 80%.
3. Accounts of Western disarray after Afghanistan are plentiful. A few examples: George H. Quester, "The Superpowers and the Atlantic Alliance," William G. Hyland, "The Atlantic Crisis," and Robert R. Bowie, "The Atlantic Alliance," in *Daedalus* (Winter 1981), pp. 23-70; Josef Joffe, "European-American Relations — the Enduring Crisis," *Foreign Affairs* 59 (Spring 1981), pp. 835-851; Pierre Hassner, "Moscow and the Western Alliance," *Problems of Communism* 30 (May-June 1981), especially pp. 48-49.
4. See Chapter 7 in this volume.
5. Helmut Schmidt, "The Alastair Buchan Memorial Lecture," *Survival* 20 (January/February 1978), pp. 3-4.
6. For an excellent account and criticism of the military justifications for the deployment, followed by tempered support on the ground that the deployment would contribute to strengthening deterrence and increasing survivability: Christoph Bertram, "The Implications of Theatre Nuclear Weapons in Europe," *Foreign Affairs* 60 (Winter, 1981-1982), pp. 307-309; on the problem of Soviet pre-emption and survivability, Jeffrey Record, "Theatre Nuclear Weapons: Begging the Soviet Union to Pre-Empt," *Survival* 19 (September/October 1977), pp. 208-211; the LRTNF decision has been scathingly criticized by Michael Howard and by McGeorge Bundy. For a telling critique by the latter, "America in the 1980s: Reframing Our Relations with Our Friends and Among Our Allies," *Survival* 24 (January/February 1982), pp. 24-28.

7. Bertram, "The Implications of Theatre Nuclear Weapons in Europe," p. 308. Why such systems would provide more coupling than the fate of several hundred thousand American soldiers attacked by nuclear weapons remains a puzzle.

8. Josef Joffe, "German Defense Policy: Novel Solution and Enduring Dilemmas," in Gregory Flynn (ed.), *The Internal Fabric of Western Security* (London: Croom Helm, 1981), pp. 87-88.

9. Bertram, "The Implications of Theatre Nuclear Weapons in Europe," p. 309.

10. For example, the comments by Richard Perle, Assistant Secretary of Defense for International Security Policy, *The New York Times*, November 22, 1981, p. 2E.

11. Excerpts from the speech are reprinted in *Survival* 24 (March/April 1982) pp. 87-89.

12. McGeorge Bundy, George F. Kennan, Robert S. McNamara and Gerard Smith, "Nuclear Weapons and the Atlantic Alliance," 60 (Spring 1982), pp. 765-766.

13. The author is grateful to Kenneth Oye for this tripartite categorization of American justifications.

14. Interview with James Reston, *The New York Times*, January 3, 1982, p. 14.

15. Hanns W. Maull, *Natural Gas and Economic Security* (Paris: Atlantic Institute for International Affairs, 1981), p. 49. Maull's account is perhaps the best defense of the pipeline decision, although combined with cautions and recommendations for measures to guard against Soviet leverage. For a more skeptical American view, see Thomas Blau and Joseph Kirchheimer, "European Dependence and Soviet Leverage: the Yamal Pipeline," *Survival*, 23 (September/October 1981), pp. 209-214.

16. Leslie H. Gelb, *International Herald Tribune*, February 4, 1982, p. 2.

17. See the accounts by Hedrick Smith, *International Herald Tribune*, June 8, 1982, and John Wyles, *Financial Times*, June 7, 1982.

18. The French were also pleased that the "limiting" was not defined quantitatively, as the Americans had wished, and that the agreement for periodic review of East-West transactions had not found its way into the communiqué. Paul Fabra, "Certains ambiguïtés demeurent sur les questions monétaires et commerciales," *Le Monde*, June 8, 1982, p. 4.

19. For the highly orthodox statements of Mauroy at the meetings, see *Le Monde*, June 12, 1982.

20. Report by Patricia Clough in *The Times (London)*, June 18, 1982; John Vinocur of *The New York Times* offers a different point of view, emphasizing the divisions in the movement over Reagan's visit, and the distancing of some church groups from the demonstrations (*New York Times*, June 3, 1982, p. A10).

21. John Vinocur, "Few New Pledges in Pact, Allies Say," *The New York Times*, pp. A1, A25; Bernard Gwertzman, "U.S. and France Agree on Strategy for Handling Trade with Moscow," *The New York Times*, 15 December 1982, pp. A1, A13.

22. For example, see Karl Kaiser, *et al.*, *Western Security: What has changed? What should be done?* (New York: Council on Foreign Relations, 1981).

23. The observation of resurgent "Gaullism," on both sides of the Atlantic, is made by André Fontaine, "Tous gaullistes!" *Le Monde*, July 6, 1982, pp. 1, 6.

24. A similar explanation can be given for the Italian Socialist Party's anti-Soviet and Atlanticist positions: governing status plus Communist rival.

25. Hedrick Smith, "Reagan forced by events abroad to temper his hard-line policies," *The New York Times*, January 22, 1982, pp. A1, 8. Smith describes the multilateralist vs. unilateralist split in the administration.

26. Leslie H. Gelb, *The New York Times*, February 7, 1982.

27. Lawrence Freedman, "NATO Myths," *Foreign Policy* (Number 45, Winter 1981-1982), p. 67.
28. Two contributions to the debate between advocates of traditional coalition defense and those who favor a new division of labor are Robert W. Komer, "Maritime Strategy vs. Coalition Defense," *Foreign Affairs*, 60, 5 (Summer 1982), 1124-1144, and Admiral Stansfield Turner and Captain George Thibault, "Preparing for the Unexpected: The Need for a New Military Strategy," *Foreign Affairs*, 61, 1 (Fall 1982), 122-135.
29. Stanley Hoffmann, "NATO and Nuclear Weapons: Reasons and Unreason," *Foreign Affairs* 60 (Winter 1981/1982), pp. 327-346.
30. For the views of one wing of the peace movement, which argues for a European security system independent of the superpowers, see Edward Thompson, "Notes on Exterminism, the Last Stage of Civilization," *New Left Review* 121; and contributions of Lucio Magri, Rudolf Bahro, and Ken Coates in *New Left Review*, 131 (January-February 1982), pp. 5-43. Also see Alan Wolfe, "Europe in Search of Autonomy," *The Nation* (February 27, 1982), pp. 226, 241-244.
31. William H. Kincaide, "Over the Technological Horizon," *Daedalus* 110 (Winter 1981), p. 125.

10

Ronald Reagan and Latin America: Coping with Hegemony in Decline

Abraham F. Lowenthal

Ronald Reagan and his administration came to Washington determined to improve United States relations with Latin America and to restore the predominance of the United States in the Western Hemisphere. During its first few months, the Reagan administration devoted very significant attention — rhetorical, political, and economic — to Latin America: to El Salvador and Central America generally; to Cuba and the whole Caribbean; to Mexico; and to Argentina, Brazil, and Chile. As had been true of Jimmy Carter's administration and of John F. Kennedy's, President Reagan's new team concentrated a high share of its foreign policy concern on the Americas during its first year.

By the end of 1982, however, United States relations with Latin America and the Caribbean were as troubled as ever, if not more so. Having set out to reverse the decline of United States hegemony in the Western Hemisphere, the Reagan administration encountered sharp limits on the exercise of United States power in Latin America and the Caribbean, including some limits resulting from its own policies.

It is impossible to know how the Reagan administration will ultimately respond to the accumulating evidence that hemispheric frictions are intensifying and that United States dominance is on the wane. Internal deliberations within the administration, triggered first by the South Atlantic war between Argentina and Great Britain and then affected by the substitution of George Shultz for Alexander Haig as Secretary of State, have already caused some shifts in policy. President Reagan's own trip to

Abraham F. Lowenthal, former director of studies at the Council on Foreign Relations, heads the Latin American program at the Woodrow Wilson International Center for Scholars in Washington. Dr. Lowenthal has also worked at Harvard, Brookings, Princeton, and the Ford Foundation. His publications include The Dominican Intervention, The Peruvian Experiment, *and numerous articles.*

Latin America in December 1982 seemed to portend further changes, but it is not yet clear how far these will go.

What can already be analyzed, however, is the Reagan administration's approach toward Latin America and the Caribbean during its first two years in office: its initial character and underlying premises, its evolution, and its immediate effects.

II

On no other foreign policy issue was the contrast between the opening stance of Ronald Reagan's administration and the initial posture of Jimmy Carter's sharper than with regard to Latin America and the Caribbean.

The Carter administration came to office in 1977 intent on reshaping inter-American relations.[1] From the start, it focused on what it took to be the key issues in the hemisphere, issues deriving from a changed international context: the diffusion of power, "detente" with the Soviet Union, and the rising importance of North-South relations.

The Carter administration gave immediate priority to trying to improve United States relations with Latin America by recognizing Panama's sovereignty over the Canal Zone. Almost as early, the administration began to explore the prospects for moving, on a measured and reciprocal basis, toward renewing United States relations with Fidel Castro's Cuba. It sought to convey more broadly an increased tolerance for ideological pluralism in Latin America, even in the Caribbean and Central America; Mrs. Carter's friendly visit to confer with Jamaica's Prime Minister Michael Manley symbolized the new approach. The new administration also indicated its aim to improve bilateral relations with Mexico; the coincidence of new presidents in Washington and in Mexico City provided a special opportunity to do so.

The Carter administration moved forcefully to show its concern with protecting fundamental human rights, to try to disassociate the United States from authoritarian repression, and to build closer relations with the region's democratic forces. It also signaled that it wished to respond positively to Latin American views on a host of North-South issues with mainly economic content but significant political overtones: trade, aid, finance, and technology transfer. More generally, the Carter administration moved away from the concept of a regional "special relationship" with Latin America that had so often in practice masked paternalistic, discriminatory, and even interventionist treatment. Rather, the new administration announced it would deal with underlying hemispheric problems in a global context — but without mindlessly projecting back to the region extrahemispheric concerns not relevant to the Americas. It promised to fashion new policies to respond to changing world and regional realities. In Latin America — as in Africa, Europe, and Asia — the Carter foreign policy began by seeking to adjust to underlying transformations in international affairs. The president himself decried past policies that reflected an "inordinate fear of Communism" and urged concentration instead on more fundamental issues: promoting economic development, conserving energy and other resources, protecting human rights, curbing nuclear proliferation, limiting arms races, and keeping the peace.

As the Carter administration's policies toward Latin America were implemented, however, notable gaps emerged between rhetoric and actions.

Washington's desire to win Latin American cooperation for dealing with major global problems turned out to be tangible mainly with regard to those issues the United States itself deemed most urgent, especially energy, narcotics, and nuclear nonproliferation. The issues that most deeply concerned many Latin American countries — improved access for middle-income countries to the markets, capital, and technology of advanced industrial countries; more automatic and generous concessional aid to the least advantaged countries; more predictable and favorable returns to developing countries from international trade in commodities; more responsiveness by multinational corporations to the interests of host countries — got short shrift. Concessional resource flows from the United States and other industrial countries to support economic growth in Latin America failed to expand, and the administration's "basic human rights" approach called for most of Latin America to be weaned from further aid. A proposal to increase assistance for Caribbean development was adopted but then cut back sharply in the administration's budgetary process. Specific United States decisions — to raise tariffs on imported sugar, to sell surplus tin from the government stockpiles in order to lower the price, to deny certain airline routes to Latin American carriers, and to tighten tax regulations regarding exemptions for business conventions abroad — hurt Latin American and Caribbean countries considerably. On matters of dollars and cents, the Carter administration produced, in sum, small change.

On other issues, too, the Carter administration's policies evolved away from their original articulation. The announced intent to improve relations with Mexico was largely undercut by unilateral and even peremptory United States decisions on immigration and on natural gas, and it was further frustrated by maladroit presidential diplomacy. Relations with Cuba soon reverted to frostiness, especially after Cuban forces entered Ethiopia and the United States belatedly "discovered" that Soviet combat troops were stationed on the island. The administration's initially cautious response to Central America's revolutionary movements, particularly in Nicaragua, gave way over time to an increasingly hostile approach. The immediate United States reaction to Grenada's leftist coup in 1979 was, for the most part, antagonistic. And the Carter administration's attempts to distance the United States from South America's "bureaucratic authoritarian" regimes and to support processes of redemocratization — important in their specific impact on several countries — were eventually soft-pedaled as Washington sought ways to reinforce what it regarded as improved performance on human rights issues and also to prevent tensions over human rights from overwhelming the pursuit of other United States objectives.[2]

By the time the Carter administration left office in January 1981, it had retreated considerably toward earlier United States policies. The president's decision on January 15 (just five days before leaving office) to provide military assistance to El Salvador's embattled government highlighted this return, but the trend had already been unmistakable: as implemented over time, the Carter administration's policies toward Latin America turned out not to be very different from previous United States approaches.

III

The incoming Reagan administration and its principal campaign advisers on Latin American policy did not criticize the Carter regime for failing to implement fully its initially innovative approach to Western Hemisphere affairs. On the contrary, the new administration's advisers made it clear — both in what they wrote before the election and in what they said and did soon after taking office — that they fundamentally rejected the original Carter approach, which they saw as misguided, vacillating, and counterproductive. Even more so than in most other foreign policy areas, the new administration deliberately fashioned policies toward Latin America designed to reverse what they saw as the self-defeating thrust of Carter's new policies.

Although Ronald Reagan as a candidate had vigorously opposed the Panama Canal treaties — and although prominent Reagan supporter Senator Jesse Helms, the lone member of the Senate Foreign Relations Committee to vote against them, now became chairman of the committee's Western Hemisphere Subcommittee — the new administration did not move to undo the Panama accords.

The Reagan team did attempt drastic change on many other matters, however. The Carter administration's early interest in North-South issues and in economic problems was replaced by a primary concern with East-West issues, a focus on security questions, and a decision to play down the concerns of developing countries. This shift was epitomized by the Reagan administration's decisions to neglect substantive global negotiations, to vote against imposing an advertising code for infant formula, and especially to reject the long-negotiated Law of the Seas Treaty. The

Carter administration's early initial tolerance (at least in some sectors of the administration) of ideological diversity in the hemisphere gave way to a uniform insistence by Washington on the advantages of political and ideological harmony in the Americas, including support for private enterprise, the free market, and United States investment.

For the Carter administration's initiative to improve relations with Cuba, the Reagan administration substituted stark threats to punish Havana, which was portrayed as the "source" of violence and instability in Central America and the Caribbean. The Carter emphasis on human rights was replaced by a primary concern with non-state terrorism and by a desire to quickly patch up frayed United States relations with the authoritarian regimes of the Southern Cone. Finally, President Reagan and his new team decried the Carter administration's "globalism." The president himself, during his campaign, had called for a "North American accord" to institutionalize special relations with Mexico and Canada. The new administration began soon to explore preferential arrangements with Central America and the Caribbean nations. Some within the government called for a resurrection of the inter-American system and pan-American harmony.

The Reagan administration, thus, initially promised a sharp course correction in the United States approach to Latin America and the Caribbean, perhaps the most dramatic of the twentieth century. In concepts, rhetoric, personnel, and incipient implementation, the Reagan administration in 1981 began radically to reverse United States policy.[3]

This major shift was foreshadowed in several essays and reports published before January 1981 by persons who subsequently entered the new administration.[4] The basic thrust of these several essays was that Carter's policies had contributed to undermining United States influence in the hemisphere by destabilizing friendly governments (including Somoza's in Nicaragua), by alienating major nations (such as Brazil), and by facilitating the spread of Cuban and Soviet influence. The Carter approach was attacked for its supposed bias in favor of Latin American leftist movements, for its "utopian" pursuit of human rights concerns in alleged disregard of regional political realities and of United States interests, and for its apparent eschewal of available instruments for the direct and indirect exercise of United States influence. Several argued that the Carter administration's views and those of the liberal "Establishment" from which many of Carter's top foreign policy advisers had been recruited paralleled those of the New Left.[5] Some even seemed to suggest that the Carter approach had actually been crafted by leftists in order to advance Cuban and Soviet aims.[6]

Whatever their views on the ultimate aims of the Carter entourage, various commentators who eventually entered the Reagan government agreed that the Carter approach had accelerated the decline of United

States power in the hemisphere. They called for new policies: to assert and protect United States ideological influence; to build more solid alliances with like-minded forces; to contain and reduce perceived Cuban and Soviet inroads in the hemisphere; and to strengthen inter-American institutions. Rather than accommodate to international and hemispheric tendencies they regarded as disagreeable, these advisers recommended energetic measures to reverse undesirable trends.

A combination of urgency and anticipatory exhilaration characterized much of this writing. The *Report of the Committee of Santa Fe* — written by five specialists, of whom Roger Fontaine, General Gordon Sumner, and Lewis Tambs entered the new administration — warned that World War III was already underway, that Latin America was the "soft underbelly" of the United States, and that the region was in danger of being overcome by Soviet-Cuban advances. The report called for bold steps — even for launching a "war of national liberation" against Fidel Castro.

Other experts, outside the "Santa Fe group," shared these basic concerns. Jeane Kirkpatrick, soon to be appointed Ambassador to the United Nations, was much more circumspect in expression; but she, too, outlined "serious vulnerabilities" in the hemisphere; Kirkpatrick declared that "one of the first and most urgent tasks of the Reagan administration will be to revise the U.S. approach to Latin America and the Caribbean" in order to reverse the deterioration of United States influence.[7] Constantine Menges, months before being appointed Western Hemisphere National Intelligence Officer, argued that an "enormous failure of political will and prudence has resulted in the establishment of governments in Grenada and Nicaragua that are now nearly under complete Marxist-Leninist control" and that these developments and others like them pose an "urgent, specific danger to the security of the United States."[8]

The Reagan administration began its tenure aiming to reverse United States policies toward Latin America and the Caribbean. Having attacked Carter during the electoral campaign for "losing" Nicaragua, the new administration saw evidence that some of the arms used in the January 1981 "final offensive" by the Salvadoran left had been provided externally as proof of its fears that United States softness under Carter had paved the way for Communist gains.[9] Secretary of State Alexander Haig, with one eye on Central America and the other on his standing with the administration's core constituency, pointedly drew a line in El Salvador and affirmed that resisting leftist insurrectionaries there by whatever means necessary was a "vital interest" of the United States. Implicitly and even explicitly, the administration suggested that military force could not be excluded as a United States option in Central America or Cuba. A blitz of diplomatic and informational activity revealed that the new administration aimed not only to halt what it characterizes as a "textbook case of Soviet aggression" but to use El Salvador to show its own resolve and effectiveness. The process of leftist advance in Central America would be decisively reversed.

Within weeks, the Reagan administration began taking steps designed to isolate and to intimidate the fledgling revolutionary regime in Nicaragua led by the Sandinistas; United States aid was delayed and then suspended, anti-Sandinista paramilitary groups were allowed to train in Florida, and clandestine United States "destabilization" measures against Nicaragua were not only reported in the press but were explicitly not denied by administration spokesmen.[10] Secretary Haig warned that the United States would "go to the source" (that is, to Cuba) to prevent further leftist advances in Central America, and administration representatives revealed that a broad range of possible anti-Cuba measures, including the use of force, were being studied. A major effort to support the Jamaican regime of Edward Seaga — pro-United States, anti-Cuba, and market-oriented — was rapidly put into place. The newly elected Jamaican leader was invited to Washington as Reagan's first official state visitor, and plans were unveiled to provide major infusions of aid and to stimulate and facilitate private capital flows.

Within its first year, the new administration moved on many other fronts as well. Several officials who had been influential in implementing the Carter policies toward Central America — including senior career foreign service officers — were purged from the service, thus breaking with a long-standing bipartisan approach.[11] New personnel were appointed, including a number of political appointees presumably imbued with the administration's ideological approach to hemispheric affairs, as well as several career diplomats without significant previous experience in Latin America, apparently chosen because they were not committed to or implicated in previous policy.[12] Personnel decisions were followed, too, by budget choices, including a major emphasis on security-related assistance and a correspondingly increased reliance on private investment to transfer resources for economic development.[13]

The administration's initial moves to revise human rights policies were equally decisive. Even though the president's first nominee for the post of human rights coordinator, Professor Ernest Lefever, was forced to withdraw his name because of congressional opposition, the nomination signaled the administration's intent to transform United States policies on human rights, to concentrate more on abuses in Communist countries and less on those in friendly authoritarian regimes. Washington lifted its previous ban on Export-Import Bank loans to Chile, invited Chile to participate again in the joint naval exercises from which the Carter administration had excluded it on human rights grounds, moved early toward eliminating Congressional restrictions on military aid and sales to Argentina, Chile, and Uruguay, and indicated its desire to do the same for Guatemala.

Special efforts were undertaken quickly to improve United States relations with several countries and regions. Ronald Reagan's personal aim to focus on Mexico was reflected in his unprecedented preinaugural visit there to confer with President José López Portillo, and in his four summit meetings during 1981 with the Mexican leader. The administration's strong desire to restore harmonious relations with Brazil led to an early visit by Vice President George Bush to Brasilia and to the vice president's announcement that the United States would not invoke penalty clauses against Brazil in connection with refueling the Angora I nuclear reactor. The effort to woo Argentina included not only visits to Buenos Aires by key Reagan troubleshooters and talk of forming a "South Atlantic Community," which would also have included South Africa, but also the administration's embrace of the newly installed (and ultimately short-lived) Argentine president Roberto Viola and its warm hospitality to future president Leopoldo Galtieri. And the administration's hope to strengthen United States relations with the Caribbean was illustrated not only by the support extended to Seaga but also by its active consideration of a possible "mini-Marshall Plan" for the Caribbean, a concept originally advanced by Seaga himself.

By the middle of 1981, then, the Reagan administration had begun to implement a distinctive approach to inter-American relations. The administration's concepts, objectives, premises, and instruments had been set forth. The new government was neither neglecting Latin America and the Caribbean, nor simply continuing past policies.

IV

By late 1982, however, the Reagan administration's policies toward Latin America and the Caribbean had evolved in important respects. In their implementation — and even often in their iteration — the new administration's specific measures have turned out to be much less radically different from preceding lines than at first appeared likely. Some important differences between the Reagan and Carter approaches remain, to be sure — and these should be emphasized — but they have not been nearly as sharp as campaign rhetoric or early official formulations had suggested.[14]

In El Salvador, for example, the possibility of United States direct military intervention has for all practical (and rhetorical) purposes been eliminated as a policy option. The Reagan administration, despite its criticisms of the Carter policies, has continued the Carter approach of supporting El Salvador's centrists, especially reformist elements of the military and the Christian Democrats, against opposition from the left and right. The Reagan administration's stance has turned out to be so similar to the earlier United States posture that United States Ambassador Deane Hinton was vigorously attacked in late 1982 by the Salvadoran right for being allegedly indistinguishable from former Ambassador Robert White, whose resignation the Reagan administration had demanded within its first weeks.[15]

The administration's systematic review of its options for undertaking overt or clandestine actions against Cuba apparently led to a judgment that feasible steps are strictly limited. Both those who decry the United States government's failure to act forcefully against Fidel Castro and those who believe the United States should move toward normalizing its relations with Cuba agree that the Reagan policy has not amounted to any significant departure from previous approaches.[16]

Hostile United States policies toward Nicaragua and Grenada, evident by the end of the Carter period, have continued and intensified under Reagan, but they have stopped short so far of decisive counter-revolutionary activity, despite Nicaragua's major arms build up and Grenada's increasingly public relationship with the Soviet Union. Clandestine action against these countries appears to be significant, but there are some signs that also this aspect of the Reagan administration's posture may be altering — as has much of the rhetoric of confrontation.[17]

Other features of the original Reagan approach have also been attenuated. Various congressionally mandated legal and administrative restrictions on United States military and economic assistance to Argentina, Chila, Uruguay, and Guatemala are still in effect, though some provisions have been circumvented and the administration apparently aims to lift others. The Caribbean Basin Initiative — President Reagan's salient new foreign policy proposal during his first year and a half — evolved from its first articulation so that it becomes less single-mindedly anti-Communist and considerably more development oriented than was initially apparent. The Initiative was whittled down, moreover, from a "mini-Marshall Plan" to a much more modest set of measures, and from a multilateral effort to a series of loosely linked unilateral schemes.

What had begun early in 1981 as a radical reversal of United States policy toward Latin America and the Caribbean thus did not seem so overwhelming a change by the end of 1982. Both the early Carter policies and the early Reagan approach seemed to depart from the previous norms of United States policy, albeit in different directions, but they were both modified in similar ways, gravitating back toward a center course.

Perhaps even more significant, the decline of United States influence in the Western Hemisphere — so forcefully lamented by the Reagan administration's key advisers — had, if anything, accelerated. Cuba, far from succumbing to United States pressures, found itself somewhat less isolated by late 1982 than it had been for several years, partly as a result of the South Atlantic crisis. José Napoleón Duarte's loss in the March 1982 elections in El Salvador showed how limited United States leverage is in that country and further diminished United States influence. The United States presence in Nicaragua and Grenada continues to be minimal, and Soviet ties with both countries have steadily strengthened. Nicaragua's election to the United Nations Security Council in November 1982 represented a major diplomatic setback for Washington, as did the support Nicaragua obtained from several key Latin American nations. Steps to improve United States relations with Argentina gave way to intensified embitterment after the South Atlantic crisis. Relations with Venezuela were strained by the South Atlantic war as well as by differences over Central America and even Puerto Rico. Colombia's new president Belisario Betancur, elected in 1982, moved quickly after his inauguration to distance his administration from the United States, at least at the symbolic and diplomatic level. President Reagan's visit to Brazil in December 1982 significantly improved the climate for United States-Brazil relations but even so tended to underline how many unresolved substantive clashes the two countries face: on energy, tariffs and subsidies, nontariff barriers, international monetary policy, and other economic conflicts.[18] Relations with Mexico face new tests as Mexico begins to cope with its severe financial crisis and fears of United States efforts to exploit it; deep divisions over Central American and Caribbean policy have already been evident. Curiously, the most notable improvement in United States relations with a Western Hemisphere nation during the Reagan administration's first two years was with Jamaica, precisely the country with which the Carter administration had managed a dramatic rapprochement during its first two years, but the latest improvement might well be as fragile as the one four years earlier.[19]

V

What accounts for the fact that both the Carter and the Reagan administrations began with bold, innovative, and contrasting policies toward Latin America — and that each so quickly retreated from its initiative? And what explains the evident failure of both administrations to arrest the decline of United States influence in the Americas, or even to reduce inter-American frictions?

The first step toward answering these questions is to note that both administrations are repeating an old pattern.[20] Whether calling its approach a Good Neighbor Policy, an Alliance for Progress, a Mature Partnership, a New Dialogue, or a Caribbean Basin Initiative — or pointedly eschewing labels, as Carter did — one United States administration after another has promised to improve United States-Latin American relations. Always goaded by a period of perceived tensions in hemispheric relations and often responsive to domestic political exigencies, successive administrations have announced new policies, pledged greater attention to the region, vowed their support for Latin America's development, and expressed their interest in the region's political evolution.

The next phase in this historic cycle has generally seen the newly expressed policy toward Latin America vitiated. Despite promises that Latin American interests will receive enhanced consideration, they are slighted or contravened. Despite United States pretense of consultation and negotiation, Latin Americans find themselves victims of unilateral decisions taken in the United States. Despite the hoopla of state visits, efforts to improve bilateral relations between the United States and individual Latin American countries often founder on the shoals of specific disagreements.

The Carter period fits this classic mode: the attenuation of human rights pressures, the failure to make significant progress on trade and commodity negotiations and the lack of effective follow-up on technology transfer proposals, the sugar tariff increase, the persistent imposition of countervailing duties, the sale of surplus tin, the curtailing of Carter's proposed aid program for the Caribbean, the retreat from attempted rapprochement with Cuba, the unilateral proposals to deal with undocumented aliens, and the turn toward a more conservative stance in Central America.

The Reagan period so far closely follows the same pattern, despite its radically different initial premises. Like the Carter administration, the Reagan government has backed off from its initial stance on key issues. It has diluted its boldest initiatives, undertaken some measures directly contradictory to others, and failed to follow up effectively precisely on the measures potentially of greatest interest to Latin America. Central American policy, the Caribbean Basin Initiative, human rights policy and relations with the Southern Cone countries, trade and tariff policies, sugar policy: all illustrate the return toward previous lines.

Why does the resolve of new United States administrations to improve inter-American relations repeatedly come to naught? What can we learn from the experiences of the Carter and Reagan administrations?

First, focusing on Latin American policy as such tends to obscure what should be obvious: Many United States government actions importantly affecting Latin America are not taken for that purpose at all but are initiated in other policy arenas, domestic or foreign, with little or no consideration of their likely impact in the hemisphere. Examples are plentiful. A one percent fluctuation in the interest rate in the United States is estimated to affect Brazil's annual current account deficit to the extent of $400-500 million. A domestically motivated United States decision on sugar quotas makes a crucial difference to the Dominican Republic and affects several other nations as well. Protectionist legislation on textiles hurts Mexico, the Caribbean, and Peru. Sales of tin or silver from United States government stockpiles significantly affect Bolivia and Peru. These and many other decisions — on energy, trade, money, arms transfers, agriculture, and a host of other issues — are typically taken with little consideration of their regional effects and with little input by United States government personnel primarily working on inter-American affairs. Those within the administration devoted to hemispheric affairs may sincerely push for alternate policies. That they usually fail reflects the relative lack of real priority for improving regional relations, official rhetoric to the contrary notwithstanding. Other interests of the United States ultimately outweigh those involved in inter-American relations. The decision by Peru's president Fernando Belaúnde to cancel his state visit to the United States in November 1982 because of the scheduled imposition of countervailing duties on Peruvian textile exports poignantly illustrates this point.

A second observation, equally obvious but also often ignored, is that much of inter-American relations is shaped by a multiplicity of non-governmental forces that no administration can easily control. Multinational corporations, labor unions, commercial banks, universities and research institutes, church groups, even private individuals: all operate within an overall structure powerfully influenced by past and present United States government decisions. Still, what the United States government decides to do (or to refrain from doing) in Latin America cannot by itself alter the main impact of the United States as a whole. Paradoxically, it is much easier for the United States government to manage this country's relations with Russia or with China than with Chile, Peru, or especially with Mexico. Latin American and Caribbean countries are much influenced by decisions taken by United States companies and banks, by investors, by labor unions, by tourists, and by the media. Many of the main issues in inter-American relations, moreover — especially access to capital, markets, and technology — are matters on which the United States government has considerably less influence than non-governmental actors.

Several other reasons for the contrast between an administration's announced intentions and its subsequent actions also have to do with the process of policy making.

First, within the executive branch, policy emerges over time from a process of struggle among three main sources: those with primary control of "declaratory" policy, those who specialize on regional issues, and those who work primarily on functional matters.

Those who shape "declaratory" policy — the National Security Council staff, the president's personal advisers and speechwriters, and the State Department's policy planners — are typically recruited from outside the permanent bureaucracy and may indeed be chosen precisely because of their political or ideological affinity with the newly elected leadership. These new policy makers are determined to distinguish themselves from and to outdo their predecessors; they bring with them concepts forged in task forces and reflected in their own individual writing. The recruits draw on this background to draft policy directives and presidential speeches. They contribute quickly at precisely the point in the policy making process at which their access is greatest, and at the time of their maximum influence.

The new recruits' zealous advocacy of new policy directions is predictably opposed by the career bureaucracy, including regional and functional specialists. The regional specialists tend to "represent" the countries of Latin America in pushing for continuity of United States policies. The functional specialists work year in and year out on the issues that comprise the warp and woof of inter-American relations: trade, finance, investment, migration, and security. Their views tend not to be changed much by partisan transitions or political considerations, and they, too, tend to push for continuity. The career bureaucracy's capacity to restrain new initiatives is considerable, especially after an administration's first few months. Passive resistance, especially by regional specialists, accounts in significant measure for the tendency of new initiatives to give way to old habits.

Finally, the bureaucratic imperatives toward continuity are reinforced by the learning process new personnel engage in, as at least some of them come to see issues in more complex terms. As new officials involve themselves in dealing with real problems in the context of trade-offs, deadlines, and myriad pressures, they absorb the accumulated experience of past administrations.

These process-related reasons why new Latin American policies tend to fade away are further reinforced by the role of Congress, by the broader involvement of nongovernment actors in policy making, by the role of public opinion, and by the influence of international pressures, especially from allies.

The legislative branch influences Latin American policy through general legislation (often adopted, again, without seriously considering its effects on the hemisphere), as well as by taking up particular issues in inter-American relations. The assertive role Congress has played in foreign policy making since the Vietnam War has been particularly evident on Latin American policy issues, such as aid to El Salvador, human rights certification processes, and the licensing of Radio Martí. By a curious but logical "reverse pendulum" effect, Congress tends to combat whatever new policy directions the administration moves in and thus to reinforce continuity of approach.[21]

Trade policy, human rights, agriculture, arms transfers, foreign aid — these and other matters important in the hemisphere are strongly influenced by Congress. Almost any new policy initiative must run the gauntlet of congressional scrutiny, influenced by constituent pressures of all sorts, before it can be adopted. Few proposals survive this ordeal unscathed. President Reagan's Caribbean Basin Initiative — amended, whittled down, and delayed by Congress — illustrates the process.

Broad and consistent shifts in United States policy — toward Latin America and toward many issues — are also hard to achieve because private interests can pursue their particular claims through so many differing access points. A proposed measure that penalizes some well-organized group — copper companies, sugar or citrus growers, shoe manufacturers, auto or textile workers, church groups, or whatever — can be shelved by a blocking coalition within the highly fragmented structure of United States foreign policy making. Although the proposed change may promise substantially to benefit United States society as a whole, a group likely to be influenced often can prevent the measure's adoption; the history of sugar tariffs and quotas amply illustrates this point. Nor does it necessarily require congressional action to frustrate an administration's initiatives; sustained criticism in the media, criticism by church groups, or other evidence of public disapproval may serve to restrain the Executive directly, as seems to have occurred in 1981, at least to some extent, regarding El Salvador.

An administration may, therefore, take office thinking that a new policy toward Latin America is urgent but it may not be able to sustain its resolve when it is faced with the proliferating crises United States foreign policy encounters each year. The record of the Carter and Reagan periods suggests that efforts to focus on inter-American relations are easily overwhelmed by other priorities, domestic and foreign.

All of these internal reasons for a tendency to dilute new policy initiatives toward Latin America have been further reinforced, especially during the Reagan administration, by the influence of external pressures, including those of close allies. The Reagan administration encountered strong resistance from both European and Latin American allies to its initial formulation of a Latin American policy. France, Germany, Mexico, Venezuela, and other nations opposed the original Reagan approach, especially toward Central America, and have both pressured and cajoled for a more moderate United States stance.[22] The Reagan administration, learning that unilateral fiat no longer works in the Americas, has had to take these representations into account.

Even when a new policy is formally adopted, an administration must assure its full implementation at all levels of sharply divergent bureaucracies. To be sure that all segments of the United States government will cooperate to put a new policy fully into effect, an administration must be willing to give the policy significant and sustained priority. A number of agencies need to be coordinated: the State, Treasury, and Defense Departments, the Departments of Agriculture, Commerce, Energy, and Justice, the Central Intelligence Agency, the Export-Import Bank, the Civil Aeronautics Board, and so on. Constant monitoring, innovative coordination, and energetic follow-up are required. That kind of priority is, and necessarily must be, rare.

VI

Domestic and international imperatives, then, cause one new United States administration after another to seek a new approach to hemispheric policy. Domestic, international, and bureaucratic factors combine in predictable ways, however, to frustrate these initiatives. United States-Latin American relations, therefore, are not much improved by promised transformations of United States policy. Indeed, they continue to be difficult and even to deteriorate.

The underlying reason why inter-American tensions continue to accumulate goes well beyond the shortfalls of the announced United States policies, however. The fundamental flaw of United States policy toward Latin America and the Caribbean during the past twenty years is not so much the failure to implement announced new policies as the failure ever to deal, except at the rhetorical level, with the underlying tendency of contemporary inter-American relations: the redistribution of power. The unmet challenge of United States policy during the past twenty years has been how to respond to the erosion of the brief postwar period of virtually unchallenged dominance in the Western Hemisphere — how to cope with hegemony in decline.[23]

United States influence in Latin America reached its apogee after World War II, when the striking global predominance the United States had achieved on many different dimensions of power was particularly evident in the Western Hemisphere. United States investment displaced that of Britain and Germany, and the United States became the dominant trading partner of most Latin American nations. The cultural presence of the United States steadily increased. The United States achieved a virtual monopoly of military advisory missions, and it supplied almost all the region's arms. Washington extended to all of Latin America the "hegemonic presumption" previously confined to the Caribbean basin, and the United States involved itself deeply in South American domestic politics. The interAmerican system, meanwhile, was institutionalized, both to legitimize United States influence and to limit the effects of United States dominance.

During the past generation, however, the countries of Latin America have become increasingly assertive, autonomous, and diverse. The region as a whole is demographically, economically, and politically far more consequential than it was. The power of the major Latin American nations has exploded, the influence in Latin America of extrahemispheric countries has steadily increased, and the relative position of the United States has inevitably diminished.

A few facts amplify this fundamental point:

— In 1950, Latin America's population was about equal to that of the United States. Now it is 65 percent higher, and by the year 2000 Latin America's population may be double that of this country. And Latin America's rates of urbanization and literacy have increased in unprecedentedly rapid fashion.
— Latin America's average annual rate of economic growth for the past twenty years — until the global recession of 1981-1982 — has been about 6 percent, compared with 3.5 percent annually during the same period in the United States. Latin America's electric power consumption, its production of steel, petrochemicals, and automobiles has multiplied many times. Latin America's aggregate economic activity has quintupled in thirty years and by now approximates that of all Western Europe in 1950; by 1985, if the current international economic downturn can be reversed, it is estimated that Latin America's aggregate economic might may approximate that of Western Europe in 1970.[24]
— Latin America's economic structure has been changing dramatically, as the region's major countries turn from resource extraction increasingly to the export of manufactured goods. During the 1970s, the annual rate of expansion of manufactured exports from Brazil, Mexico, Argentina, and Colombia exceeded 30 percent. The region's share of worldwide industrial production climbed from 4.6 percent in 1964 to 5.7 in 1977, while that of the United States was falling from 29.4 percent to 22.4 percent in the same period.[25]
— As Latin America's political economy changes, the countries of the region necessarily look for additional markets and for new sources of capital, technology, and other imports; their need and their capacity for diversified international relationships expand. As Latin America's extraregional trade grows — and as political relationships mirror commercial links — the United States becomes less central to the international ties of most Latin American nations.

In recent years, therefore, United States predominance in the Western Hemisphere has steadily declined, regardless of the particular United States administration in Washington or of its specific policies. The United States share of Latin America's imports decreased from over 50 percent in 1950 to less than 30 percent in 1979. The United States share of Latin American exports fell from over 48 percent in 1950 to 34 percent in 1980. These aggregate trends are even more dramatic in South America, for Mexico and the countries of the Caribbean have actually become more closely integrated to the United States economy in recent years.[26]

The relative cultural, educational, and political influence of the

United States has diminished, as has the military presence of the United States. United States government-sponsored international visitors and students from Latin America numbered 521 in 1977, compared to 1,450 in 1968, and this decline has continued since then.[27] The number of United States military advisers in Latin America dropped from over 800 in 1965 to fewer than 100 in 1980. By the late 1970s four or five other nations outranked the United States in the sales of heavy weapons to the region.[28]

During these years, the Soviet Union has established a limited presence in the Western Hemisphere: increasing its diplomatic representation from three countries in 1960 to nineteen in 1979; expanding its trading partners in Latin America from four in 1964 to twenty by 1979; sending trade missions and technical assistance to a number of nations; training over 10,000 students from Latin America and the Caribbean in Soviet bloc countries; furnishing military training and over $600 million in military equipment in Peru; establishing itself as Argentina's principal trading partner by purchasing vast quantities of grain; and building close political, economic, and military relations with Cuba, Nicaragua, and Grenada.[29] Except for the military links, however, the Soviet presence is eclipsed by that of Germany and Japan, both expanding very rapidly in the region. Japan's trade with Latin America multiplied 17 times from 1960 to 1980 (from $610 million to $10.6 billion, compared with about $1 billion in Soviet-Latin American trade). German investment in Latin America is booming, and German political and cultural foundations are intensely active in the region. And there are other foreign influences: of the European Social Democrats and Christian Democrats, of Israel and of the Arab nations (as well as the Palestine Liberation Organization), of Spain and Canada, of the Council for Mutual Economic Assistance (COMECON), and especially of the European Economic Community.

In recent years, thus, a pattern of international relations reminiscent of that prevailing in the 1920s has been establishing itself in South America. Then the United States was a dominant but not a domineering power in South America. The United States had significant but not exclusive influence. Germany, the United Kingdom, France, and Italy also had important interests and engagements: commercial, financial, cultural, and military. A few of the South American nations then ranked themselves as middle powers on the world scene, comparable in economic and political terms to all but the seven or eight major nations of the world. The United States recognized the stature of the South American nations and their diverse links; it confined its most intense involvement in domestic affairs to those nations in its immediate border area — the Central American and Caribbean countries — thought of in geopolitical and security terms. Many aspects of the 1980s are new, of course: the influence of Japan and of the Soviet Union in Latin America; the emergence of Brazil and other nations as major industrial exporters; even the beginnings of significant arms manufacture in South America; and especially the region's transformed political economy and the changed nature of United States economic involvement in Latin America. But the relative influence of the United States in the Hemisphere is probably closer to that of the 1920s than to that from 1945 to 1965.

VII

No United States administration to date has dealt successfully with the decline of United States hegemony and its implications, nor with the full consequences of Latin America's profound social and economic transformation.

Jimmy Carter's approach took some account of Latin America's emergence, recognizing explicitly the increased efficacy of key Latin American countries in pursuing their own interests and the legitimacy of their doing so, as well as the growing international significance of the middle powers in Latin America and elsewhere in the Third World. The Carter policy also began to respond to the social and political evolution of Latin America by attempting to loosen the close ties between the United States and unpopular authoritarian regimes. And the Carter administration tried to adapt to declining hegemony by changing the style of United States policy, particularly by negotiating the Panama Canal treaties and by purging the lingering rhetoric of "special relationship."

But although the Carter administration made these and other symbolic moves — epitomized by the President's trips to Venezuela and Brazil, by its aid package for the Caribbean, and by its activist human rights policies — it never responded very substantively to the effects of Latin America's changed political economy. Few steps were taken under Carter in the direction of restructuring the international economic order to accommodate the claims of the main newly industrialized countries. Most Latin American nations (except for the smallest) no longer care about obtaining bilateral concessional assistance from the United States. They, and other Third World countries, primarily want new international rules and practices that will improve their access to markets, capital, and technology in the industrialized world. These steps, beneficial to Latin America, would hurt marginal industries and sectors in the United States and other industrialized nations, however, and would therefore require painful domestic adjustments. The Carter administration never faced these costs and consequently never adequately addressed a basic issue in contemporary United States-Latin American relations.

Ronald Reagan's initial approach to the Western Hemisphere was essentially to ignore or even to deny Latin America's transformation, and to attempt to restore United States dominance: by declarations and demonstrations of force; by emphasizing security assistance; by reinforcing established pro-United States regimes; even by switching allegiances to favor previously shunned groups; and by covert action.

The Reagan administration soon began to learn, however, that some of Latin America's changed realities are intransigent, that many limits on United States influence are objective, and that restoring United States dominance will therefore be hard, if not impossible. Even more, the administration is finding that some of its own policies might be exacerbating the problems the United States is facing. In Nicaragua, for example, it seems that by harassing the revolution from the outside and seeming to align itself with ex-Somocistas, the United States has been undercutting the opposition and reviving the failing popular support of the Sandinista government. More generally, the administration's confrontational rhetoric and actions in Central America and the Caribbean seemed to be increasing the distance between Washington and some of the major Latin American nations. And the Reagan administration's rush to embrace authoritarian regimes cost Washington credibility with opposition groups and democratic forces in Latin America while giving it very little leverage with the regimes themselves.

All these problems were illustrated by the South Atlantic crisis of mid-1982. The Reagan administration failed to dissuade Argentina from launching its ill-fated invasion, could not persuade Argentina to accept various compromise solutions for ending the conflict, and was unable to convince many other Latin American countries to oppose Argentina's adventure: the limits of United States influence were thus starkly revealed. Like a streak of lightning in a summer storm, the South Atlantic crisis illuminated the craggy landscape of United States-Latin American relations, with its deep fissures. No simple rhetorical adjustment in United States policy can paper over these differences. An insistent emphasis by Washington on presumed regional harmony — and an implicit assumption of continued United States dominance — would simply sharpen those differences.[30]

VIII

The central feature of United States-Latin American relations during the next few years will be conflict. As Latin American and other Third World economies try to expand — and as their export potential and their thirst for capital, technology, and markets grow — tensions will inevitably arise between them and the earlier industrialized countries. The specific issues will include tariffs, subsidies, and countervailing duties; commodity prices; technology transfer; debt management; local content and processing requirements; export performance conditions; remittances and royalties; the conservation and management of resources; the law of the seas and fishing rights; energy policies; proliferation; pollution; the terms on which capital and labor migrate; and the making and management of international regimes to govern these and related problems. As Brazil, Mexico, Venezuela, Argentina, Colombia, and other Latin American countries strive to fulfill their potential and to satisfy the aspirations of their citizens, they will increasingly encounter a growing tendency in the United States and other established powers to defend the status quo through protectionism, the preservation of international monetary "law and order," and non-proliferation policies. All these measures, Latin Americans perceive, are based on presumed dominance or the self-serving but dubious assumption that what serves the immediate interests of the industrialized countries automatically satisfies the needs of all. No matter how many trips are taken, speeches are made, or new approaches are announced, a real basis for conflict between the United States and Latin America will persist, therefore. No lasting improvement in United States-Latin American relations will occur until that is taken into account.

To achieve a major and enduring advance in United States-Latin American relations, Washington would have to help nurture an international economic and political order within which the needs of Latin American and other aspiring powers are more fully accommodated. Substantially more of the world's manufacturing would have to take place in the South, for instance, even though this would adversely affect particular sectors and regions in the United States. Increased benefits from international trade in raw materials and other primary products would have to accrue to the less industrialized countries. The advantages derived by the rich countries from prior accumulations of capital and technology would have to decrease significantly. The present and prospective benefits from the world's commons — especially from the seas, the seabeds, and outer space — would be distributed in a much more equitable manner. The costs of adjustment to international economic downturns would be shared more fully, and the special needs of developing countries would be more adequately met. The rules and regimes affecting these and other international issues would be made in fora where the interests of Latin America and other Third World countries would be better protected than in the complex of institutions established just after World War II. To a large extent, market forces could be used to make such a new international order work. But substantial structural change would be required to assure that markets would operate effectively in a world where leverage, influence, and rewards are now so unevenly distributed that markets reinforce inefficient distortions.

No United States administration so far has seriously attempted to reform the structure of the international order from which the United States has obviously gained so much. Economic concessions granted by

Washington to Latin America or Caribbean countries (or to others) have always been extended grudgingly, from a dominant posture, in exchange for cooperation on specific political or strategic matters. Never has the United States Government seen a need to transform the nature of its relationship with Latin America. The forces shaping United States policy — during Ronald Reagan's term but also under other presidents — make such a change unlikely. Interests, perceptions, and process combine to shape a long-standing United States approach to Latin America and the Caribbean that Latin Americans will find increasingly unsatisfactory in the years ahead.

IX

Will United States policy toward Latin America ever change? Will the United States ever be more responsive to Latin America's claims and needs?

If the familiar reasons Latin Americans and their sympathizers in the United States traditionally advance to support their pleas for more United States attention were still the only motives for this country's concern with Latin America, the United States could (and probably would) pay less heed to the region during the next few years, not more.

The traditional litany of United States security, economic, and political interests in the Western Hemisphere is less relevant every year. No direct and substantial military threat to the United States is likely to be mounted from locations in the Western Hemisphere in the foreseeable future, and the importance of United States military assets in the region has been declining for years. Latin America's relative importance as a source for strategic materials has declined as the United States has multiplied its international links and as synthetics have increasingly come to be used. The relative importance of Latin America for United States direct foreign investment has also been dropping, as has the relative share of United States trade accounted for by commerce with Latin America. Politically, Latin America's historic international solidarity with the United States is both much less assured and considerably less important than it used to be. Ritualistic incantations by Latin America area specialists (in government, international organizations, foundations, business, and academia) to the contrary notwithstanding, the familiar rationale for focusing on improving United States relations with Latin America and the Caribbean has been steadily undercut for years. The secular trend toward inattention by Washington has been understandable.

The next few years, however, may well bring a significant change, for it is increasingly obvious that the countries of the Western Hemisphere will affect the United States much more than ever in the 1980s, not less. United States national security in the narrowly defined sense of safety from direct military attack is not likely to be seriously threatened in the hemisphere. But United States security in the broader sense — the capacity to protect individual and collective welfare — may be decisively influenced by events in Latin America and the Caribbean.

The international financial crisis of 1982 dramatically illustrates this point. Nine of the largest banks in the United States have 85 percent of their equity, or balance, exposed in Mexico and Brazil alone.[31] Foreign lending was 7.6 percent of all United States bank lending in 1970, but had risen to 26 percent by 1980, much of it in Latin America.[32] How Latin American nations fare in coping with severe recession will directly and importantly affect the health of our national economy.

The financial bind that ties the United States to Latin America is one example of Latin America's considerably increased significance for the world economy and for that of the United States. Latin America will also be more important for the United States in other ways.

First, the major Latin American nations — together with "newly industrialized countries" in other regions — will help determine whether revised international rules and structures can evolve to permit the continued peaceful expansion of interdependence, or whether the world will retreat to "beggar thy neighbor" policies and practices.

Second, Latin American countries, especially the larger ones, are well situated either to help resolve or to substantially worsen some of the central world problems of the 1980s: food and energy production and distribution, the law and use of the seas and other resources, industrial pollution and environmental protection, narcotics control, and nuclear proliferation. How successfully the United States can engage the positive cooperation of Latin American nations in solving these shared problems will significantly affect our national future.

Third, a few Western Hemisphere nations — particularly Mexico, the insular Caribbean islands, and some Central American countries — will directly influence life in the United States through the massive migration of their citizens. The major flow of immigrants, not likely to be reduced or even regulated without cooperation from Latin American governments, will profoundly shape this country in spheres ranging from education, employment, public health, business, labor, and politics to culture and cuisine. Whether the influence is mainly positive or primarily divisive will depend to a significant degree on United States-Latin American relations.

Finally — less demonstrably but not less significantly — circumstances in Latin America and the Caribbean will importantly condition the ambience for the expression of basic United States values, especially respect for individual human rights. Alliances, explicit or even tacit, between the United States government and authoritarian regimes inevitably strain this country's domestic consensus, based on core values shared by Americans and fundamental to the society.

These four interests — not hoary axioms nor the national *in*security concerns that cause decision makers to focus on threatened United States hegemony in Central America — suggest that substantially increased United States attention to and involvement with the Western Hemisphere will be required in the 1980s. They suggest that Washington should pay more attention to Brazil, Mexico, and Venezuela than to Cuba, Nicaragua, and Grenada. They indicate that the United States should concern itself more with underlying economic issues than with United Nations votes or the rhetoric of nonalignment.

President Reagan's trip to Latin America at the end of 1982 may be Washington's first response to this insight. Whether that will turn out to be so depends, as policy usually does, on follow-up and implementation.

Notes

1. This review of the Carter administration's policy draws on Abraham F. Lowenthal, "Jimmy Carter and Latin America: A New Era or Small Change?" in Kenneth Oye, Donald Rothchild, and Robert Lieber (eds.) *Eagle Entangled* (New York, 1979) pp. 290-303. See also Richard R. Fagen, "The Carter Administration and Latin America: Business as Usual," *Foreign Affairs*, vol. 57, No. 3 (January 1979).
2. See Lincoln R. Bloomfield, "From Ideology to Program to Policy: Tracking the Carter Human Rights Policy," *Journal of Policy Analysis and Management*, vol. 2, No. 1 (1982), pp. 1-12. See also Lars Schoultz, "The Carter Administration and Human Rights in Latin America" in Margaret Crahan (ed.) *Human Rights and Basic Needs in the Americas* (Washington, D.C., 1982), pp. 301-340.
3. See William D. Rogers and Jeffrey A. Meyers, "The Reagan Administration and Latin America: An Uneasy Beginning," *Caribbean Review*, vol. 11, No. 2 (Spring 1982), pp. 14-17. For a left-radical perspective, see Robert C. Armstrong, "Reagan Policy in Crisis: Will the Empire Strike Back?" *NACLA Report on the Americas*, vol. 15, No. 4 (July-August 1981). A Latin American evaluation is provided by Luis Maira, *América Latina y la crisis de hegemonía norteamericana* (Lima, Peru, 1982).
4. Examples include Roger Fontaine, Cleto DiGiovanni, Jr., and Alexander Kruger, "Castro's Specter," *The Washington Quarterly*, vol. 3, No. 4 (Autumn 1980), pp. 3-27; Pedro San Juan, "Why We Don't Have a Latin American Policy?" *The Washington Quarterly*, vol. 3, No. 4 (Autumn 1980), pp. 28-39; Jeane Kirkpatrick, "United States Security and Latin America," *Commentary*, vol. 71, No. 1 (January 1981); James Theberge, "Rediscovering the Caribbean: Toward a United States Policy for the 1980s," *Commonsense* (Spring 1980); Constantine Menges, "Central America and Its Enemies," *Commentary*, vol. 72, No. 2 (August 1981); and especially Lewis Tambs (ed.), *A New Inter-American Policy for the Eighties: Report of the Committee of Santa Fe* (Washington, D.C.: Council for Inter-American Security, May 1980).
5. See, for example, Kirkpatrick, "United States Security in Latin America."
6. This view is suggested, albeit more by innuendo than by outright allegation, by Fontaine, DiGiovanni, and Kruger in "Castro's Specter."

7. Kirkpatrick, "United States Security in Latin America."

8. Menges, "Central America and Its Enemies."

9. The new administration rapidly went public with its claims that captured documents and other new intelligence confirmed substantial Cuban and Soviet involvement in El Salvador. The Department of State's "White Paper" on "Communist Interference in El Salvador" (Special Report No. 80, Department of State, Bureau of Public Affairs, 23 February 1981) was soon critically analyzed in *The Wall Street Journal, The Washington Post*, and elsewhere and shown to be flawed. One suspects this was a classic case of intelligence supporting policy rather than shaping it.

10. See, for example, Alan Riding, "Rightist Exiles Plan Invasion of Nicaragua," *The New York Times* (April 2, 1981); "Reagan Backs Action Plan for Central America," *The Washington Post* (February 14, 1982); and Patrick E. Tyle and Bob Woodward, "U.S. Approves Covert Plan in Nicaragua," *The Washington Post* (March 10, 1982).

11. See Carla Anne Robbins, "A State Department Purge," *The New York Times* (November 3, 1981).

12. Statistics on political versus career appointments are provided in Foreign Service Association, "Status Report on Ambassadorial Appointments" (Washington, D.C., mimeo, April 1982). On the career appointments of persons without previous experience in Latin America, see Phil Keisling, "The Tallest Gun in Foggy Bottom," *The Washington Monthly* (November 1982) 50-56 and Christopher Dickey, "The Gang that Blew Vietnam Goes Latin," *The Washington Post* "Outlook" (November 28, 1982). Keisling argues that Assistant Secretary of State Thomas O. Enders's lack of previous experience in Latin America made his appointment acceptable to Senator Helms; Dickey argues that the Reagan administration's approach to Central America has been shaped by the previous experience in Indochina of Enders, Central American desk officer Craig Johnstone, and John Negroponte, U.S. Ambassador to Honduras.

13. See "U.S. Assistance to Latin America: Profound Reorientations," *WOLA Occasional Paper No. 2* (Washington, D.C.: Washington Office on Latin America, May 1982).

14. See Paul E. Sigmund, "Latin America: Change or Continuity?" *Foreign Affairs*, vol. 60, No. 3 (1982), pp. 629-657; Susan Kaufman Purcell, "Carter, Reagan et l'Amérique Central," *Politique Etrangère*, vol. 47 (June 1982), pp. 309-317; and Howard J. Wiarda, "The United States and Latin America: Change and Continuity" paper presented at the University of Pittsburgh (October 28-29, 1982). See also Thomas O. Enders, "Building the Peace in Central America," address to the Commonwealth Club, San Francisco, August 20, 1982.

15. See Ed Cody, "Salvadoran Businessmen Assail U.S. Ambassador as Roman Pro-Consul," *The Washington Post* (November 3, 1982).

16. Wayne Smith, for several years a principal figure in U.S.-Cuban relations, first as the State Department Cuban Desk Officer and then as head of the United States "Interests Section" in Havana, argues that the Carter and Reagan administrations have been nearly equally inattentive to Cuban overtures for changing bilateral relations. See Wayne Smith, "Dateline Havana: Myopic Diplomacy," *Foreign Policy* (Fall 1982), pp. 157-174. Also see, Max Singer, "The Record in Latin America," *Commentary*, vol. 74, No. 6 (December 1982), pp. 43-49.

17. See Philip Taubman, "U.S. Supports Raids in Nicaragua but Says their Scope Is Limited," *The New York Times* (November 2, 1982) and *Newsweek* (November 8, 1982), featuring a cover story on "A Secret War for Nicaragua." The administration's decision to postpone scheduled joint military maneuvers with Honduras near the Nicaraguan border, the tone of President Reagan's remarks on his visit to

Central America in December 1982, and reports of Secretary Shultz's reaction to the *Newsweek* revelations all tended to suggest a decision not to escalate anti-Nicaraguan actions, although it is possible these signals mask further clandestine intervention.

18. Many of these issues are discussed in Albert Fishlow, "The United States and Brazil: The Case of the Missing Relationship," *Foreign Affairs*, vol. 60, No. 4 (Spring, 1982).

19. See J. Daniel O'Flaherty "Finding Jamaica's Way," *Foreign Policy* (Summer 1978), pp. 137-158.

20. The following pages draw substantially on Abraham F. Lowenthal, "Jimmy Carter and Latin America," pp. 297-300, and on Abraham F. Lowenthal and Gregory F. Treverton, "The Making of United States Policies toward Latin America," *Working Paper No. 4* (Washington, D.C.: Woodrow Wilson International Center for Scholars, 1978).

21. See I. M. Destler and Patricia Cohen "Congress Swings," *Foreign Service Journal* (July-August 1982), pp. 19-21, 38.

22. See Wolf Grabendorff, "The Central American Crisis and Western Europe: Perceptions and Reactions," *International Politics* (Germany, 1982).

23. Some of the points that follow were first presented in Abraham F. Lowenthal, "The United States and Latin America: Ending the Hegemonic Presumption," *Foreign Affairs* (October 1976).

24. See Margaret Daley Hayes, *Latin America and the U.S. National Interest: A Basis for U.S. Foreign Policy*, Westview Press (Boulder, Co., January, 1983).

25. University of Cambridge *World Trade and Prospects for the 1980s* (December 1980), Tables 1.14 and 1.12.

26. For 1950-1970, based on the *UN Yearbook of International Trade Statistics, UN Monthly Bulletin of Statistics*, see SELA (LAES) Ley de Comercio *Internacional de Estados Unidos de América* (June 1979). For 1970-1979, University of Cambridge, *World Trade and Finance: Prospects for the 1980s* (Cambridge, England, December 1980), App. B. For 1980, United States Department of Commerce, *Highlights of US Exports and Import Trade* (Washington, D.C., 1981).

27. See Constantine Menges, "The United States and Latin America in the 1980s," in *The National Interests of the United States*, Prosser Gifford (ed.), Woodrow Wilson International Center for Scholars, 1981, p. 54.

28. Figures and numbers of United States military advisers and/or arms trade have been obtained from various governmental sources.

29. Robert Leiken, "Soviet Strategy in Latin America," *The Washington Papers*, vol. X, No. 93, Praeger Publishers, 1982.

30. Francisco Orrego Vicuña, "The Elusive Understanding between Latin America and the United States," paper presented to the Inter-American Dialogue, October 15-16, 1982. (Washington, D.C.: Woodrow Wilson International Center for Scholars).

31. See William R. Cline, "The Debt-Trade Nexus and Global Growth," speech presented to a Global Interdependence Center (Philadelphia), March 9, 1982.

32. *Economic Report of the President*, 1982.

11

From Carter to Reagan: The Global Perspective on Africa Becomes Ascendant

Donald Rothchild and John Ravenhill

From 1946 to 1976, successive United States administrations adopted low-profile and cautious policies toward Africa. The styles of different administrations were distinctive, but their substantive involvements, with their various emphases on stability and gradualism, entailed consistent support for the existing structure of the international economic system. As Africa emerged as a major locus for superpower rivalry, and as the struggle for black majority rule in the continent's southern tip intensified, the United States became a more active player on the African stage. Policies adopted by successive administrations have differed according to whether African issues were viewed from a regionalist or a globalist perspective. Regionalists perceive African problems with a sympathetic eye, placing emphasis on the uniqueness of the African environment and attempting to accommodate the aspirations of African peoples. Globalists, on the other hand, tend to perceive African issues from the perspective of an all-encompass-

Donald Rothchild is Professor of Political Science at the University of California, Davis. He has lectured at universities in Uganda, Kenya, Zambia, and Ghana. His books include Racial Bargaining in Independent Kenya *(Oxford University Press, 1973), (coauthor)* Scarcity, Choice and Public Policy in Middle Africa *(University of California Press, 1978), (coeditor)* Eagle Entangled *(Longman, 1979), and (coeditor)* State Versus Ethnic Claims: African Policy Dilemmas *(Westview, 1983).*

John Ravenhill is Lecturer in international politics at the University of Sydney, Australia. He previously taught at the University of Virginia. He has published articles in a number of journals on North-South issues and African international relations.

The authors wish to thank the coeditors and Harvey Glickman, Stephen Low, Richard Feinberg, Michael Clough, and Michael Foley for their help and advice on this chapter.

ing East-West conflict in which there can be no neutral parties. The simplicity of the globalist perspective gives it a certain inner consistency but one that may entail high costs in terms of misperceptions of the issues at stake in regional conflicts and in terms of misallocation of scarce resources from the point of view of national interest. Where the Carter administration adopted a rather complex and low-profile regionalist orientation, the Reagan team has moved decisively to embrace a globalist view in which emphasis is placed on the unrelenting Soviet threat.

American interests in Africa are real but limited: to promote human rights and racial justice, to secure African diplomatic support at the United Nations and other multilateral bodies, to gain strategic advantage, to obtain raw materials, and to promote trade and investment. Africa plays a relatively minor role in United States foreign trade and investment. But the continent is a major source of vital minerals — platinum, asbestos, ferromanganese, fluorine, antimony, and vanadium from South Africa; mica from Malagasy; cobalt from Zaire; tantalum from Nigeria and Zaire; manganese from Gabon, South Africa, and Zaire; chrome from South Africa and Zimbabwe (formerly Rhodesia); and petroleum from Angola, Nigeria, Gabon, Libya, Algeria, and Cameroun. Currently, the dependence of the American economy on such African strategic minerals as platinum, ferromanganese, chrome, and cobalt is critical, with some 40 percent of the first three imported from South Africa and a similar percentage of cobalt from Zaire. Even so, it is necessary to be cautious in assessing the importance of southern African suppliers. Not only is it doubtful that any new regime would curb exports of these minerals to the United States, but the possibilities for alternative suppliers, new sources (in particular, the seabed nodules), stockpiling, and recycling make grave apprehensions over a minerals cutoff seem overstated.

Increasing trade with Nigeria (America's second largest supplier of crude oil) and other black African countries complicates any policy tilt toward South Africa justified on the grounds of global security interests. A rational definition of national self-interest (including the promotion of American egalitarian values, domestic racial harmony, and security ties as well as trade relations with black Africa) would indicate a need to accommodate the aspirations of black Africa. But the globalism of the Reagan administration posits a narrower interpretation of American interests: the global struggle against Communism has led to a change in priorities in relations with the minority white regimes of southern Africa.

At the same time, it is apparent that American capabilities are more circumscribed than once assumed. Only in a few cases is the United States a major trading partner for African countries (mainly such oil and commodity exporters as Algeria, Nigeria, Angola, Cameroun, Burundi, and Sierra Leone); similarly, the American share of bilateral development aid to Africa (with the exception of Egypt) is relatively small, and is likely to decrease as the Reagan administration continues to cut back on non-military overseas assistance. In most of black Africa the European Economic Community is by far the most significant economic partner, and former European colonial powers maintain better contacts and greater influence in many African capitals than does the United States. In part because of Vietnam, but also because of American interests in South Africa and the failure of recent administrations to respond sympathetically to demands of less-developed countries (LDCs) on restructuring the international economic order, the political capital enjoyed by the United States in contemporary black Africa has not remained as high as in the early 1960s. As a consequence, motivations are often regarded with great suspicion. Yet the United States alone is in a position to exert significant pressure on South Africa to modify its apartheid policies and to provide the wherewithal for African states to resist unwanted incursions by Soviet proxies. These are the major parameters within which current American policy must operate. How the United States got there and how American policy makers perceive and respond to these parameters are the subjects of this chapter.

Minimal Engagement, 1946-1976

By current standards, all the United States governments in the 1946-1976 period adopted low-profile stances toward Africa.[1] In the late 1950s, as independence neared, American spokesmen, anxious to avoid disruptions in the world system, encouraged African leaders to retain close ties with Europe after the transfer of power. The themes of moderation, orderly transition, and international stability were reiterated time and again during this period and were sometimes accorded a higher priority than African claims for rapid independence (for example, the Eisenhower administration's abstention at the UN on the 1960 vote on the Declaration on the Granting of Independence to Colonial Countries and Peoples).

As the trauma of independence came and went, American policy makers began to adjust to the new world of African states. President Kennedy, not hesitating to bypass European capitals, increased United States bilateral assistance and built effective relations with nationalist leaders. Although African nonalignment was no longer viewed as immoral, the fundamental thrust, competition with Soviet expansion, remained unaltered. The United States continued to seek to contain Soviet expansion in the area, in particular giving its support to the UN initiative in the Congo. If the Kennedy administration made conscious efforts to establish personal ties with radical as well as moderate African leaders, the Johnson administration moved steadily toward the center, both in its policy positions and in its preference for reformist-inclined rulers. And with material and psychic resources heavily committed to Vietnam, it was little inclined to become embroiled in other regions or issues that could, it seemed, be safely left to future leaders.

It is possible to distinguish two periods in African policy during the ensuing Nixon and Ford administrations: Kissinger phase I, which lasted from President Nixon's inauguration in 1969 until the spring 1976 change in policy, and Kissinger phase II, which followed. Preoccupied with the Vietnam war and predisposed toward "benign neglect," Kissinger was only minimally engaged with African issues during much of phase I. Nevertheless, a policy tilt to the right became manifest. Not only did Kissinger I prefer an alignment with moderate and conservative African leaders, but he pursued policies that had the effect of identifying the United States with white racist regimes in southern Africa. Kissinger I accepted the major premise of National Security Study Memorandum 39 [2] that "the whites [of southern Africa] are here to stay and the only way that constructive change can come about is through them." Following from this premise, NSSM 39's option 2, which Kissinger embraced, called for a "selective relaxation of our stance toward the white regime." Thus in 1971 Nixon failed to offer resolute leadership to Congress in opposition to the Byrd amendment, which permitted the United States to import Rhodesian chrome and other strategic minerals in direct violation of UN sanctions. Significantly, the United States cast its first veto in the UN Security Council in 1970 on a resolution condemning Britain for failure to overthrow by force the illegal white minority regime in Rhodesia. This and other votes on arms embargoes aimed at South Africa isolated the United States from the mainstream of world public opinion.

Kissinger clearly conceived of global stability in terms of a relative equilibrium between major international actors. Hence, when the Soviet Union moved outside its immediate orbit and intervened in mineral-rich Angola — sending to the Popular Movement for the Liberation of Angola (MPLA) support teams of military technicians and advisers, some $200 million in military equipment, and some 11,000 Cuban combat troops — Kissinger saw it necessary for the United States, as the leader of the non-Communist states, to back its African allies there. Senate liberals, drawing analogies to earlier defense appropriations for Vietnam, effectively resisted Kissinger's arguments for confrontation. No one seriously questioned Angola's importance as a supplier of raw materials or its strategic significance. But the paralysis-of-will argument advanced by neoconservatives to explain congressional opposition seems unconvincing. More important was the feeling that the limits of accommodation, with Africa and the Soviet Union, had not yet been reached. Unlike Kissinger and the global confrontationists, the Senate liberals did not believe American interests required a strong response to Soviet-backed MPLA power. Two forms of realpolitik were engaged head-on, and in this instance the confrontationists failed.

Accommodations with Black Africa:
Kissinger II and Carter

With the failure of a confrontationist stance in Angola, Kissinger recognized that minimal engagement with a tilt toward white Africa was increasingly counterproductive. As he declared in early 1976, "The radicalization of the Third World and its consolidation into an antagonistic bloc is neither in our political nor our economic interest." Thus was born phase II of Kissinger's African policy and its rationale, in North-South relations, of a movement from confrontation to cooperation. In a speech in Lusaka, Zambia, in April 1976, Kissinger set forth a ten-point program aimed at facilitating southern African negotiations and blocking external encroachment in the area. He called for the establishment of majority rule prior to independence in Rhodesia and outlined a program of action that included direct diplomatic pressures on the Salisbury regime, repeal of the Byrd amendment, and provision of political and economic support to Rhodesia during the transition to majority rule. As regards Namibia, the former German colony illegally administered by South Africa, Kissinger sought to promote movement toward a peaceful settlement while an opportunity for bargaining existed. He called upon the South Africans to announce a timetable on self-determination acceptable to the international community and promised that once progress toward a settlement was apparent, the United States would ease its restrictions on trade and investment.

Stressing that South Africa's independence set it apart from Namibia and Rhodesia (still technically a colony), Kissinger contended that South Africa's government "represents a legitimate government which carries out practices with which we disagree." It therefore required a different type of American response. He refused to intervene openly in the struggle against South Africa's institutionalized racism, preferring to rely upon domestic pressures, assisted externally by quiet diplomacy. Kissinger's handling of South Africa was predicated on a need to secure Prime Minister John Vorster's cooperation in achieving accommodationist objectives in southern Africa. In something of a tacit exchange, Kissinger held out the possibility of respectability, even international legitimacy, to South Africa while attempting to secure critically needed support for majority rule in Rhodesia and Namibia. In linking South Africa to the wider strategy of accommodation, Kissinger redefined the southern African question, but to no one's liking, least of all in black Africa.

Although early responses to Kissinger's proposals were encouraging, final agreement on Namibia proved elusive. And on the Rhodesian issue, nationalist leaders and front-line presidents refused to agree to terms which allowed the ministries of defense and law and order to remain in white hands. The gulf between white and black Africa proved as wide as ever, and the Kissinger package became unwrapped.

The Carter administration's advent to power marked something of a shift in United States foreign policy style. Highly moralistic in tone and pro-black in inclination, this administration sought to fashion a "liberal" African approach that would shun mechanical cold war responses to African issues and put the United States more in step with black aspirations at home and abroad. If, in substance, there was considerable continuity with the policy outlined by Kissinger II, the "principled pragmatism" of the Carter team meant a more concerted effort to reconcile the symbols of idealism with effective restraints on Soviet expansionism. Carter policy makers sought to deal with African problems in their African context. Rather than ignoring the Soviet global factor, they believed that the best way to confront it was by trying to resolve the problems the Soviets were exploiting for their own purposes. In this sense, Carter's accommodation joined liberal purposes with considerations of national self-interest.

Both domestic and international pressures pushed the Carter administration to be sensitive toward African aspirations. On the domestic side, a liberal bloc including intellectuals, professional Africanists, church groups, and black Americans (who contributed in no small part to Carter's close electoral victory) emerged as an important element influencing his policies on African-related issues. The appointment of Andrew Young as ambassador to the UN was more than symbolic. Young's highly accommodative style received support from many professional policy makers at the State Department's Africa Bureau and Policy Planning Staff, the National Security Council, and the United Nations who were determined to erase all traces of the Kissinger I tilt on southern Africa.

Developments in economic relations with Africa reinforced the Carter accommodation stance. Trade with black Africa was increasing, although South Africa remained a significant export market. Nigeria, which replaced South Africa as America's largest African trading partner, was courted as one of the administration's "new influentials." For Nigeria, southern African racism was deemed a nonnegotiable issue on which there could be no straddling by Western interests, a position the Carter administration could well understand. It responded by rhetorically disavowing the Kissinger strategy of dividing the Rhodesian, Namibian, and South African issues into distinct negotiating tracks. Carter's opposition in principle to all compromises with white racism in southern Africa led to an improvement in United States-Nigerian relations, one of the major successes for his liberal internationalist approach.

How successful was an accommodative policy style when applied to southern African issues? Accommodation meant a generally similar game plan in all three conflicts: to come to terms with moderate elements and thus preclude a radical takeover. What was desired were regimes acceptable to black Africa and linked to the global economy through Western capital and technology. In the case of Rhodesia, the accommodation stance led to a major symbolic achievement soon after Carter took office when Congress moved swiftly to overturn the Byrd amendment. With its support for all-party negotiations and its efforts at mediation, the Carter administration contributed substantially to a successful resolution of the conflict. But the eventual settlement of the Rhodesian issue occurred with the Americans limited to a behind-the-scenes role. An African-sponsored motion approved by the UN Security Council declared "illegal and unacceptable" the internal settlement being negotiated with moderate black nationalists under Rhodesian Prime Minister Ian Smith's auspices. Despite the logic of accommodation, and the warning by Young of the possibilities of a "black on black" civil war, the United States abstained on this resolution. Under considerable domestic conservative pressure, it was all the administration could do to resist resolutions in the House and Senate calling for the lifting of economic sanctions against Zimbabwe once elections under Smith's internal settlement were held. The new Thatcher government in Britain, publicly supported by Secretary of State Cyrus Vance, moved quickly to renew the search for a mutually acceptable constitution. It invited all parties to a conference to work out a constitution providing for "genuine" black majority rule, and after protracted negotiations, a complex formula for free elections, majority rule, and rigid minority safeguards was hammered out. Carter's consistent support for such an outcome had successfully identified the United States with progressive forces in Africa.

The course pursued with respect to Namibia paralleled that in Rhodesia, but without the same success. Again, a white-backed administration, under severe military pressure from the South West Africa People's Organization (SWAPO) and from African nationalist and world opinion generally, recognized the need to transfer power to a majority-backed regime. A South African sponsored solution, based on ethnic representation in the legislature, was opposed by American officials, who maintained that no settlement was likely to endure in the face of intense SWAPO resistance. To secure a comprehensive settlement, a "contact group" of five Western UN Security Council members (the United States, Britain, France, Canada and West Germany) met separately in 1977 and 1978 with SWAPO and South African spokesmen. On various occasions the contact group presented a package plan to the two sides and managed in July 1978 to reach an understanding with SWAPO leader Sam Nujoma that augured well for a peaceful settlement of the dispute. Although the two sides remained far apart on the status of Walvis Bay (claimed by South Africa on the basis of its annexation in 1884), a wide measure of agreement had been secured on UN-supervised elections, the release of political prisoners, South African troop levels, and the size of the UN peacekeeping force. But the accord, as the American negotiator predicted, proved a "fragile soufflé." In September, outgoing South African Prime Minister Vorster rejected the UN's Namibia plan and, despite strong UN opposition, South African authorities went ahead with a December election for a constituent assembly. SWAPO and two other nationalist parties boycotted this exercise, leaving the Democratic Turnhalle Alliance a winner by default.

New UN and contact group initiatives to find an internationally acceptable accord followed. The United States carried on discussions in the summer of 1979 with Angola's President Agostinho Neto, which produced a proposal for a demilitarized zone 31 miles wide on both sides of the Namibia-Angola border. Throughout this frustrating period the various parties had little difficulty finding new problems at every stage; the central difficulty was less one of specific provisions than of a general lack of confidence in the other side's intentions: SWAPO feared that South Africa would deny it political power based on genuine majority backing, and South Africa worried that UN favoritism would prejudice the results. In all this, the Carter team played an important facilitative role, supporting an all-party agreement embracing the principles of majority rule and minority protections.

If an accommodative stance remained a reasonably steady guide to strategy in Rhodesia and Namibia, it was applied less consistently to South Africa. In line with its accommodative stance, the United States curtailed official sports contacts; reacted harshly to violations of civil liberties; suspended nuclear cooperation unless South African authorities agreed to adhere to the nonproliferation treaty; endorsed the Sullivan code on fair labor practices; and voted favorably on UN resolutions condemning apartheid, imposing a mandatory arms embargo, and criticizing South Africa's continued attack against its neighbors. Vice-President Mondale asserted, following talks with Vorster in Vienna in May 1977, that without "evident progress" toward ending apartheid, the United States would have to take "actions based on our policy ... to the detriment of the constructive relations we would prefer with South Africa." Although these actions were considered evidence of good intentions in the Third World, African leaders urged more forceful and effective measures. During Carter's trip to Nigeria, General Olusegun Obasanjo expressed his government's "strong disappointment" over the continued pursuit of "policies of outright collaboration with South Africa." In practice, the United States arms embargo still did not eliminate all gray areas, and the Carter administration continued to extend Export-Import Bank loan guarantees to South Africa until October 1978 when Congress, despite administration opposition, overturned the policy. Moreover, faced with a bitter South African attack on Mondale's call for full political participation, American officials stressed that they offered no blueprint or timetable for South Africa's democratization.

The administration's efforts appeared even less satisfactory in middle Africa. Given America's low involvement in black Africa's struggle for independence, nonintervention and deference to African preferences seemed a logical framework for Carter policy. In line with Young's formula, "African solutions for African problems," the early Carter team limited its involvement in middle African struggles, declining in 1977 to be drawn directly into a series of conflicts of questionable concern to the United States: the April invasion of Zaire's Shaba Province by 2,000 former Katanga gendarmes ("Shaba 1"); the growing conflict in Western Sahara; and the Ethiopian-Somali and Ethiopian-Eritrean disputes. Should the parties to inter-African disputes be unable to resolve their differences among themselves, the standard American prescription was OAU mediation, not great-power interference.

By November 1977, the utility of an accommodative stance on such issues was called into question. That the Soviets would become involved in a large buildup of the Somali army and would establish an extensive military complex in Berbera was disturbing to those who had assumed a more conciliatory Soviet Union. Concern increased as the Soviets dispatched massive military assistance to the new Marxist-oriented government in Ethiopia. For a time, it seemed just possible that the Soviets might be able to reduce tensions between these ideologically similar regimes, but President Siyad Barre's determination to include all ethnic Somalis in an enlarged Somali state proved fundamentally at cross purposes with Mengistu Haile Mariam's efforts to maintain a shaky Ethiopia against all challengers — Somali, Eritrean, or other nationality dissidents. Inevitably, the Soviet straddle failed, and in October the Soviets cut off further arms shipments to Somalia. The Somalis, meanwhile, invaded Ethiopia's Ogaden region. The United States retreated from any assurances it may have given the Somalis on arms shipments, viewing such assistance as intensifying the conflict as well as violating OAU findings on changing the border by force. The Soviet Union provided Mengistu with all the human and material support needed to defeat the Somalis in the Ogaden, thereby consolidating its alliance with Ethiopia and demonstrating its capabilities and resoluteness to Africa.

National security advisor Zbigniew Brzezinski, a prominent conservative internationalist, warned Moscow that its activities in Africa would "inevitably complicate" the SALT negotiations. Another indication of a tougher Carter stance on Africa was the refusal to extend diplomatic recognition to the MPLA government unless Cuban troops were withdrawn from Angola. With the second invasion of Shaba Province in May 1978 ("Shaba 2"), Washington seized the initiative and responded quickly to a request from Zaire, France, and Belgium for logistical support. This invasion of Zaire by Katangan exiles from Angola (allegedly trained and equipped by East German and/or Cuban forces) involved a violation of OAU principles.

With the departure of Young and Vance from government service, a more traditional approach to global competition became apparent. Growing concern regarding American interests in the Middle East had brought about a noticeable hardening of attitudes toward Soviet activities in Africa. In August 1980, a United States-Somali agreement was signed permitting American forces to make use of the Berbera facilities in exchange for $45 million in credits for defensive equipment. Despite firm assurance from the Siyad Barre government that American equipment would not be used in the Ogaden,[3] the political costs of a military identification with Somali irredentism might prove high. Clearly the optimistic, initial visions of the Carter policy makers on the possibilities of accommodation in Africa had been shaken as they came up against the cold realities of global competition, domestic pressure, African demands, and South African intransigence.

The New Administration's African Guidelines

A new administration in Washington frequently entails a change in approach to world issues as the incoming team seeks to distinguish itself from its predecessors. Although basic perceptions of American interests have shifted little from the late Carter-Brzezinski period, something of a change has taken place in how these interests might best be pursued. Reagan has stressed the importance of rooting foreign policy "in realism, not naïveté or self-delusion." [4] The essential element of Reagan's realism has been the restoring of America's military "credibility," its economic dynamism, and its psychological vigor. Administration spokespeople have castigated policies they see as responsible for decreasing American influence or for uncertainty over the country's future, including a supposed failure to recognize the global Soviet threat, an attempt to accommodate Soviet client states, and a neglect of Third World allies on the grounds of human rights violations. Taking a more traditional view of the role of power in international relations than did the Carter administration, the Reagan team has concentrated more singlemindedly on resisting "Soviet adventurism" in Africa as elsewhere. Such a predisposition toward globalism carries with it a lower priority on accommodating African claims as well as a more independent American effort to arrest the general decline in Western power.

The Reagan administration's African policy has represented a rare instance in which the views of the senior State Department official responsible for the area — Chester Crocker, the assistant secretary of state for African affairs — were clearly articulated in advance of his taking office and have largely been pursued since then.[5] Crocker was among the principal academic critics of the African policies of the Carter administration's liberal internationalism. Arguing that there had been a preoccupation with clichés and rhetorical abstractions, Crocker asserted that "the Cyrus Vance-Andrew Young litany of 'Africa for the Africans' is a state of mind, not a policy." American interests in Africa were growing more rapidly than American influence, leading to a dangerous gap between rhetoric and reality. Washington had attempted to conduct an ambitious regional policy on the cheap by sidestepping tough choices; Crocker therefore called for an integration of the regionalist and globalist views. Both regionalists, who perceived all foreign conflicts as potential Vietnams, and globalists, who were preoccupied with avoiding future Angolas, misperceived African realities. At a time when Africa was of growing importance to American economic and security interests, it was also becoming an arena of East-West rivalry, a fact that could not be altered through disengagement.

Crocker identified a number of reasons why these African security issues were of growing salience in the late 1970s: (1) continuing withdrawal of European powers from their previous security roles; (2) an increasing disparity in power and domestic cohesion among different states in Africa, coupled with a new willingness to challenge OAU principles supporting the integrity of colonial boundaries and the legitimacy of member states' governments; (3) the failure of Western countries to adopt a coherent policy toward African development and security issues; and (4) the rapid growth of military involvement by the Soviet Union and its allies in the continent. "This military activity," Crocker asserted, "is the single most destabilizing factor in an already fragile environment." Soviet and Cuban adventurism would end only when the West increased the costs of such activity: American restraint would only open the way for others to step in. Hence the United States should cease treating all forms of outside involvement in African affairs as equally illegitimate.

The United States had tied its own hands in Africa by adopting an aid program that lacked "coherence of purpose and focus of effort." Not only was the American aid program too small, its focus on meeting basic human needs "almost rules out using aid as a tool for the promotion of *any* U.S. interest — either developmental or political." Crocker also criticized the distribution of American aid, observing that "a relatively large chunk of aid is sent routinely to socialist Tanzania," while pro-West, capitalist Ivory Coast received virtually nothing. He concluded, "Washington needs to stop thinking of African policy as a philanthropic venture and start defining *U.S. interests* in the economic relationship with Africa." After chiding American aid givers for running "rural welfare programs" in Africa, he urged attention to "more mundane tasks" — export promotion, investment incentives, regional infrastructure aid projects, and industrial free zones. Not only should greater assistance be given to the American private sector through the Overseas Private Investment Corporation (OPIC) and the ExIm Bank, but military assistance to such long-standing American clients as Zaire and Morocco should once again be emphasized. As regards which governments the United States should support, Crocker suggested that the criteria should include an African government's past and current attitude on issues of direct importance to the United States, its posture on foreign investment and nationalization, its current and potential contribution to regional and international peace keeping, and an estimate of its likely durability as a governing group.

Four key areas were identified on which United States policy should focus: the Horn, where the objective should be, by supporting clients in the Sudan and Kenya, to contain Soviet-inspired damage to American interests; Zaire, where a joint Western effort should be made to preserve the integrity of the country and the survival of an acceptable government; West Africa, where the objective should be to contain the spread of radical Arab influence; and southern Africa, where an internationally acceptable solution to the Namibian question should be sought. In the crucial southern African subregion, Crocker had initially supported the internal settlement in Rhodesia and criticized the "utopian" nature of proposals for a United Nations-administered transition to majority rule. He later reversed himself to applaud "British diplomatic virtuosity" in negotiating the settlement. On Namibia, he argued that only an agreement backed by the UN would bring an opportunity for peaceful transition in the subregion. Although normalization of relations with Angola was desirable, recognition should result in increased American leverage within the subregion and be timed to ensure some quid pro quo.

Shortly before taking office, Crocker published a major statement in *Foreign Affairs* that provides a number of insights into his thinking on American policy toward South Africa. Noting the need to strengthen the "fragile centrist consensus" in American political circles, Crocker criticized the policies of previous administrations for either acquiescing to Pretoria or sending false signals. The objective of American policy toward South Africa should be to promote the emergence "of a society with which the United States can pursue its varied interests in a full and friendly relationship, without constraint, embarrassment or political damage." The present apartheid system precluded this. But American influence would be achieved only if there were an appreciation of South Africa's internal dynamics (including the importance of Afrikaner nationalism). Crocker stressed the necessity of sympathy "for the awesome political dilemma in which Afrikaners and other whites find themselves" (without suggesting that this dilemma might be largely of their own making).

Crocker's prescription was for "constructive engagement." He ruled out economic warfare or even more moderate economic instruments of foreign policy against the South African system and contended that the United States should not judge the legitimacy of a sovereign South Africa's rules and regulations. Crocker did argue, however, that there should be no support for the independent homelands unless a "meaningful" test of opinion of those affected by the policy was obtained. Moreover, the United States should encourage those changes that would enable blacks to acquire the economic and organizational base from which they could effectively demand a larger share of political power. Noting that the "political and attitudinal preconditions for significant change have emerged in recent years," Crocker asserted that American interests might best be pursued by encouraging evolutionary change: The United States should maintain consistent pressure on Pretoria, but there must be a recognition that "the power to coerce Pretoria is not in America's hands." In taking this position, Crocker appears to have underemphasized the ability of the United States to wield the stick against South Africa.[6] Curiously, Crocker's realism regarding the prerequisites for bargaining with the Soviet Union contrasts with his kid-glove, all-carrot-and-no-stick approach to South Africa.

Reagan's Strategic Globalism

On African security issues, the Reagan administration's new assertiveness distinguishes it from its predecessor. As Crocker told the Council on Foreign Relations on October 5, 1981, "It is . . . time to recognize . . . that the solution to regional disputes does not lie in Western abstinence at a time when Libyan, Soviet, and Cuban policies seek actively to exploit and fuel the fires of instability." The Reagan administration states clearly that it will not remain on the sidelines, allowing its Soviet adversary to probe with a free hand. Rather, it asserts its intention to counter Soviet involvement with American involvement. This includes the provision of bilateral aid and military assistance to "proven African friends" to enable them to resist possible aggression — whether in the form of direct Soviet expansion or indirect expansion through the agency of local proxies. The effectiveness of such a globalist posture appears questionable, however. By stressing military solutions to political problems, the Reagan orientation tends to overplay the force variable. The consequence is to underestimate Africa's commitment to nonalignment, to the ending of racism in southern Africa, and to the New International Economic Order.

The American commitment to identify openly with friends and shun adversaries appears at first glance to be consistent with the Reagan team's focus on East-West rivalries. Yet the costs of such an orientation seem relatively high in terms of grappling effectively with complex intraregional issues. An emphasis on globalist issues brings the United States into dangerously close proximity with regimes disliked by the majority of their own populations for their racist tendencies (South Africa) or for their corrupt and arbitrary practices (Zaire); its open commitment of support can at times also be embarrassing to friends who are sincerely pledged to nonalignment (Kenya, Zimbabwe, Zambia). Targets of Reagan's displeasure are likely to be characterized by a hostile "Marxist" ideology, the stationing on their territories of substantial numbers of Communist-bloc troops (of an estimated 41,000 such forces in Subsaharan Africa, most were concentrated in Angola and Ethiopia), or a conscious posture of maintaining a substantial distance from American influences. Reagan's proven allies, on the other hand, are largely the less ideologically inclined states that are receptive to American strategic and economic influences and adjacent to Soviet-backed countries. To be sure, anomalies abound. The People's Republic of the Congo, for example, espouses a Marxist world view, yet it shuns the export of its ideology to other countries and remains generally receptive to Western multinational investments. Zimbabwe's leaders also proclaim radical policy positions but have acted pragmatically in their relationships with racial minorities and multinational companies. The Reagan administration, recognizing such pragmatism as conducive to regional stability, has extended economic assistance to both these countries, including pledges of $300 million for Zimbabwe rehabilitation.[7]

In addition to Libya, those radical African states most frequently identified by Reaganites as Soviet surrogates include Ethiopia, Angola, and Mozambique. Namibia's SWAPO and the regimes in Mali and Tanzania have also evoked Reaganite ire for the way they have distanced themselves from American purposes. Not surprisingly, Mali, Mozambique, and Tanzania have tended to fare poorly under Reagan's revisions in the FY1982 budget for foreign assistance; moreover, the United States blocked the bid of Tanzania's foreign minister to become UN secretary general. In Mozambique, from which four American diplomats were expelled for alleged espionage and interference, the Reagan team responded with alacrity, charging extraordinary harassment and suspending food assistance.

Although Mengistu's regime proclaims a commitment to Marxist-Leninist principles, Ethiopian-Soviet links have been based on common perceptions of interest as well as ideology. The Soviets have continued to maintain a close relationship with Ethiopia since the 1977 struggle with Somali and Eritrean secessionists, shipping arms and garrisoning Soviet-Cuban forces (estimated at 18,000 men in 1978). In exchange, Mengistu reportedly allows the Soviets to operate naval facilities in the Dahlak islands and is considering making Ethiopian air facilities available to them. Deepening Soviet-Ethiopian ties, highlighted by the signing of a twenty-year friendship treaty and Ethiopian backing for Soviet intervention in Afghanistan, have been the source of uncertainty in Washington. Despite the Reagan administration's indicated concern over the continued Soviet-Cuban presence in Ethiopia as well as the buildup of the Dahlak islands facilities, it has acted cautiously, refusing to sever links with Ethiopia and extending only $20 million in increased military credits to Somalia under FY1982. Moreover, the 250 American troops sent to Berbera to participate in the "Bright Star" exercises of November 1981 were quietly withdrawn at the conclusion of these maneuvers, and current outlays to improve

Berbera have been held to a minimum. Certainly, it is too early to rule out the possibility of further serious fighting on the Horn, with all that that implies for American involvement; thus as anti-government forces attempted to topple the Siyad Barre government in the summer of 1982, the United States speeded up deliveries of previously ordered weapons and supplies. Even so, for the moment East-West rivalries have remained at a low level.

In Angola, the advent of the Reagan administration has signaled a more combative stance against the MPLA regime. Although the Carter administration had refused to establish diplomatic relations with Angola because of the continued presence of some 20,000 Cuban troops there, it had nonetheless pursued a hands-off approach regarding that country's internal affairs. The Reagan administration, however, has attempted to exert greater pressure on the Luanda government. Reaganite preferences have been apparent: to raise the costs of Soviet adventurism by repealing the 1976 Clark Amendment (which banned American assistance to rebel units in Angola); to increase pressure for a pullout of Cuban forces; and to support the claims of UNITA leader Jonas Savimbi to a legitimate political role in a coalition regime in Luanda. Although Congress eventually resisted the Reagan call for a repeal of the Clark Amendment, the administration's advocacy of such a policy nonetheless has had a considerable symbolic import for African observers. The Africans viewed terminating the restraints of the Clark Amendment and giving military support to UNITA as destabilizing acts, helpful only to the South African design for subregional hegemony. This perception was reinforced by the administration's failure to take a strong stand in criticism of South African raids against Angola. For Nigeria's president, Shehu Shagari, such American support to "rebel organizations in a sovereign country . . . would be in defiance not only of Angola but of all Africa." Not only would such an approach antagonize friendly states and destabilize the area, it would risk an expanded and intensified conflict.

The pressures for a moderation of policy have been many-sided. They have come not only from the usual liberal internationalist spokesmen but from diplomats seeking Angolan government support on the Namibian issue and from multinational corporation executives whose firms (for example, Gulf Oil, General Tire, and Chase Manhattan Bank) have extensive Angolan investments.[8] With Angola's President José Eduardo dos Santos sending clear signals in November 1981 of a desire to avoid an open confrontation, and even to normalize relations with the United States, the Reagan team appeared to move grudgingly toward a more pragmatic position. To be sure, its rhetoric on the Soviet-backed regime in Luanda continued to be hard line; yet the effect of its policies was movement toward a more flexible stance. As the issues of the Clark Amendment and the role of Savimbi became intertwined with the drive to secure a Namibian settlement, the Reagan team's approach became less ideological. The administration allowed the ExIm Bank to extend an $85 million loan to Angola and entered into a quiet dialogue with Angolan officials. In January 1982, in talks in Paris with Angolan Foreign Minister Paulo Jorge, Crocker appears to have linked a Namibian settlement to Cuban withdrawal, and he indicated that once the process of normalization was under way, United States-Angolan diplomatic relations, as well as an allocation of American economic assistance to Angola, could be expected to follow. A hint that such a strategy was more likely than confrontation to further American objectives can be seen in the Soviet warnings to the Angolans on American imperialistic ambitions in the area, issued following Crocker's talks. All the evidence suggests that the Angolans desired a settlement, were eager to eliminate the costs of maintaining the Cubans, and wanted to distance themselves from the Soviets and forge closer economic links with the West.

Even in support of "proven friends," Reagan administration motives are mixed. In addition to a desire to back allies (Morocco, Tunisia, Zaire, Angola's UNITA) or to stabilize what are perceived as critically important countries (Zaire, Zimbabwe, Namibia, South Africa), there are two related globalist objectives: to secure naval and air facilities for use by the United States Navy and the Rapid Deployment Force (Somalia, Kenya, Diego Garcia), and to resist Libyan adventurism (Liberia, Chad, Sudan, Somalia). Colonel Muammar el-Qaddafi's messianic anti-American style, his close military links with the Soviet Union, his alleged support of international terrorism, and his apparent penchant for intervening abroad are profoundly repugnant to the Reagan team. As part of a get-tough policy former Secretary of State Alexander Haig ruled out a "business as usual" relationship with a regime said to distort the rules of international behavior. The Libyan People's Bureau in Washington was closed, Americans living in Libya were asked to return home, an embargo was put on American imports of Libyan oil, curbs were placed on the sale of American technology to Libya, and an aerial encounter took place off the Libyan coast.

This get-tough policy has also included pledges of American military assistance to African states resisting Libyan interventionism, including major increases in military assistance to such Libyan neighbors as Tunisia, Morocco, Egypt, and the Sudan; a (rather meager) allocation of $12 million to help the OAU peacekeeping force which arrived in Chad following the withdrawal of Libyan troops; joint military exercises with Egyptian and Sudanese forces; and an extensive economic and military aid program, including the dispatching of a 100-man Green Beret unit, to bolster the Liberian military regime. Qaddafi's much-publicized adventurism had indeed provoked the United States to respond; however, questions remain as to whether such wide-ranging measures, especially the embargo on Libyan oil imports, are in fact warranted by Qaddafi's actions, and whether the measures serve American national interests (possibly, in a worst case scenario, leading to a greater Libyan dependence on the Soviet Union).

If the United States sought to counter Qaddafi's actions as destabilizing to his subregion, it attempted to play the role of peacemaker in southern Africa, again in pursuit of greater stability. Such a status quo approach follows logically from the Reagan administration's perceptions of economic and political interests. Seeing the United States as the hub of the world economic system, Reaganites naturally place great emphasis on buttressing a global order that contributes to American strength and well-being. Thus a September 1980 working paper prepared for Reagan observed, with continued access to southern Africa's mineral resources plainly in mind, that "we can't afford to de-stabilize such an important subregion." [9] Though the administration has subsequently played down a sense of urgency over access to these minerals (since a South African embargo is most unlikely in any event), the unresolved question at hand remains: What is the main cause of instability in southern Africa — racial inequality and poverty or Soviet-inspired subversion? To stress the latter, as Reaganites are all too prone to do, is to miss genuine African grievances that produce the opportunities for Soviet interference.

The Reagan team's stability objectives, pursued in a context of racial domination, have led to a tortuous diplomatic process in Namibia and South Africa. As an avowedly conservative regime, the administration raises grave doubts at home and abroad about its intentions in southern Africa. Thus its May 1981 veto of the UN Security Council resolutions for sanctions against South Africa did strengthen its standing in Pretoria but possibly at a high cost elsewhere. Since no other government is both so sympathetic and so powerful, appeals by the United States cannot be cavalierly dismissed by the friendless South Africans. What is not clear at this juncture is whether this administration will press the South Africans with sufficient vigor for an internationally acceptable Namibian settlement and rapid internal liberalization at home.

Thus far, the Reagan administration's efforts to negotiate Namibian independence have appeared to be a kind of high-risk diplomacy that has yet to display conclusive results. As the Johannesburg *Star* recognized in a May 19, 1981, editorial, Reagan went "out on something of a limb" with his policy of "constructive engagement" toward South Africa. Either he could deliver on Namibian independence and South African internal reform, or the new relationship would be seen as diplomatically damaging. Delivering on Namibia, in the sense of hammering out a settlement minimally satisfactory to both black and white interests, was a chancy undertaking at best. If, in April, Crocker found Nigeria and the front-line states adamant on the need for Western pressure to support an unchanged Security Council Resolution (SCR) 435 of 1978 (providing for the withdrawal of South Africa's illegal administration, a cease-fire, and free elections under UN supervision), he found the South Africans equally unyielding in their opposition to UN-administered elections and the prospect of a SWAPO government in Windhoek. Inevitably, the mediator became part of the problem.

For all the assurances Haig made to Nigerian Foreign Minister Ishaya Audu in March 1981 that United States policy "would not change substantially" on Namibia, the American role in the peacemaking process has shifted noticeably.[10] The new administration's refusal to send an observer to the Geneva conference on Namibia in January 1981 suggested the possibility of a separate American initiative. Its policy appeared to be closer to the South African position; this perception was reinforced by hard-line Reaganite statements on convergent United States-South African political, economic, and strategic interests in countering Soviet influences in southern Africa and the Indian Ocean. Further indications of a policy tilt followed as the Reagan team took hold — the call, early in the administration's tenure, for a repeal of the Clark Amendment; the welcoming to Washington of UNITA's Savimbi, leaders of Namibia's ruling Democratic Turnhalle Alliance, and even South African military officers; the linking of Namibian independence to the withdrawal of Cuban troops from Angola; a reference to SCR 435 as a basis for a transition to Namibian independence rather than as a final settlement; the veto of UN sanctions against South Africa; the easing of restrictions on the sale of "nonmilitary" food, industrial chemicals, computers, and other items to South African police and military organizations; and strong support for a $1.1 billion International Monetary Fund loan to South Africa.

If further evidence of a change of policy were necessary, the revelations contained in several leaked documents made the tilt seem unmistakable. Thus, in April, Crocker told South Africa's leaders that "our objective is to increase SAG [South African Government] confidence" in American abilities to stand up to African pressures. While backing SCR 435, Crocker called for "Pretoria's cooperation in working toward an internationally acceptable solution to Namibia which would . . . safeguard U.S. and South African essential interests and concerns." Provided the South Africans cooperated on this and the domestic reform issue, Crocker saw no difficulty in pledging to work toward ending that country's "polecat status" in the world.[11] The African response was sharply critical. At the Eighteenth Summit Conference of the OAU in Nairobi in June, resolutions were passed criticizing the abandonment of SCR 435 and denouncing "the emerging unholy alliance between Pretoria and Washington."[12] The conflict in Namibia was described as a colonial one, not "one of global strategic consideration." Such criticism might be shrugged off by the Reagan administration as part of the price of getting both sides to the bargaining table, for if the administration succeeded in bringing about an internationally accepted settlement, many of the misgivings voiced by African countries might soon be forgotten.

It was the Reagan team's tinkering with SCR 435 that at times evoked heated African disapproval. The new Reagan thrust on the Namibian constitution represented a considerable departure from the procedures originally envisaged under SCR 435. Where the UN plan proposed UN-supervised elections leading to the selection of a constituent assembly that would work out a constitution, the Crocker compromise formula called for agreement on a Namibian independence constitution — including entrenched provisions on elections, private property, minority rights, and the harboring of guerrilla forces — prior to elections and the withdrawal of the South African administration. Describing this compromise, which incorporated aspects of the successful Zimbabwe settlement, as a strengthening of SCR 435, not its abandonment, Crocker sought simultaneously to allay South African strategic fears and African anxieties on a manipulated independence. The immediate reactions to the proposal were largely negative. In June 1981, SWAPO leader Nujoma dismissed American proposals for a Namibian constitutional conference to work out minority guarantees as "sheer nonsense" and described white minority interests as "already taken care of."

In the fall, intensive American discussions with the South Africans and the front-line leaders on revised American proposals rekindled hopes of ending the Namibian deadlock. These proposals provided the foundation for a revised Western plan released in Lagos in late October. This Western plan outlined the principles to be used by the constituent assembly in drawing up the constitution (Phase I); the implementation of the cease-fire, the positioning of the UN force, the withdrawal of SWAPO and South African forces, and the arrangements for the election (Phase II); and the holding of the election and adoption of the constitution (Phase III). The constitutional principles under Phase I called for the establishment of a unitary state under a constitution adopted by a two-thirds vote of all the members of the constituent assembly. The constitution would assure fair representation of the different political groups in Namibia by a system of proportional representation or by appropriate determination of constituencies, or by a combination of the two. It could not be amended except by a designated process of legislative action or popular referendum and would also contain a declaration of fundamental rights enforceable in the courts.

With respect to military arrangements, the plan provided for the monitoring of the elections by UN troops drawn largely from the forces of the five contact countries, wearing their national uniforms (a concession to South African charges of UN partiality toward SWAPO). SWAPO forces would be confined to bases in Angola under UN supervision during the elections, and Cuban troops would be kept in northern Angola. South African armed forces would be removed from Namibia prior to the elections; and SWAPO pledged not to use Namibian territory as a base for future terrorist attacks. South Africa would retain Walvis Bay temporarily;

after independence it would become the subject of separate negotiations. Clearly, by increasing the Western role in the monitoring force, safeguarding minority rights and participation, and placing constraints on SWAPO's ability to establish a one-party state after the elections, the framers of this plan sought to coax South African authorities into agreeing to a timetable for Namibian independence.

Reactions to the Western plan were cautiously positive. Soon after its issuance, the Nigerians and the front-line states, while voicing criticisms on certain issues (such as a complex combination of proportional representation and single-member constituency systems, and the separation of powers), nonetheless accepted the underlying strategy of the plan. Although SWAPO spokesmen expressed a general reluctance to tamper with SCR 435, Nujoma indicated a willingness to include provisions on minority rights in the independence constitution. Moreover, in a November interview, SWAPO Secretary General Moses Garoeb stated that a SWAPO regime would be "extremely pragmatic" on a number of issues; in particular, he noted that SWAPO would not nationalize multinational companies after taking office, impose a one-party state, or allow guerrillas to establish bases in Namibia.[13] South Africa's Prime Minister Botha said the plan could open the way to a settlement, and Namibia's Democratic Turnhalle Alliance, though not joined by the extreme right-wing whites, expressed a readiness to participate in elections under the proposed guidelines. By December 1982, agreement had been reached on many of the Phase I and Phase II principles: a voting system on the basis of either proportional representation or single-member constituencies, but not both; a United Nations force to guarantee free elections for an assembly to work out Namibia's independence constitution; and four of the seven countries to make up the supervisory force (Sudan, Bangladesh, Yugoslavia, and Panama). Nevertheless, with no agreement on a date for a cease-fire between South Africa and SWAPO or on a Cuban troop withdrawal from Angola, the possibilities for further delays and disputes seem well-nigh endless. The main point at contention — formal linkage of a Namibian settlement with a Cuban troop withdrawal — seems as unresolved as ever. In this respect, Vice-President George Bush's statement during his November 1982 tour of seven African countries publicly backing a linkage position can only compound the difficulties in the way of coming to an agreement, as it seems likely to harden South Africa's determination to maintain its current insistence on a Cuban troop withdrawal from the area.

Reaganomics as Applied to Africa

The "New Orthodoxy" in vogue in the Reagan administration has minimized the importance of international economic relations in general and the North-South dialogue in particular. International economic policy has been subordinated to the needs of supply-side and monetarist domestic economic policies. In its relations with the Third World, the administration has emphasized military security rather than issues of economic welfare. And both in its rhetoric and policies, it has shown a strong preference for bilateral foreign assistance rather than for working through multilateral development institutions. The third component of its approach to the Third World has been to underline the present and potential role of the private sector and of market forces. Among other things, the administration's hostility to government intervention and to multilateral aid institutions, coupled with its budgetary problems, have caused it to cut back on its contributions to the World Bank. And, at a time when many African economies are suffering from the simultaneous effects of high prices for their oil imports and low revenues from their principal exports, the administration has put pressure on both the World Bank and the IMF to tighten the terms on which funds are made available to help developing countries overcome balance of payments problems and undertake structural adjustment.

As Richard Feinberg shows in Chapter 5 of this volume, African countries, like other LDCs, have been victims of the side effects of the administration's domestic economic policies. High interest rates in the United States, which have caused other developed countries to implement similar policies, have had a deflationary effect on the principal markets for African exports. One consequence of this has been a decline in the prices of many of the raw material exports on which African economies depend — the International Monetary Fund's composite commodity price index reached its lowest level ever in early 1982. In addition, high interest rates add to the debt servicing burden of those African countries that have been able to borrow in private international financial markets.

At the same time, Reagan's emphasis on the private sector and a more prominent role for market forces has not fallen entirely on deaf ears in Africa. There appears to be a growing disillusionment on the part of a number of African countries with the performance of the parastatal sector (public enterprises that operate on a commercial basis), and increasing enthusiasm for both local and international private enterprise. An emphasis on market forces was endorsed by an important policy paper issued by the World Bank in 1981. While the Reagan administration has applauded this, it has ignored the report's other principal conclusion and proposal — that there will be no significant economic progress in African countries unless a substantial increase in foreign aid occurs. (The report recommends that aid to Africa be doubled in real terms in the 1980s.)[14] Even though the administration's position that "the most important contribution any country can make to world development is to pursue sound economic policies at home" cannot be faulted on strictly logical grounds, the worldwide recession to which Reagan policies have contributed in the short term has placed African countries among its principal victims. Reagan's somewhat paternalistic emphasis on "the magic of the marketplace" and seeming lack of sympathy with the economic difficulties faced by many developing countries has further alienated many African leaders. Ironically, the administration's faith in the virtues of the private sector, and in particular in the positive role that American business can play overseas, has not been reflected in increased support for all government programs to spur American business activities in Africa. While the OPIC lending role has been strengthened, funding for the ExIm Bank is down 15 percent from 1981.[15]

The administration's aid record is a mixed one. The Carter administration had been sympathetic to African aspirations in its rhetoric; this sympathy was limited, however, when applied to the pocketbook. Although from 1975 Africa was the fastest growing geographical program of the Agency for International Development, this growth leveled off in 1978 and the real value of aid to the region actually declined by 3 percent in 1980. Matters were complicated by the Carter administration's inability to persuade Congress to pass an International Security and Development Cooperation Act.

The new administration began on a negative note: In accordance with its desire to cut overall government spending, it slashed $177 million from the Carter administration's request for development assistance to Africa in FY1981. Yet for 1982, the administration proposed an increase in the real value of aid, plus an increase from 23 to 29 percent in the African share of AID's regional programs. Most noticeable is a change in aid priorities; as outlined to Congress by Lannon Walker, former deputy secretary of state for African affairs, "security interests" were placed uppermost. In line with the American emphasis on building a strategic framework to protect interests in the Middle East, Sudan, Somalia, Djibouti, Kenya, and the Indian Ocean states became priority recipients, receiving close to 40 percent of the administration's proposed African aid program for FY1982.

Second, the administration put a high priority on its economic and political interests in southern Africa, a subregion with "enormous potential for mutual economic advantage," which "is threatened by conflict and Soviet troublemaking." Accordingly, the administration proposed devoting 22 percent of its aid budget to this area. The third category was "old friends." Walker noted that Haig had expressed the desire to demonstrate that "it pays to be America's friend and that we can be counted upon in times of need." Singled out for attention were Liberia, Zaire, Senegal, Ghana, and Cameroun, which together would receive 15 percent of the total assistance to Africa. "Last but certainly not least" (in Walker's words) were humanitarian and political interests. In particular he noted American assistance to the Sahel, a subregion where security interests had been added to humanitarian concerns as a result of Libyan adventurism.[16]

Most dramatic of all was the new Reagan emphasis on military assistance. In its original proposal for FY1982, the administration had proposed a $1.7 billion cut in development assistance for the Third World as compared with Carter administration requests; in part this represented a shift in allocations toward the Economic Support Fund (over which the administration had greater discretion) as well as toward military assistance, which rose by $900 million. In the final accounting, Africa's share of development assistance actually increased somewhat, but it was military aid that was programmed to rise most rapidly, increasing by 260 percent — from the 1981 total of $79 million to $210 million for FY1982. Although the administration proposed a $44 million reduction in the PL 480 "Food for Peace" program for Africa (from its existing level of $259 million to $215 million), major military training programs were recommended for Kenya, Sudan, and Zaire, with new ones slated for Cape Verde, Congo, Djibouti, Equatorial Guinea, Guinea Bissau, and Zimbabwe. A useful comment on the administration's priorities was provided by the House Subcommittee on Africa, which described the emphasis on military assistance as "shortsighted": "This approach does not take into account the fact that America's national and security interests throughout the world — but particularly in Africa and the Third World — are best protected by helping nations eliminate poverty and reduce the economic and social disparities which give rise to political instability and armed conflict." [17]

Conclusion

Globalism and regionalism are two prominent perspectives on how United States foreign policy objectives in contemporary world arenas might be secured. On African policy, globalists and regionalists may well agree as to basic American interests and capabilities as well as to the gravity of superpower rivalries on the current global scene. Within the Reagan administration, as was the case with the Carter administration before it, moreover, a wide spectrum of opinion is present, ranging the full gamut from unrestrained globalist to unbridled regionalist thinking. It is also evident that this entire spectrum shifted with the advent of the new Reagan administration. Thus Crocker, prior to taking office, criticized the Carter team as underestimating America's global strategic concerns. In power, however, he falls near the regionalist side of the new administration's continuum — perhaps reflecting his institutional role as assistant secretary of state for African affairs. In true globalist fashion, former Secretary of State Haig pointed to the Soviet Union's "ominous objective" of positioning itself on the Horn to strike against countries near vital Western resource lines;[18] yet Haig also spoke with the sensitivity of a committed regionalist regarding the implications of Soviet military aid to Africa. "Many are very free," he wrote, "about labeling these recipient states as Marxist. Some have suggested they will be Marxist or democratic depending on their assessment of which label will bring them the progress for their people that they seek. And I am one that shares that view." [19]

In brief, the globalist-regionalist distinction is situational and relative, not located at some fixed point or position. On certain issues, proponents of African policies have distinctive overviews with respect to their ranking of priorities on strategic, economic, and social concerns. Nevertheless, it is unwise to overemphasize the significance of these distinctions. Individuals, even factions within the bureaucracy, are likely to display different tendencies on diverse policy questions, and these may vary in turn as the time or place context shifts. During its first year in office, the Reagan administration acted in a cautious and pragmatic manner in its dealings with the Somali government; its relations with the Nimeiry regime in the Sudan seemed less guarded and judicious, no doubt reflecting its determination to respond forcefully and effectively to perceived Libyan threats in the area. Hence globalist and regionalist foreign policy perspectives, long employed by Washington participant-observers themselves, can be said to be generally useful for analytical purposes — provided it is recognized that these labels are intended to represent no more than overarching perspectives, and not fixed or necessarily opposed policy positions.

With this in mind, we wish to turn to the shift from Carter to Reagan and to some tentative conclusions about the implications of this change for the foreign policy process. In this regard, we view the Reagan team's globalist approach as perceptibly different from Carter's thinking, even during the final, difficult days of Carter's term in office. The following points of difference seem critical:

1. Whereas the Carter administration gave high attention to African issues, the Reagan administration has tended to accord them a lower priority. In part this difference reflects a conscious Reagan choice to restrict the agenda, especially on foreign policy matters.[20] Thus except as African questions affect East-West rivalries or economic concerns, Reaganites are less inclined than their immediate predecessors to be attentive to African issues.

2. Unlike the Carter team, which tended to emphasize the regional sources of regional problems, the Reagan administration perceives a planned and organized Soviet global threat as the origin of regional difficulties. For Haig, Libya's pressures against Sudan and Tunisia were part of a broader external challenge, and suggested a central point: "*the interrelationships between threats and events in different theatres*" (italics Haig's).[21] Thus Soviet penetration in the Horn and southern Africa is not restricted to the Soviet Union's own regionalist goals; it also involves broader globalist objectives (for example, the possible denial of strategic minerals or sea lanes to Western adversaries).

3. In contrast to Carter's willingness to suffer criticism, hostility, and even adventurist actions on the part of radical African states, the Reagan administration is determined to raise the cost of what it perceives as antagonistic or reckless behavior. Thus Mozambique's decision to deport American officials or Libya's expansionist moves directed at such American friends as Liberia, Sudan, and Tunisia encountered a strong American response. Foreign critics and adversaries were to be alerted to a changed attitude on the part of the United States government that was intentionally more assertive. In reckoning on gaining respect commensurate with its status as a superpower, the United States seems to be acting in line with its perception of successful Soviet practices in the Third World in recent years (e.g., extensive military support to Ethiopia, Libya, and Angola). The tentativeness that marked the post-Vietnam era is over; Reaganites are resolved to take the rhetoric of their African critics at face value and to act against these presumed opponents.

4. Contrary to Carter's somewhat flexible stance regarding the continued presence of Cuban forces in southern Africa, the Reagan policy makers firmly insist on linking a Cuban troop withdrawal to a settlement of the Namibian issue. The Carter administration assumed that if an agreement could be reached on an internationally acceptable Namibian independence formula then a Cuban withdrawal would follow. The Reagan administration, unwilling to make such an assumption, argues that "realism" requires a parallel withdrawal of Cuban troops from Angola and South African troops from Namibia.

5. Differing from the Carter administration's strong rhetoric on human rights (it did not come down as hard on Mobutu and South Africa as this commitment might imply), the Reagan team has explicitly proclaimed its support for "proven friends" despite their human rights and development records. To be sure, this position brought the Reagan administration somewhat closer to certain African regimes, such as the corrupt dictatorship in power in Zaire. However, the identification of American interests with oppressive regimes such as Mobutu's may well prove costly in the future should conditions deteriorate further and an alternative regime seize power.

6. The Reagan administration gives a noticeably higher priority to military arms transfers to African allies than did its predecessor. This policy orientation reflects its greater concern over what it perceives as a threat from the Soviet Union and its African clients (particularly Libya) to regional stability.

Clearly, the policy preferences of the administration have altered somewhat with the shift from Carter to Reagan. American interests and capabilities remain much as they were, but the objectives of policy and the manner of securing these objectives have undergone change. Although it is apparent that tradeoffs may be present in each type of policy orientation, how is one to assess the realism of the Reagan administration's current globalist orientation as it affects American relations with Africa? Such a Reagan-style globalist thrust, we conclude, tends to be dysfunctional for broader United States-African interests for the following reasons:

1. A globalist approach, with its primary concern for East-West competition, may cause the United States to be insensitive to African goals and priorities. The uniqueness of Africa tends to be overlooked, even dismissed, and a kind of new paternalism is adopted, which places the ultimate responsibility for policy in non-African (that is, Western and Soviet) hands. Those who hold such a view refuse to accept Africa's primary responsibility for its own security and well-being; instead, they assume that the United States and its allies can best decide Africa's true interests and that these interests in time will be seen as identical with those of the West. Such a view inclines the United States toward a status quo orientation that may prove counterproductive. To the extent the United States comes to lack rapport with African leaders and ideas, it may well frustrate the achievement of its most critical objectives in Africa.

2. Globalism, with its emphasis upon strategic factors, tends to lead to false priorities being set in dealings with African states. Thus the stress upon the protection of sea lanes, access to strategic minerals, the right to make use of military facilities, bases, and so forth complicates dealings with African host countries who find themselves identified with American purposes. In acceding to American wishes with respect to the use of naval facilities in Mombasa, for example, the Moi government in Kenya has been placed somewhat on the defensive in its relations with domestic political opponents.[22] More seriously, perhaps, the desire to protect sea lanes and access to minerals contributes to the special American treatment given to certain resource-rich African lands (as witness the policy of "constructive engagement" with South Africa and the conciliatory stance toward Mobutu's Zaire). Unless these approaches bring demonstrable progress toward majority human rights, and, in the case of Namibia, independence, they will likely identify the United States with racism and reactionary impulses in Africa for a long time to come.

3. A globalist orientation, which includes an inclination to punish enemies, leads the Reagan administration to an exaggerated sense of threat from the Soviet Union and its perceived military allies, such as Libya. Such a perspective results in irrational, self-defeating policies (the embargo on Libyan oil, for example), which are not the most effective means of containing Soviet influences. When it is remembered that

Libya was one of only two Arab states that did not take part in the 1973 oil embargo against the United States, then an oil cutoff that pushes Qaddafi closer to one's superpower rival, and risks future access to petroleum reserves in times of need, seems imprudent.

4. A high-risk policy in regard to a Namibian settlement may jeopardize the long-term position of the United States should it fail. External mediation is a chancy undertaking under the best of circumstances, and given the high stakes as well as the evidence of Soviet interference and South African intransigence, steady progress toward an internationally accepted settlement seems an unlikely prospect. Hence, by focusing so much attention upon the American role in resolving the Namibian dispute, the Reagan administration risks major problems in the event that its policy package becomes unraveled.

5. Globalism, by its very nature, lacks a vision of future objectives in Africa. In the case of Namibia, even if a settlement should be hammered out, what program will follow? Constructive engagement with South Africa is likely to remain unacceptable to African opinion throughout the continent. African states are, quite rightfully, to be expected to continue to strive for majority African rule in the rest of southern Africa and will not be diverted for long by any progress on Namibian independence. A globalist orientation seems of little help in understanding the forces for self-rule at work here or in setting long-range priorities in line with Africa's values and expectations.

6. Globalist influences on aid priorities may work against American objectives on the long-term stability of the African state system. Anti-American populism arises in such friendly countries as Ghana precisely because economic deterioration has led to a sense of desperation in the populace at large. With its tendency to direct an increasing proportion of its assistance in Africa to defense-related purposes, the United States is courting further economic, political, and social breakdown, with all its attendant effects on United States-African relations.

In brief, the new Reagan "realism" on Africa must be examined in terms of its near and longer term consequences. To the extent that the qualitative costs seem to outweigh the benefits, a reappraisal of policy seems imperative. "As a matter of fact," writes Arnold Wolfers, "the moral dilemmas with which statesmen and their critics are constantly faced revolve around the question of whether in a given instance the defense or satisfaction of interests other than survival justify the costs in other values." [23] Genuine realism, then, eschews an ideological mind set and requires an accurate assessment of the regional forces at work. An anti-Soviet orientation *not grounded in regional reality* is not likely to prove effective in the long run. Hence an enlightened realism, which places these interrelated regional-global perspectives in balance, seems to hold out the greatest promise for achieving various American purposes in a constructive and morally fulfilling manner.

Notes

1. For further information on the points covered in this section, see Donald Rothchild, "U.S. Policy Styles in Africa: From Minimal Engagement to Liberal Internationalism" in *Eagle Entangled*, pp. 304-335.
2. See the documents in Colin Legum (ed.), *Africa Contemporary Record, 1975-76* (New York: Africana Publishing Co., 1976), pp. C97-106.
3. See the letter from President Siyad Barre to Ambassador John L. Loughran, April 23, 1978, as quoted in U.S. Congress, House Subcommittee on Africa, Committee on Foreign Affairs, *Hearings on Reprograming of Military Aid to Somalia*, 96th Cong., 2nd Sess., 26 August 1980, p. 15.
4. President Reagan's State of the Union Message, as reprinted in *The New York Times*, January 27, 1982, p. 8.
5. Crocker's positions were outlined in a series of articles including "Lost in Africa," *New Republic* 178, 7 (February 18, 1978), pp. 15-17; "Making Africa Safe for the Cubans," *Foreign Policy* 31 (Summer 1978), pp. 31-33; "Missing Opportunities in Africa," coauthored with W. H. Lewis, *Foreign Policy* 35 (Summer 1979), pp. 142-161; "Voilà, Zimbabwe!" *New Republic* 181, 35 (December 22, 1979), pp. 10-13; and, with Mario Greszes and Robert Henderson, "Southern Africa: A U.S. Policy for the '80s," *Freedom at Issue* 58 (November-December 1980), pp. 11-18. See also the article, quoted below, which appeared shortly after his nomination, "South Africa: Strategy for Change," *Foreign Affairs* 59, 2 (Winter 1980/81), pp. 323-351.
6. See Michael Clough, "Why Carrots Alone Won't Work," *African Index* 4, 10 (June 30, 1980), pp. 1-14.
7. *The New York Times*, November 27, 1982, p. 27.
8. On this, see the statement of the president of Gulf Oil Exploration and Production Co., in U.S. Congress, House Subcommittee on Africa, Committee on Foreign Affairs, *Hearings on United States Policy Toward Angola — Update*, 96th Cong., 2nd Sess., 17 September 1980, pp. 10-13.
9. *West Africa*, November 17, 1980, p. 2285.
10. On a reported threat by Nigerian leaders to use their "oil weapon" as a last resort if they felt the Reagan administration tilted too far toward South Africa, see *Weekly Review* (Nairobi), April 10, 1981, p. 16.
11. Several of these leaked documents appear in *Counterspy* 5, 4 (August-October 1981), pp. 48-57.
12. Quoted in *Africa Research Bulletin* 18, 6 (July 15, 1981), p. 6069.
13. *Africa Research Bulletin* 18, 11 (December 15, 1981), p. 6261.
14. International Bank for Reconstruction and Development/The World Bank, *Accelerated Development in Sub-Saharan Africa: An Agenda for Action*, Report No. 3358 (Washington, D.C.: IBRD/World Bank, 1981).
15. Susan Gilpin, "Reagan's Private-Sector Thrust," *Africa Report* 27, 1 (January-February 1982), p. 52.
16. U.S. Congress, House Subcommittee on Africa, Foreign Affairs Committee, *Hear-

ings on Foreign Assistance Legislation for Fiscal Year 1982, Pt. 8, 97th Cong., 1st Sess., pp. 123-124.

17. *Ibid.*, p. ix. For the initial figures, see pp. ix-x of the Subcommittee's statement, as well as Walker's presentation, *ibid.*, pp. 122-187. For the final budget requests and comparisons with previous spending levels, see U.S. Agency for International Development, "Congressional Presentation, Fiscal Year 1982," Main Volume, Amended, in U.S. Congress, House Subcommittee on Foreign Operations, Appropriations Committee, *Hearings on Foreign Assistance and Related Appropriations for 1982*, Pt. 6, 97th Cong., 1st Sess., especially pp. 451-465.

18. *Ibid.*, Pt. 2, 28 April 1981, p. 91.

19. U.S. Congress, Senate Subcommittee on Foreign Operations, Appropriations Committee, *Hearings on Foreign Assistance and Related Programs Appropriations, FY 1982*, Pt. 1, 97th Cong., 1st Sess., 26 March 1981, pp. 32-33.

20. See Thomas L. Hughes, "Up From Reaganism," *Foreign Policy* 44 (Fall 1981), p. 9.

21. House Appropriations Committee, *Hearings on Foreign Assistance*, Pt. 2, 28 April 1981, p. 102.

22. Expressing a radical Kenyan viewpoint, one newspaper noted: "They [Moi's Kenya African National Union] have finally given our entire country over to U.S. imperialism to use as a political and military base." *Pambana* (Nairobi) 1 (May 1982), p. 1.

23. Arnold Wolfers, "Statesmanship and Moral Choice," *World Politics* 1, 2 (January 1949), p. 190.

12

The Reagan Administration and the Middle East

Barry Rubin

The Reagan administration's policy toward the Middle East was characterized at the start by three features. First, it focused overwhelmingly on a single issue and a single contingency — the threat of Soviet invasion or international aggression by Soviet-backed radical states in the Gulf. Second, other problems were generally neglected until they forced their way to center stage as full-blown international crises. Third, a lack of clarity and predictability in Washington's policy toward most local issues did more to undermine the American regional position than any question of America's will and power.

This last problem continued even after September 1982 when the administration changed its focus and made progress on an Arab-Israeli settlement its main priority in the region. The Reagan plan of September 1, 1982, restated many past positions of the United States, but it also established a strong administration commitment to work on the issue. Presented, for the first time, was an American conception of a final settlement: A Jordanian-Palestinian federated state on the West Bank and Gaza strip, coexisting alongside Israel.

It is certainly difficult to formulate clear and successful policies for the Middle East. This region presents the United States with a large set of conflicts and problems whose mere listing leaves one breathless. They include: the war in the western Sahara between Morocco and Algerian-backed guerrillas, the ambitions and activities abroad of the Libyan government in supporting terrorism and subverting other states, the

Barry Rubin is a Senior Fellow at the Center for Strategic and International Studies and a professorial lecturer at the Georgetown University School of Foreign Service. His books include Paved With Good Intentions: The American Experience and Iran *(Oxford University Press, 1980) and* The Arab States and the Palestine Conflict *(Syracuse University Press, 1981).*

desire to maintain correct Egypt-Israel relations in the post-Camp David era, the Arab-Israeli conflict, the Palestinian question and the future of the West Bank, the Lebanese civil war and the lack of an effective government in that country, the demands of local countries for increasingly larger amounts of arms from the United States, the Iran-Iraq war, the rapid economic development of Gulf oil producers with its social and political problems and threat of instability, the aftermath of the Iranian revolution and the breakdown of United States-Iran relations, the Soviet invasion of Afghanistan and the struggle of Afghan guerrillas against Soviet occupation, and the threat posed to Pakistan by Afghan events. The fact that the region is the location of the four largest recipients of American aid (Egypt, Israel, Pakistan, and Turkey) as well as the main purchasers of American arms, indicates its centrality in U.S. foreign policy.

Past Policies: Consistency of American Interests

The Middle East has become a prime focus — often the only focus — of American foreign policy in recent years. Not only has the region increasingly been the site of major international crises, it has also been significant in setting the tone of overall American diplomacy. Developments in the region also played an important role in shaping American public opinion toward international affairs in general and in influencing domestic politics, including the 1980 election.

American interests in the Middle East are simply stated, but the way of best ensuring them can be defined only with difficulty in the face of tremendous controversy. Different politicians, administrations, and portions of the government agree more often on the ends than the means of American Middle East policy.

The first of these interests, particularly significant since 1973, is the continued flow of oil. The West remains heavily dependent on the Middle East for this vital energy source. The argument can be made that existence of a reliable petroleum supply is relatively independent of the regime ruling any country since the export of oil is usually that state's only major economic asset. This is more true than many policy makers recognize; yet, during a war or crisis the supply of oil may be governed by factors contrary to the normal procedures of trade and commerce. Further, control over oil could be used by unfriendly forces to gain political leverage against Western Europe and Japan, who are far more dependent on Middle East petroleum supplies than is the United States itself.

A second American interest is to keep Soviet influence in the area at the lowest possible level. The Soviet Union and its allies must not be allowed to gain control over the oil fields. The region's strategic location at the crossroads of three continents and vital shipping lanes also makes it critical in the East-West conflict. Furthermore, the huge amounts of capital the oil-producing countries hold is another asset that must be denied the Soviet camp.

Regional stability represents a third American interest, as access to oil will be more reliable if countries in the area are not disrupted by internal and external strife. Revolutions might cause nonaligned states to move closer to the Soviet Union or disrupt states that maintain close relations with the United States. Radical change may also produce regimes more hostile to their neighbors, eager to fight or subvert them. Finally, wars between Middle Eastern countries might create significant problems for the United States in the event that it has good relations with both sides.

A fourth interest is to preserve close contacts with friendly states, especially Egypt, Israel, Saudi Arabia, Turkey, and Pakistan, and to a lesser extent, Jordan, the small Arab sheikdoms of the Gulf, Tunisia, Sudan, and Oman. Prior to the Iranian revolution, the shah's regime was also included in the former category. These ties provide the United States with political allies in the regional and international arenas, and in turn deny them to the Soviet Union and its allies.

Many of the debates over the American Middle East policy revolve around how to weigh these four main interests. Both stability and alliance are concepts whose promotion and delineation is subject to many different interpretations. Political change is sometimes inevitable, the Carter administration argued, and the problem for the United States sprang not so much from the fact of change itself as from Washington's decision to side with the status quo. Such an approach encouraged or even forced existing oppositions, once they came to power, to look upon the United States in adversarial terms. Is support for allies necessarily the best way to deter Soviet influence? Will American pressure or accommodation with friends help maintain greater stability? Despite United States-Soviet rivalry in the area, the question remains how high a priority to place on these aspects of American concern. Would the East-West conflict be regarded as primary in all circumstances, or would American influence be best served and Soviet leverage most effectively circumscribed by a proven American ability to cope with regional problems? [1]

During the 1950s, the United States dealt with the Middle East as an area of Cold War conflict. This policy corresponded with the existing Arab tensions between traditionalist states and the radical military regimes allied with Moscow. With the 1967 war, Israel emerged as a major regional military power and United States-Israel relations grew extremely close, given their often parallel enmities and global alignments. After the 1973 war, Secretary of State Henry Kissinger put more emphasis on a policy of building bridges to Egypt and oil-rich Saudi Arabia. Given America's interests on both sides of the Arab-Israeli conflict, the United States government sought to maintain good relations with the various combatants. Not surprisingly, this found expression in an effort to defuse the points of conflict as much as possible.

The Carter Administration

The Carter administration's approach to the region emphasized local problems rather than the East-West conflict and stressed political relations rather than military/security considerations. At the same time, it continued the Nixon Doctrine and the "two-pillar" Gulf policy; this policy eschewed direct American involvement in that subregion, placing reliance on Saudi Arabia and especially Iran to maintain stability there. The shah's fall destroyed this policy and undermined much of the thinking behind it.

Within this framework, Carter set out in the first half of his term to make progress in resolving the Arab-Israeli conflict. The Soviet Union, lacking a similar standing with the two sides, could not compete in such efforts. Washington initially explored possibilities of a broader settlement, including contacts with Palestinian groups, but finally, after President Sadat's trip to Jerusalem, turned to the best achievable option, the Camp David accords. Although two major goals were achieved — a peaceful relationship between Egypt and Israel and the completion of Israeli withdrawal from the Sinai — the talks on autonomy for the residents of the West Bank and Gaza strip did not make much progress. Significantly in this regard, other Arab states did not enter this negotiating process or propose a realistic alternative.

During the Carter administration's second half, the regional position of the United States was affected primarily by the great traumas of 1979: the Iranian revolution, the taking of American hostages in Teheran, and the Soviet invasion of Afghanistan.[2]

The two Iranian crises had very different psychological effects on the United States. Many Americans saw the revolution as retribution for excessive American proximity to an unpopular and repressive dictatorship: American actions in that country may have helped lead to Iranian anti-Americanism. The Carter administration was slow throughout 1978 to recognize the extent of the upheaval in Iran; by late December, however, the White House decided to try to negotiate a moderate transition from the shah. The interim government that followed was unable to mobilize significant support from monarchists or Islamic fundamentalists, and, in February 1979, the Khomeini forces took power.

The revolution's strategic and political impact was enormous. The collapse of a regime previously thought to have been a pillar of regional stability created doubts about every government in the Gulf area. The Islamic nature of the revolution led many American observers to expect a series of similar explosions, and Carter's national security advisor, Zbigniew Brzezinski, dubbed the area the "arc of crisis."

The taking of American diplomats as hostages by Khomeini-supported militants in November 1979 intensified the crisis. In addition, it negated the earlier, "liberal" interpretations of the Iranian revolution that traced it to the shah's violations of human rights, excessive arms buildup, the indulgence of the United States for the Iranian regime, and other similar causes. Instead, the Islamic republic's "irrationality" and extreme hatred and contempt for America were seen as characteristic of the revolutionary change. The revolution had, in the eyes of most Americans, produced a situation detrimental to the interests of both the American and Iranian people. Change, it was concluded, could be quite a frightening process, and the shah, with all of his faults, came to be viewed as a more attractive figure in retrospect.

In short, the hostage crisis accelerated or created the victory of a "conservative" interpretation of Iranian events. According to this interpretation, Khomeini dared to act as he did only because the United States was weak or, at least, acted weak. Other foreign leaders watching the American handling of the crisis would conclude that Washington did not really support its own allies and was not a reliable friend. The failure of the April 1980 hostage rescue mission further undercut public confidence in the competence of the Carter administration. This image of Carter's weakness was consistent with the thinking of Ronald Reagan and his supporters. Thus the experience of the hostage crisis reinforced the ideological perspective of this group and made it far more acceptable to the general public.[3]

Former Secretary of State Henry Kissinger provided an influential version of this critique of weakness. American failings, presumably arising after he left office, had transformed "inchoate unrest into a revolution. . . . To my mind," he explained, "the combination of Soviet actions in Ethiopia, South Yemen, Afghanistan, plus the general perception of an American geopolitical decline, had the consequence of demoralizing those whose stock in trade was cooperation with the United States, undermining their resolution towards potential revolutionaries." The shah did not resist the revolt more forcefully "because he must have had doubts about our real intentions," but concessions could not stop revolutions and should come only when order is restored. "Whether we like it or not," Kissinger concluded, "the shah was considered our close ally in that area for 37 years. He left office under the visible urging of the United States. Other local rulers might fear similar treatment by America and would seek alliances elsewhere."[4]

The idea of White House responsibility for the shah's collapse was as irresistible as it was erroneous. Then vice-presidential candidate George Bush accused Carter of "pulling the rug out from under the shah." The president's "on-again, off-again statements . . . did much to hasten his departure," and the administration's policy of "splendid oscillation" severed the links between the United States and its allies.[5]

The shah's fall forced adjustments in American strategic thinking on the Middle East. Ironically, as in the case of detente, the challenged theory had been formulated by the Nixon rather than the Carter administration. The Iranian revolution was taken to show that the indirect approach favored by the Nixon Doctrine did not work. If the United States wanted something done it must do it itself.

Such conclusions were further reinforced by the Soviet invasion of Afghanistan in December 1979. President Carter's statement that this was the greatest crisis since World War Two was generally taken as exaggeration, but the occupation of Afghanistan was a shock to American policy makers. Speaking of the Middle East in the 1950s, veteran diplomat Raymond Hare once commented, "It's hard to put ourselves back into this period. There was really a definite fear of hostilities, of an active Russian occupation of the Middle East physically, and you could practically hear the Russian boots clumping down over hot desert sands." In the early 1980s the psychological state of American Middle East policy reverted to that earlier era.

The invasion's impact was particularly strong given its echo of the events that first began the Cold War in the post-World War II period. The United States was generally prepared to accept an Eastern Europe friendly toward the Soviet Union, but it assumed at the same time that those states would be independent of Moscow's control — a "Finlandized" but sovereign Eastern Europe. The brutal suppression of all opposition forces and democracy there convinced American policy makers that the Soviets, whether through an excessive appetite for security or aggressive designs, would continue to extend their power until stopped.

The same framework was applied to Afghanistan, long a neutralist country with a large amount of Soviet influence. Precisely because Kabul had made such efforts to appease Moscow, the takeover was seen as a sign of Soviet insatiability; political accommodation as a way for neighboring states to maintain good relations with the Soviet Union was deemed to be impermanent. Whatever the reasons for Moscow's action, whether "offensive" or "defensive" in conception, whether as a step toward the Gulf or to prevent the overthrow of a pro-Soviet Marxist government, objectively the new situation marked a major advance for Soviet forces and a possible stepping stone for new attacks.

In January 1980, national security advisor Zbigniew Brzezinski called for the United States to establish a "cooperative security framework" of Middle East nations against the Soviet Union.[6] A few days later, President Carter's State of the Union message outlined the approach that later became known as the Carter Doctrine. "The steady growth and increased projections abroad of Soviet military power," he said, had combined with "the overwhelming dependence of Western nations, which now increasingly includes the United States, on vital oil supplies from the Middle East" to form a serious threat to American interests.

"The pressure of change in many nations of the developing world," and particularly the possibility of internal upheavals in the Gulf states, provided "some of the most serious challenges in the history of this nation," the president continued. "The denial of these oil supplies — to us or to others — would threaten our security and provoke an economic crisis greater than that of the Great Depression 50 years ago, with a fundamental change in the way we live." [7] This situation required, Carter concluded, an increase in American military strength and ability to project it through a Rapid Deployment Force, a regional security framework, some covert aid to Afghan guerrillas, and a warning to Moscow that aggression in the Gulf would be met by a strong American response.

Thus, the conclusions drawn by the Carter administration from these experiences were first, that the East-West conflict must be given a more central place in any consideration of the Middle East and particularly of Gulf security, and second, that the ability to project American forces into the area must play a more important role in American military thinking. These ideas were both accepted and extended by the Reagan administration.

The Reagan Administration: Policy Premises

It became quite fashionable, both in the United States and the Middle East itself, to state that the Reagan administration had no Middle East policy. This misconception arose because the Reagan policy was not in fact comprehensive. The administration consciously ignored some regional problems that it judged to be unimportant. Excessive emphasis on the necessary incompleteness of policy has diverted attention from a fundamental change in approach. The Reagan administration, rejecting the view that changes in international politics limited the ability of the United States to shape regional developments, asserted that American power should and could be used to determine the course of events. The refusal to do so rather than an inability to do so was at fault, they argued. The shah's incompetence, the shortcomings of Nixon-Kissinger policy, and socioeconomic changes in Iran were not regarded as responsible for the revolution's success; rather, the fault lay with a failure of will and toughness on the part of the Carter administration.

The Reagan administration's view of the region was based on three premises that broadly defined its strategy. The first of these was the primacy of the Gulf as an area for American concern and activity. This resulted both from changes in regional financial power and strategic importance (with the rise of the oil exporting countries) and from the crises in Iran and Afghanistan. Hence the Gulf was to become the focus of the administration's "strategic consensus" — a broad regional alliance against the Soviets, pivoted on Saudi Arabia. The implications of this new emphasis were varied: an increased arms sales program, a theater for the training of American troops, and a network of support facilities.

Obviously, this emphasis on the Gulf meant less attention on the Arab-Israeli conflict generally and on the autonomy negotiations between Egypt and Israel in particular.[8] From the administration's point of view, this was no oversight. The limits placed on Camp David (caused by the intransigence of the Palestine Liberation Organization and Israel and the refusal of more Arab regimes to join the talks) made a breakthrough seem unlikely. Also, since the Camp David agreements were the Carter administration's creation, the administration's successors felt much less commitment to them.

Further, the Reagan team saw no attractive plan in sight. The Palestine Liberation Organization (PLO) was considered a terrorist and pro-Soviet group — two factors defining it as an enemy in the Reagan administration's book. A Palestinian state was seen as destabilizing for the region. A "Jordanian solution," involving a Jordan-West Bank federation, was preferable and was indeed later taken up by the September 1982 Reagan plan, but required Jordanian support and possibly even PLO acquiescence. Finally, Israeli annexation of the territories, which the permanent settlements seemed headed toward, would carry high costs for American interests in the Arab world and was also opposed by the administration. Given the complexity of the issue and the difficulty in making progress, it was more expedient to focus on other questions.

The second main administration premise was that the Soviet Union posed the greatest clear and present danger to the region. The invasion of Afghanistan lent credence to this view. However, with the exception of Pakistan, this perspective did not correspond to regional perceptions. Middle Eastern countries, including the Arab states of the Gulf, were far more worried about regional and domestic problems than they were about the external Soviet threat.

In this context, the administration emphasized, and sometimes overstated, the capabilities of Moscow's prospective and real regional allies. Richard Allen, then national security advisor, explained in September 1981, for example, that the threat to the Gulf "could come from a destabilized Iran, from Ethiopia, from Yemen or elsewhere.... The situation has changed dramatically in the last four years."[9]

Given the unexpected explosion in Iran, American leaders believed anything was possible in the Middle East, an attitude conducive to panic. For example, when the Sudanese government claimed that Libya was about to launch a cross-border attack — an unlikely contingency on logistical, military, and political grounds — Senator Richard Lugar, an administration ally, said, "It seems to me ... invasion is imminent." Even Senator John Glenn, who expressed concern about White House commitments on Gulf intervention, added that the Libya-Ethiopia-South Yemen pact was "probably under Soviet leadership."[10]

As Gulf Arabs remained uninterested in an anti-Soviet alliance, however, and as Iran won victories in its war with Iraq, American concern partly shifted to Teheran. By mid-1982, Washington, while remaining ostensibly neutral in the Iran-Iraq war, gave some covert aid to Iraq and its Arab allies against Iranian invasion or a possible revolution by radical Islamic forces in the Gulf.[11]

The third premise, based on the emphasis on Gulf security and on a Soviet threat, produced the conclusion that American regional policy must be primarily military and unilateralist. If the greatest danger was from the Soviet Union, only the United States could confront it successfully. If local states were unable to insure regional security against the Soviets or Soviet-backed aggressors, then the United States would have to respond directly. On this point, analysts often misunderstood the administration's conception as a revival of 1950s regional alliance policy. Instead, the United States now emphasized its own responses and the use of its own forces; local states were mainly expected to supply bases or facilities.[12] Thus, while Egypt, Israel, and Saudi Arabia sometimes competed for the position of America's best friend and favored ally in the region, Washington was not seeking any regional policeman. This job would in principle be reserved for the United States itself.

At the same time the United States, as part of its military posture, continued and expanded previous large-scale arms sales programs to the area. These, it should be remembered, came at the insistence of the local governments. Failure to provide such equipment could carry with it political costs. As the *Washington Post* correctly noted in regard to the sale of intelligence and surveillance aircraft: "The Saudis evidently asked for AWACS not so much to prepare for either a Soviet or an Israeli attack, although both contingencies continually bob up and down in their minds, as to test the strength of their American connection."[13] In many cases, there were legitimate defensive requirements. For example, Saudi oil fields were relatively unprotected, and keeping these assets safe was not only in Saudi interests but those of the West as a whole. However, as in Iran, the equipment purchased was not always the most effective for preserving internal stability; rather, the most advanced, sophisticated armaments for international warfare were provided.

Policy Implementation: Military

The United States Rapid Deployment Force (RDF) and a whole network of support facilities behind it were explicitly designed to oppose any Soviet attack on the region. The RDF might also be used in state-to-state or internal conflicts, and this led to much distrust of American intentions in the Gulf. President Reagan hinted at additional missions for the force in an October 1981 press conference, "Saudi Arabia we will not permit to be an

Iran." [14] The implication of American willingness to intervene in internal Saudi upheavals was of extraordinary significance, but Secretary of Defense Caspar Weinberger had some difficulty in defining this pledge. What the president had in mind, he said, "is that we would not stand by and allow in the event of Saudi requests . . . a government . . . totally unfriendly to the United States and the Free World to take over." [15] By failing to define the RDF's role with clarity, the administration invites major controversy in the United States and abroad should it ever be used.

Both the Carter and Reagan administrations had little success in gaining European cooperation for Gulf security; most local countries, including those friendly to the United States, were reluctant to become publicly involved or to provide bases. Some facilities were found, however, on the region's periphery in Kenya, Somalia, Oman, and the Indian Ocean island of Diego Garcia. In June 1980, a United States-Kenya agreement provided for the use of Mombasa port and an adjacent airfield in exchange for military and economic aid; a United States-Oman accord at the same time allowed for access to bases, including the air force base on Masirah island. Two months later, an arrangement was made with Somalia for use of facilities in Mogadishu and Berbera.

All of these facilities required large-scale spending to make them usable and all of them remained rather far from the Gulf. But the maintenance of naval units in the Arabian Sea with stored supplies supplemented these efforts. The presence of AWACS, first under complete American control and then to be sold to the Saudis, provided intelligence information to the United States on the activities of a variety of potentially inimical forces in the region. Further, despite their public criticism of any American military involvement in the region, there was ample evidence that the Saudis and other Gulf Arab states were overbuilding their own bases in case the American forces would ever need to use them. Much of the local military cooperation, including the new Gulf Cooperation Council, was also consistent with American objectives.

Policy Implementation: Government Organization

The administration's choice of Middle Eastern policy makers reflected its globalist priorities and premises. This was clearly true for former Secretary of State Alexander Haig and those chosen for the National Security Council and the State Department's Policy Planning Staff, among others. Because of the region's importance, Middle East policy was conducted from the top to a greater degree, and with less reference to the State Department's career service, than was the case for any other part of the world. As a consequence, American policy was framed with insufficient sensitivity to and knowledge of regional concerns.

The Department of Defense, particularly in the person of Secretary of Defense Caspar Weinberger, was more influential in shaping Middle East policy than it had ever been before. Given the general lack of experience and diplomatic talent in the administration, a great deal of the burden was placed upon retired Ambassador Philip Habib, whose seemingly interminable shuttle trips were a major asset in resolving the fighting in Lebanon.

While the Reagan team shared many assumptions about the Middle East, there was no shortage of sharp disagreements, particularly pitting Weinberger against Haig until the latter's resignation in June of 1982. Since no individual or institution was placed in clear charge of American Middle East policy, not to mention American foreign policy as a whole, the American stance was often vacillating and contradictory, especially on the Arab-Israeli conflict. The Reagan team apparently failed to understand that Middle East distrust of the United States came not from derision of American weakness, but rather from the frequent shifts in American foreign policy that make it so unpredictable.

Further, in the aftermath of Iran's revolution, the White House, State Department, and CIA spoke of the obvious need to improve national intelligence assessments on the international and domestic developments in the Middle East. Yet despite the proven inadequacies of reporting and policy making procedures in the Iranian case, there were no major improvements. American leaders continued to have little understanding of radical Islamic movements and of the motives and mechanisms in regional politics.

Moreover, the fact that American actions often reflect internal bureaucratic conflicts provokes much confusion in the Middle East. The greatest substantive conflict within the administration was over the policy to be pursued on the Arab-Israeli conflict. Haig considered the Arabs far more concerned about Gulf insecurity and an increasingly vociferous Islamic Iran than about Israel. He thought that internal and international security considerations would prevent the Arabs from turning toward the Soviets or reducing their links with Washington, and he rated highly the importance of the United States-Israel link in preserving American interests.

Weinberger's view was partly shaped by the Defense Department's responsibility for arms sales and for military cooperation with Saudi Arabia, which he believed could play an important leadership role in the region. He considered pressure on Israel and progress on negotiations over the Palestinian question necessary to maintain good United States-Arab relations. In brief, Weinberger was much more worried about a decline of the American position in the Arab world.

Sometimes these battles seriously damaged United States policy. For example, when Weinberger visited Jordan in the summer of 1981, he publicly announced American intentions to sell Amman F-15 planes and Hawk antiaircraft missiles, even though this decision had not been fully approved within the United States government. In another case, the Lebanon crisis in the summer of 1982, at a time when Haig was trying to pressure the PLO to leave Beirut (using the leverage of a possible Israeli attack), NSC advisor William Clark told the Saudis that Israel's troops would not advance against the PLO-held section of the city. Because of disputes over such conflicting actions on Middle East and other issues, Haig resigned. His replacement, George Shultz, was an economist who had most recently worked with Weinberger at the Bechtel Corporation, which held large contracts in the Arab world. Shultz put a higher priority on dealing with the Arab-Israeli conflict and was the main force behind President Reagan's major initiative of September 1, 1982, which adopted a Jordanian solution approach for the future of the occupied territories. The new secretary of state depended to a greater extent on Assistant Secretary of State for Near East Affairs Nicholas Veliotes and on the State Department staff. But given Shultz's easygoing ways, authority on Middle East policy was still diffused throughout the administration.

Policy Implementation: United States-Saudi Relations

Saudi Arabia played a central role in administration policy as the region's most important oil producer and as a potential leader among the Arabs.[16] The main controversy of American Middle East policy in 1981 was over the sale of AWACS to the Saudis. The request to buy AWACS was accompanied by orders for Sidewinder air-to-air missiles, auxiliary fuel tanks, and bomb racks for already purchased American-built F-15s, as well as for refueling planes able to extend those fighter-bombers' range. In 1978 the Carter administration, to gain Israeli acquiescence on the original sale, promised Israel that such equipment would not be sold; this was reversed two years later, however.

Advocates of the $2 billion sale argued it would enhance Saudi security, help protect the oil fields and the Gulf against aggression by Soviet or local radical forces, aid American military and intelligence efforts, and strengthen bilateral relations. Failure to deliver the AWACS would severely undermine American credibility in the Gulf.[17] Opponents saw this step endangering America's secret technology by exposure in a country whose security, stability, and friendship were questionable; threatening to Israel's security; and entangling the United States with a regime whose fall might be hastened by excessive military transfers. After a heated congressional debate, the Senate narrowly supported the sale.[18]

As for the political side of United States-Saudi relations, President Reagan himself gave a succinct explanation of American goals: "Moderate Arab states like Egypt want peace, and Israel wants peace. Together they can be a force to keep the biggest troublemaker in the world, the Soviet Union, from making mischief in the Mideast.... Saudi Arabia is a leader of the moderate Arab states. I believe the Saudis are the key to spreading the peace throughout the Mideast instead of just having it confined to Israel and Egypt." [19]

Policy Implementation: Libya

The Reagan administration's antagonism toward the Libyan regime was an important part of its Middle East policy. Colonel Muammar el-Qaddafi's support for international terrorism, his alliance with Moscow — though he was hardly the Soviet surrogate perceived in Washington — and his destabilizing actions in Africa, made this position understandable. The Reagan government considered him a test case to show they would not be bullied by petty dictators.

During its early months in office, the administration explored overthrowing him. The White House stated it would not block Egyptian action against Libya, a reversal of Carter administration policy. As the difficulties and dangers of direct action against Qaddafi became clear, the administration turned to other strategies. The administration tried to convince American oil companies operating there to withdraw, but with limited effects. In May 1981, the United States expelled Libyan representatives from Washington; six months later the State Department ordered Americans out of Libya, and in March 1982 the United States stopped buying Libyan oil.

President Carter had sought to avoid confrontation with Libya by canceling American maneuvers in the Gulf of Sidra, which Qaddafi claimed as territorial waters, a view not accepted by the United States and many other countries. For the Reagan administration, however, the reassertion of American strength was primary; a confrontation was considered a salutary demonstration of American power.

During August 1981 naval exercises, American carrier planes were attacked by Libyan fighters 60 miles off the coast. Two of Qaddafi's planes were shot down. This incident, said *The New York Times*, was "impressive to the enemies of freedom." But while the event might have been generally well received at home, it was not as favorably regarded by most people in the Islamic Middle East who saw the United States as acting in a bullying and unnecessarily provocative way. Qaddafi was also strengthened both at home and regionally by his new image of a David confronted with the American Goliath. [20]

Policy Implementation: United States-Israel Relations

Despite the administration's desire to emphasize the Persian Gulf, a series of events nonetheless tended to highlight the Arab-Israeli conflict. These events provoked a rising degree of tension in United States-Israel relations, without substantially altering their nature. These episodes included the movement of Syrian antiaircraft missiles into Lebanon; an artillery battle between Israel and the PLO on the Israel-Lebanon border; the June 1981 Israeli raid destroying Iraq's nuclear reactor; the July Israeli air attack on PLO offices in Beirut, which resulted in civilian casualties; the controversy over AWACS sales to Saudi Arabia; Israel's step toward annexing the Golan Heights in December; the firing of West Bank mayors in March and April 1982; and the Israeli invasion of Lebanon in June 1982.

Initially, the Reagan administration seemed tolerant of the Begin government's assertive policies. Washington's prime goal was to preserve quiet on the Arab-Israeli front, fearing that trouble there might lead to war or weaken any impetus toward Gulf cooperation. The United States government alternated between the view that the Begin regime was endangering that balance and the concern that pressure on Israel might only encourage precipitate action by Jerusalem.

Israel's policies were based on expectations of continued Arab hostility and a mistrust of foreign allies, seen as inevitably selling out Israeli interests. While the country tended to rally against outside pressure, the government's ability to work with and maintain the American connection remained an important domestic asset. In the fight for survival, words were far less important than the military balance of forces and the situation on the ground. Foreigners saw Israel as all-conquering, but Israelis were conscious of security dangers; they would make concessions on security issues only if offered acceptable alternatives. In line with these priorities, the Begin government claimed that safety lay in continued West Bank settlement leading to permanent Israeli control over the occupied territories.

American vacillation over bilateral relations affected Israel's political culture in the worst possible way. Since Israel was afraid of what the United States might do the following month, it repeatedly acted quickly to grab any possible advantage during periods of apparent American support. The September 1981 strategic understanding was a good example of the effect of administration policy shifts, which inspired neither concessions nor restraint from Israel. As Shlomo Avineri, former director-general of Israel's foreign ministry, wrote, "It just does not reflect seriousness of purpose when the United States hastily signs a strategic memorandum of understanding with Israel merely to placate the Israelis in the wake of the AWACS sale to Saudi Arabia and then, just as hastily, voids the understanding after Israel's *de facto* annexation of the Golan Heights." [21]

The main conflict between the United States and Israel came during Jerusalem's invasion of Lebanon in the summer of 1982. During the early months of the administration, the anti-Syria and anti-PLO stance of the United States seemed to support strong Israeli measures. Thus, former national security advisor Richard Allen contended that "to the extent that one reaches to the source of terrorism, then, of course, there's ample justification ... for taking actions. ... I'm just saying that reaching to the source is generally recognized as a 'hot pursuit' of a sort and therefore justified." [22]

Later, however, Haig recognized that Lebanon was the most likely place for a general war to break out in the Middle East; although the State Department had no particular blueprint for dealing with this situation, he set a high priority on ending the civil war there. Simultaneously, the United States worked hard to restrain Israel from invading Lebanon. More than once, these pressures worked, but they finally failed in June of 1982.

Even though the United States had strongly opposed any Israeli invasion, Washington was slow and confused in responding to the attack. The military success of the Israeli move seemed to prompt Haig's acceptance of the idea that a defeat for the PLO and Syrians was a setback for forces inimical to the United States and was a breakthrough in ending Lebanon's civil war. But Haig soon resigned, and despite Ambassador Philip Habib's strenuous labors, Israel's demand for Lebanese political concessions before it would withdraw its troops heightened Washington's frustration and anger.

President Reagan's September 1 proposals produced further tension for United States-Israel relations, since Israel was not consulted and did not agree with the new initiative. To a great extent, the carefully worded speech reiterated past American thinking. Reagan called for a solution based on a federated Jordanian-Palestinian state ruling the occupied territories under King Hussein's control. Border adjustments might be made for Israel's security, but construction of Jewish settlements on the West Bank should be frozen as soon as possible. The United States would not accept either Israeli annexation of the territory or an independent Palestinian state under PLO leadership.

There were several reasons for the timing and shape of this proposal. Israel's invasion of Lebanon provided opportunities for United States policy by weakening Arab hard-liners, demonstrating the lack of a viable Arab military option and forcing them to seek protection from Israeli power. The United States clearly held the cards for any diplomatic settlement. But in order to take advantage of these developments, Washington had to dissociate itself from the policy of Israel's government and make gestures toward the Arabs. A moderate solution could for the first time build a consensus in the United States over how to resolve the conflict. Finally, the administration became convinced that a slow and confused response to the Lebanon crisis was damaging its credibility and prestige at home.

Future United States-Israel relations hinge on the extent to which Washington finds Israeli actions detrimental to its interests and to regional stability. A conflict could also arise from attempts to pressure Jerusalem to give up occupied territories, stop settlement construction there, and negotiate on terms that the Israeli government finds unacceptable. While

Israel's popularity in the United States seemed to have suffered some erosion during the friction of 1981-1982, proposals for foreign aid indicated that it still enjoyed a large measure of support in the United States Congress.

Limitations of Administration Policy: Regional Politics

Arab politics tend to be volatile because of the great strains on the legitimacy of governments and states. The tenets of both Islam and of Arab nationalism are difficult for any regime to fulfill. Islamic tenets demand adherence to Islamic laws, while Arab nationalism demands the unity of the Arab world and the cooperation of Arab states, failing to take into account the very real factors that divide them. Both considerations allow states to intervene constantly in each other's affairs, support internal opposition forces, and form a dizzying series of alliances and enmities.

Modernization also produces social and psychological changes that makes governing difficult. The failure of various types of regimes to fulfill Islam's ideals, unite the Arabs, defeat Israel, bring rapid and painless increases in living standards, or prevent outside forces from intervening in the region, produces great dissatisfaction. Radical, fundamentalist Islam has become the most important antiestablishment ideology, causing those in power to try to establish Islamic credentials while simultaneously campaigning to increase loyalty to their own nation-state. To be sure, Islamic radical movements have spread; yet in light of the defensive measures taken by state elites, such movements have not come close to taking power elsewhere since Iran's revolution.

The Manichaean view of Middle East states as pro-West or pro-Soviet, so characteristic of the Reagan administration, is based on a fallacy. Islam and Arabism make these governments and countries loyal to their own interests, limiting the extent of alliances with outsiders. Foreign involvement can encourage local xenophobia and undermine regimes. Not surprisingly, therefore, both the United States and the Soviet Union have discovered the difficulty of obtaining leverage in the Islamic Middle East.

These factors also shape Arab policies in the conflict with Israel. Support for the Palestinians is coupled with knowledge that failure to maintain militancy opens Arab regimes to attack at home and abroad. Similarly, the PLO leadership realizes that even if it wanted to compromise on a political settlement, this would split its ranks and allow Arab governments to attack it. Such considerations put heavy constraints on Arab political maneuverability. Consequently, the safest course is usually the one of least innovation or deviation from the mainstream Arab line. Still, the very rivalries that discourage Arab states from becoming too conciliatory also limit their willingness to take risks for the PLO and permit them to place priority on their own interests.

The Administration's Arab Strategy

An understanding of these dynamics, so necessary in formulating any policy toward the region, has been sadly lacking in the Reagan administration. The constant public rhetoric about American security plans in the Gulf and the insistence on a high profile in various countries literally forced moderate Arabs to dissociate themselves from Washington. Examples of this were public statements by the administration requesting bases from Egypt. Foreign bases are anathema for Cairo: Opposition to Britain's Suez base was a central issue during the 1940s and early 1950s, while resentment of Soviet bases was a major factor in Sadat's expulsion of the Russians.

Certainly, some Middle Easterners questioned American reliability after Iran's revolution, yet the argument heard so often during the Vietnam war — that American commitments must be pursued whatever the cost to show Washington's determination — proved counterproductive. Not only was the United States bogged down in an increasingly costly and damaging conflict, but it reaped no perceivable political benefit for its persistence; the audience was not impressed with the show.

Yet Reagan officials greatly overestimated the ease with which military interventions could put down internal conflict. Their misunderstanding of revolutions and Islamic societies had frightening implications for their own performance in the face of such a crisis. Further, the blithe optimism about the effects of willpower was based on a misreading of past American ability to shape regional events. Even in the 1950s, the peak of America's international power, Washington had been unable to stop a series of radical military coups and the alignment of the three most important Arab states — Egypt, Syria, and Iraq — with the Soviet Union.

A similar problem beset the administration's Gulf policy. Was such a public and assertive American posture really more conducive to preserving internal stability and regional order? Sometimes, American policy itself seemed a major source of unrest and anti-Americanism. Many Arabs in the Gulf worried that the RDF might be used to take over their oil fields or change their governments should they refuse to follow American wishes.

Unfortunately, while in military thinking even the slenderest contingency and worst-case analysis must be taken into consideration, in diplomacy, governments are loathe to embark on any effort that does not have the greatest promise of success. A credible deterrent to any direct Soviet attack was necessary, but the problem was that this single issue became so overwhelmingly dominant in shaping American regional policy. Ironically, despite American fears of further Soviet interventions and of pro-Soviet, Islamic revolutions, Moscow's influence and prestige in the area descended to their lowest point in a quarter-century.

In this context, Washington overestimated Soviet control over Syria, Ethiopia, Libya, and South Yemen. These countries, especially the first three, were far from being Soviet surrogates or puppets. The United States had learned nothing from the past mistake of labeling Egypt, Iraq, and the Sudan in this manner. The Reagan administration totaled Moscow's regional gains without considering its equally impressive losses and defeats over the last decade. The result was an overly high estimate of the Soviet Union's strength and capabilities.

In addition, the excessive emphasis on Soviet influence meant overdependence on direct American responses, particularly of a military nature. The decision to use the RDF in a regional crisis might be hasty and ill-considered. Rather, the most likely contingency — internal revolution in the face of rapid modernization and social change — required different kinds of policies. These were problems the United States was least prepared to deal with or to help avoid.

Relatively bereft of a regionalist political overview, United States-Arab relations in the Reagan administration focused increasingly on arms sales, particularly in regard to Washington's two most important bilateral links in the Arab world, Saudi Arabia and Egypt. The belief by some American officials that Saudi Arabia would be a strong regional force and bulwark of the status quo was based on a serious misunderstanding: Saudi Arabia's financial strength is not matched by political or military power. The vulnerable Saudis usually pursue a timid diplomatic path, seeking to avoid antagonizing more powerful Arab forces. Riyadh is incapable of regional leadership, though it remains an important country whose security and stability are very much in the American interest.

If Arab countries were to join an anti-Soviet strategic grouping and were to identify clearly with the United States, these states would be exposed to domestic and international instability. In this, Haig failed to understand the Saudi concern over the Arab-Israeli conflict, and Weinberger could not formulate a program that would actually promote greater regional stability. The Arabs would never enlist in a United States-led anti-Soviet alliance or openly acquiesce to American intervention in the Gulf. The Washington debate over tactics missed the unworkable nature of the strategy.

While the Reagan administration focused on Saudi Arabia, Egypt was curiously neglected. Development of a close relationship with the single most important Arab country was a major achievement of the Nixon and Carter administrations. President Sadat's trip to Jerusalem and involvement in the Camp David accords greatly changed regional politics. Yet, despite large amounts of American aid, the Reagan administration avoided coordi-

nation with Cairo and was uninterested in using Cairo's strength to preserve regional security.

The Reagan plan of September 1982 saw Jordan as the key factor in
solving the Palestinian issue and the Arab-Israeli conflict. While Amman
wanted to end the battle and repossess the West Bank, this was no easy
undertaking. King Hussein sought a mandate from the other Arab states
and from the PLO. Again, Saudi Arabia was not willing to go out on a
limb and support Hussein or Reagan's proposal. The Arab belief that only
the United States could mediate a settlement and force Israeli concessions
was coupled with warnings that failure to achieve a breakthrough would
bring retaliation. But the glut in the petroleum market, Arab military
weakness, tightening Israeli control over the West Bank, and limits to
Soviet support have reduced Arab leverage.

The United States can only produce results with a moderated Arab
bargaining position and cooperation from Israel's government — neither
easily obtained. The Reagan administration faced the problem of having
policies toward Egypt, Jordan, Saudi Arabia, and Israel that did not mesh.
The United States was helping all four countries. They, in turn, recipro-
cated with cooperation on specific bilateral issues but provided little assistance on regional problems.

The Arab-Israeli Conflict

The Reagan administration's original problem with the Arab-Israeli conflict was not a failure to gain some dramatic diplomatic breakthrough —
this was unlikely in any case. The administration had to define its proxi-
mate objectives. Did it want Palestinian, Jordanian, or Israeli rule over the
occupied territories? Was there a place for the PLO in a peace settlement?
Should the Saudis be involved in this effort? What was the best way to
bring together the different parties?

With the September 1982 Reagan plan, the administration finally succeeded in producing a reasonable proposal, albeit one very difficult to
implement. Since the administration wanted Arab cooperation on security
issues and the Cold War, it was not in a position to pressure the Arabs to
cooperate. And, because of American domestic politics, the Begin government's determination, and Arab unwillingness to recognize the Jewish
state, the United States could not effectively put pressure on Israel. The
positions of the Arab and Israeli regimes were mutually reinforcing in
creating a deadlock. The Reagan proposal was well formulated and did
help secure United States regional interests and move forward the peace
process by a step. At the same time, by effectively undermining the already knotted Camp David autonomy talks, Washington undertook the
risky burden of promising further progress. Although most of the responsibility for the intractability of the conflict lay with regional forces, the

administration's earlier actions weakened American prestige and leverage.

Second, there was a serious failure of planning in the face of clear and present contingencies. Middle Easterners found it hard to believe that the United States had no program to present after Israel's final withdrawal on April 25, 1982, from the Sinai. Although the United States opposed an Israeli invasion of Lebanon, there was no policy set forth in advance on what to do should this happen; nor, despite much talk about the need to rebuild a unified Lebanon, was there any American plan as to how this might be accomplished. Similarly, there was no link between the AWACS sale to Saudi Arabia and other forms of strategic cooperation.

The administration was unable to prod the Saudis toward either a leadership or a peacemaking role, and the only possible opening in this regard, the Fahd peace plan, was poorly handled by America, both publicly and privately. In the end, Washington succeeded in alienating both sides. Crown Prince Fahd's proposal sharply attacked Israel and called for a Palestinian state; nevertheless, it held out the possibility, more clearly than ever before, of Saudi recognition for Israel. The Reagan administration generally ignored the initiative. Only at the last minute, immediately after the AWACS sale and just before an Arab summit meeting called to discuss the idea, did President Reagan offhandedly make a partial endorsement, which provoked the Israelis without offering the Saudis much comfort. The Arab failure to accept the plan was hardly the fault of the United States, but Washington might have handled such a promising initiative more effectively.[23]

Third, the United States did not set forth in any credible way its stand on bilateral relations with Israel. A failure to continue past American policy opposing more Israeli settlements on the West Bank and to disagree strongly with any change in the area's status allowed the government of Prime Minister Menachem Begin to continue tightening Israeli control without any serious costs in its international relations.

Fourth, Washington continually vacillated on whether it wanted to punish or woo Syria, crush or moderate the PLO, pressure or accommodate Israel, encourage the Saudis to play a larger regional role or expect them to concentrate on their own stability, strongly aid or ignore the guerrillas in Afghanistan, and so on. In international affairs, and particularly in the rapidly changing Middle East, a certain amount of ambiguity is useful, and a willingness to shift ground is necessary. Yet the Reagan administration did not stand still long enough to register any effective influence on events.

These varying signals entailed real costs. To cite one example, the administration's early stress on antiterrorist and anti-Soviet moves led Israeli policy makers to believe Washington would welcome their attacks on Syrian and PLO forces in Lebanon. They were surprised when the United States disapproved. Neither Arabs nor Israelis deliberately acted to embarrass or take advantage of the United States; they simply ceased to consider it as a predictable factor. And both sides came to resent and distrust the vagaries of American policy. This was related to the continuous struggles within the administration between those advocating different courses, but even these altercations had more to do with bureaucratic infighting in Washington than with the regional situation.

Confusion and Reification

The Reagan administration's picture of the Middle East was formed mainly out of ideological abstraction, lack of knowledge, indecision, and internal conflict. Its definition of regional threats and solutions did not generally correspond with the actual forces and dangers on the scene. Within the Middle East, the policy struck chords far different from those intended in Washington.

Even when local thinking corresponded relatively well with the administration's premises, as in Afghanistan, American passivity was striking. The amount of American assistance for the anti-Soviet guerrillas remained limited, and Afghans spoke with increasing bitterness about the contrast between America's public relations use of the issue and its lack of real support for anti-Soviet forces in the field. Similarly, American policy makers paid little attention to Sadat, who also stressed the Soviet regional threat and the need for cooperation to reinforce stability. Israeli trust was dissipated without gaining Israeli concessions. The same could be said for a number of Arab countries.

Most of the region already accepted Reagan's main image objective — that America was strong. Middle East governments, however, saw the United States not as a pitiful, helpless giant, but as a dangerously erratic one, discomfiting in its lurches to friend and foe alike. As they see it, Washington does not have policies, it has only moods. *Al Akhbar*, Egypt's largest newspaper, complained, "President Reagan's administration is the least competent of the U.S. governments and the most pitiful in the field of foreign policy in the 20th century." [24]

Yet despite these shortcomings, developments within the region by no means amounted to the series of disasters perceived by many observers. Arab fears of Iran, the discrediting of Moscow, the failures of leftist economic policies, and real concerns about internal and external instability all led to a greater appreciation of the importance of the American factor in the region. Both the Gulf and Arab-Israeli crises heightened an appreciation on all sides that the United States held the cards necessary to defuse major regional problems. Only America seems in a position to mediate the Arab-Israeli conflict and only Washington can insure the Gulf against Soviet ambitions. The United States remains the sole supplier, moreover, of many types of weapons and technologies.

The story of Reagan's Middle East policy, then, is not one of catastrophes created but of the misuse of American leverage. Few criticisms could be more telling than the administration's failure to create an active, able, and reliable policy. As Alexander Haig correctly noted, "No other region is less forgiving of political passivity than the Middle East. So many interests are at stake and so many factors are at work that the alternative to shaping events is to suffer through them." [25]

Notes

1. Harold Saunders, *The Middle East Problem in the 1980s*, American Enterprise Institute Special Analysis (Washington, 1981) is one attempt to analyze American regional interests. See also John Campbell, "The Middle East: A House of Containment Built on Shifting Sands," Foreign Affairs, *America and the World 1981*, pp. 593-628.
2. Barry Rubin, *Paved with Good Intentions: The American Experience and Iran* (New York, 1980), and "American Relations with the Islamic Republic of Iran, 1979-1981," *Iranian Studies*, Vol. 13, Nos. 1-4 (1980), pp. 307-326.
3. On the effect of the Iranian crisis on the elections, see *The New York Times*, November 16, 1980.
4. Interview in *The Economist* (London), February 10, 1979.
5. *Washington Post*, January 26, 1979.
6. *The New York Times*, January 21, 1980.
7. *Washington Post*, January 22, 1980.
8. On Washington's low profile on the autonomy negotiations, see *The New York Times*, December 16, 1981.
9. Interview on "The Today Show," September 23, 1981.
10. Interview on "The Today Show," October 14, 1981.
11. Barry Rubin, "The Iranian Revolution and Gulf Instability," in Shirin Tahrir-Kheli, *et al.*, *The Iran-Iraq War — Old Conflicts, New Weapons* (New York, Praeger, 1982).
12. Christopher Madison, "U.S. Balancing Act in the Middle East," *National Journal*, November 28, 1981; Christopher Joyner and Shafqat Ali Shah, "The Reagan Policy of 'Strategic Consensus' in the Middle East," *Strategic Review*, Fall 1981.
13. *Washington Post*, September 4, 1981.
14. *The New York Times*, October 2, 1981.
15. "Face the Nation," October 4, 1981.
16. *Washington Post*, November 3, 1981; *The New York Times*, December 16, 1981; William Quandt, *Saudi Arabia in the 1980s* (Washington, 1981); Department of State, "Saudi Arabia and U.S. Security Policy," September 25, 1981, *Current Policy* 320; Alexander Haig, "Saudi Security, Middle East Peace and U.S. Interests," *Current Policy* 323, October 1, 1981.
17. On the debate, see the *Washington Post*, September 27, 1981; *The New York Times*, September 28, October 1, October 6, 1981; and *The Economist*, October 3, 1981.
18. Polls showed 56% of Americans were against and only 29% were in favor of the sale, *Los Angeles Times*, October 8, 1981.

19. *Washington Post,* November 1, 1981.
20. The strange, tangled tale told by the U.S. government in December 1980 of an alleged Libyan hit team dispatched to kill American leaders only added to the regional image of Washington as somewhat foolish and irresponsible.
21. Shlomo Avineri, "Beyond Camp David," *Foreign Policy,* Spring 1982, pp. 35-36. Text of accord in *Department of State Bulletin,* January 1982.
22. Interview, April 2, 1981, in Congressional Research Service, *Documents and Statements on Middle East Peace 1979-1982* (Washington, 1982), p. 229.
23. *The New York Times,* November 2 and 4, 1981.
24. *Al Akhbar,* June 27, 1982.
25. Alexander Haig, "Peace and Security in the Middle East," May 1982, U.S. Department of State, *Current Policy 395.*

Index